Presented To

_____

By

_____

CLIMBING HIGHER

IN **REVERATION**

DANIEL YORK

Copyright © 2013 Daniel York All rights reserved. Unlimited permission to copy this devotional without altering text or profiteering is allowed subject to inclusion of this copyright notice and so long as the purpose for which the material is copied glorifies God. For information, email Daniel York at dan@firstcause.org.

Unless otherwise noted, all Scripture quotations are taken from the Holman Christian Standard Bible ®, Copyright ©1999, 2000, 2002, 2003, 2009 by Holman Bible Publishers. Used by permission. Holman Christian Standard Bible®, Holman CSB® and HCSB® are federally registered trademarks of Holman Bible Publishers. Other Scripture references are from the following sources: The Contemporary English Version (CEV) ©1991, 1992, 1995 by the American Bible Society. Used by permission. The Holy Bible, English Standard Version (ESV) ©2001 by Crossway Bibles, a publishing ministry of Good News Publishers. Used by permission. All rights reserved. The New International Version (NIV) copyright ©1973, 1978, 1984 by the International Bible Society. Used by permission of Zondervan Publishing House. The New Living Translation (NLT) copyright 1996. Used by permission of Tyndale House Publishers, Inc. Wheaton, Illinois 60189. All rights reserved. The New Testament in Modern English Translated by J.B. Phillips Copyright ©J.B. Phillips 1958, 1960, 1972, 1986, and 1988.

York, Daniel L., 1958-
    Climbing Higher in Reveration/Daniel York
    ISBN-13: 978-1492184898
    ISBN-10: 1492184896
    Library of Congress Control Number: 2013919961

    1. Devotional   2. Spiritual Growth   3. Christianity   4. Inspiration

Special thanks to Dr. John George, Michael O'Laughlin and Mark Tegtmeier for editing. I'm also grateful to Pneuma33 for their help in designing the First Cause logo and front and back cover. Their web design services are incredible—visit www.pneuma33.com.

This book is dedicated to Jesus-followers, those who are motivated to love and obey the Savior, unashamed, committed for life and joyful in telling His story!

Thoughts from Reveration readers the past 12 years . . .

- Daily, I am in **Reveration** and inspired to go deeper into God's word...I have opportunity to share the day's devotion with others and they are inspired to download or buy the devotional themselves. A must have for anyone who seeks God's presence.—Mary Anderson, Bend, Oregon

- Your devotionals start my day and it's amazing to me how timely they are! I love that the 'meditation' speaks to my heart, sometimes as a reminder and other times as a deeper message that encourages further study and application. I've come to count on these devotionals . . . I read with expectation, that God will use your message to teach me what I need at that moment and, He never fails.—Linda Sheets, Beaverton, Oregon

- **Reverations** have breathed life into my spirit in ways few others have. I have used them in my ministry, especially to men, with great success.—Pastor Glenn Wade, San Diego, California

- I take this opportunity to thank God for the ministry of **Reveration**. God is using you mightily. God is speaking to me in a very personal way, every time addressing my present circumstance.—Pastor Mwangangi, Nairobi, Kenya

- Dan is a story teller with a unique ability to weave God's truth into a digestible daily format.—Kevin Cady, Sherwood, Oregon

- I don't recall it, but is there a gift of "hitting the nail on the head?" If so, you've got it, brother.—Pastor Tim Arensmeier, Sonoma, California

- The pictures that Dan paints in **Reveration** makes it easy for me to "hide God's Word in my heart!"—George LaDu, Beaverton, Oregon

- **Reverations** provide huge encouragement for dealing with the everyday issues of life.—Colonel (ret) Bryan Newkirk, Denton, Texas

Ecclesiastes 12:10—The Teacher sought to find delightful sayings and write words of truth accurately.

Scripture Abbreviations

Books of the Bible

Genesis	Gen	Matthew	Mat
Exodus	Exo	Romans	Rom
Leviticus	Lev	1 Corinthians	1 Co
Numbers	Num	2 Corinthians	2 Co
Deuteronomy	Deu	Galatians	Gal
Joshua	Jos	Ephesians	Eph
Judges	Jud	Philippians	Php
1 Samuel	1 Sa	Colossians	Col
2 Samuel	2 Sa	1 Thessalonians	1 Th
1 Kings	1 Ki	2 Thessalonians	2 Th
2 Kings	2 Ki	1 Timothy	1 Ti
1 Chronicles	1 Ch	2 Timothy	2 Ti
2 Chronicles	2 Ch	Titus	Tit
Nehemiah	Neh	Philemon	Phi
Esther	Est	Hebrews	Heb
Psalms	Psa	James	Jam
Proverbs	Pro	1 Peter	1 Pe
Ecclesiastes	Ecc	2 Peter	2 Pe
Song of Songs	SoS	1 John	1 Jn
Isaiah	Isa	2 John	2 Jn
Jeremiah	Jer	3 John	3 Jn
Ezekiel	Eze	Revelation	Rev
Daniel	Dan		
Hosea	Hos		
Obadiah	Oba		
Jonah	Jon		
Micah	Mic		
Nahum	Nah		
Habakkuk	Hab		
Zephaniah	Zep		
Haggai	Hag		
Zechariah	Zec		
Malachi	Mal		

Climbing Higher—The Year Ahead!

Title	Topic	Scripture	Date
Eating the Right Fruit	Goal-Setting	Gen. 2:16,17	Jan 1
Judged By Our Cover	Image	Gen. 1:27	2
But He Lingered	Holding on to Sin	Gen. 19:16	3
Moving	Following God's Plan	Gen. 46:3,4	4
He Has Become My Salvation	Salvation	Exo. 15:2	5
Move On!	Spiritual Growth	Exo. 24:9-11	6
Karoshi	Rest	Exo. 31:15	7
Bourbon Street	Salvation	Exo. 32:9,10,30	8
Unauthorized	Obedience	Lev. 10:1-3	9
Leave Them For the Poor	Generosity	Lev. 19:9,10	10
Spiritists	Occult	Lev. 19:31	11
The Lord Spoke	God's Voice	Num 1:1	12
Grasshoppers	Faithlessness	Num. 13:33	13
Sign Twirlers	Obedience	Num. 20:10-12	14
Perversity	Evil	Deu. 1:26,27	15
Molly Tsurtsid	Distrust	Deu. 1:32,33	16
Commissioning	Commission	Deu. 3:28	17
Priorities	Priorities	Deu. 6:5-7	18
Filling Moses' Sandals	Victory	Jos. 1:3	19
Spiritual Ofuros	Meditation	Jos. 1:8	20
Buck Up!	Strong & Courageous	Jos. 1:9	21
Melting	God at Work	Jos. 2:10,11	22
Background Checks	Waiting on God	Jos. 9:14,15	23
Two Courses	Life Choices	Jos. 24:14,15	24
Storytelling	Testimonies	Jud. 2:10-12	25
You Are Not Forgotten	Deliverance	Jud. 16:28	26
Purging	God's Judgment	Jud. 20:26	27
Lam's Escape	People Fleeing	Jud. 20:46,47	28
Kinsman Redeemers	Guardians	Ruth 2:20	29
God-Centered	Creativity	1 Sa. 7:3	30
Maasai	Profile	1 Sa. 17:37	31
Weeping	Mourning	1 Sa. 20:41	Feb 1
Seeking Direction	God's Will	1 Sa. 23:4	2
Founder's Day	Prayer	1 Sa. 23:10-12	3
Divine Appointment	God's Leading	1 Sa. 25:23,24	4
Letting Pride Go	Trust	1 Sa. 25:32,33	5
Super Bowl	Priorities	1 Th. 4:16,17	6

Title	Topic	Scripture	Date
Wavering	Doubt	1 Sa. 27:1,2	7
Inconsistent	Inconsistency	2 Sa. 13:21	8
Subtleties	Discernment	2 Sa. 14:19	9
Undercover Boss	God Observing	2 Sa. 22:26,27	10
Keep Your Obligation	Obedience	1 Ki. 2:2,3	11
Angels	Angels	1 Ki. 19:5-7	12
Grab His Feet!	Struggling with God	2 Ki. 4:28	13
Valentine's Day	Loving God	Pro. 18:22	14
The Last 100 Yards	Significance	2 Ki. 5:17	15
He Tore His Robe	Accountable	2 Ki. 23:2,3	16
Void or Valid?	Cost of Sin	1 Ch. 5:1	17
It Was God's Battle!	Faith	1 Ch. 5:20-22	18
First to Kill	Character	1 Ch. 11:6	19
Akaba	Revival	2 Ch. 7:13,14	20
The Approaching Army	Fear	2 Ch. 20:2-4	21
Paying Homage	Finding Favor	2 Ch.24:17,18	22
Heroic	Faithfulness	2 Ch. 31:17,18	23
Failed Marriage	Discouragement	Ezr. 9:3,4	24
Billy Graham Came to Seoul	Teaching	Neh. 8:7,8	25
Self Control	Self Control	Neh. 5:14,15	26
George Mueller	God's Guidance	Neh. 9:19-21	27
Primary Purpose	Life's Purpose	Est. 10:3	28
Sorry I Was a Jerk	Insensitive	Job 16:3,4; 33:3	Mar 1
Crises	Character Formation	Job 27:9,10	2
Turning Away	Fleeing Evil	Job 28:28	3
Mount Fuji	Awe for God	Job 38:4-7	4
Positivity	Happiness	Psa. 1:1-3	5
The Lifter	God's Encouragement	Psa. 3:2,3	6
Joint Pains	Affliction	Psa. 4:1	7
Jupiter	God's Handiwork	Psa. 8:3,4	8
Scheming	Plotting Evil	Psa. 10:4	9
Liberty Lowered Her Torch	Immorality	Psa. 17:3; Mat. 12:36	10
Despair	Suffering	Psa. 17:15	11
Pathway	Growing Faith	Psa. 18:36	12
Mold	Unintentional Sin	Psa. 19:12	13
Fallen	Willful Sin	Psa. 19:13	14
Bowling	God's Way	Psa. 25:4,5	15
Terrified	Adversity	Psa. 30:7	16

Title	Topic	Scripture	Date
Water on the Head	God's Goodness	Psa. 31:19	17
Should've Been	Willfulness	Psa. 32:5,10	18
Delivered	Deliverance	Psa. 34:4	19
Coaching Eighth-Grade Boys	Impressionable	Psa. 34:11	20
Storm Power	Trusting God	Psa. 40:2	21
Unwelcome Visitors	Temptation	Psa. 40:8	22
Longing For You	Desire	Psa. 42:1	23
Down the Tennessee River	Rescue	Psa. 46:1	24
No Referees	Honesty	Psa. 51:6	25
From the Roof	Reputation	Psa.51:12,13	26
Jungle Prisoners	Praising God	Psa. 56:4; 86:12	27
Peruvian Concert	Evangelism	Psa. 96:2	28
Heritage	Eternal Home	Psa. 61:5	29
Rendering Judgment	God's Judgment	Psa. 64:9,10	30
Colonel R	Mentoring	Psa. 71:18	31
Home	Heavenly Focus	Psa. 73:24,25	Apr 1
Wise Sayings	Telling God's Story	Psa. 78:2-4,7	2
Restoration	God's Work in Us	Psa. 80:3	3
Seven Themes Regarding Truth	Truth	Psa. 85:11	4
This Awesome Affirmation	God's Love	Psa. 89:1	5
Kneeling	Prayer	Psa. 95:6,7	6
Destitute	Destitute	Psa. 102:17	7
Gloom	Overcoming Gloom	Psa. 107:13,14	8
The Road to Wisdom	Wisdom	Psa. 111:10	9
Our Compassionate God	God's Compassion	Psa. 116:5	10
Empty Tomb	Easter	John 20:1,2	11
Real Freedom	Freedom	Psa. 119:45	12
Kelcy's Rescue	Salvation	Heb. 10:12	13
Covenant	Promise Keeping	Psa. 119:50	14
Walking on Ice	Help from Scripture	Psa. 119:104,105	15
Fencing Sadie	Steadfast	Psa. 119:112	16
Maria	Resiliency	1 Sa. 2:6-8	17
Word from God	God Speaking	Psa. 119:130,133	18
Check Engine	Tune Up	Psa. 120:1	19
Casa de Niños	Protection	Psa. 121	20

Title	Topic	Scripture	Date
Immanent	Omnipresence	Psa. 139:8-10	21
Two Words to Avoid	Giving Up	Psa. 139:23,24	22
Finding Answers	Scripture	Pro. 1:5, 2:1-6	23
Against My Wife's Better Judgment	Counsel	Pro. 1:23	24
Delnora's Life	Example	Pro. 3:7,8	25
Critters	Rest	Pro. 3:24	26
Knecht the Dots	Doing Good	Pro. 3:27	27
Milestone	God's Healing	Psa. 90:12	28
What's Wrong with You?	Ignoring Insults	Pro. 12:16	29
The Power of Language	Words Matter	Pro. 12:18	30
Initiative	God's Leading	Pro. 16:1	May 1
Work in Progress	Discernment	Pro. 16:23	2
Opinions	Opinions	Pro. 18:2	3
The Balance of Justice	Justice	Pro. 18:5	4
Scientism	Scientism	Pro. 20:12	5
Dan's Letter to Cole	A Good Heart	Pro. 21:2	6
Consideration	Kindness	Pro. 21:10	7
Peruvian Patriarch	Missionary Example	Pro. 27:19	8
Time	Using Time	Ecc. 3:11	9
Comradeship	Ministry Partners	Ecc. 4:9,10	10
Annie's Grief	Grieving	Ecc. 7:3	11
Unflappable	Courage in Adversity	Ecc. 9:17	12
Hero Hit a Jetta	Patience	SoS. 5:6	13
Snow in May	Gratitude	Isa. 1:18	14
Under the Flight Path	Peace	Isa. 26:3,4	15
Certain	Confident in Christ	Isa. 28:16	16
Gracious	God's Graciousness	Isa. 30:9,10	17
Afraid to Share	Fainthearted	Isa. 35:3,4	18
Cross Country Racing	Hope to Run	Isa. 40:31	19
Consider these Thoughts	Warriors	Isa. 42:13	20
Anodyne	The Ultimate Cure	Isa. 45:12	21
Forgetting	God Remembers	Isa. 49:14-16	22
Lean on His God	Trust	Isa. 50:10	23
Liberty	Thankful for Freedom	Isa. 61:1-3	24
Contrite	Humility	Isa. 66:1,2	25
I Don't Know How to Speak	Courage	Jer. 1:6,7	26
Deception	Deception	Jer. 9:6	27
Knowing God	Knowing God	Jer. 9:23,24	28
Customs	Inspection	Jer. 17:10	29

Title	Topic	Scripture	Date
I Will Listen to You	Finding God's Will	Jer. 29:12,13	30
Faithfulness	Faithfulness	Jer. 31:37	31
Motivation	Motivation	Jer. 32:39,40	Jun 1
Hidden	Trusting God	Jer. 36:26	3
Hasty Words	Truth Finding	Jer. 37:11-14	2
Hesitant	Fearful	Jer. 38:15	4
A Deeper Kindness	God's Kindness	Jer. 39:18	5
Consequences	Accountability	Jer. 40:2,3	6
Lamenting	Lamenting	Lam. 1:12	7
Inspection in Ranks	Examined	Eze. 11:5	8
Lenience	Redemption	Eze. 18:21,22	9
Saber's Annoying Habit	Holiness	Eze. 36:23-28	10
Abundant Compassion	God's Compassion	Dan. 9:18	11
Promiscuous	Disobedience	Hos. 4:1-14	12
Get Your Own Dirt!	God's Existence	Hos. 13:6	13
Word Pictures	Telling Stories	Joel 2:31	14
Revealer	God Speaking	Amos 3:7, 4:13	15
Gloating	Gloating	Oba. 12	16
Illogical	Illogical	Jon. 1:12	17
Taken for Granted	Valuing God	Mic. 7:1,2	18
Contemptible	God's Hatred of Evil	Nah. 1:14	19
What Makes a Good Father	Fathers	Pro. 4:1-5	20
Made a Spectacle	God's Punishment	Nah. 3:3,5,6	21
What Constitutes Security	Security	Hab. 3:19	22
Jenny	Affliction	Zep. 3:19	23
Self-Centered	Self-Centered	Hag. 1:9	24
Fow Diow	Fear of God	Zec. 8:20-22	25
Immutable	God's Nature	Mal. 3:6	26
Geneology	Scripture Gems	Mat. 1:1	27
One Star	God's Leading	Mat. 2:1-3	28
Where's the Excitement?!	Caring	Mat. 2:3-5	29
Leadership	Leadership	Mat. 4:19,20	30
Billboards	Shining as Lights	Mat. 5:16	Jul 1
Practice Secret Acts of Kindness	Kindness	Mat. 6:1	2
The Narrow Gate	Choosing Life	Mat. 7:13,14	3
Insecurity	Insecurity	Psa. 4:8, 7:10	4
Getting Away	Time Alone	Mat. 14:13	5
Prayer Walks	Prayer	Mat. 18:19,20	6

Title	Topic	Scripture	Date
Creeds	Legalists	Mat. 23:23,24	7
Living Off Small Strips	Lacking Vision	Mat. 25:24,25	8
Jed	Reaching the Difficult	Mark 6:19,20	9
The Ghost	Fear	Mark 6:49,50	10
Interference	Discretion	Mark 10:14	11
Generous Peruvians	Generosity	Mark 12:42-44	12
Prove Yourself!	Finding God	Mark 15:39	13
A Mother's Milk	Glorifying God	Luke 1:46-49	14
Overwhelmed	God's Mercy	Luke 1:57,58	15
I Will Be Yours	Consecration	Luke 2:29-32	16
Watching Him Closely	Scrutinized	Luke 6:7	17
Meet Manasseh	Profile	Luke 6:39,40	18
Building the Foundation	Knowing Jesus	Luke 6:47,48	19
Proclaiming	Evangelism	Luke 8:1	20
Down to Hades	Rebellion	Luke 10:15	21
Panya	Meeting Needs	Luke 10:33,34	22
Crystallize	Eyes on Jesus	Luke 11:34	23
Ready for Service	Serving	Luke 12:35	24
Challenges	Following Jesus	Luke 14:26,27,33	25
Stewardship	Stewardship	Luke 16:10-12	26
The Road Down to the City	True Followers	Luke 19:35,36	27
Two Swords	Listening	Luke 22:36-38	28
Blessing	God's Blessings	John 1:16	29
Sin Responsibility	Sin	John 3:19-21	30
Universalism	Universalism	John 3:36	31
Reported	Betrayal	John 5:15	Aug 1
The Work of God	Following Christ	John 6 27-29	2
Skepticism	Truth	John 7:12	3
Sickness	Healing	John 9:2,3	4
Live Each Day as if it Were My Last	Resolve	John 10:27,28	5
Status	Status	John 12:42,43	6
Washing Feet	Serving	John 13:12-15	7
Trinity	Trinity	John 15:26	8
Slapped	Suffering	John 18:22,23	9
Vasa	Weak Design	Eze. 13:10-12	10
Pardoned	Salvation	Acts 2:20,21	11
Pierced to the Heart	Convicted	Acts 2:36,37	12
"Get up and Walk!"	Power to Heal	Acts 3:6,16	13

Title	Topic	Scripture	Date
"We are Unable to Stop Speaking"	Evangelism	Acts 4:18-20	14
His Power at Work	Power	Acts 4:29,30	15
Simplicity	Simple Lifestyle	Acts 6:3,4	16
Crystal Elements	Assumptions	Acts 7:24,25	17
Conversion	Transformation	Acts 9:4-6	18
Hollow	Process Theology	Acts 9:40,41	19
Off to the Jungle	Encouragement	Acts 11:22-24	20
Missionaries	Support	Acts 13:2,3	21
Mega Shift	Miracles Worldwide	Acts 14:3	22
James	Profile	Acts 15:13	23
Decision Making	Decision Making	Acts 15:22	24
Flexible	Flexible	Acts 16:6-8	25
Storms	Prayer	Psa. 109:4	26
Ron's Phone Parable	Evangelism	Acts 21:21	27
Tested	Character	Acts 24:16	28
Called a Slave	Servant of Christ	Rom. 1:1	29
Covered	Forgiven	Rom. 4:7,8	30
Disposition	Attitude	Rom. 8:11,12	31
On a Grassy Plain	Creation	Rom. 8:19-21	Sep 1
Not According to Knowledge	Zeal	Rom. 10:2	2
Wow	Praise	Rom. 11:33-36	3
How to Become a Living Sacrifice	Spiritual Worship	Rom. 12:1,2	4
In Reality	Sensible Living	Rom. 12:3	5
Success	Racing for God	Rom. 12:10	6
Meddling	Meddling	Rom. 12:16	7
Authlicism	Respect for Authority	Rom. 13:1-4	8
Cheyenne Disaster	Putting God First	Rom. 13:14	9
Alone With God	Alone	Rom. 14:7,8	10
Valor	Valor	John 16:33	11
Pursuing Peace	Peace	Rom. 14:19	12
Endurance and Encouragement	Persevering Well	Rom. 15:4	13
Manifestation	Manifestation	1 Co. 1:4-6	14
Song Selection	Uncompromising	1 Co. 3:1,2	15
Memorial	Memorial	Exo. 12:14,26,27	16
Wizdumb	Living God's Truth	1 Co. 3:19,20	17
Responsibility	Faithfulness	1 Co. 4:2	18
Marriage	Marriage	1 Co. 7:3,4	19

Title	Topic	Scripture	Date
Demons	Demons	Luke 1:1-4	20
Manny	Training Hard	1 Co. 9:25-27	21
Sacrament	Communion	1 Co. 11:25,26	22
Symphony Orchestra	Playing Our Part	1 Co. 12:12,27	23
The Great Advancer of Power	Kindness	1 Co. 13:4	24
Doors	New Opportunities	1 Co. 16:7-9	25
Three Good Men	Encouraging Others	1 Co. 16:17,18	26
The Reality of Trouble	Suffering	2 Co. 1:3,4	27
Ethics	Ethics	2 Co. 1:12	28
Naked Mole Rats	God's Workers	2 Co. 1:24	29
Healthy Devotion	Balance	2 Co. 6:3-10	30
Priorities	Setting Aside Riches	2 Co. 8:9	Oct 1
Giving Wisely	Discernment Giving	2 Co. 8:14,15	2
The Dentist	Investing	2 Co. 9:13	3
A Tiny Seed	Destiny	2 Co. 11:14,15	4
Failure	Putting God First	2 Co. 13:5,6	5
Building Up	Edifying Others	2 Co. 13:10,11	6
Strategic	Nigeria	Gal. 1:3-5	7
Outsiders	Living Rightly	Gal. 2:11-13	8
Identification	Identifying with Jesus	Gal. 3:27	9
COG Card	Our Status With God	Gal. 3:28,29	10
Distortions	Biased Reporting	Gal. 4:17,18	11
Gori	Overcoming Oppression	Gal. 5:1	12
Revelation	God Speaking	Eph. 1:17	13
Flying	Opportunity to Share	Eph. 3:7,11,12	14
Dunamis	Profile	Eph. 3:20	15
Costly Grace	Understanding Grace	Eph. 4:7	16
Don't be a Sledge Hammer!	Applying Love With Truth	Eph. 4:14,15	17
Changing of the Guard	Serving Well	Eph. 4:15,16	18
Purpose	Waiting on God	Eph. 5:8-10, 15-17	19
Humanism	Humanism	Eph. 6:7; Rev. 4:11	20
Spiritual Fitness	Spiritual Fitness	Eph. 6:10	21
Prayer Walk Report	Prayer Walking	Eph. 6:18	22
Spiritual Battle	Spiritual Battle	Php. 1:14	23
Retirement	Serving God	Php. 1:20	24
Worthy of the Gospel	Living Right	Php. 1:27	25
Seeing Others First	Others-Focused	Php. 2:1-4	26

Title	Topic	Scripture	Date
Kenosis	Jesus' State	Php. 2:6-8	27
Grumbling	Grumbling	Php. 2:14,15	28
Pura Vida	Pure Life	Php. 4:8	29
Bee Stings	Calm Witness	Php. 4:9	30
Glue	Preeminence of Christ	Col. 1:17	31
Mindset	Looking Above	Col. 3:1,2	Nov 1
Infatuation	Infatuation	Col. 3:5	2
The Three P's	Persevering Marriage	Col. 3:5,8,12,13	3
Outlook	Thankful	Col. 3:15	4
Lengkat	Profile	Php. 4:5-7	5
Cleaning Toilets	Hearty Service	Col. 3:23,24	6
Falling Away	Leaving the Faith	Col. 4:14	7
Letter to You	Encouragement	1 Th. 1:2	8
Be a Blessing!	Blessing Others	1 Th. 3:11,12	9
Tribute	Honored	2 Th. 1:11,12	10
Enlightened	Sharing Christ	Phi. 6	11
I Grabbed a Rifle	Discipline	2 Th. 3:11	12
Suicide	Suicide	1 Ti. 1:15,16	13
A Noble Work	Leaders Needed	1 Ti. 3:1	14
Fearing Failure	Trusting God	2 Ti. 1:7	15
Learned, Received, Heard, and Seen	Jesus-Followers	2 Ti. 1:13	16
Treasure Hunting	Valuing Christ	2 Ti. 1:14	17
Refreshed	Encouraging Others	2 Ti. 1:16,17	18
I Don't Know	Honesty	2 Ti. 2:19	19
Preparation	Responding	2 Ti. 2:20,21	20
Joseph	Profile	2 Ti. 4:2	21
Sound Beyond Reproach	Reputation	Tit. 2:8	22
New Thought	False Psychology	Tit. 3:5	23
Dividers	Divisive People	Tit. 3:9-11	24
Thanksgiving	Thanksgiving	1 Ti. 4:4,5	25
Bernoulli's Spiral	God's Design	Heb. 1:10	26
Drifting	Spiritual Drifting	Heb. 2:1	27
What Causes Immaturity	Immaturity	Heb. 5:11,12	28
Write Your Will	Spiritual Investing	Heb. 9:16,17	29
Savonarola	Profile	Heb. 11:13-16	30
Endurance	Toxic People	Heb. 12:3	Dec 1
Climbing the Staircase	Self Denial	Heb. 12:4-6	2
He Never Played a Down	Commitment	Heb. 13:16	3

Title	Topic	Scripture	Date
Maturity	Maturity	Jam. 1:5	4
More Than Intellectual	Active Faith	Jam. 2:14-17	5
Negative Emails	Speech	Jam. 3:7-9	6
Selfishness	Selfishness	Jam. 3:14-16	7
Hypocrisy	Hypocrisy	1 Pe. 2:1	8
Lovemic	Strong Love	1 Pe. 4:8	9
Prison	Testimony	1 Pe.4:16	10
Elders	Elders	1 Pe. 5:1-4	11
Koi	Lessons from Fish	2 Pe. 1:3	12
Climbing Higher	Shining Witnesses	2 Pe. 1:19	13
Change	Change	1 Jn. 3:2,3	14
Intimacy	Spiritual Intimacy	1 Jn. 4:16	15
Paper and Ink	Communicating Value	2 Jn. 12	16
Tracks	Leaving Signs of God	3 Jn. 3,4	17
Partnership—A Better Perspective	Partnership	3 Jn. 5-8	18
Taps	Contend for the Faith	Jude 3	19
Choices	Choosing Right	Jude 24,25	20
Bold Despite Their Fear	Courage to Share	Ezra 3:3	21
Loving Kindness	Loving Kindness	Psa. 36:5-7	22
When They Saw the Star	Shining for Jesus	Mat. 2:9,10	23
Joy and Sorrow	A Costly Grief	Mat. 2:16	24
Ransom	The Gift of Jesus	Psa. 49:7,8	25
Busyness	Busyness	Rev. 3:20	26
Mortification	Dying to Self	Rev. 3:21	27
Worship	Worship	Rev. 15:4	28
War	God's Victory	Rev. 17:14	29
Mutiny	Rebellion	1 Ki. 12:18,19	30
Come	God's Invitation	Rev. 22:17	31
Bible Marking	Code		433
About	First Cause		434
Books by	Daniel York		435
Music by	Daniel York		436
About	The Author		437
Endnotes			438

Before You Begin . . .

Matthew 14:23—After dismissing the crowds, He went up on the mountain by Himself to pray. When evening came, He was there alone.

Jesus seemed to love hiking the mountains of Israel to get time alone with His disciples but also time alone with His Father. There is something very therapeutic about climbing high into the hills. I love hiking in Oregon. First, the rich aroma of fir trees is invigorating. Second, the higher I hike the more grand the view. Third, traversing the forest, grassy meadows and rocky knolls on an ascent draws me closer to the Lord. Not only do I sense His presence, it is heartwarming to admire His creation.

This devotional is meant to be a companion and friend to you as you climb higher in your walk with God. We all need a lifting word to encourage us as we seek to know Him better. The purpose of this devotional is to cheer you on in your spiritual journey.

Following the format of *Something to think about . . . in Reveration*, this devotional will also take you through the Bible from Genesis to Revelation. Like its predecessor, it is written for you to *chew on*, to meditate on both the Scripture readings and the content so that you are motivated to grow! Sometimes cheering means a kick in the pants through a word of exhortation. Other times a whisper of encouragement and loving affirmation is the right touch. My prayer is you will find an array of writing that the Holy Spirit will use to bless you at just the right time. May you have divine appointments!

If you would like to sign up to receive Reveration each week via email, send me an email at dan@firstcause.org and asked to be placed on the mailing list. If you would like to read devotionals online, go to our website: www.firstcause.org.

As you read this devotional, my prayer is that Paul's words to the Philippians in chapter three, verses 12-14 will be true for you and me.

Not that I have already reached the goal or am already fully mature, but I make every effort to take hold of it because I also have been taken hold of by Christ Jesus. Brothers, I do not consider myself to have taken hold of it. But one thing I do: Forgetting what is behind and reaching forward to what is ahead, I pursue as my goal the prize promised by God's heavenly call in Christ Jesus.

Eating the Right Fruit

January 1

Genesis 2:16,17—And the LORD God commanded the man, "You are free to eat from any tree of the garden, but you must not eat from the tree of the knowledge of good and evil, for on the day you eat from it, you will certainly die."

God warned Adam and Eve not to eat from *one* tree. They had an entire garden and the ability to enjoy 99% of creation, instead they listened to a crafty serpent's tempting proposition. They set aside God's best for their own ideal and immediately failed. We are no different. We set out to reach our idea of ideal when we ought simply to please God by listening to His voice and by appropriating His power.

The Bible tells us in Luke 2:52 that Jesus grew in four areas—intellectually, physically, spiritually and socially. What enabled Him to be perfect was more than His deity or the author of Hebrews could not write, *"For since He Himself was tested and has suffered, He is able to help those who are tested"* (Heb. 2:18). Jesus was perfect because He chose each moment to submit to God's will.

At the beginning of each year people love to make resolutions. How many times do we say or hear someone say, "I am going to lose 30 pounds," or "I am going to quit smoking!" Well meaning Christians proclaim, "This year I am going to read my Bible and pray every day." So what happens to these good intentions? Perhaps the problem is we focus on ideals and immediately our vision blurs. What we need to do is be faithful and that is where the battle comes. It is impossible for imperfection to create perfection. Only God can give us the strength to change, to be holy as He is holy. Therefore we must discover what it is He wants for us.

Oswald Chambers wrote in *The Highest Good*, "It is not more ideals we want, but the power to live up to what we know we ought to and don't." Jesus didn't come to complicate our lives and make us miserable. He came that we might have life and be stoked living it! There is nothing wrong with goals or the setting of goals so long as we determine to go after what is on God's heart and not get trapped pursuing those things He never intended for us. God is not ambiguous in His direction—follow Him and be blessed!

Inspiration †††

There are certain things that you do not need a calling to do. You've already been commanded to do them.—Erwin Raphael McManus in *Chasing Daylight*

Judged By Our Cover

January 2

On my music CD titled "Evidence," Misha, the graphics designer, created a lightning bolt across a dark sky reflecting vividly off a placid water surface. We labored for a long time in looking for the right picture. Without an amazing cover many people won't pick up or even consider a CD. With respect to marketing, the saying "Don't judge a book by its cover," doesn't apply.

Genesis 1:27—So God created man in His own image; He created him in the image of God; He created them male and female.

Like it or not, we too are judged by our cover. God created Adam and Eve in His own image but sin irreparably damaged the human race. Yet, through the second Adam, Jesus Christ, the One who knew no sin, we see the image of God in human form. The Apostle Paul wrote in 2 Corinthians 3:18, *"We all, with unveiled faces, are looking as in a mirror at the glory of the Lord and are being transformed into the same image from glory to glory; this is from the Lord who is the Spirit."* The beauty of this verse is the reality of spiritual transformation. When we put our faith in Jesus and pursue Him, the transformation journey begins! We take on the image of Christ and the world sees again what God intended.

With transformation comes responsibility. A sloppy (unholy) life is a poor reflection of God's glory. If our cover (life) does not glorify God, who cares who lives inside us? God wants the world to know Him. He wants those who are lost in sin to find Him by seeing the change that occurs in those who follow His Son. Likeness *is* profoundly important. God never sacrifices His image and neither should we.

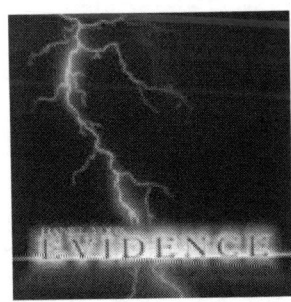

Inspiration †††

Much of our difficulty as seeking Christians stems from our unwillingness to take God as He is and adjust our lives accordingly. We insist upon trying to modify Him and to bring Him nearer to our own image.—A.W. Tozer in *The Pursuit of God*

But He Lingered

January 3

In Genesis 19, we read one of the saddest stories in the Bible. The awful behavior of the valley inhabitants of Sodom and Gomorrah caused the Lord with two angels to come down to investigate. Abraham was concerned because his nephew Lot lived in the city. Fearfully, Abraham asked the Lord if He would spare Sodom if He found just ten righteous people there. The Lord replied, *"For the sake of ten I will not destroy it"* (18:32, ESV).

Two angels arrived at Sodom just before nightfall and as it happened, Lot saw them and insisted that they stay in his home. He knew it was not safe for them in the town square. *"But before they lay down, the men of the city, the men of Sodom, both young and old, all the people to the last man, surrounded the house"* (19:4, ESV). They insisted that Lot give his guests up so they could have sex with them. When he refused, the Sodomites threatened Lot and attempted an assault on his home. The angels intervened and struck the men with blindness. These people were so evil that even when blind, rather than seeking forgiveness or help, they wore themselves out groping for the door. In the morning, the angels urged Lot to flee with his wife and daughters before God torched the valley.

Genesis 19:16—But he lingered. So the men seized him and his wife and his two daughters by the hand, the LORD being merciful to him, and they brought him out and set him outside the city. (ESV)

Without God's help, the men in Sodom could easily have ravaged Lot. He saw their wickedness in full display. So I find it incredible that instead of taking off *he lingered.* He hesitated! Are you kidding me!!! Only God's mercy kept him from becoming toast. Yet, when fleeing, his wife ignored the angel's warning not to look back or stop anywhere in the valley and she became a pillar of salt. Disobedience always begins with lingering.

But he lingered . . . May I ask several tough questions? What's your threshold for sin? It was easier for Lot and his family to live with sin than to move away. How much evil are you tolerating around you?

But he lingered . . . When a merciful Father asks you to do something, do you hesitate or do you obey? Very rarely does evil walk up to us and smack us in the head. It comes alongside us subtly. It whispers in our ear. It seduces the flesh with clever promises and feeds the appetite with decorated garbage. Slowly we become wrapped in wrongs we don't even notice. We compromise. We rationalize. We die. I don't know about you, but I would hate to have on my tombstone, *"But he lingered . . ."*

Inspiration † † †

There is no sin known to man that the human mind cannot rationalize away!—Dr. Bill Gothard in *How to Conquer Habits and Addictions*

Moving

January 4

I've moved so many times in my life that I've never had to reorder business cards. But with increased age moves are more complicated. First, I wonder if my knee will give out when I carry the desk down the stairs. Second, it seems like furniture keeps getting heavier. Third, I thought I was doing a good job downsizing, so how in the world did we get so much stuff? Ah, but it's all good. Moving is an opportunity to start afresh, to trust God around new bends and to meet new people.

Genesis 46:3,4—God said, "I am God, the God of your father. Do not be afraid to go down to Egypt, for I will make you into a great nation there. I will go down with you to Egypt, and I will also bring you back. Joseph will put his hands on your eyes."

If anyone ever had reason to protest moving, it was Jacob. After all, he was living in the land the Lord promised to give his grandfather, Abraham. But God had other plans. First, He sovereignly used jealous brothers to relocate Joseph to Egypt. Second, with His hand of favor securely on Joseph's life, He made him second only to Pharaoh in authority. Third, He caused a massive famine which resulted in Jacob and his entire family moving to Egypt for food. Why were these machinations necessary?

Do you believe it is God's intent for the world to know Him? By uprooting Joseph and then Jacob, He wove an amazing story. Instead of calmly building the nation of Israel in the promised land of Canaan, He jerked them around through rising stress. The family of 70 morphed from favored status in Egypt to a nation of slaves. Yet, God deftly worked over 400 years later to free them through Moses. "Then God spoke to Moses, telling him, 'I am Yahweh. I appeared to Abraham, Isaac, and Jacob as God Almighty, but I did not reveal My name Yahweh to them'" (Exo. 6:2,3). The Israelites experienced God in a way unknown to their forefathers. The world heard about God's mighty acts. The *move* became a movement.

So, if it seems like God is uprooting you, or sending you down windy roads when you can see a much easier way, take heart! He knows what is best for you. He sees the world and forms the future. His plan is flawless. We don't have to understand, we have to trust Him. And though the move may be a pain, so long as we keep Him at the center of our vision, the end will be better than we deserve as we climb higher . . . in reveration.

Inspiration ✝✝✝

We chose to trust God's longer-range provision rather than invest in our own short-term security.—Russ Johnston in *Activate Your Faith*

He Has Become My Salvation   January 5

Open the newspapers after a tragedy and a swarm of hornets would make less noise than the clattering keys of a million writers typing manmade solutions to a marred society. When the hum of their common sense solutions reaches its apex, the sound will be as useful as a compass attached to a magnet. The needle waves wildly, then breaks.

History reveals that no civilization has ever escaped moral deterioration. Despite the best trumpet calls of would-be saviors, only Jesus has erased the reality of sin and the sting of death.

Exodus 15:2—The LORD is my strength and my song; He has become my salvation. This is my God, and I will praise Him, my father's God, and I will exalt Him.

Salvation comes from God. Only the Creator can rescue His creation from a rebellion He providentially allows to exist. Only a slain Messiah capable of overcoming death and taking on the sins of a world can hold the torch of salvation and not get burned. Is it baptism, or speaking in a mysterious tongue, or attending the right church that saves us? Is it ritual, birth heritage, sacraments, or clean living that guarantee eternal life? Or is it grace that rescues us—God's divine and holy grace? *"For you are saved by grace through faith, and this is not from yourselves; it is God's gift—not from works, so that no one can boast"* (Eph. 2:8,9).

The credit for salvation goes to the Savior not the one being rescued. Is not our work to believe that the one who extends His hands is able to pull us in—and not let go! Only the grace of a merciful Jesus can transform a sin-stained life into a redeemed soul! The Apostle Peter stated, *"There is salvation in no one else, for there is no other name under heaven given to people, and we must be saved by it"* (Acts 4:12). The Apostle Paul noted, *"For God did not appoint us to wrath, but to obtain salvation through our Lord Jesus Christ"* (1 Th. 5:9). We follow Jesus and He is our salvation!

God revealed to the Apostle John that one day there will be:
... a vast multitude from every nation, tribe, people, and language, which no one could number, standing before the throne and before the Lamb. They were robed in white with palm branches in their hands. And they cried out in a loud voice: Salvation belongs to our God, who is seated on the throne, and to the Lamb!" (Rev. 7:9,10)

I am so glad that I have a rescuer named Jesus! No matter how bad the world becomes, we know that He will bring transformation.

Inspiration ✝✝✝

Our salvation is entirely from God; there is no reason in us at all why He should save us ... If the source of our life is in God, so also is everything else.—Watchman Nee in *Changed into His Likeness*

Move On!

January 6

Exodus 24:9-11—Then Moses went up with Aaron, Nadab, and Abihu, and 70 of Israel's elders, and they saw the God of Israel. Beneath His feet was something like a pavement made of sapphire stone, as clear as the sky itself. God did not harm the Israelite nobles; they saw Him, and they ate and drank.

This is one of the most amazing yet obscure stories in the Bible. Seventy-four men on God's invitation, partially climbed Mount Sinai to fellowship with Him. Later in Exodus 33:20, the Lord said to Moses, "*You cannot see My face, for no one can see Me and live.*" Moses and his leaders saw only a part of God and not His face.

It was important to God to build in the spiritual lives of Israel's leaders His own authority and presence. There is no other example of God corporately permitting people in His presence in the Old Testament. But what amazes me the most about this story is what happens just a month or so later. While Moses remained on the mountain receiving God's laws, the people grew restless. In Exodus chapter 32 we find Aaron appeased their desire to make idols by fashioning them a golden calf. How could this happen? Aaron, with his two sons and the 70 elders witnessed miraculous deliverance from Egypt. They had just beheld the glorious presence of the Almighty God. How could they now forsake Him?

Never assume that your spiritual life will be strong on the basis of your mountain-inspired experiences. What the presence of God did for you yesterday is no guarantee of how you will act today. When we descend into the valley, the temptation is to rest on what we knew on the mountain. That will not sustain us when the crowd grows restless and we are envious that someone else is getting cloud-time.

Spiritual life must constantly be nourished. Growth is not achieved by memories! Jesus never said to His disciples, "Your faithfulness was great last week! You can take a break now and when you feel like following Me, come on!" He said, "*If anyone wants to come with Me, he must deny himself, take up his cross daily, and follow Me. For whoever wants to save his life will lose it, but whoever loses his life because of Me will save it*" (Luke 9:23,24). Losing my life means refusing to glory from what happened before, placing no value in position, and no merit in haphazard obedience. It means I fix my eyes on Jesus this moment and the next. Is your spiritual life sullied today by your contentment with yesterday? Move on! Seek God's presence and let Him inspire you anew with His fresh will.

Inspiration † † †

The will is the ruler of our understanding our memory.—Jeanne Guyon in *Final Steps in Christian Maturity*

Karoshi

January 7

In 1969 the Japanese reported their first case of karoshi—death from overwork. More recently about 10,000 Japanese die annually for reasons attributed to karoshi.[1] If that is a frightening statistic for an island of high achievers, one can only wonder how many die for the same reasons in the United States where even longer work hours are kept! King Solomon once wrote, "Therefore, I hated life because the work that was done under the sun was distressing to me. For everything is futile and a pursuit of the wind" (Ecc. 2:17). How many people die each year hating what they do—filled with work anxiety—wishing desperately to find meaning in life?

Exodus 31:15—Work may be done for six days, but on the seventh day there must be a Sabbath of complete rest, dedicated to the LORD. Anyone who does work on the Sabbath day must be put to death.

In Hebrews 4:4, we read that after God spent six days creating the earth, He "*rested from all His works.*" God commanded the nation of Israel, through His servant Moses, to take a day off to rest each week. Failure to do so brought a death sentence. I suspect God required the life of a person for disrespecting life in the first place and for blatantly disobeying a command He instituted for their own welfare!

Harm is the inevitable outcome from continuous overworking. The cost of not knowing when to stop easily leads to irritability, poor decision-making, decreased time with those we love, inability to concentrate, poor health, depression, anger and accidents. While there will be times in life when we cannot escape deadlines or the need to bring a project to conclusion, to create time platforms devoid of rest is ultimately fatal.

Regularly I challenge my subordinate leaders to schedule one day a quarter to get away and rest and make time for reflection. I will do the same thing I asked of them. Most army reservists have the challenge of balancing two careers, and it is not easy! As much as I can, I program one day a week to spend away from work. I need the time with God and to be alone to relax and recharge my batteries. I suspect it is the same with you. If a timeless, omnipotent God saw the need to rest, what in the cosmos makes us think we can exert our energy with reckless abandon? Rest leads to rejuvenation, reclamation, recuperation, restoration, calming, quiet and joy—sound inviting? Let's rest for God's glory and our health!

Inspiration ✝✝✝

All life requires a rhythm of rest.—Wayne Muller in *Sabbath*

Bourbon Street   January 8

I once stayed at the Crown Astor in New Orleans for a military conference. On Friday night I got almost no sleep. On the fifth floor near my room was a group of university students engaged in loud and vulgar revelry. It made me wonder how many parents have any idea of what their college children are really doing.

Saturday, after a delicious dinner with my commanders at the Pelican Restaurant, we walked along the infamous Bourbon Street where Mardi Gras occurs each year. The road was lined with bars geared towards illicit sex, people drinking and looking for entertainment. We did not linger long.

Exodus 32:9,10,30—The LORD also said to Moses: "I have seen this people, and they are indeed a stiff-necked people. Now leave Me alone, so that My anger can burn against them and I can destroy them. Then I will make you into a great nation" . . . The following day Moses said to the people, "You have committed a grave sin. Now I will go up to the LORD; perhaps I will be able to atone for your sins."

In the heart of Bourbon Street was a sign proclaiming Jesus and help for anyone in need. A group of men and women stood ready to talk to passersby. Two things occurred to me. First, it was not surprising that followers of Jesus would be here. It is not the healthy who need a doctor but the spiritually sick. Second, I saw no people offering help through Buddha, Muhammad, or any other religious figure. Why is it that in the most desperate, evil places, Jesus can often be found? To me, the greatest proof that He is God's Son and the world's sole Savior is His presence on a street the demons manage and where His name is a swearword and object of derision. Jesus rescues where lust destroys, voodoo threatens, hearts are broken, minds are bent on evil, and wickedness is fed by hands moved by the vilest imaginations.

God will hold accountable those who reject Him for their own evil agendas. His judgment will be fierce and terrible. But where we find Jesus we find hope. We discover that it is not religion that assuages the empty soul—it is a faith relationship with a Messiah slaughtered by the same stiff-necked people who rejected Yahweh for a golden calf. On a day when He was determined to wipe out an entire nation, He listened instead to the pleas of Moses to spare them. We should not be surprised, then, that on a street named for whiskey, God still mercifully offers Living Water.

Inspiration ✝✝✝

Judgment isn't a matter of geography. It doesn't matter where you are. No place is far enough away, and no refuge strong enough.—Jonathan Cahn in *The Harbinger*

Unauthorized

January 9

I find the book of Leviticus to be hard reading. For the first nine chapters, God instructs Moses in how the Israelites are to bring offerings and the priests are to conduct themselves. I struggle to see anything even remotely interesting in this. Then chapter ten comes along and I read the shocking verses below.

Leviticus 10:1-3—Aaron's sons Nadab and Abihu each took his own firepan, put fire in it, placed incense on it, and presented unauthorized fire before the LORD, which He had not commanded them to do. Then flames came from the LORD and burned them to death before the LORD. So Moses said to Aaron, "This is what the LORD meant when He said: I will show My holiness to those who are near Me, and I will reveal My glory before all the people." But Aaron remained silent.

Do you ever have questions about why God acts the way He does? I do. While Moses was gone 40 days receiving instruction from God, his brother Aaron caved in to the wishes of his countrymen and forged an unauthorized golden calf for them to worship. He let them get out of control. His dereliction of duty initially resulted in 3000 Israelites killed. God struck the people with a plague (Exo. 32) yet He did nothing to Aaron.

We read above of God burning to death Nadab and Abihu! Where was their father when they went before God? Did he know his sons were possibly drunk and therefore irresponsible in their actions? Again, God did nothing to Aaron.

In Numbers chapter 12, Moses' sister Miriam and Aaron criticized Moses because of his Cushite wife and challenged his authority. God struck Miriam with temporary leprosy for speaking against His servant and did nothing to Aaron. Eight chapters later, Moses and Aaron disobeyed God's explicit instruction to speak to the rock so water might pour out. Instead, an angry Moses struck the rock while Aaron took no action to stop him. Then God punished them. He took away their right to enter the Promised Land and shortly thereafter, He ended the life of Aaron.

Was not Aaron's treasonous golden calf far more heinous than the quirky fire his sons brought before God? It scares me to think that God can be, dare I say, fickle. Or could it be that He has His purposes for doing what He does? He sees into the hearts of men and women what we cannot see. He knows when it is time to strike and when it is better to refrain from striking. Perhaps it was not fitting to terminate His anointed high priest. Maybe Aaron's service was more important for a season than leaving Moses alone to cope with his rebellious countrymen. Maybe Aaron's days were filled with unimaginable grief and pressure trying to appease complainers. Maybe his silence at the execution of his sons was as remarkable as his ability to later worship the Executioner. Maybe his criticism was the overflow of a heart fed up by desert life where people dropped dead on a daily basis and he didn't always like the decisions of his younger brother. Maybe, just maybe God decided to extend grace.

I don't understand. It doesn't matter. The point is that God expects me to live in a pure manner. You and I have no right to do what is unauthorized. The consequences may be immediate and shattering or God may seemingly do nothing. He sees. He knows. He loves. He judges. Our responsibility is to make the fire the way He prescribed.

Inspiration †††

A fault once denied is twice committed.—Japanese proverb

Leave Them for the Poor

January 10

Leviticus 19:9,10—When you reap the harvest of your land, you are not to reap to the very edge of your field or gather the gleanings of your harvest. You must not strip your vineyard bare or gather its fallen grapes. Leave them for the poor and the foreign resident; I am Yahweh your God.

The Bible was written when agriculture and not industry dominated society. Fear of droughts in the Middle East was a real and present threat and one could understand why people would hoard or even be stingy about collecting food. But God's design for His people never included the word miserly or the notion that they would focus solely on feeding their own appetites. He wanted the Israelites to be generous and that extended to the very thing they considered precious—food.

Only in Scripture when God's people are deliberately living in disobedience to His commands does *He* turn His back on the poor. Otherwise, seven different books in the Old Testament admonish the Israelites to help the foreigners, the fatherless and the widows. And in three of those books with the addition of Hosea, God promises Himself to look after those who are vulnerable.

Jesus told His disciples, "*Sell your possessions and give to the poor. Make money-bags for yourselves that won't grow old, an inexhaustible treasure in heaven, where no thief comes near and no moth destroys*" (Luke 12:33). His brother James wrote, "*Pure and undefiled religion before our God and Father is this: to look after orphans and widows in their distress and to keep oneself unstained by the world*" (James 1:27). Whether it be Christmas, a birthday, time of harvest or time of paycheck, what sets us apart as people of faith is our ability to see beyond "I" to help others.

Oswald Chambers wrote in *Studies in the Sermon on the Mount*:

Much of our modern philanthropy is based on the motive of giving to the poor man because he deserves it, or because we are distressed at seeing him poor. Jesus never taught charity from those motives: He said, 'Give to the one who asks you, not because he deserves it, but because I tell you to.' The great motive in all giving is Jesus Christ's command.

If God has filled your hands, your heart and your house, look around for those in need of help and be grateful to have the ability to give! May God bless you as you obey Him by blessing those in need of gleaning!

Inspiration † † †

Much of our modern philanthropy is based on the motive of giving to the poor man because he deserves it, or because we are distressed at seeing him poor. Jesus never taught charity from those motives.—Oswald Chambers in *Studies in the Sermon on the Mount*

Spiritists

Nadjya* came into our center to get food. As Bryan had her fill out forms, she shared she was mentally struggling. He forewarned me that she seemed kind of bizarre. I called her in and asked her questions to determine her financial and spiritual status. I was impressed with her faith in God's mercy and forgiveness and grasp of the Bible.

Nadjya recounted the abuse and pain she suffered from her husband. When she went for help, she ended up meeting a female naturopathic doctor who confessed to being an Ascended Master ("a being who has become Self-Realized and serves humanity; a being who has raised his/her vibration to a sustained frequency of light. He/she can come and go at will from the earth plane without the Birth/Death cycle.")[3] This woman told Nadjya she would work with guiding spirits to help her. The result of this therapy was an inability to sleep for five days. She began hallucinating and her husband, intent on hurting her, told the police she was violent and had her briefly committed to a mental ward.

Leviticus 19:31—Do not turn to mediums or consult spiritists, or you will be defiled by them; I am Yahweh your God.

Nadjya wondered if perhaps God was punishing her. I was able to pray for God's peace to be restored to her life and to point her repeatedly back to Christ and the need to be grounded in Scripture. I prayed for God to protect her and to undo and remove the false teaching poured into her mind, poisoning her spirit.

I understand why consulting spiritists is forbidden by God. Nadjya's spirit and demeanor reflected defilement. For those who dabble in astrology and the occult there are drastic consequences. King David once prayed, "Teach me Your way, Yahweh, and I will live by Your truth. Give me an undivided mind to fear Your name" (Psalm 86:11). Only when we walk in God's way can we experience the grace and peace of the Almighty that grants clear thinking. When we turn for help to those who worship any other god or follow a self-made path, we immediately suffer a divided mind and the foolishness of the world clouds the wisdom of God. Consider the statement of a man claiming to be an Ascended Master, he writes, "There is but one path to knowledge and that is the path that you are on now." It sounds like a wise and true statement but if that path is not God's path it is the way of destruction—don't go there!

*Not her real name.

The Lord Spoke

January 12

Kathleen and I worked hard to find the right company to help us refinance our home. Each broker we spoke with gave us compelling reasons to refinance with his or her particular company. Finally, we sat down with a broker who before he went into his pitch told us about his family and about a solar energy project he was working to help people bring their energy costs down. At some point in the meeting, I distinctly in my heart "heard" the Lord tell me that this was the man who would help us refinance. It was sort of a surreal moment. Yet, I instantly had peace about our choice and course of action.

Numbers 1:1—The LORD spoke to Moses in the tent of meeting in the Wilderness of Sinai, on the first day of the second month of the second year after Israel's departure from the land of Egypt.
Acts 18:9—Then the Lord said to Paul in a night vision, "Don't be afraid, but keep on speaking and don't be silent."

We all need to hear from the Lord. We need His direction. We need His encouragement. And here is the good news—the Lord wants to speak to us.

Some people wander away from His voice and are not sure He is willing to speak to them anymore. Others have heard His voice and resisted. They don't want to hear Him speak for fear of what He is going to say. Still others are so discouraged they have concluded that God isn't interested in speaking to them. Thankfully, there are many who hear Him speak regularly and have an intimacy that is refreshing.

Jesus told His followers in John 16:13 *"When the Spirit of truth comes, He will guide you into all the truth. For He will not speak on His own, but He will speak whatever He hears. He will also declare to you what is to come."* I met with a friend discouraged about his relationship with God. He admitted consistently running from Him so as to exercise his own will. Burdened by alcohol and broken relationships with women he was a broken man. He wanted to do the right thing but he was not sure he could even hear God speaking. I encouraged him to take one day off a week to rest, to spend time studying Scripture and to give God the opportunity to speak to his life.

Let's set aside time to let the Holy Spirit communicate with us. Let's trust that even when we are engaged in our daily activities, we can still hear Him speak. Life lived obediently before God is the precursor to joy. A life deaf to His leading is a formula for tragedy. Choose wisely and listen!

Inspiration †††

When God speaks, we tremble. God is looking for a man who trembles at His word. Such a man will find the Spirit of God resting upon him; he will become a dwelling place for the Almighty.—Francis Frangipane in *Holiness, Truth and the Presence of God*

Grasshoppers January 13

Numbers 13:33—We even saw the Nephilim there—the descendants of Anak come from the Nephilim! To ourselves we seemed like grasshoppers, and we must have seemed the same to them.

They felt like grasshoppers? The people living in the land were too strong to conquer! After forty days of scouting about 240 miles of traveled distance, they could see the beauty and the potential of "the promised land" but it took second place to their fears. Ten spies counseled rejecting God's plan while two passionately pressed for victory with complete confidence that God would certainly go before them. The Israelites opted for the pessimistic majority; after all, it matched their morbid pattern of perpetually complaining against their Redeemer-Deliverer despite all the incredible miracles He performed on their behalf.

Before we condemn them let's take personal inventory. When was the last time we had to walk across a harsh desert daily beneath an unforgiving sun? Have we ever had to carry all our belongings, herd animals, keep children happy, while wiping the grit of sand from our eyes, nose and mouth from one more ridiculous sandstorm! How often were our mouths parched from thirst, and our body sick of pesky sand fleas and aggressive flies? Imagine answering for the millionth time, "Daddy, are we there yet?"

Exodus gives us a pretty accurate picture of what people are like. Two see in stones a future temple. Ten see objects worthy of hurling in protest. We tend to fall in line with the ten because after all they are the majority. But watch out. This is where we go wrong. We take counsel from the crowd. We remember Egypt and its leeks, its relative safety and the security of sameness. But the Lord made Canaan and its fruit. He requires faith and the certainty of salvation. We deify comfort at His expense. We forget He killed His Son for our salvation.

If we are grasshoppers, it's not in comparison to tall people, it's because we jump with the prevailing wind. God forgive us for our attitudes of defeat, pessimism and the rottenness of demanding OUR rights. God help us to be like Caleb and Joshua—uncommon men with the right stuff. God will save us if we'll just trust Him and that's something no mound of sand can overcome!

Inspiration †††

A barking dog is no hunter.—Japanese proverb

Another reason that we are tempted to substitute outer conformity for inner obedience is that behavior conformity gains for us instant acceptance, approval, even status, with others.—Margaret Thatcher in *The Freedom of Obedience*

Sign Twirlers

January 14

As the minivan I was riding in stopped at a red light, I noticed a teenager twirling a sign. He was one of those persons paid by a business to hold up a sign advertising their products along busy roads. But no matter how hard I tried to read the large letters on the board I could not. He was so busy spinning it behind his back and over his head that it was impossible to read the message.

Numbers 20:10-12—Moses and Aaron summoned the assembly in front of the rock, and Moses said to them, "Listen, you rebels! Must we bring water out of this rock for you?" Then Moses raised his hand and struck the rock twice with his staff, so that a great amount of water gushed out, and the community and their livestock drank. But the LORD said to Moses and Aaron, "Because you did not trust Me to show My holiness in the sight of the Israelites, you will not bring this assembly into the land I have given them."

The Israelites were sick of wandering through the desert. They had lost trust in their God. They were thirsty and wanted water. So they quarreled with Moses and Aaron and accused them of failing them by bringing them to that barren place. Moses was also sick. He was sick of leading people who constantly complained. He was worn out by their incessant grumbling to the point that he lost his temper with them. I suspect he was also mad at God.

Yahweh asked Moses to take his staff and speak to what must have been a prominent rock in the presence of the people (v. 8). Instead he banged his stick twice and railed at his countrymen. He ruined the sign the Lord meant to be seen of His power and authority. Water does not come out of rocks by verbal commands—unless the Lord is at work.

What God says to do, we must do. He says to hold and manage our sign so others will read it. We don't believe the message will make a difference because every driver seems oblivious or ignores us. We twirl our board to get their attention. We get tired of a boring task. We perform so that people will see *us* and notice *our talents, our position, our authority*. By disobeying the Lord's instruction, we distort His message and incur punishment for our lack of trust and respect.

How badly Moses regretted his hotheaded words and actions. He lost the privilege of leading his people into the Promised Land. Who but God knows what blessings we miss because we twirl our signs and the message was lost.

Inspiration ✝✝✝

Unbelief thrives on cheap grace, for it is determined to persist in disobedience.—Dietrich Bonhoeffer in *The Cost of Discipleship*

Perversity

January 15

Have you ever tried to help someone only to be second guessed, accused of manipulating, or of having some hidden, evil agenda? I once had a subordinate leader who was quick to complain about the personnel in my headquarters. Despite the faults he found in others, his performance was consistently weak. For his own betterment I removed him from his position. I shared with him my intentions and then explained why his behavior was detrimental to our organization.

He thanked me for being candid and said I was the first leader he served who had shared such observations. He finally admitted that his conduct was poor and agreed it was best to move to another job. But behind my back he sang a different tune. He badmouthed me to his replacement. He threatened to attack me physically if he ever got the chance. He was bitter and vile instead of grateful.

Deuteronomy 1:26,27—But you were not willing to go up, rebelling against the command of the LORD your God. You grumbled in your tents and said, "The LORD brought us out of the land of Egypt to deliver us into the hands of the Amorites so they would destroy us, because He hated us."

The Israelites did not want to leave Egypt. It was easier to endure abuse than to move and suffer the inconveniences of change and facing the unknown. Listen to their complaint. *"Isn't this what we told you in Egypt: Leave us alone so that we may serve the Egyptians? It would have been better for us to serve the Egyptians than to die in the wilderness"* (Exo. 14:12). They complained like petulant children. Somehow they didn't believe that the Lord who miraculously extracted them could actually feed and provide water. It wasn't their idea to survive in the desert! They preferred leeks and onions to manna.

Moving wasn't their idea. It was easier to grumble in their tents. First, they would rather live by their own flawed plan than inherit God's promise. Second, it was far easier to grouse than to believe in a Lord they did not trust.

Complaining is not a technique to improve poor conditions, it is a statement of condemnation against another's agenda. Oswald Chambers wrote in *Philosophy of Sin*, "Perversity means to turn away from one to whom I have been devoted because he or she says things that do not suit my ideas." Perversity is the logical outflow of complaining. *If I can't have my way, I will sabotage your way.* Never tolerate perversion. It will suck the life from all who abide it and spoil the spirit of any who are infected. Avoid it like the plague it is!

Molly Tsurtsid

January 16

Molly Tsurtsid* works as a mechanical engineer for a firm in Duluth, Minnesota. She got the job through the recommendation of a friend at church, and it was an answer to prayer. Her boss is cantankerous but she enjoys the work. So it came as a surprise to her friends when she announced that she was secretly looking for a new job. They counseled her against this. Why risk losing a position God clearly provided? In truth, she also felt a check from the Holy Spirit to remain where she was. Even when reading her Bible, she sensed God directing her to stay.

One subtle thing keeps Molly from developing an intimate relationship with her Father. She doesn't really trust Him. Growing up she watched her father, a deacon in the church, leave her mother and abandon them for another woman. She remembers the time she prayed and asked God for help on a crucial history test in college—only to fail. She's not sure God is reliable. She follows Him, but only on her terms.

Molly proceeded to submit resumes with four other firms. Unbeknownst to her, one of the other managers was a personal friend of her boss. When he discovered what she was doing, she was promptly fired.

Deuteronomy 1:32,33—But in spite of this you did not trust the LORD your God, who went before you on the journey to seek out a place for you to camp. He went in the fire by night and in the cloud by day to guide you on the road you were to travel.

Distrust can be cloaked in clever disguise. When the Israelites approached Moses about sending men to spy and then report on the Promised Land, it sounded to him like a good idea. So he sent out twelve leaders. But was it necessary to spy out the land? God faithfully led the people each day through the desert. There is no indication that when they reached Canaan His leadership would cease. In fact, because of His promise, He was committed to their successful journey. Did the Israelites send out spies because they did not trust God? If their faith had been strong, they would have believed their Lord would finish what He started and fulfill what He pledged. They actually moved ahead of His leading and by so doing fell victim to their own unbelief. A plan that sounded good was flawed by ulterior motives shaped by distrust. Ten unbelieving men ratified the suspicion of a nation of doubters.

While distrust may at times be warranted, being skeptical and unbelieving concerning God's will dishonors Him and robs us of the blessing that He longs to provide us. I wonder what boon we miss stuck in our own desert of disbelief?

*Fictional name

Commissioning

January 17

Twice I had the privilege of delivering the commissioning speech to the ROTC graduates at the University of Portland. Cadets in front of their friends and relatives raised their right hands and swore to support and defend the constitution. Each stood before a noncommissioned officer to render their first salute and then gave the NCO a silver dollar in keeping with Army tradition. On each occasion, I was impressed by the quality of the young men and women ready to serve their nation.

Deuteronomy 3:28—But commission Joshua and encourage and strengthen him, for he will cross over ahead of the people and enable them to inherit this land that you will see.

Moses was reluctant to commission Joshua. In 3:23-25 we learn that he begged the Lord to let him cross over and see the Promised Land. He wanted to fulfill what God initially called him to do. But God was angry with His humble servant for disobeying an earlier command (see Numbers 20:12) and told Moses to stop asking to cross the Jordan. Instead, He took him to the top of Mount Pisgah, a mountain in west Jordan, about 10 miles east of the Dead Sea and let him look down upon what would one day be the land of Israel.

One of the most important acts godly leaders perform is to commission new leaders. It's not easy to come to the end of life and watch someone else take on the mantle of leading. Moses was in great health, sound mind and full of drive when God determined his *enough*. But true to form, the Exodus Patriarch obeyed His Master.

Moses encouraged Joshua. I imagine they went on some long walks, or sat down on some ledge where they could see for miles while Moses told his longtime friend, "Don't be afraid Joshua. You've been with me for 40 years. You've seen what I do and how God works. He will help you. You can do it!" Just as God asked, he strengthened his protégé.

Commissioning is all about the mission and uncompromising loyalty to the one in charge. It is not about the perks of leading, the servitude of others, or the power of holding office. If we lose the ability to commission capable leaders of integrity and wisdom, eventually we lose our ability to exist as a nation—whether it be a free republic or as a kingdom of priests.

Inspiration † † †

Pastors are sometimes afraid to commission lay ministers to supervise cells for fear that they will lose the strokes that come from being the only chief.—Carl George in *Prepare Your Church for the Future*

Priorities

January 18

Deuteronomy 6:5-7—Love the LORD your God with all your heart, with all your soul, and with all your strength. These words that I am giving you today are to be in your heart. Repeat them to your children. Talk about them when you sit in your house and when you walk along the road, when you lie down and when you get up.

Phil Downer once served as the President of Christian Business Men's Committee (CBMC). Before leading CBMC he was a senior partner in a large law firm. He is the father of six children and the author of several books. *A Father's Reward "Raising Your Children to Walk in the Truth"* is an outstanding book that reveals unvarnished lessons from a dad intent on challenging fathers to parent their children as God intended.

I observed five of Downer's children present at a family retreat, and saw them model poise, respect, maturity and a deep love for God uncommon among most children. Two parents cared deeply enough to invest heavily in their children and the results spoke for themselves.

If my wife ignores our rose bushes they don't produce gorgeous flowers. Aphids, fungus and an assortment of other enemies all conspire industriously to destroy them. In the same way children left to themselves rarely grow up to be sterling adults. Immoral peers, ungodly teachers, an internal sin nature and Satan and his vile underlings are all capable of causing moral meltdowns. Children need training—godly training.

Before you trot off on another spectacular assignment, or give your best time and energy to work and to those needing your help consider the welfare of your children. God says we are to impress upon them His commandments. What impresses your young ones—the television, computer games, drugs, sex, depraved music, pornography etc.? I can't afford to not prioritize spending time with the most precious gifts God entrusted to my care. Neither can you.

If you don't have children of your own have you ever considered teaching a Sunday School class or leading a youth group or coaching a sports team? The fact that we cannot determine how our children will live when they become adults should not detract us from imparting as much of God's truth as we can. It is all a matter of priorities isn't it!

Inspiration † † †

. . . the great concern of our lives is not God, but how we are going to fit ourselves to live. Jesus Christ says, "Reverse the order, get rightly related to Me first, see that you maintain that as the great care of your life, and never put the concentration of your care on the other things.—Oswald Chambers in *Studies in the Sermon on the Mount*

Filling Moses' Sandals   January 19

Joshua 1:3—I have given you every place where the sole of your foot treads, just as I promised Moses.

There are times when I am reading my Bible and a verse stops me in my tracks. The verse above qualifies. Let's consider the context. Moses just died. To appreciate his loss, think of losing your parents as a child or your nation's best leader right before a major war. The Israelites were poised to move into Canaan, a land full of bigger, stronger nations and now the man who spoke with God was buried somewhere in a Moab valley (see Deu. 34:6).

God told Joshua, the heir to Israel's greatest leader, *"Moses is dead now get moving!"* (1:2, paraphrased). Imagine for a moment even trying to fill Moses' sandals! But what is amazing is the promise God uttered in verse three. Before the Israelites crossed the Jordan River, He guaranteed their victory. They just had to walk forward into a land whose inhabitants they feared not knowing that the Canaanites were even more afraid of them (2:9-11).

How many times in life have we missed triumph because we failed to understand or claim God's promise of victory? How many times have we wallowed in the slough of fear unwilling to move forward? The world longs to see God at work. He longs to work through us! The former cannot experience the latter unless we are willing *to live* by faith. We don't have to go earn the victory, we already *have* the victory! The problem is we don't live out God's reality because we get stuck in our inferiority.

No, in all these things we are more than victorious through Him who loved us. For I am persuaded that not even death or life, angels or rulers, things present or things to come, hostile powers, height or depth, or any other created thing will have the power to separate us from the love of God that is in Christ Jesus our Lord! (Rom. 8:37-39)

Triumph is not a fictitious possibility it is a realized hope. God smashed Satan's play for supremacy on the cross. Jesus' conquest of sin and death fashioned all we need to live victoriously so long as our trust remains squarely in Him. If we want to know God, we have to know triumph—anything less is just religion.

Inspiration † † †

Satan's primary object is not to get us to sin, but simply to make it easy for us to do so by getting us off the ground of perfect triumph on to which the Lord has brought us.—Watchman Nee in *Sit Walk Stand*

Spiritual Ofuros

January 20

Dennis the Menace and I would have got along great when it comes to our dislike of bathtubs. He didn't like to get clean, I don't like the time it takes to wait for a tub to fill up. I'd rather be in the shower, get clean and get going. Maybe that's a problem—I'm in too much of a hurry to get to the next thing.

The Japanese have the ultimate Jacuzzi. It's called the ofuro and wow is the water hot! It's not a place to wash, you do that before you ever climb in the tank. It's a place to sit and let the steaming water work its magic. It's a place to think and relax. It's a place to burn away the tension of a long day. It's a place to find rest and be renewed. It's a place where one can socialize or be left to wander the inner halls of thought.

Joshua 1:8—This book of instruction must not depart from your mouth; you are to recite it day and night so that you may carefully observe everything written in it. For then you will prosper and succeed in whatever you do.

Spiritual growth would come much more readily if we would make the time for spiritual ofuros. God's approval should be our motivation to honor the spiritual thoughts He bestows us in the Bible—not to be legalistic or because we have to but rather because it is good for us. I have found it to be true in my life, that whenever I establish periods to meditate over Scripture and apply it to my life an amazing peace transpires that carries me through the tides of time. Meditation is like oil. It lubricates the physical, emotional and mental gears so that they turn smoothly without freezing up. If soaking can be so invigorating, perhaps it's time to be more patient about letting the tub fill up! If your day looks especially challenging, decide to set aside <u>more</u> time early on to ponder God's truths. Then watch what happens! You won't be disappointed!

Buck Up! January 21

Living in Oregon over the past twenty years gives me an economic perspective of the state. In the past six years a large number of companies shut down or left the state to do business in other places. Times are tougher. For every headline proclaiming bad news there are real lives effected, like David in Salem. In tears he grapples with the virtual elimination of his savings as stock once worth $89 a share is now 40 cents a share. Like Mike in Beaverton, he went in to work to find his plant had closed down—unannounced. He returned home without a job.

Joshua 1:9—Haven't I commanded you: be strong and courageous? Do not be afraid or discouraged, for the LORD your God is with you wherever you go.

When God says to be strong, He means "Buck up! Get your eyes off adversity and look to Me!" Strong in the Bible implies living by faith in the power of God.

Why did God need to tell Joshua three times to be strong and courageous? Well, for one thing, Joshua knew full well what a rebellious nation he led. The Israelites tested God to the limit and Joshua knew how unruly they were. But God did not want Joshua's eyes focused on his countrymen. Second, imagine the task of leading over a million people across the Jordan river to conquer a land inhabited by larger and stronger nations! Just getting across the river was a logistical nightmare. But God did not want Joshua's eyes focused on the obstacles. Third, Joshua no doubt felt insecure, overwhelmed by the responsibilities upon his shoulders. Look whose shoes he had to fill, and Moses never wanted the job! But God did not want Joshua's eyes focused on himself.

God worked through Joshua to part the Jordan just like He ministered through Moses to part the Red Sea, so the people could cross on dry land. *"On that day the LORD exalted Joshua in the sight of all Israel, and they revered him throughout his life, as they had revered Moses."* (Jos.4:14)

Be strong and courageous. I don't know what challenges you are facing, but God does. You don't need to be afraid. Friend, don't lose sleep trying to figure out how you and your family will make it. I've seen God part lots of rivers in my short life. If you think about it carefully, you probably have too! I've never encountered a situation too difficult for my Father to handle. He's quite awesome! He is able! He is worthy of trust. He will see you through—count on it, live like it, start crossing the river. Remember, the waters did not part until the priests entered the river!

Melting

January 22

Joshua 2:10,11—For we have heard how the LORD dried up the water of the Red Sea before you when you came out of Egypt, and what you did to the two kings of the Amorites who were beyond the Jordan, to Sihon and Og, whom you devoted to destruction. And as soon as we heard it, our hearts melted, and there was no spirit left in any man because of you, for the LORD your God, he is God in the heavens above and on the earth beneath. (ESV)

Joshua sent two men from Acacia Grove as spies primarily to investigate the city of Jericho. The Israelites were preparing to move across the Jordan River to invade Canaan. When the spies entered Jericho, they hid at the home of Rahab, a prostitute. She protected them from getting captured and made them promise to spare her family when they conquered the city. We can understand why she had no hope that Jericho would withstand an assault by her words in the above meditation.

Whenever Israel followed God's plan amazing things happened. First, He caused their enemies to lose heart because they saw His muscle at work. Divine power breaks the spirits of those opposed to heaven's agenda. Second, He encouraged Joshua and his countrymen by revealing the effect He had on those resisting them. But for them to see melting there had to be heat. God dried up the Red Sea so Israel could escape the Egyptian army. Moses led his countrymen to defeat the two Amorite kings, Sihon and Og. Those actions sent massive fear shivers down the spines of Jericho's citizens.

When was the last time you saw hearts melting? If you are willing to do what God asks of you, it is impossible not to see Him at work. It may be imperceptible at first. Discouragement may set in as those against you seem unbeatable. So walk in faith. Press forward! E. Stanley Jones noted, "My life in my hand is a pain and a problem; my life in God's hand is a power and a possibility!" Too often we won't progress because we would rather control our own destiny—not understanding that our unwillingness keeps us from God's best for us.

Obey your Lord and you will surely experience His power at work. Erwin Raphael McManus wrote in his book *Chasing Daylight*, "When the people of God relinquish the purpose of God, when there is no movement, we lose the power to change lives."[4]

Inspiration † † †

The characteristic of those who truly know God is that they have no faith in their own competence, no reliance upon themselves.—Watchman Nee in *Changed into His Likeness*

Background Checks

January 23

A team of four of us conducted interviews for a top supervisor position in a Brigade I commanded. There were three job applicants. One of the individuals on the hiring team, Jack,* clearly favored one of the applicants and pressured the rest of us to hire her. His choice did the best job fielding questions and technically seemed the most competent for the job. By the end of the interviews the team leaned towards hiring her. Inwardly I did not feel comfortable selecting her. It felt like we were rushing to make a hire—squeezed by time and loyalty to select a woman who had served in our organization a long time. I silently asked God for His help that we would do the right thing. Instead of immediately offering her the position I gained approval from the other three leaders to conduct a more thorough background check.

Joshua 9:14,15—Then the men of Israel took some of their provisions, but did not seek the LORD's counsel. So Joshua established peace with them and made a treaty to let them live, and the leaders of the community swore an oath to them.

The Gibeonites heard the stories of how God delivered the Israelites from Egypt and destroyed their enemies as they journeyed to Canaan. Cleverly they concocted a ruse to convince Joshua and the Israelite leaders that they were a distant community that traveled far to make a treaty of peace with Israel. Joshua and the elders fell for the deception and made a peace treaty with them without seeking God's direction or taking the time to research the claims of the Gibeonites. Whatever their reasoning, three days later they discovered they were deceived by an idolatrous people marked by God for destruction. Joshua and his leaders lost credibility in the eyes of their followers and in the process learned a valuable lesson—don't make important decisions without consulting God!

Most of us live with pressure routinely. How we manage making decisions determines how we grow spiritually. The best thing we can do is to run to God and try to run in our own strength. Rely on His help through prayer. Examine His Word and consult with those who abide with Him. Trust Him for the results.

Proverbs 19:2 says, "Even zeal is not good without knowledge, and the one who acts hastily sins." Never let the weight of decision-making preclude the wait of hearing God's voice. By the way, a background check revealed serious problems with the applicant Jack wanted us to hire. God spared me from making a hasty decision under pressure. Praise His name!

*Not his real name

Two Courses

January 24

Joshua 24:14,15—Therefore, fear the LORD and worship Him in sincerity and truth. Get rid of the gods your fathers worshiped beyond the Euphrates River and in Egypt, and worship Yahweh. But if it doesn't please you to worship Yahweh, choose for yourselves today the one you will worship: the gods your fathers worshiped beyond the Euphrates River or the gods of the Amorites in whose land you are living. As for me and my family, we will worship Yahweh.

There are two courses in life—walking with God or walking without God. Walking with God requires several elements:
- Repentance—I must agree that my own sin separates me from God and be sorrowful over my sin such that I am willing to change.
- Humility—(The evidence of repentance)—I must agree that I cannot secure a permanent relationship with God because of anything I earn or deserve. I am a sinner in need of grace—God's awesome grace.
- Faith—(The evidence of humility)--I must believe that God can defeat the death I'm helpless to stop, forgive the sin I have committed and give me a new body, a cleansed soul, and the joy of living with Him and His followers forever.
- Love—(The evidence of faith)—God is not a puppet master but rather a Heavenly Father who is not only trustworthy but also love-worthy. Pursuing God means I jettison selfishness in order to love Him and thereby learn to love others as He loves them.
- Obedience—(The evidence of love)—I must be willing to follow God's will, to obey His Word and to allow Him to lead me. If I'm not willing to obey God, anyone could rightly question whether I truly even know Him for the preceding elements would all be questionable.

Though I'm not immune from wrongdoing, pain, and suffering, the result of walking with God is inner peace and gratification. I'm no longer afraid of death because I know who owns the future and I'm no longer afraid of life because I know God loves me and will take care of me as He promises.

The second course, walking without God, also requires several elements:
- Pride—I must decide that I don't need God. I'm a pretty good person who can go my own way and shape my own destiny.
- Rebellion—(The evidence of pride)—My theme song is "I Did It My Way." God cannot make me follow Him. I can believe whatever I choose to believe.
- Self-centeredness—(The evidence of rebellion)—The problem I have with following after God is the fear that He might ask or want me to do something I don't want to do. It's easier to please myself than to serve an invisible God with His heavenly agenda.
- Rationalization—(The evidence of self-centeredness)—I use questions to justify my position: 1. What about people who have never heard

about Jesus—surely God cannot condemn them! 2. There are many paths to heaven—Christianity is just one path among many. 3. Christians are a bunch of hypocrites so why would I want to become one? 4. How can a loving God send anyone to hell? 5. The Bible was written by men and therefore is fallible how can we know for sure it is true? 6. If God is perfect, where did evil come from and why do "good" people suffer? My questioning allows me to avoid the responsibility of having to accept or reject who the Bible says God is and what He expects of me.

- Audacity—(The evidence of rationalization)—It takes foolish bravado to choose not to follow God, to refuse to put my faith in Him and trust that I am right.

The result of walking without God is inner turmoil. Outwardly I appear calm or like I have my act together. Inwardly I wrestle with uncertainty about the future, lack of peace, and an emptiness that revolves around the issue—there must be more to life than what I am experiencing.

Oswald Chambers wrote in *The Pilgrim's Song Book:*

The course of deliberately remaining independent of God ends in damnation, by God's direct decree, not as an inevitable happening; and the course of dependence upon God ends in heaven, by God's decree, not by chance.

Two courses, one decision—choose wisely!

Storytelling

January 25

Eight months into his tour of duty in Vietnam, Navy gunner Dave Roever was burned horrifically when a phosphorous grenade exploded in his hand. This mild mannered Texan spent fourteen months in a hospital undergoing several major surgeries. By God's grace, he lived. Yet, what he does with his survival is truly heroic.

Instead of feeling sorry for himself and leading a private life away from the eyes of people who naturally recoil at the sight of burn victims, Dave is a public speaker. Combining humor and hope, he internationally shares the awesome love of Jesus to all who will listen. His accounts of God working through his pain, recovery, challenges, and victories both past and present inspire his listeners.[5]

Judges 2:10-13—That whole generation was also gathered to their ancestors. After them another generation rose up who did not know the LORD or the works He had done for Israel. The Israelites did what was evil in the LORD's sight. They worshiped the Baals and abandoned the LORD, the God of their fathers, who had brought them out of Egypt. They went after other gods from the surrounding peoples and bowed down to them. They infuriated the LORD, for they abandoned Him and worshiped Baal and the Ashtoreths.

In Judges 2:10 above we can surmise that *know* does not mean ignorant to God's existence. What it suggests is that there was no longer a relationship with Him. Gideon said to a visiting angel, *"Please Sir, if the LORD is with us, why has all this happened? And where are all His wonders that our fathers told us about? They said, 'Hasn't the LORD brought us out of Egypt?' But now the LORD has abandoned us and handed us over to Midian"* (Jud. 6:13). Gideon knew *about* God but his family was worshipping Baal, a local spirit deity and cult image (see 6:25). It is poignant that he blames God for abandoning Israel when clearly the opposite is true.

When idolatry is prevalent, stories of what God used to do become irrelevant. There is a reason churches are decreasing across America—just listen to the stories. Our challenge and privilege is to know God and experience His working today! Our responsibility is to share our stories. When we do so, we give credible evidence to the certainty of God; we proclaim His transforming, salvific work; we plant seeds of hope in our listeners; and we provide information that is most easily remembered and retold!

Inspiration †††

Stories are the coat pegs of the mind.—Mark Sanborn in *You Don't Need a Title to be a Leader*

You Are Not Forgotten   January 26

    Step after step in unison they marched, accenting the weight of each boot upon the carpet so that everyone in that banquet room could hear. Not an eye wandered, each man in his dress uniform staring straight ahead as they slowly moved across the assembled guests. Near a small round table, the squad leader halted them and faced them to the center. He moved to the second man and slowly saluted him, before taking from his outstretched hands the folded flag. In return, the one no longer carrying his nation's colors, saluted. Next, the sergeant marched in silence to the empty table and placed the folded flag upon it. Returning, he aligned himself in front of the next man. From this one's hands, he took another folded flag. Then he turned to his right and waited while the last man in formation moved to join him. Slowly the two unfolded the mostly black flag. With reverence and precision, the younger soldier snapped the flag in place on a thin pole, beside the empty table set for one. Across the bottom of that flag were printed the words, "*You are not forgotten.*"

    We who are soldiers pledge not to forget our fallen and missing comrades—those brave men and women who never came home. Where they languish in captivity, or died on lost and lonely landscape is unknown. That is only part of what fills our minds. What matters more is that we honor them. In this case, to remember is to value—it is a spiritual concept breathed by our Creator! Moreover, tugging our hearts is that inner hope that if we were in their place, we would not be forgotten.

Judges 16:28—He called out to the LORD: "Lord GOD, please remember me. Strengthen me, God, just once more. With one act of vengeance, let me pay back the Philistines for my two eyes."

    Samson the warrior knew he sinned badly against God. Blinded, shamed, and mocked by his enemies, he cried out hoping God would remember him and give him the power once more to inflict damage on the Philistines. God did remember and Samson's last feat of strength killed more Philistines than all his other exploits combined.

    Imagine if God forgot us. Imagine if we died and our bodies turned to dust and our souls were nothing more than some wind-carried, siren song. Imagine if there were no homecoming because the Maker saw no need to forgive, restore, and perpetuate. Fortunately, the same God who promised never to forget the nation of Israel, sent His Son who promised us, *"My sheep hear My voice, I know them, and they follow Me. I give them eternal life, and they will never perish—ever! No one will snatch them out of My hand"* (John 10:27,28).

Purging

January 27

Sometimes we can do what God asks of us and suffer disastrous consequences. When this happens, we can do one of two things: turn away from God and blame Him for our misfortunes; or, humble ourselves and continue to do exactly what He asks.

The Israelites were forced to do the unthinkable—attack one of their own tribes. The stage was set because of the wicked inhabitants of a town called Gibeah. A band of men brutally gang raped and killed the wife of a Levite. You can find the disgusting account in Judges 19 to capture the full context. The leaders of the collective tribes demanded Benjamin turn over the criminals for punishment. Incredibly, they refused and took up arms to defend their vicious brethren. Why would the Benjaminites defend such a heinous crime? What were they thinking? Clearly, they had abandoned their love for God and conviction to follow His laws.

At God's direction, Israel banded to attack Benjamin with the tribe of Judah drawing the assignment to lead the charge. Four hundred thousand soldiers moved to combat 26,700 warriors from Benjamin. Incredibly they lost 22,000 troops. Stunned, but undeterred, full of tears but submitted to God, they asked Him if the attack should continue. The Lord said, *"Fight against them"* (20:23). In the second day of battle 18,000 men were slaughtered by Benjamin's fighters. God let 40,000 men die and still the evildoers were unpunished! Why? Imagine what was running through the minds of the Israelite warriors as they gathered again before God. Feel their pain!

Judges 20:26—The whole Israelite army went to Bethel where they wept and sat before the LORD. They fasted that day until evening and offered burnt offerings and fellowship offerings to the LORD.

Again Israel sought God's desire. Once more He told them to fight. On day three they were victorious, destroying 25,100 Benjaminites (20:35). Such an awful cost was shouldered to accomplish justice. It is conceivable that God was not just purging evil from Benjamin; He was refining all the tribes. Very rarely is sin localized or monopolized. If immorality was ripe in Benjamin, it was probably seasoned throughout the land.

As difficult as it may be, we have to trust God's punishment. When we follow the trails of second guessing, excuses, or blaming we reach a destination far from where God would have us tread. We allow small sins to exist until they become much bigger. Slowly a tribe of saints becomes a rebellious clan. Purging is not pleasant work but for God to get our attention, He must thoroughly punish. From deeper wounds comes deeper healing. We have to trust His purging.

Lam's Escape

January 28

I met Lam in a dining facility at Fort McCoy, Wisconsin. As we chatted I asked him when he came to the United States. Lam escaped from Viet Nam at the age of eleven with an uncle and his older brother. His parents feared that when he turned thirteen he would be forced to serve in the military and potentially die or come back maimed as so many of their countrymen compelled as children to fight the Cambodians.

Lam left Ho Chi Minh City crossing through Cambodia (Kampuchea) into Thailand where he remained as a refugee. He nearly starved to death in that camp waiting daily in line for three hours to get a bowl of soup. Eventually an uncle in the United States paid for him to travel to Chicago. Now serving at the age of 44 as a Captain in the U.S. Army, he is filled with gratitude for his freedom and God's hand of protection on his life.

Judges 20:46,47; 21:13,14—All the Benjaminites who died that day were 25,000 armed men; all were warriors. But 600 men escaped into the wilderness to the rock of Rimmon and stayed there four months . . . The whole congregation sent a message of peace to the Benjaminites who were at the rock of Rimmon. Benjamin returned at that time, and Israel gave them the women they had kept alive from Jabesh-gilead. But there were not enough for them.

Behind the action of escaping is a palpable sense of fear. Six hundred Benjaminites felt the terror of battling countrymen outraged at the conduct of Gibeah. As thousands were cut down by spears, arrows, and swords, they managed to flee to Rimmon. Imagine what emotions cascaded through their minds as they foraged for food and water for four months just to survive. It was a dark time in Israel. While the outcome for those traumatized soldiers was the provision of women to marry, they would never forget the cost of a city's sin and the consequence of fighting for an immoral cause.

We are surrounded by people escaping. Some are distant like Lam and flee from oppression. Some like the warriors of Benjamin flee punishment as a consequence of their own ill-fated decisions. But the most tragic flight is those trying to escape Satan and his evil designs without a knowledge of Jesus.

Paul wrote Timothy, "*Perhaps God will grant them repentance leading them to the knowledge of the truth. Then they may come to their senses and escape the Devil's trap, having been captured by him to do his will*" (2 Ti. 2:25b,26). Lam knows what it means to be free spiritually and physically. Let's pray for those who are without hope, that they will find the only One who can bring them to their senses.

Kinsman Redeemers

January 29

Recently I had the opportunity to speak to a group of Army officers and noncommissioned officers. I asked the question, "How many of you grew up with a mom and a dad?" Almost all of them raised their hands. I then asked, "How many of your cadets (college students) come from homes with a mom and a dad?" The crowd guesstimated that about 50% came from two-parent homes. They underscored a point I hoped to make which is that today there is a huge need for mentors. Too many of those exiting high schools across our land have had insufficient parenting and manifest a great craving for meaningful relationships.

Ruth 2:20—Then Naomi said to her daughter-in-law, "May he be blessed by the LORD, who has not forsaken his kindness to the living or the dead." Naomi continued, "The man is a close relative. He is one of our family redeemers."

There is a fascinating concept in the Old Testament called the kinsman redeemer. God established for the Israelites a plan to perpetuate and protect a family's name and heritage. If a woman's husband died and she had no sons, it was the responsibility of the nearest relative, on the husband's side, to marry the widow or her daughter to ensure through children her deceased husband's name and land inheritance continued. Naomi and her daughter-in-law Ruth returned to Israel as widows. As we discover in the book of Ruth, Boaz married Ruth and through her offspring came David and later Jesus.

Today's New International Version translates, *"family redeemers"* as *"family guardians."* Guardian conveys a protective quality that is inherent in redemption. Today we don't have men marrying multiple women to perpetuate family lines. But wouldn't it be fantastic if we spiritually ministered to our extended family members? We could do this through:
1. Prayer.
2. Mentoring.
3. Resourcing.

I can't help but think of the many young men and women raised in single-parent households. I wonder how many of them have relatives in love with Jesus who have never considered becoming spiritual guardians—redeemers serious about ensuring the blessing of needy family members. What a difference we could make in society if we took on this privilege with joy and diligence!

Inspiration †††

What you want costs far more than what you can pay. You don't need a system, you need a Savior. You don't need a resume, you need a Redeemer.— Max Lucado in *The Applause of Heaven*

God-Centered

January 30

Junior High School was the worst period of my life. My family moved from Tokyo, Japan, to Seoul, Korea in the middle of my 7th grade. I didn't find a niche in the new school, so I compensated by handling adversity by being funny. Mr. Eng, the principal of the Crusaders, assisted my cause. Once I pulled a rubber band back as if to shoot him and his immediate response was, "That's stretching things too far!" My life was being stretched, but my coping ideas weren't working. I was a teenager and I was self-centered when I needed to be God-centered.

1 Samuel 7:3—Samuel told them, "If you are returning to the LORD with all your heart, get rid of the foreign gods and the Ashtoreths that are among you, dedicate yourselves to the LORD, and worship only Him. Then He will rescue you from the hand of the Philistines."

Samuel, the Old Testament prophet gave his people, the Israelites, four pieces of spiritual advice that revealed that they were not walking with God in the right manner. We too can learn much from his exhortation.

1. Following God is a wholehearted matter. If we are not willing to give God our undivided attention we will constantly be buffeted by the idols of our own choosing.
2. Whatever distracted them from following God was vain! The Ashtoreth was a goddess of love, fertility, and war worshiped by many people in the ancient Near East. When the Jews bowed before idols, God withheld His blessing and the Philistines smote them.
3. Worship God only! He is a jealous God (Exo. 20:5). That may sound bad, but think about it! He wants our undivided love because He undividedly loves us!
4. The benefit of following God was His protection and deliverance. So often we wonder why we struggle when if we would just obey and follow after God He would bless us with His deliverance.

Self-centeredness if pursued enslaves us to our own conceptions. A God-centered life results in clarity, peace and a joy that is unquenchable!

Inspiration †††

Life in the kingdom is God-centered. We don't think first of getting our needs met and our problems solved. We concentrate on what makes God happy, what gives our Lord pleasure, and what makes Him look good. That always turns out to be the best choice for us as well.—Jan David Hettinga in *Follow Me*

Maasai

January 31

David Ole Kereto was born in Narok, Kenya, the Maasai son of a witch doctor. By tradition he was expected to follow in his father's footsteps. One of the highest honors for a Maasai male is to become a warrior. To achieve warrior status, one must kill a lion or a man. To kill a lion, tribesmen will surround the big cat and agitate it by shouting. One of the men then steps forward making himself a target. He holds a spear in his right hand and a stick sharpened to a point on both ends in the other hand. When the lion attacks, it usually lunges for the spear hand. Just as it leaps, the Maasai shifts the stick to his right hand and as the lion opens its mouth he thrusts it between its jaws. David accomplished this at age 15 thereby becoming a Maasai warrior!

A fellow tribesman, who followed Jesus, began to share with David about Him. At first David said, "I'm headed for the most honored position in the village to be a witch doctor. I have no need for your Christ." Steadfastly his friend pursued him, repeatedly inviting him to attend Christian meetings. Finally, David attended a youth rally where he heard what Christ had done for him. In faith, he decided to place his trust in Jesus and become His follower.

David's father found out and, though angry, took no action, concluding that his son would not remain a Christian. Yet, over time, he saw his influence over his son decrease. Finally, David's uncompromising loyalty to Christ so provoked his father that he went to the village elders and secured their agreement that David must die. His father placed a curse on his son. The sun is a Maasai god. So he prayed, "Sun, when you go down tonight, take my son with you so he will not be alive in the morning." David's mother wept. His dad told her, "This is a test between my god and His God." But in the morning David was still alive. So his father took a machete to chop him up. David grabbed his father's arm and they struggled. The elders rescued David from his irate father but because he knew his father was intent on killing him, he fled.

A Maasai who worked for World Vision as an electrician took David into his home. He and his family helped David grow spiritually by studying the Bible. Eventually David went on to college and graduated at the top of his class. Then he went to England and studied theology. He came back to the Maasai and became a powerful evangelist, especially among the youth. Then the Lord called him into starting new churches.

1 Samuel 17:37—Then David said, "The LORD who rescued me from the paw of the lion and the paw of the bear will rescue me from the hand of this Philistine." Saul said to David, "Go, and may the LORD be with you."

Recently, this warrior-turned-servant of God again was confronted with an enormous challenge. The British owned a 99-year lease on a large section of Maasai fertile land. (The Maasai are concentrated in Kenya and Tanzania). In 2005 that lease expired. Maasai leaders wrote to their government asking for them to honor the expiration yet received no response. So David led a march upon the Kenyan National leadership to return the land to his people. The government responded by surrounding them with soldiers. But the same warrior who overcame the lion and a violent father, walked right through the soldiers brushing their weapons aside. That act of courage catapulted David to the forefront of his tribesmen. He was selected to be the leader of the Maasai nation. God has used David to plant more than 30 churches working with the Africa Inland Mission (AIM).

David married Jane at the age of 42. He and his wife have five children. They own cattle and land and have their own safari company. Like his Biblical namesake, David provides his nation with a powerful example of why following Jesus is truly transformational.

Maasai warrior

Weeping

February 1

Jack Deere wrote in *Surprised By The Power Of The Spirit:*
> The ability to weep over the words of Scripture and over our failure to keep God's Word is something that ought to be cultivated and desired today. It is not a sign of weakness or emotional instability. Rather, it is a sign of sensitivity to God's Word and of our abhorrence of sin. It is also a sign of spiritual and emotional health. The inability to weep over these things, on the other hand, is a sign of a traumatized or hardened heart.[6]

1 Samuel 20:41—When the young man had gone, David got up from the south side of the stone Ezel, fell with his face to the ground, and bowed three times. Then he and Jonathan kissed each other and wept with each other, though David wept more.

1 Samuel 20 gives us the tragic story of Prince Jonathan having to validate David's fear that King Saul truly did want to kill him. No longer was it safe for David to serve a jealous leader out for his head. As the two best friends embraced they understood that life would no longer be the same for them. A deep sadness filled the air.

Jonathan wept; shamed by an evil dad who abandoned honor for power. No doubt his grief and fear swirled with the guilt of a king's betrayal, the knowledge that David would live like some hunted animal and the realization that the good times they shared hunting, swapping stories and listening to David's songs were over. But David wept more. His grief was the severance of peace, the pain of rejection and premonition of judgment. There could not be two kings and he was anointed.

In Luke 23:28, Jesus walking towards crucifixion, turned and said, *"Daughters of Jerusalem, do not weep for Me, but weep for yourselves and your children."* On that fateful Friday, women wept: shamed by corrupt religious leaders who abandoned honor for power and embarrassed by men who forsook loyalty to avoid arrest. Their grief and fear swirled with the guilt of the King's betrayal, the knowledge that Jesus must die like some despicable criminal and the realization that the good times they shared eating, ministering to Him, and listening to His parables and teaching were over. Did Jesus weep more? His grief was the severance of peace, the pain of rejection, and foreknowledge of judgment. There could not be two kings, and He was anointed.

For what do you weep?

Inspiration † † †

The sultan felt great pity at seeing the king weep, and he wept also; then he sent thirty thousand loaves to the poor as well as the rich; and sent the same quantity daily during four days.—Joseph Francois Michaud in *The History of the Crusades Vol. II*

Seeking Direction

February 2

1 Samuel 23:4—Once again, David inquired of the LORD, and the LORD answered him: "Go at once to Keilah, for I will hand the Philistines over to you."
Psalm 37:23—The steps of the godly are directed by the Lord. He delights in every detail of their lives. (NLT)

What King David sang as truth he experienced as reality. At some point in his life, he made the remarkable decision to ask God for direction before taking action. Repeatedly thereafter he succeeded. He relied upon the Lord to lead him and then complied with His instructions.

Taking direction from God requires several key components:

1. Our lives must be in alignment with God's word. This morning I toasted two bagels. If I set the oven mark too high, no amount of coaxing will keep those New York beauties from burning! If I set the mark too low, no amount of encouragement will make them brown. When we neglect to obey God, we will not obtain His leading and the effect of sin will show.

2. Our focus must remain on God. Taking direction from God means we must contain and rightly direct our zeal. Often we discern our Lord's will but we become over eager in our attempts to make it happen. Beware of falling more in love with the work or word God has for you than in love with Him. The results can be disastrous! God shows a woman she is to be a nurse in Zimbabwe and that He will provide for her schooling. Years go by and the funds have not come in. So she takes out a huge loan. She obtains her degree but now her indebtedness blocks her ability to go. Choosing quick fixes often does not show dependence on God.

3. Our intentions must be pure. So often we live with an enduring need to do something great or to be viewed as important. Honestly, this bears the smell of pride. If we hold hidden agendas, or seek glory for ourselves, we are in grave danger of distorting God's direction to further our own cause. God is not impressed by what we do for Him. Scripture resoundingly reveals that His intent is that we love and fear Him wholeheartedly. I believe we will be quite amazed in heaven to see the rich rewards heaped on custodians, shop-workers, seamstresses, cooks and workers who humbly went about their work faithfully all the while building an abiding love for God that touched all who worked around them. Cease striving to do something great. Let go of what the world says matters and then you can listen to what God directs. This is the key to true joy in living.

Inspiration ☦☦☦

A life lived listening to the decisive call of God is a life lived before one audience that trumps all others—the Audience of One.—Os Guinness in *The Call*

Founder's Day

February 3

West Point graduates celebrate around the world an annual banquet called Founder's Day. Within this fellowship tradition the youngest and oldest graduates in attendance are asked to give a short speech. Recently at a Portland, Oregon gathering, retired Lieutenant Colonel Jeffrey Knight, class of 1952, delivered the "old grad" speech. He shared a story of "but for God's grace," he should not even be in attendance. His soft spoken delivery gave all of us pause to consider the simple importance of asking the right question.

Before Christmas in 1951, a special opportunity was afforded cadets whose homes were on the West Coast to catch a military Douglas C-47D flight from Massachusetts. Cadet Knight was excited to get home for the holidays without having to purchase a commercial ticket. But before he placed his name on the manifest he asked what flight arrangements were made to return the cadets back to West Point? The answer he received was that no arrangements were made. Afraid that he might be late in returning to school and potentially get into trouble, he declined the offer. On December 30, near Phoenix, Arizona, the west bound flight crashed. Nineteen optimistic young cadets on board all perished.

1 Samuel 23:10-12—Then David said, "LORD God of Israel, Your servant has heard that Saul intends to come to Keilah and destroy the town because of me. Will the citizens of Keilah hand me over to him? Will Saul come down as Your servant has heard? LORD God of Israel, please tell Your servant." The LORD answered, "He will come down." Then David asked, "Will the citizens of Keilah hand me and my men over to Saul?" "They will," the LORD responded.

What made David such a great leader was that he rarely made assumptions. Instead, he asked God questions. Rather than taking matters into his own hands or solving problems by his wits, he asked God what he should do. It is an American joke that men may get lost when traveling because they are too proud to ask for directions. I suspect there are many women who could share with us hilarious stories about their "lost" spouses! The simple truth is not only is there no shame in asking for directions, we would all negotiate life far better by querying God for His wisdom. Jesus said, *"Keep asking, and it will be given to you. Keep searching, and you will find. Keep knocking, and the door will be opened to you. For everyone who asks receives, and the one who searches finds, and to the one who knocks, the door will be opened"* (Mat. 7:7,8). Words to live by as we climb higher . . . in reveration!

Inspiration † † †

I am finding every day that the best of the five or six ways in which I try to keep contact with God is for me to wait for His thoughts, to ask Him to speak.—Brother Lawrence & Frank Laubach in *Practicing His Presence*

Divine Appointment

February 4

Previously I wrote about meeting Jeff Knight at a Founder's Day Banquet. Five days after meeting him, I was standing beside the plane at the Denver airport waiting for my bag to be delivered. Next to me was an elderly gentleman, Chuck, who asked me what my job was (I was in uniform). I explained to him that I was responsible for Reserve Officers' Training Corps (ROTC) for the United States Army Reserves. He then shared that he once served as the Professor of Military Science (PMS) for Wheaton College. Knowing Wheaton's admission standards for the PMS position, I asked the gentleman if he was a Christian. Indeed he was. Then I noticed that he was wearing a sweater with the Army mule emblem. I asked him if he graduated from West Point. Indeed he had, graduating in 1952. He then shared that his wife's brother-in-law was also a classmate of his and that his name was (are you ready!!!) Jeff Knight.

1 Samuel 25:23,24—When Abigail saw David, she quickly got off the donkey and fell with her face to the ground in front of David. She fell at his feet and said, "The guilt is mine, my lord, but please let your servant speak to you directly. Listen to the words of your servant."

David was on the way with his men to kill Nabal, a man who refused to help him in his time of need and who treated him rudely. David's anger was justified but his intended course of action was not. God was merciful and through a servant of Nabal, warned Abigail, Nabal's wife, what her husband had done. She quickly put together provisions and hastened to meet David. Through her words in the passage above and actions in providing food, she prevented David from taking rash action. He said to her, *"Praise to the LORD God of Israel, who sent you to meet me today!"* (25:32). Abigail was a divine appointment.

Chuck was a divine appointment. Through meeting him, I gained two more men who want to pray for their classmates as part of the Long Eternal Line. Chuck bought me dinner in the airport and shared some of his life story which was fascinating. I gained a new friend and was encouraged to keep doing the ministry God called me to do.

Never underestimate how God might work through you. He may protect you from doing something rash by bringing an Abigail at the right moment to stop you. He may bless you with words of encouragement from a stranger. He may use you to bring hope to someone in despair. God loves to work in and through our lives if we will but trust Him and give Him the glory! You never know who you might run into at the airport, but God does!

Letting Pride Go

February 5

I personally find it a challenge to submit my reputation, rights and responsibility to God's sovereignty. When wronged by someone else, my instinct is to seek retribution. For most of my life I've possessed a fierce need to defend myself. If my family, friends or teachers pointed out flaws in my conduct or character, I was adept at making excuses. Of course all of this posturing can be explained by one word—PRIDE.

We establish our importance yet neglect to ascertain the value of the One who gave us life. Perhaps one of the greatest spiritual truths we can learn is that we do not belong to ourselves. God made us for His enjoyment. Therefore, if we want to gain the greatest benefit from living, we must discover what brings Him joy. Scripture makes it abundantly clear that God takes great pleasure in those who lose their own sense of importance because they are so enamored with Him. In obeying Him they become less to become more.

1 Samuel 25:32,33—Then David said to Abigail, "Praise to the LORD God of Israel, who sent you to meet me today! Your discernment is blessed, and you are blessed. Today you kept me from participating in bloodshed and avenging myself by my own hand."

As evidenced in the verses above, David recognized that God warned him against avenging himself and bringing guilt upon his name. Approximately ten days later the Lord put Nabal to death. I believe that this lesson was instrumental subsequently in keeping David from killing King Saul twice when he had opportunity. Rather than acting by his own strength, he recognized that God was able at any time to depose the unjust king. David grasped the sovereignty of God.

Those who are full of themselves do not please God. Those who recognize and submit to His absolute authority please Him. Understanding the sovereignty of God means that we no longer act in our own strength. We have the freedom to trust Him! We have the responsibility to give up our timetable so as to carry out His timeless will.

If our Father is not sovereign, then we are at the mercy of people. What makes a profoundly fulfilling life is when we believe that God deserves to be Lord and that He is capable of carrying out His will regardless of whether we understand. Are you willing to be broken of your need to be in control to experience His perfect handiwork?

Inspiration † † †

The manifestation of the answer in time is a matter of God's sovereignty. Time is nothing to God.—Oswald Chambers in *My Utmost For His Highest*

Super Bowl   February 6

February 6, 2011 the Green Bay Packers defeated the Pittsburgh Steelers in one of the most watched Super Bowls ever. I admit I was pretty excited because I've always been a diehard Packers fan. Pittsburgh held the most Super Bowl wins in the National Football League with six. But on this day of battle, Green Bay won its fourth coveted Lombardi trophy.

Companies advertising for this monstrous event paid Fox Sports about 3 million for 30 seconds of airtime or $100,000 per second! About 110 million viewers watched the game (that's more than the entire population of Mexico). We were entertained by companies that peddled shoes, candy bars, chips, cars and beer. I couldn't help but think about how convoluted our values are! It costs anywhere from $1500 to $30,000 (depending on the depth) to dig a well in India or Africa. A well can give clean water to 500 or more people. Just imagine if the average cost of digging a well were $15,750, then 190 wells could be drilled for that money and serve clean water to over 95,000 people. Who knows how many lives would be spared of death to disease and dehydration just because a well was dug! As much as I like Green Bay, I would much rather see people excited about giving their time and money to helping those who will never see a game on television and wonder how they will survive the week.

Many woke up on Monday depressed because their team lost while those who backed the winner were elated. Yet, if 22 men and a pigskin can generate that much electricity, here's a far more profound thought.

1 Thessalonians 4:16-17—For the Lord Himself will descend from heaven with a shout, with the archangel's voice, and with the trumpet of God, and the dead in Christ will rise first. Then we who are still alive will be caught up together with them in the clouds to meet the Lord in the air; and so we will always be with the Lord.

As much as I like football, I would much rather see people consider what side they will be on when the game of life ends and God pronounces His judgment. The greatest event in history won't be a championship sports match. It will be the return of Jesus in triumph to an earth filled with those who cheer His every move and those who refuse to believe His life even matters. I'd rather be caught up in the air than catch a ball for a touchdown. How about you? Are you ready for the final event and on which sideline will you be found?

Inspiration ✝✝✝

The typical individual who allocates some energy to personal spiritual growth spends an average of four hours per week on these endeavors.— George Barna in *Growing True Disciple*

Wavering

February 7

1 Samuel 27:1,2—David said to himself, "One of these days I'll be swept away by Saul. There is nothing better for me than to escape immediately to the land of the Philistines. Then Saul will stop searching for me everywhere in Israel, and I'll escape from him." So David set out with his 600 men and went to Achish son of Maoch, the king of Gath.

What happened? Why did David, the Middle Eastern heartthrob and most popular combatant on the planet decide it was time to flee the country? He had just filled King Saul with shame by sparing him when by all rights he could have speared him. Saul even admitted knowing David would prevail. David knew that God promised him the kingship. God never reigns through dead bodies. So why did he give in to the notion that Saul could end his life?

Maybe he was tired. Fatigue can make us second guess anything.

Maybe he was afraid. Instead of trusting God as was his normal pattern, perhaps he looked at circumstances and let them dictate his next course of action.

Maybe he was discouraged. Often after a major victory or emotional high, we are subject to a letdown. Remember Elijah after defeating 400 of Baal's prophets and making King Ahab look ridiculous, fled in abject fear when Queen Jezebel vowed to kill him? David knew he was God's anointed, but that did not mean that every day he woke up feeling positive about his life expectancy. Even oil dries up.

Maybe he was stuck—his options seemed dismal. If he went back home to Judah and Saul came after him again, he put his entire family in jeopardy. He knew Saul was spiritually unstable yet held the power so today's peace was no guarantee of tomorrow's security. What else could he do but run and seek the protection of Gath's king?

Before deploying to the Sinai, our task force needed a chaplain. The chaplain who was scheduled to deploy with us begged his boss to find someone else to go. Faced with a scary unknown, he wavered. Another chaplain was found who agreed to deploy. Troy Carter not only became part of our organization, I believe he logged more miles on his jeep than any other leader in our battalion. Tirelessly he visited troops at the farthest outposts. He shared the gospel with them, he prayed for their needs, and he comforted them when they were anxious about their spouses or children at home. His messages at each service were inspiring. Troy was a man of God and we all learned much from him. Troy died with 247 other peacekeepers when our next to last plane returning to Kentucky crashed in Gander Newfoundland. He finished well!

Right now, you may be facing a big decision. You may be tired, afraid, or at wits end. At this moment of choice look to the Lord for wisdom and strength. Ask for His help. Share with Him what you are feeling. He understands. He will guide and protect you. You don't have to waver!

Inconsistent

February 8

We can learn a lot from a cat. We bought a puppy, a yellow Labrador we named *Hero*. As is often the case with puppies, he is a chewer—nothing is safe from his razor-like teeth—except for Misty, our cat. Every time Hero tries to chew on Misty he takes one-two combinations to the head from a not-amused feline.

Most vets and dog owners say "never hit a dog." But our "no bite" admonitions, and inconsistent techniques in disciplining Hero have little effect on him. He thinks biting is all part of a game. As our cat bemusedly watches us, she is free of his assaults. He knows that anytime he invades her space he is sure to get swatted. So he follows her around, wags his tail affectionately and acts responsibly.

2 Samuel 13:21—When King David heard about all these things, he was furious.

Horace Smith said, "Inconsistency is the only thing in which men are consistent." King David was a godly man. He was also royally inconsistent. After his son Amnon raped his half-sister Tamar, the Bible says David was furious. But he took no action. Because he failed to punish his son, Tamar's brother, Absolom, avenged his sister and murdered Amnon. David wept bitterly but again took no action. Absalom, having little respect for his father, led a revolt to take his dad's throne. In the end, David lost another son. When a father is inconsistent in the application of discipline, the family cannot help but suffer.

In the face of improper behavior, when it is philosophically inconvenient, the norm today is to be non-judgmental. If you want proof, read the "Letter to the Editor" section of newspapers or peruse the blogs on the aftermath of scandals. "Don't swat the little puppy he's just acting like puppies act!" A furious application of nothing is a fatal invitation for anarchy. An inconsistent application of something leads to a confused dog. Wouldn't it be nice if Scripture said, "When King David heard about these things, he punished Amnon"? Who but God knows how the story might have changed?

Inspiration † † †

Inconsistency is the only thing in which men are consistent.—Horace Smith

Subtleties

February 9

According to our guide, if a person spent four seconds looking at each item in the Musee du Louvre in Paris, it would take four years to see everything! Ranging from paintings like Michelangelo's Mona Lisa, Tiziano Vecellio's Titien, and Antonio Puccio's Pisanello, to amazing clay and marble sculptures, to the architecture and ceiling paintings on the edifice itself, the Louvre was both inspiring and thought-provoking.

One man who particularly fascinated me was Jacques-Louis David. This famous French artist was born August 30, 1748 and died December 29, 1825. David was a brilliant thinker who was very aware of the politics and moral condition of his countrymen. First, he was annoyed by the superficial Rococo artistic style which matched the frivolous government under King Louis the XVI. David became an active supporter of Napoleon I during the French Revolution and was a friend of Maximilien Robespierre, one of the most influential leaders of his time.[7] Second, David knew if his feelings towards his government were expressed through contemporary art, he would likely lose his life. Using a style later categorized as neoclassic, he utilized subtlety in painting historical scenes that spoke against the vices and problems of his day.

2 Samuel 14:19—The king asked, "Did Joab put you up to all this?" The woman answered. "As you live, my lord the king, no one can turn to the right or left from all my lord the king says. Yes, your servant Joab is the one who gave orders to me; he told your servant exactly what to say."

Joab was the Commanding General of King David's army. During part of David's reign, the king banished his son Absalom from the land for murdering his brother Amnon. But David understood that Absalom's action was in revenge for Amnon raping his sister Tamar and the king longed to have his son restored. Joab recognized the complexity of David's situation and realized that to directly approach David with advice would not work. Instead, he recruited the services of a wise woman from a town called Tekoa. In 2 Samuel 14 you can read how Joab invented a dilemma for her to tell the king. By gaining his counsel regarding her situation, she used David's words to advise him to restore Absalom.

It is not always prudent to be direct in our communication. Sometimes subtleties in what we convey work best for those not listening or thinking clearly. A restrained approach avoids enflaming another person's temper. It gives the listener an opportunity to reflect. It affords the messenger or artist a variety of ways to convey a message—such as humor, art, drama or narrative. God gives us the ability to be clever for a reason.

With good intentions and well-crafted delivery, a shrewd depiction may prevent dereliction. According to our scholarly guide, Jacques-Louis David's painting, The Oath of the Horatii, conveyed to a corrupt court the value of honor, the pain and casualties of battle, and the magnitude of loyalty.

Inspiration †††

Integrity is acting for what is right . . . Integrity has three parts:
1. Discern right from wrong.
2. Act for what is right regardless of risk to self.
3. Teach others from that act of integrity.—Stephen L. Carter in *Integrity* and Gus Lee in *Courage*

Undercover Boss
February 10

There is an insightful television program called Undercover Boss. Each episode, the owner of a company is disguised and then works for several days with different employees with differing responsibilities. Often the boss is inept at the tasks the employee is to teach him which puts pressure on him to do better. As he works with each selected person he also finds out what life is like in their shoes. Some are struggling financially or dealing with challenges that make life difficult.

At the end of each show, the owner meets with each employee he worked with and reveals who he is. Then things get very emotional. For those employees who demonstrated great character, professionalism and dedication, the boss gives out lavish rewards and the overwhelmed recipients often cry. In a more recent episode the boss was a woman and her heart was deeply touched by a mom who not only was a great technician but a wonderful wife and mother. Both women openly wept as the owner gave the young mother $25,000 and a promotion so she would not have to take a second job. She also gave a brand new truck to a young man who was a stellar leader. Before the show ended I was reaching for Kleenex.

2 Samuel 22:26,27—With the faithful You prove Yourself faithful; with the blameless man You prove Yourself blameless; with the pure You prove Yourself pure, but with the crooked You prove Yourself shrewd.

Undercover Boss provides its viewers a rich experience in leaders learning first-hand what their employees do and feel. Viewers celebrate with those who are rewarded. They also get the chance to see competent and incompetent employees. The program illustrates in a different way a profound spiritual truth.

Do you ever consider that God is with you every day? He sees what you think and how you act. I suspect King David understood this and his heart swelled with praise. He knew that he could completely depend on his rock, fortress, and deliverer (22:2). David discerned that when he was in trouble, he could call out to God and He would not just hear his cry, He would help him. More importantly, he recognized that when his attitude, character, and behavior conformed to God's standard of right, he could count on the Lord's favor.

What would I change today if I remembered God is with me? What would I do differently if my Undercover Father was suddenly visible? If I see unseen as absent, I am apt to loosen His standards. If I see unseen as present, I am apt to know His love.

Inspiration † † †

Be faithful in small things because it is in them that your strength lies.—Mother Theresa

Keep Your Obligation

February 11

1 Kings 2:2,3—As for me, I am going the way of all the earth. Be strong and be courageous like a man, and keep your obligation to the LORD your God to walk in His ways and to keep His statutes, commands, ordinances, and decrees. This is written in the law of Moses, so that you will have success in everything you do and wherever you turn, and so that the LORD will carry out His promise that He made to me: "If your sons are careful to walk faithfully before Me with their whole mind and heart, you will never fail to have a man on the throne of Israel."

As the time approached for him to die what thoughts crossed his mind? *"I am going the way of all the earth."* Death was knocking. Was he afraid? Probably not—his words give no hint of terror. I suspect his strong walk with God more than equipped him for his final steps.

"Be strong and be courageous . . ." David wrote the book on strength and courage. A lion, a bear, a giant, vast armies, he vanquished them all with fierce audacity. He watched his predecessor Saul, decay and fail. David's son must follow the father's lead.

"Keep your obligation to the LORD your God to walk in His ways . . ." Surely a country of vacillators vexed his soul! How many of them despite his edicts were still closet idol worshipers? How many failed to listen to God's commands because it was far more pleasurable to do whatever they wanted? He himself knew the price of sin. If Solomon would only be faithful to God, he would succeed.

Unfortunately, Solomon, the world's wisest man, chose the path of fools. He started out praying great prayers, built a colossal temple and secured the Lord's blessing. But his wisdom turned inward. He decided to play and find the meaning in foolishness. His dominant obligation became pleasing his foreign wives. To stem their incessant whining and to gain favor, he built them temples to their gods. He compromised his convictions to fulfill his sex drive. He became the world's most famous playboy and a first-hand expert on the word *meaningless*.

Keep your obligation. God gave you more than Solomon ever had. You have His ever-present Holy Spirit! It is hard to be enamored with rules. It is an honor to follow the Messiah. Let nothing come between you and your responsibility to love the Lord and to keep His ways.

Obligation is a noble word. It is the stuff of duty. It is the essence of binding and covenants. When we lose sight of this, we compromise; we settle for pleasing our whims and find ourselves wimps. Love is not enhanced by fickle behavior. We don't make champions out of two-faced people. Power and dignity, holiness and worship grow strong because you keep your obligation. When those around you see that you are faithful, is it any wonder that they want what you have? Keep your obligation.

Angels

February 12

On several occasions, I have read or heard amazing testimonies of people who experienced God's deliverance via angels from an enemy intent on their destruction. God's Word extensively teaches us about angels with over a 105 references to them in the Old Testament and more than 170 times in the New Testament. The Bible teaches that angels:

- were created by God prior to earth's creation—Psa. 148:2-5.
- initially were all good; when Lucifer turned against God, he coaxed multitudes into following him. We call evil angels demons—Rev. 12:9.
- take orders from God and serve Him by intervening, instructing or rescuing God's children—Gen. 16:9; 19; 24:40; Psa. 91:11; Luke 1:26-28.
- drive out/destroy enemies to help God's people and serve as instruments of punishment and judgment; one day they will gather and separate the wicked from the righteous—Exo. 33:2; 2 Sa. 24:16,17; 2 Ki. 19:35; Psa. 103:20; Mat. 13:41,49; Rev. 7:2.
- are without material form and often are invisible—Num. 22:25-31; Heb. 1:14.
- can appear as people—Gen. 18:1-8; Heb. 13:2.
- immediately transport from place to place not effected by fire or elements on earth—Jud. 6:21; 13:20.
- are completely reliable as God's servants—1 Sa. 29:9.
- are able through God to predict future events to people—Jud 13:3.
- eat food in heaven—Psa. 78:25.
- praise the Lord and live in His presence—Psa. 103:20, 148:2; Rev. 7:11.
- appear to people in dreams to provide instruction—Mat. 2:13.
- may actually be assigned (guardians) to protect people—Mat.18:10.
- are unmarried and pattern what we will experience after the resurrection—Mat. 22:30.
- bring healing to people—John 5:4.
- bring the gospel message to the lost—Acts 10:22.
- will return with Jesus when He comes back—Mat. 25:31.
- are prominent in heaven and seem to have a rank structure—Luke 12:8,9 Eph. 1:20,21; Col. 1:16.
- experience emotions such as joy and have their own mind and will—Luke 15:10; 2 Sam. 14:20; Rev. 22:8,9.
- are eternal—Luke 20:36.
- are not to be worshiped but must themselves worship God—Col. 2:18; Heb. 1:6.
- are countless in number—Rev. 5:11.
- fight against Satan and his demons—Rev.12:7.

1 Kings 19:5-7—Then he lay down and slept under the broom tree. Suddenly, an angel touched him. The angel told him, "Get up and eat." Then he looked, and there at his head was a loaf of bread baked over hot stones and a jug of water. So he ate and drank and lay down again. Then the angel of the LORD returned a second time and touched him. He said, "Get up and eat, or the journey will be too much for you."

Elijah, on the heels of a great victory over false prophets went into a panic when the wicked queen of Israel, Jezebel, threatened to murder him. He fled for his life and yet in the midst of great despair to the point of giving up on life, God sent an angel to minister to him. Elijah didn't ask God to dispatch an angel to rescue him. The Bible doesn't tell us if he even recognized his benefactor as an angel. It just informs us that he was strengthened by the food and water he received.

Do you ever wonder if God protects your life or provides for you supernaturally through an angel? Angels did not cease working after the time of the apostles—nowhere does the Bible even hint to such a thing. So we can safely assume that they are active on the earth serving God's purposes today. This encourages me to be more alert for them, to live more obediently since angels may be observing my behavior, and to be more mindful that when I am in trouble, it makes good sense to call out to God for His help. He has an enormous body of beings able to make a difference.

Grab His Feet! February 13

She was a wealthy woman of the best kind— thoughtful and generous. She noticed a man of God in need and she fed him. As he often frequented her town, she talked her husband into building a home addition so the man would have his own room furnished to meet his needs. Grateful for her kindness, the godly man asked her what he could do for her. She declined his offer. So he asked his helper what could be done for her. He saw that her husband was old and she had no children. So he called her to his room and as she stood in the doorway told her she would have a son the following spring. She asked him not to lie to her, but sure enough she gave birth to a boy. Years later the woman's son became ill and died. His mother immediately traveled to Mount Carmel where she found Elisha, fell on the ground and grabbed his feet.

2 Kings 4:28—Then she said, "Did I ask my lord for a son? Didn't I say, 'Do not deceive me?'"

A Shunammite woman held God to account for His action. She recognized the Lord blessed her with a son she never requested. His death then became a grave affront—for God is not cruel and His reputation was at stake—at least in her mind. In laying the responsibility for her son's life at Elisha's feet she in truth grabbed God's feet. Elisha had nothing to do with his illness and death but as God's representative, he had everything to do with his birth and life. I suspect her son's demise rendered God unjust before this righteous woman. His gift came into question. I imagine she was bitter in mind but better in heart— rather than accept bereavement and grieve she trusted that the same man who brought her unexpected joy could make things right. And he did.

Elisha stretched his body over her son's still form. God restored his life honoring her faith. This (2 Kings 4) is the story of a determined woman who pressed ahead until a holy God did what she knew to be right. In the process she honored God by her understanding and moxie.

What we know of God determines what we do before Him. Sometimes the best way to honor Him is to challenge from His hand what is incongruent with His word. So long as His glory is upheld our story is not finished. Do you struggle with God? Do you wonder why you lost what He gave you, or endure an ordeal that started with promise? Tell Him! Unload your grief and grab His feet. If the gift was from Him without your seeking it and tragedy ensues, plead for His restoration. He will either honor your persistent faith or give you eyes to see His deeper purpose for His higher glory.

Inspiration ✝✝✝

When God asks large steps of faith from us, he has already worked to prepare us through his deliverance in the past.—Russ Johnston in *Activate Your Faith*

Valentine's Day

February 14

When it comes to romance, maybe the wise thing for us to remember is that one day cannot offset 364 days. How we love the rest of the year speaks infinitely louder than the most creative gifts given on February 14.

I believe there are four keys to making a marriage prosper and endure and guys if we don't get this, we are doomed to a lot of hardship. (Apologies to the unmarried and to gals, but this message is for married men or those engaged to be married).

1. My first and most important priority is to love and fear the Lord! *"So be very diligent to love the LORD your God for your own well-being"* (Jos. 23:11).

> *How happy is everyone who fears the LORD, who walks in His ways! You will surely eat what your hands have worked for. You will be happy, and it will go well for you. Your wife will be like a fruitful vine within your house, your sons, like young olive trees around your table. In this very way the man who fears the LORD will be blessed.* (Psa. 128:1-4)

One of the reasons relationships fail or are miserable is we put our focus squarely on our wants at the expense of our walk with God. Often when I am most discouraged with my marriage, I am also most off-focus in my walk with God. My center of attention has shifted to my own needs. We see this problem in the life of Samson. In Jud. 14:3 we read:

> *But his father and mother said to him, "Can't you find a young woman among your relatives or among any of our people? Must you go to the uncircumcised Philistines for a wife?" But Samson told his father, "Get her for me, because I want her."*

2. My second priority is to marry someone who loves and fears the Lord. *"Charm is deceptive and beauty is fleeting, but a woman who fears the LORD will be praised"* (Pro. 31:30).

> *For if you turn away and cling to the rest of these nations remaining among you and if you intermarry or associate with them and they with you, know for certain that the LORD your God will not continue to drive these nations out before you. They will become a snare and a trap for you, a scourge for your sides and thorns in your eyes, until you disappear from this good land the LORD your God has given you.* (Jos. 23:12,13)

If your wife or fiancée does not love and fear the Lord, your marriage is doomed to pain and sorrow.

3. My third priority is to love and take pleasure in my wife. *"A man who finds a wife finds a good thing and obtains favor from the LORD"* (Pro. 18:22). *"Let your fountain be blessed, and take pleasure in the wife of your youth. A loving doe, a graceful fawn—let her breasts always satisfy you; be lost in her love forever"* (Pro. 5:18,19). *"In the same way, husbands are to love their wives as their own bodies. He who loves his wife loves himself"* (Eph. 5:28).

The key to romance is to really enjoy your mate! Therefore you meet her needs and have fun doing so. If I don't enjoy my wife or she does not enjoy me, I'm not emotionally and physically satisfied.

4. My fourth priority is to make sure my wife has all she needs to thrive. In Proverbs 31 we find key behavior from the husband that allows his wife to thrive. *"The heart of her husband trusts in her . . . Her husband also praises her . . . Give her the reward of her labor, and let her works praise her at the city gates."*

God prepares and gives us a wife that will complement us in the ways we need help and vice versa. Don't try to carve your wife into your own image or concept of what she should be! *"Husbands, in the same way, live with your wives with an understanding of their weaker nature yet showing them honor as co-heirs of the grace of life, so that your prayers will not be hindered"* (1 Pe.3:7).

The next time you feel critical toward your spouse or find yourself angry because of something she has done or not done, or said or not said, consider this. God chose us to be His bride. Despite our sins, He forgave and loved us. In spite of our inadequacies, He chose to have an eternal relationship with us. When we responded to His love, He covered our imperfection with grace. Isn't it awesome that Jesus models the way for us in the way He treats us!

The Last 100 Yards February 15

The Last 100 Yards is the National Infantry Museum's signature exhibit. Figures cast from current soldiers make up the life-like scenes representing eight wars fought by Americans. As guests make their way into the museum, they walk up a 100-yard-long inclining ramp, which signifies the infantry's role in taking the last 100 yards of any battle. As I walked the ramp with four other officers, the sights, sounds and solemn feel of the exhibit breathed sacrifice. We had progressed part way when Mr. Talley, an elderly guide, asked if he could share with us the significance of what we were seeing. He proudly discussed the detailed planning and symbolism behind each section. He shared about the tears and the deep emotion felt by many veterans and their families who visited the museum just outside Fort Benning, Georgia.

Mr. Talley directed our gaze out the window to the new parade field. Enlisted soldiers attending Officer Candidate School (OCS) now graduate before a grandstand instead of on a parking lot. Soil was transported to this field from eight actual battlegrounds fought in the Revolutionary War, War of 1812, Civil War, World Wars I & II, Viet-Nam, Korea and Iraq. Among the soil spreaders were descendants of Alexander Hamilton, Theodore Roosevelt and Alvin York, as well as Lieutenant General Hal Moore and Command Sergeant Basil Plumley, who led the historic assault on the Viet Cong at Landing Zone X-Ray. Before OCS graduates march onto the parade field, they learn they will take their oath of allegiance on grass grown in dirt their descendants once shed blood to liberate.

2 Kings 5:17—Naaman responded, "If not, please let your servant be given as much soil as a pair of mules can carry, for your servant will no longer offer a burnt offering or a sacrifice to any other god but Yahweh."

We come from dirt and dirt holds meaning. General Naaman, commander of the King of Aram's army, became a worshiper of Israel's God after He healed him of his leprosy. Naaman asked the prophet Elisha to allow him to take dirt from the land of Israel back to his own country so he could offer burnt offerings to God on earth he considered special. His cause was made certain by His Liberator.

If the stuff of dust can stir our hearts, imagine what the new earth God is planning will be like when we live with Him and all His glory! No longer will sin-infected blood spill on tainted soil. We will live with Jesus in our new eternal bodies. Each of us will testify forever to the truth and light of Him who made us and loves us.

Inspiration ✝ ✝ ✝

Our chief want is someone who will inspire us to be what we know we could be.—Ralph Waldo Emerson

He Tore His Robe

February 16

Have you ever served shifty leaders—men or women who despite the problems faced somehow evaded responsibility? I am reminded of politicians perhaps because their actions are most visible to the public. While there are certainly upright politicians, too often it seems that the majority of our elected leaders spend more time blaming the other party for the country's misfortunes than working to fix the crisis. Blaming others is attention shifting—a flawed technique applied by weak leaders. Unfortunately, we feed weakness by allowing those we vote in office to create and perpetuate a system that rewards them with lifetime perks and privileges. No matter what their convictions, once elected their need to stand answerable before us in fixing what is broken is compromised.

There is no corrupt-free government or form of governance in the world. Yet even in the darkest of times, a leader may emerge who devotes his authority and applies his power to doing what is right regardless of the cost. Meet King Josiah. Seated on Judah's throne at the age of eight, he ruled for thirty-one years. Around 623 B.C. in the eighteenth year of Josiah's reign, the high priest Hilkiah while repairing the temple, discovered the Book of the Law. Eventually the book was read to Josiah who after listening became so upset he tore his clothes. The 26 year-old ruler recognized that his nation was guilty of disobeying God's edicts (2 Kings 22:13).

Josiah, knowing his father and grandfather were corrupt could have rationalized that he was not accountable for Judah's problems. He could have blamed the people for worshiping idols and disobeying God. He could have criticized the priests for misplacing God's Word and failing to uphold their duties. Instead, he made himself answerable. By tearing his robe he took personal responsibility. What he did next is inspiring!

2 Kings 23:2,3—Then the king went to the LORD's temple with all the men of Judah and all the inhabitants of Jerusalem, as well as the priests and the prophets—all the people from the youngest to the oldest. As they listened, he read all the words of the book of the covenant that had been found in the LORD's temple. Next, the king stood by the pillar and made a covenant in the presence of the LORD to follow the LORD and to keep His commands, His decrees, and His statutes with all his mind and with all his heart, and to carry out the words of this covenant that were written in this book; all the people agreed to the covenant.

Henry & Richard Blackaby wrote in *Spiritual Leadership*, "Spiritual leaders seek God's will, whether it is for their church or for their corporation, and then they marshal their people to pursue God's plan."[8]

Lord, raise up Josiahs. Empower us with courage to do what is right and not to make excuses or shift blame. Help our leaders to be morally fit, answerable problem solvers!

Void or Valid?　　　　　　　　　　　　　　　　February 17

Have you ever boycotted a product because its maker was associated with wrongdoing? A company that endorses corruption or whose reputation is tainted by sleazy actions will not last long. Reputation is not something to be taken lightly.

1 Chronicles 5:1—These were the sons of Reuben the firstborn of Israel. He was the firstborn, but his birthright was given to the sons of Joseph son of Israel, because Rueben defiled his father's bed. He is not listed in the genealogy according to birthright.

Reuben could have been one of the most popular names in the Mideast and western world. As Jacob's firstborn of twelve sons, he was the possessor of the birthright which entitled him to a double portion of inheritance (see Deu. 21:15-17) and royal succession might have followed through his sons. Unfortunately, Reuben made a huge blunder. Genesis 35:22 records, *"While Israel was living in that region, Reuben went in and slept with his father's concubine Bilhah, and Israel heard about it."* This was an outrageous affront, a brazen act of disrespect to his father. Unfortunately, it was not the only thing Reuben did wrong. He had a reputation for being *"turbulent as water."* On Israel's deathbed as he spoke final words over his sons, he refrained from blessing Reuben, instead telling him he would no longer excel (Gen. 49:4). His birthright went to Joseph's sons Ephraim and Manasseh. Rueben's tribe never really amounted to much: they became void.

If history ran its normal course, do you realize that you and I would be void? Because a holy God cannot associate with evil, by His own right standard of justice we should be eternally separated from His presence. In effect, we would have no spiritual inheritance. I don't know about you, but I, to my shame, can think of many things I have done that were wrong, that clearly violated God's law. I am guilty. I have no excuse. My tribe of one, would be exiled forever to some superheated plot in hell were it not for Jesus.

If sin makes us void, grace makes us valid. But we have to renounce our sin and follow Jesus to receive that grace. If we continuously choose to ignore what God wants, to have what we want, then grace clearly is not at work in us. A life changed by the Holy Spirit resists sin. A life continually running after sin will fill a space void of God and void of meaning.

Inspiration ✝✝✝

"Void" means the aftermath of destruction by judgement, or the result of Divine judgement.—Oswald Chambers in *Biblical Psychology*

It Was God's Battle!

February 18

Brian *dreamed* for a long time of building a house for his family on a wooded, five-acre plot of land nestled within the city. He did not just want to put up a simple home for his family of five. He wanted to build a ten-thousand square foot ministry center. I remember many of us thought he was overreaching. Why not just build a modest home and then, as God provided, continue to expand?

Brian started construction and soon the framing of his large home was in place. From the outset he faced continuous setbacks. He incurred costly lawsuits stemming from accounting errors. The Fire Department insisted *he* pay $28,000 for a fire hydrant. When he sought to put in a water tank at considerably less expense, they resisted his efforts and delayed for months his ability to move into the completed home. Permits took far too long to obtain from city officials who seemed intent to block his efforts to build. Neighbors filed false complaints about creek diversion which brought in the Corps of Engineers. Stairs had to be redone because they were $1/8^{th}$ of an inch off. What a battle just to construct a home.

Many people live and have lived with Brian and his family. Two groups and a house church meet every week for counseling and for worship. A small cottage for prayer sits on the property. Indeed a ministry center thrives and people's lives are impacted for God's glory.

1 Chronicles 5:20,22—They received help against these enemies because they cried out to God in battle, and the Hagrites and all their allies were handed over to them. He granted their request because they trusted in Him . . . Many of the Hagrites were killed because it was God's battle. And they lived there in the Hagrites' place until the exile.

The Israelites were commanded by God to inhabit Canaan. But knowing where they were supposed to live was far easier than actually dislodging their enemies. Notice that prayer and trust were vital in spite of the fact they were fighting God's fight.

How often do we face battles that are of our own making? Assumptions and presumptions too often are the bad fruit of self-reliance. Nowhere does it say in Scripture, "I can do all things through my own strength." Before taking action we must be clear that we are in line with God's will. A helpful question we ought to ask is, "Is this a battle that results in the advancement of God's Kingdom, or is it my own kingdom I am furthering?" Once we are sure we are doing what God laid on our heart, we still need to pray and trust Him. Prayer and faith help us keep perspective that the battle is the Lord's and in His power and provision we will prevail!

First to Kill

February 19

1 Chronicles 11:6—David said, "Whoever is the first to kill a Jebusite will become chief commander." Joab son of Zeruiah went up first, so he became the chief.

Max Depree in *Leadership Jazz* wrote, "Leaders are fragile precisely at the point of their strengths, liable to fail at the height of their success." Words definitely matter. So do our actions. On the surface, it appears that King David made a smart decision. He needed to defeat the Jebusites, the inhabitants of Jerusalem who had a successful history of repelling would-be conquerors. They told David, "*You will never get in here*" (v. 5). David needed a general to lead Israel's army so he issued the challenge in our verse for meditation. The king got what he wanted. Zeruiah's three sons, Joab, Abishai and Asahel were all warriors and Joab seized the opportunity afforded by David's challenge, and killed the first Jebusite.

David's words, "*first to kill*," would come back to haunt him. Joab was much more than a strong commander, he was a killing machine. When the king tried to reconcile Judah's army with Israel's army by giving the command to Abner, Joab stuck a knife in his stomach and killed him in retaliation for Abner killing his brother Asahel in battle. When David committed adultery and needed Bathsheba's husband, Uriah the Hittite to be eliminated, Joab supported David's treachery by ensuring Uriah was killed in battle. When David's son Absalom revolted and tried to take his throne, Joab violated the king's specific instructions not to harm Absalom by thrusting three spears in his heart. Finally, without authorization, Joab stabbed Israel's commander Amasa in the stomach. Henry & Richard Blackaby wrote in *Spiritual Leadership*, "People who are unable to admit their errors are not qualified to be leaders." Joab repeatedly justified his penchant to kill first; consequently his life ended tragically.

How might Judah and Israel's history have changed if David, instead of selecting a leader on his willingness to kill, had gone to God instead and prayerfully asked for His counsel? How might his reign have changed if instead of a cut-throat leader, he selected an honorable, God-fearing man? Courage without discretion is a recipe for recklessness. Certainly Joab was brave and did some exemplary things as a leader. But he could not restrain his anger nor govern his cruel impulses.

General H. Norman Schwarzkopf noted, "Leadership is character and competence. If you can only have one, opt for character." Macho words and crowd-pleasing heroics may make for good action footage, but if a leader's character is seriously flawed, in the end there will only be heartbreak and death. I suspect David on his deathbed wished he had done some things much differently. It may be the same for us if we fail to consult the Lord.

Akaba

February 20

In 1931, a great outpouring of the Holy Spirit took place in Rwanda. Believers in several nations prayed for God to transform Rwandan lives. Consequently, men and women became deeply convicted of their wrongdoing and in true repentance humbled themselves confessing their sins. Those who had wronged others apologized and made restitution. At the center of Rwandan revival, new believers were called *Abaka*, which meant "those on fire." As A.C. Stanley Smith wrote in his book, *Road to Revival*, joy constantly reflected in the faces of these believers and everywhere they went they modeled powerful testimony.

Wherever the Holy Spirit transforms lives there is the unmistakable sign of joy. An altered life is like a newly commissioned beacon. But a lit match is not the same as a roaring forest fire. When peace is elusive, famine common, water polluted, debt ascendant and emptiness a bestseller, one or two new believers hardly garners the attention of the lost. This is a great time for us to pray for Abaka—a large harvesting of new believers!

Imagine what would happen if your city became so convicted of sin that instantaneously people fell on their knees and cried out to God for forgiveness! Can the Holy Spirit charge dead cells of entire neighborhoods with the roaring love of Jesus if they will cry out for the Savior? I believe He can and I suspect you do as well.

2 Chronicles 7:13,14—If I close the sky so there is no rain, or if I command the grasshopper to consume the land, or if I send pestilence on My people, and My people who are called by My name humble themselves, pray and seek My face, and turn from their evil ways, then I will hear from heaven, forgive their sin, and heal their land.

Sin is a sure determinant in keeping God from awesomely working through His children to bring revival. If we are feeling the effects of divine punishment, we ought to understand that we have opportunity to apply a scriptural prescription found in 2 Chronicles 7:14. This inspired word from heaven tells us how to gain God's favor which is a huge precursor to revival. First, we who are called by God's name, must humble ourselves. Our pride is the sure symptom of spiritual dystrophy. Second, we must pray and seek God's face. This is not a one-time formulaic prayer but rather a persevering heart cry! Alongside prayer comes our third step, we must turn from our wicked ways. God never flowers what sin waters. A historical study of revivals shows that when these conditions are present, God often brings Akaba.

The Approaching Army — February 21

My friend David Brown was in a bicycle accident and broke his neck. Aside from the reality that he should be dead, I cannot imagine how he felt when he was fully conscious and realized that he was dealing with significant paralysis.

2 Chronicles 20:2-4—People came and told Jehoshaphat, "A vast number from beyond the Dead Sea and from Edom has come to fight against you; they are already in Hazazon-tamar" (that is, En-gedi). Jehoshaphat was afraid, and he resolved to seek the LORD. Then he proclaimed a fast for all Judah, who gathered to seek the LORD. They even came from all the cities of Judah to seek Him.

An approaching army of astounding size moved in confidence to destroy the nation of Judah. King Jehoshaphat faced three nations intent on his eradication. No wonder he was afraid! He had several options. He could seek help from other kingdoms—a ploy frequently used. He could surrender and pay tribute to his captors. He could fight, but his army was vastly outnumbered. Instead, he set his heart on God for help. Men, women and children from all around the country traveled to join him and they all literally stood together, waiting on the Lord to respond.

We honor God when we give our fear to Him. The Lord spoke directly to King Jehoshaphat and the gathered crowd through the prophet Jahaziel. He instructed them on how He would deliver them from their enemies (20:15-17). If you want to read an amazing battle account, read 2 Ch. 20:18-30!

Like Jehoshaphat, my friend David had several options. He could give up and despair of life—overcome by the panic of no feeling and difficulty breathing. He could blame God for his accident and live in anger and bitterness. He could turn inward and cut out those around him. Instead, like that Judah king of old, he sought God choosing to worship Him. Daily, David covers fear with praise. He ministers to the nurses and doctors and prays for them as they provide therapy. Amazingly, he is regaining movement in his feet, hands and arms. He will walk again! Those around him cannot help but see the hand of the Almighty.

When fear fills your mouth so you can barely swallow, what do you do? How you evaluate, engage and emerge from what threatens you says much about where you invest your trust. Face your greatest enemies and know that God is greater. Give your horror to Him and peace emerges. Submit your terror to prayer and experience His arms. Death is stingless if Jesus is your selected Savior.

Paying Homage

February 22

There is a slang term in the English language, *brown nose*. It means to seek favor in a fawning manner. For example, someone may pay you a compliment to make you feel good about yourself while in reality what that person wants is simply to gain your favor or a higher standing. Those who observe people brown nosing, often ridicule them directly or behind their back because the action smacks of flattery that lacks genuineness.

Brown nosing is the seamy side of paying homage, which should be a dignified act. Centuries ago in European society, a vassal might surrender himself to the feudal lord, by kneeling and giving his joined hands to the nobleman, who clasped them in his own, thus accepting the surrender.

2 Chronicles 24:17,18—However, after Jehoiada died, the rulers of Judah came and paid homage to the king. Then the king listened to them, and they abandoned the temple of Yahweh, the God of their ancestors and served the Asherah poles and the idols. So there was wrath against Judah and Jerusalem for this guilt of theirs.

The Bible tells us, "Throughout the time of Jehoiada the priest, Joash did what was right in the LORD's sight" (24:2). However, as soon as the priest died, officials from Judah came and turned his heart. How did they succeed in corrupting a good king? My hunch is it had much to do with paying homage. Those rulers appealed to King Joash's ego stroking his sense of importance such that the king viewed himself higher than he viewed God. Why else would he rebel from his Lord and authorize idol worship? Undoubtedly, those evil rulers stood to gain from the practice of idol worship. They may have resented the authority and prominence of a religious priest. Somehow, they so corrupted the king's thinking that he commanded that Johoiada's son, Zechariah, be stoned to death after the priest's son chastised the people for turning away from God. What a tragic turnaround for a leader who knew better!

Allen Bond said, "The bigger I grow in God, the smaller I become." How is your ego? What happens inside your heart when people attempt to curry your goodwill by sweet talk? If our need for importance, power, or control is out of balance, we are set up to accept hype and praise and potentially make compromising decisions. One course of action will help keep us in balance. As soon as someone gives you praise (whether it be genuine or with an agenda), deflect the glory to God. *"Not to us, Yahweh, not to us, but to Your name give glory because of Your faithful love, because of Your truth"* (Psa. 115:1). The Lord is the worthy One! If there is to be homage, let it be to Him.

Inspiration ✝✝✝

A man wrapped up in himself makes a very small bundle.—Benjamin Franklin.

Heroic

February 23

Jeff plays the game of soccer. He is not an impact player who by great talent can take over a game. In fact in many ways he is limited. But he gives all he has. At a fifty-plus age in a league where most players are in their late thirties and early forties, he is quite amazing. You see he never stops looking for an opportunity to score. By sheer persistence he manages occasionally to do what better players fail to accomplish—put the ball in the net! In my book his play is the stuff of the heroic.

The dictionary defines heroes as persons noted for courageous feats or nobility of purpose, especially those who risked or sacrificed their lives. We tend to be mesmerized by the spectacular and worship the incredible. The heroic person is the one who makes the ordinary the extraordinary.

2 Chronicles 31:17,18—They distributed also to those recorded by genealogy of the priests by their ancestral families and the Levites 20 years old and above, by their responsibilities in their divisions; to those registered by genealogy—with all their infants, wives, sons, and daughters—of the whole assembly (for they had faithfully consecrated themselves as holy).

Do you ever get tired of the regular rhythm of life? Does it seem like your relationship with God is about as exciting as canoeing down an irrigation canal? Then stop paddling. Recognize there is a current at work.

If your idea of a heroic follower of God is the crowd-enthralling evangelist, the talented pastor, or the monastery monk, is it possible you have defined importance by vocation? While any and all of those people may be heroes, in God's eyes the heroic follower is the faithful follower. Nowhere does the Bible pronounce the job as the focal point. As Dr. John George noted, "Being "full time" for the Lord is a condition of the heart, not a job title!" It is the relationship we hold with God throughout the work that we do that He values. Therefore, you are heroic by getting up each morning and dedicating the day in prayer to the Lord; by taking joy in mopping the floor or cooking or teaching or selling or building because in your heart burns a never ending blaze to know and please God.

Solomon wrote, in Proverbs 20:6, *"Many a man proclaims his own loyalty, but who can find a trustworthy man?"* Don't let the blur of time rob you of the joy of the eternal. Your relationship to God will be seasoned with joy if you see the ordinary as your opportunity to make a statement. *"Therefore, whether you eat or drink, or whatever you do, do everything for God's glory"* (1 Co. 10:31). That's heroic.

Inspiration ✝✝✝

I bring you the gift of these four words: I believe in you.—Blaise Pascal

Failed Marriage

February 24

Wando* and I drove to Tigard to pick up the parts we needed to fix the broken pipe in my garage. The first two hardware stores we checked did not have the couplings necessary to fix the half-inch pipe so we had plenty of time to chat. Wando shared about his failed marriage. It bothered him that his life bore the stain of an unsuccessful relationship. I took the opportunity to share with him about Jesus and how essential I believe the Son of God is to holding marriages together. He agreed in the importance of "a higher power."

Ezra 9:3,4—When I heard this report, I tore my tunic and robe, pulled out some of the hair from my head and beard, and sat down devastated. Everyone who trembled at the words of the God of Israel gathered around me, because of the unfaithfulness of the exiles, while I sat devastated until the evening offering.

If devastation is the sudden realization of disaster, discouragement is the lingering pain. Ezra returned to Jerusalem from Babylon. God's holy priest discovered that the Israelite people took wives from the Canaanites, Hittites, Perizzites, Jebusites, Ammonites, Moabites, Egyptians and Amorites (9:1). God strictly warned them not to do this. The act of inter-marrying often led to worshipping foreign idols and forsaking Yahweh.

Realizing the severity of their sin, the people gathered around Ezra and wept bitterly. It was the rainy season and the weather reflected their gloomy spirits. Then Shecaniah, a wise bystander, proposed a solution:

Let us therefore make a covenant before our God to send away all the foreign wives and their children, according to the counsel of my lord and of those who tremble at the command of our God . . . Get up, for this matter is your responsibility, and we support you. Be strong and take action! (10:3,4)

An energized Ezra got up and made the leaders take an oath to do what Shec proposed. A proclamation circulated calling the people to separate from their foreign wives. The people responded in agreement.

Can you imagine this happening today? The excuses not to obey God would fall thicker than a heavy rain. Perhaps this is why discouragement is prevalent among God's children. Have we become so conditioned to living as we please, that we refuse to take the difficult steps to be holy? I believe the cure to discouragement is to do what is right. God empowers us when we move in accordance with His will and not when we move by the dictates of our flesh. Friend, if you are discouraged, ask God to show you what you need to do. Get up and do it. Be strong and take action!

*Not his real name

Billy Graham Came to Seoul   February 25

When I was in Junior High School, Billy Graham came to Seoul, Korea. I was able to sit on a platform close to where the speakers stood and take pictures. At the time (early 1970's), it was the largest Billy Graham Crusade ever. Looking behind the platform there on Yoido Island there was an immense sea of people. Dr. Graham explained to this spiritually hungry audience the meaning of the gospel. He quoted John 3:16, read other Bible passages, and outlined in simple terms God's plan of salvation. Hundreds of thousands of Koreans stood and moved forward when he gave an invitation. Countless faces were wet with tears of repentance. I imagine heaven cheered watching this grand spectacle.

Nehemiah 8:7,8—Jeshua, Bani, Sherebiah, Jamin, Akkub, Shabbethai, Hodiah, Maaseiah, Kelita, Azariah, Jozabad, Hanan, and Pelaiah, who were Levites, explained the law to the people as they stood in their places. They read out of the book of the law of God, translating and giving the meaning so that the people could understand what was read.

Around 457 B.C., the Jews were spiritually impoverished. Their ancestors stopped venerating God to worship idols. They disobeyed what Moses taught to run after their own pleasures. They lost their homeland to disease, famine, and Assyrians and Babylonians who led them as captives into exile. They experienced every disaster God warned they would suffer for disobeying Him.

On the first day of the seventh month (Tishrei) in the Hebrew calendar, Ezra the scribe stood on a high wooden platform facing about 5000 people he led back to Israel. Along with thirteen Levites, he read from the Torah from daybreak until noon. When he opened up the Scripture, all the people stood and remained standing for hours.

The Hebrew-written Torah was unfamiliar to the Aramaic-speaking people. Furthermore, they did not own their own copies of the law so Moses' writing was unfamiliar to them. Consequently, it was necessary to translate and explain the law. As the people listened and comprehended, they wept. The crowd was so convicted by God's Words that Ezra and the Levites had to quiet them from grieving.

St. Alphonsus Luguori wrote in *A Good Confession*, "For a good confession three things are necessary: an examination of conscience, sorrow, and a determination to avoid sin." Confession is a great thing. It is a profound sign of a dramatic awakening to renounce sin.

Inspiration   † † †

It is impossible rightly to govern the world without God and the Bible.—President George Washington

Self Control

February 26

Before I write about self-control I must share a disclaimer. I struggle with this area. I wrestle against impure thoughts. I don't always use my time wisely. I say or do things I shouldn't. I have a long ways to go to be like my hero—Jesus. It is foolish to think I can control myself by my own doing.

Nehemiah 5:14,15— Furthermore, from the day King Artaxerxes appointed me to be their governor in the land of Judah—from the twentieth year until his thirty-second year, 12 years—I and my associates never ate from the food allotted to the governor. The governors who preceded me had heavily burdened the people, taking food and wine from them, as well as a pound of silver. Their subordinates also oppressed the people, but I didn't do this, because of the fear of God.

Governor Nehemiah did not take advantage of the perks of office. He refused to amass wealth or to eat the rich foods he could have enjoyed. He exercised self-control. What made him different from the previous rulers? He feared God. His reverence revealed his understanding of the law God passed to the Israelites through Moses on how leaders should act. Nehemiah was a great role model for us in:

How to be Self Controlled

1. Die to self. Peter the Great once said, "I have conquered an empire but I have not been able to conquer myself." Self-control is our problem; God-control is our need. Jesus said in order to follow Him we must say "no" to SELFish ambition through self-denial (Luke 9:23). We must take inventory of whatever things control us and willfully put them under God's authority.

2. Be like Christ. Whatever rules our heart dictates our behavior. If our hearts are set on pleasing Jesus, our lives will be transformed. *"Guard your heart above all else, for it is the source of life"* (Pro. 4:23). Two things help us stay Christ-centered:

- Trust God. See Proverbs 3:5,6. The reason we fail to overcome our shortcomings is we rationalize our behavior or we rely upon human remedies at the expense of believing in the sufficiency of God's power.

- Obey God. Out of reverence for God, we study His Word. Then we can discern how we should live. We work to be receptive to the Holy Spirit's leading. To rebel against His lordship pridefully suggests we know what is best.

Inspiration † † †

Biblical self-control is not a product of one's own natural willpower.—Jerry Bridges in *Respectable Sins*

George Mueller

February 27

Nehemiah 9:19-21—You did not abandon them in the wilderness because of Your great compassion. During the day the pillar of cloud never turned away from them, guiding them on their journey. And during the night the pillar of fire illuminated the way they should go. You sent Your good Spirit to instruct them. You did not withhold Your manna from their mouths, and You gave them water for their thirst. You provided for them in the wilderness 40 years and they lacked nothing. Their clothes did not wear out, and their feet did not swell.

Absolutely fantastic! Imagine if you were a logistician responsible for feeding, clothing, sheltering, providing water plus directing over one million people through a harsh barren desert for forty years! God provided manna; I'd be a maniac! Yet, God perfectly outfitted and guided a nation that often resisted, complained, and misunderstood Him. His guidance was miraculous and inspiring. The Bible gives us a thorough resume of God's accomplishments in the leadership arena!

Do you ever wonder how you might go about finding God's will for your life? George Mueller daily sought God's leading and intervention. This 19th century Englishman was led by the Lord to build four orphanages that provided care for over 10,000 children. The humble pastor distributed over $8,000,000 that God provided! His recipe for obtaining heavenly help is timeless and Biblical.

1. Beginning with prayer, Mueller sincerely sought God's direction.
2. With patience and reflection he waited on God to give him instruction (whether through godly people or circumstances).
3. He relied upon the Holy Spirit to illuminate Scripture that would guide him.
4. He learned that if he lacked honesty, lived improperly, was impatient in waiting on God, and preferred the counsel of men over the Bible, mistakes were sure to follow.
5. Once he possessed a sound peace that he was in line with God's will he proceeded to act.[9]

What could be more awesome than to have God as our guide and provider! Moses proclaimed, *"You will lead the people You have redeemed with Your faithful love; You will guide them to Your holy dwelling with Your strength"* (Exo. 15:13). May God teach us how to be faithful in following Him—for His glory and our sure footing! *"The one who has clean hands and a pure heart, who has not set his mind on what is false, and who has not sworn deceitfully. He will receive blessing from the LORD, and righteousness from the God of his salvation"* (Psa. 24:4,5).

Primary Purpose

February 28

I read a fascinating article in *The Oregonian*.
Having a sense of purpose in life seems to provide a shield against illness—particularly in old age . . . Those with the highest sense of purpose were half as likely to develop Alzheimer's disease than those with the lowest sense of purpose during seven years of follow-up . . . In an earlier study, the same group (Rush University Medical Center in Chicago) found that the risk of dying from any cause was nearly cut in half among women and men with a greater sense of purpose.[10]

Esther 10:3—Mordecai the Jew was second only to King Ahasuerus, famous among the Jews, and highly popular with many of his relatives. He continued to seek good for his people and to speak for the welfare of all his descendants.

Between 486-465 B.C. a large population of Jews lived in Persia under the reign of King Ahasuerus I. The most prominent leader under the king was a man by the name of Mordecai. The book of Esther gives a fascinating account of this leader with a clearly defined purpose—all his life he sought to promote the welfare of his people.

So what is your purpose in life? If your primary purpose is to be a great athlete, what happens when you no longer can compete with those younger and stronger? What are the consequences if your primary purpose becomes pleasing yourself? If your primary purpose is to be rich, when is enough, enough? If your primary purpose is to obtain power or popularity, how will you handle sickness and mortality? Could it be that every purpose under the sun pales before the purpose to please God?

Mordecai's intention to help his people tied into a deeper purpose of honoring and serving God. So what is your first cause? If you live to worship God, your life will radiate joy. This joy is impervious to the pain, sin, heartache, sorrow and loss that come from living in a fallen world. When we purpose to live for God, we learn by grace that our worth is not determined by age, energy level, mental capacity or social-economic status. Our worth is eternally priceless through Jesus the Savior who gave His life to make us matter. Purpose focused on pleasing God renders a hallelujah vocabulary in a *helloyuck* society. It honors the very God whose purpose is to bless us with an eternal relationship with Him in a future world where awesome will be a weak adjective.

Inspiration †††

Purpose is the foundation for everything.—Dave Kraft in *Leaders Who Last*

Sorry I Was a Jerk   March 1

Sometimes the Lord gives us opportunity to see our failings. A flaw noted should be corrected while a flaw ignored may grow into a character fissure. With about thirty other leaders, I was blessed to spend seven days learning about strategic leadership at the University of North Carolina from wise professors and senior military leaders.

One afternoon we divided into teams to work on an exercise meant to teach us about conducting negotiations. Each of us had a specific role. There were five men and one woman in our group. Knowing that we would each have to give up some conditions for the scenario to work, I came into the room and took charge. I shared that if we were honest up front and worked together without a hidden agenda, we could solve the problem we faced. The men agreed and so I stood at the marker board and began writing each point of negotiation we would have to vote.

Janet* seemed irritated. She said if she did not agree, she could veto the whole process. While that was true, it made no sense to us because she represented the company making the proposal we were debating! The more we pushed to vote, the more she resisted and became abrasive. Finally, in frustration, all the men walked out. I went back to her and asked what was wrong. She shared that she thought we were trying to "game" the exercise and were not serious about working through it diligently. I assured her that was not the case and felt like I was able to gain her support. It was not long before we solved the problem with unanimous consent. I was quite pleased with my work.

Later, each of the teams gathered to debrief and share what we learned. When it was our team's turn, the professor in charge asked me why I took the lead in the negotiations. I explained my reasoning and then she asked Janet how she felt about this. Janet shared that my actions disrupted her plan and frustrated her. It was clear that I spoiled the exercise for her. As I listened, my spirit sank. Yes, I completely overlooked Janet's role. I was so certain I had the solution that I spent no time considering that I really had no business leading. The next morning I sought her out and apologized for being a jerk. She was kind and dismissed the whole episode as a simple negotiation misunderstanding.

Job 16:3,4—Is there no end to your empty words? What provokes you that you continue testifying? If you were in my place I could also talk like you. I could string words together against you and shake my head at you.
33:3—My words come from my upright heart, and my lips speak with sincerity what they know.

Have you ever punctured a balloon and then tried to inflate it? It doesn't work! Likewise, an insensitive remark or tactless action can ruin the mental and emotional state of another person. Being right does not justify insensitivity. Conversely, being sensitive does not mean saying or doing only what someone wants. Jesus always treated people correctly—whether they liked it or not. Jesus was <u>never</u> thoughtless. Clear reflection helps us see that insensitive remarks or actions come from faulty thinking or a self-absorbed mind. *Lord, help me to treat people the way You would treat them.*

*Not her real name

Inspiration ✝✝✝

However sincere we may have been at certain times, all of us have stepped outside the will of God in well-meaning attempts to solve our own problems.— Jack Hayford in *Worship His Majesty*

Crises

March 2

There are dark days I will never forget:
- President John F. Kennedy's assassination
- the day my mother died
- the day I broke my collarbone
- 12-12-85 the Gander crash
- February 14, 1991 when Bryan's brain stem glioma was discovered
- Stephen falling from the deck
- 9-11
- Dad breaking his neck

Job 27:9,10—Will God hear his cry when distress comes on him? Will he delight in the Almighty? Will he call on God at all times?

Oswald Chambers wrote in *So Send I You* "Crises always reveal character, and we are all ignorant of our true character until it is revealed in us." Many people believe that their character is formed by tragedies or hardships. But this is not where character is shaped so much as revealed.

Character is built slowly in the workshop of daily life. My moral ethical behavior will be stellar in the midst of calamity if it is strengthened in the normative process of living. Faith cannot rise to the challenge of trusting God through pain if I have not trusted Him in my normal daily life. How can I love God when bad things happen if I don't learn to love Him when normal or good things are happening? Don't be afraid of crises. Fear complacency.

My brother found out that the $300,000 that Solace International looked forward to for its annual funding was pulled because the donor organization was too financially strapped to give. Essentially, this would end Solace's ability to survive. Instead of bemoaning this crisis, Nate saw it as an opportunity to bring about much needed change. When we leave all that we have in God's hands, we don't have to worry what others hand or do not hand us! Nate's choices were "bitter and self-reliant" or "better and God-reliant." Praise God, a tested character withstood this test.

Inspiration ✝✝✝

I like the two Oriental characters for the word crisis. In both Japanese and Chinese, they mean "threatening opportunity."—Jack Hayford, John Killinger and Howard Stevenson in *Mastering Worship*

A crisis is when you can't say: "let's forget the whole thing."—Ferguson's Precept

Turning Away

March 3

I can imagine what happened. She had lived there too long. Over time, she grew increasingly used to the sleaze to the point where the vices probably no longer shocked her. No doubt she and her family gossiped about the bizarre and strange conduct of the city's inhabitants. The two men soon to marry her daughters were resistant. Even her husband hesitated—unsure about leaving. In the end the persistent angels grabbed their hands and pulled the four of them outside the city. They warned them to run and not look back. But she didn't get far before she turned around just once to see what should not be seen. That turning away made her a pillar of salt (Gen. 19).

Job 28:28—He said to mankind, "The fear of the Lord is this: wisdom. And to turn from evil is understanding."

Very few people just run up to evil and embrace it. Rather they embark on a campaign of compromise. They rationalize. They color truth to fit their circumstances. They develop questionable habits because they feel entitled. They get angry when people question their motives. They find inconsistency and label it hypocrisy in those they observe while quietly engaging in their own pet sins.

Evil is not a hero we worship but rather a companion we tolerate until he actually grows on us, in us and over us. When we feel good about ourselves, evil pats our back and says, "That's right, you are pretty good— a lot better than so many others."

There is a cure to evil. It is called the fear of the Lord. It is the essence of wisdom, the nectar of perception. John Bunyan noted, "It is not the knowledge of the will of God, but our sincere complying therewith, that proves we fear the Lord." When we revere God, we <u>have</u> to turn away from sin—we know it violates His holiness and angers Him. John Murray noted, "The highest reaches of sanctification are realized only in the fear of God."[11]

> *The LORD hates six things; in fact, seven are detestable to Him: arrogant eyes, a lying tongue, hands that shed innocent blood, a heart that plots wicked schemes, feet eager to run to evil, a lying witness who gives false testimony, and one who stirs up trouble among brothers. (Pro. 6:16-19)*
>
> *Therefore, put to death what belongs to your worldly nature: sexual immorality, impurity, lust, evil desire, and greed, which is idolatry. Because of these, God's wrath comes on the disobedient. (Col. 3:5-6)*
>
> *Then He said, "What comes out of a person—that defiles him. For from within, out of people's hearts, come evil thoughts, sexual immoralities, thefts, murders, adulteries, greed, evil actions, deceit, promiscuity, stinginess, blasphemy, pride, and foolishness. All these evil things come from within and defile a person. (Mark 7:20-23)*

God-fearers cannot stomach the thought of hurting their loving Creator. Evil avoidance promotes purity and gives us a vibrant life. Turning away from evil deepens our friendship with our Savior and keeps us on the path He prepared for us.

The next time you are in a theater and the actors swear in God's name, use filthy language and engage in disgusting conduct, get up and walk out. So you wasted your money—at least you demonstrated understanding. The next time you watch a questionable program on television or visit an unwholesome internet site, turn the channel, escape the web, starve the desire and feed your heart with fear—godly fear.

Our character cracks into numerous fissures when we entertain evil. Forgetting about God's will and disrespecting Him for sin leads to tragedy. Conversely, our character is strengthened when we honor God's intent and live so as to be like Him. By rejecting what is wrong we experience great blessing and find heaven's favor.

Surprisingly, we don't hear much taught about the fear of God and that is particularly sad because it is a major theme that runs from Genesis to Revelation. As Jerry Bridges notes in *The Joy of Fearing God*, "There are more than 150 references to the fear of God in the Bible." In the end, God always provides the way of escape as He promises (1 Co. 10:13), but He leaves the choice to us.

Mount Fuji

March 4

From my room on the third floor we could see Mt. Fuji, a picturesque snow-capped volcano. Fuji, the glory of Japan, is the tallest and most celebrated mountain on a densely populated island. It is the celebrity of postcards. A treasured possession is a walking stick stamped with the mark of stations climbers achieve as they hike to the top. It's just a huge hill of slippery rock and snow but one would think it a god.

Job 38:4-7— Where were you when I established the earth? Tell Me, if you have understanding. Who fixed its dimensions? Certainly you know! Who stretched a measuring line across it? What supports its foundations? Or who laid its cornerstone while the morning stars sang together and all the sons of God shouted for joy?

If a mountain can cause such veneration what wonder does the Maker of mountains evoke? I watched an awe-inspiring sun send purplish hues behind the crowing peak of Mt. Fuji as it began another day. And God came to mind. There would be no life without our Father in heaven. We would have no view to admire if we had no breath to breathe. The wonder of life is the wonder of God. He is inspiring. His love goes beyond the description of man's most lofty words. I stand amazed. I bow in worship to You, O Great and Mighty God!

"If you have lost the fervor of delight in God, tell Him so . . . When wonder goes out of natural love, something or someone is to be severely blamed; wonder ought never to go."[12]

Positivity

March 5

Our headquarters folks put together a goodbye potluck for Marie. She served in the 104th Division for over 3 decades and many will greatly miss her. As I thought about what to say in my remarks to her, I remembered a quality in *Strength Finders* called "positivity." I read the description to the assembled crowd and asked them who it reminded them of as I looked at her. They knowingly laughed and applauded, for Marie is the essence of a positive and happy person.

Psalm 1:1-3—How happy is the man who does not follow the advice of the wicked or take the path of sinners or join a group of mockers! Instead, his delight is in the LORD's instruction, and he meditates on it day and night. He is like a tree planted beside streams of water that bears its fruit in season and whose leaf does not wither. Whatever he does prospers.

Do you know the way to attain genuine happiness is spelled out in the first three verses of the book of Psalms? Note the dual aspect of what God teaches. First, we learn three things that cannot happen if we hope to be happy. We cannot accept the advice of the wicked. Evil is antithetical to good and it makes sense that suggestive evil leads to collective sorrow. We cannot walk the course of sinners or join their actions. James 4:4 teaches us that *"friendship with the world is hostility towards God."* We cannot bond with those who are mockers. Mockers deify sarcasm, profane what is holy and pollute what is good.

Second, we learn that happiness has a source—God's Word. When we value His instruction, we set in our foundation a powerful principle. We recognize truth. We think about what it means for how we should live and we apply it—another way of describing meditation.

The Hebrew word for happy is *"ashrei."*[3] Leah after giving birth to her second son, in Genesis 30:13, said, *"'I am happy that the women call me happy,' so she named him Asher."* Asher means happy! When you see a happy person, you see someone who in disposition is healthy, someone who consistently prospers. This prospering in context means living according to God's instruction.

If you are not happy, go back and take personal inventory. Are you engaged in any of the actions the psalmist deplores? Are you aware of God's instruction, thinking about it and applying it? If the answer is no, the attitude will show. Happiness *can* be fabricated on a temporary basis but it will not persevere unless the conditions established in Scripture are obeyed. This is why Marie is a fruit-bearing bouquet. She is anchored in following God.

The Lifter

March 6

On a chilly Saturday I bartered for a Sheltie puppy (5 cases of dehydrated food (MREs), two music stands and an old amplifier)! I brought the 10-week-old, tri-color pup home from Silverton, Oregon and he and Hero, our Lab puppy, fast became best friends. Hero is about 55 pounds larger, but that does not seem to intimidate our newest addition—Saber. It is hilarious watching them joust and wrestle and playfully bite.

Yesterday, our neighbor Chris, rang the doorbell and informed us that Saber was trapped in our fishpond and swimming as hard as he could. I ran around to the back yard and discovered an amazing sight. Hero had jumped into the pond and was paddling right beside Saber, evidently providing moral support. As soon as Hero saw me, he easily jumped out, jumped on me and got me soaking wet as I lifted little Saber out of the water. Wow, those two dogs were so happy they just took off running!

Psalm 3:2,3—Many say about me, "There is no help for him in God." But You, LORD, are a shield around me, my glory, and the One who lifts up my head.

King David faced a time in his life when the attacks of his enemies seemed overwhelming. Even those who knew him concluded God had turned His back on His servant. I wonder how many times we encounter such severe problems or are so assailed that even our friends write us off as doomed? How many times are we rapidly paddling to keep our heads above water, unable on our own to extricate ourselves!

David did not agree with his critics. He recognized that God was his protection—the lifter of his head. *"I cry aloud to the LORD, and He answers me from His holy mountain. I lie down and sleep; I wake again because the Lord sustains me. I am not afraid of the thousands of people who have taken their stand against me on every side"* (vv. 4-6).

How about you—are you able to sleep in peace? Are you confident the Lord hears your voice and will answer? So often, we worry. God looks at *us* and desires worship. The One who made *us* is unintimidated by our fiascos. In truth, opposition and hardship ought to bring out faith not dejection. Don't accept the commentary of bystanders or believe the word of the enemy that your God does not care. That is a phony piece of interpretation from a master liar. Your God is better than your worst nightmare; more powerful than your scariest adversaries. So make Him your shield! Call on Him! He will lift your head, pull you out of the pond of despair, dry you off and bless you with the inside-out warming love of an all-compassionate Father!

Joint Pains March 7

I flew from Louisville, Kentucky to Chicago on Wednesday afternoon. My neck hurt but I suspected it was just from reading too long. The next flight was from Chicago to Portland. As I got off the plane, both my shoulders ached and I could hardly turn my head or lift my luggage. By the time I reached home, the joints in my wrists hurt. Pacing the living room at three in the morning, I wondered if perhaps this was not just some medical condition but a spiritual attack. I asked the Lord for His help and to bring healing. By that evening, the pain moved into my knees to the point that I could hardly walk. My parents urged me to go to the emergency room. I called a retired Navy Seal who served as a corpsman and he offered advice and then joined my family in praying for me.

Psalm 4:1—Answer me when I call, God, who vindicates me. You freed me from affliction; be gracious to me and hear my prayer.

On Friday, I visited a doctor and a chiropractor. Both concluded that a virus probably was responsible for the acute pain. It will take days before blood work comes back but by late in the afternoon, I was already feeling better. Talking to my friend, David, on the phone, we reflected on how little it takes to incapacitate us. Truly, the body is wonderful yet vulnerable.

"The agony of a man's affliction is often necessary to put him into the right mood to face the fundamental things of life."[4] Affliction offers God-believers the opportunity to have heartfelt conversations with Him. Words tend to be quite meaningful when pain holds us by the neck. We should be glad that we can call out to our Father when we are under assault. He gives us hope in the midst of suffering.

Affliction offers those who have strayed from God the opportunity to run back to Him. Pain is a reminder of who is really in control. But what does affliction teach those who don't believe in God? Who vindicates, frees, provides grace and listens to the one who worships no one? The same David who pled with God to answer him, later asked his afflicters in verse 2, *"How long will you love what is worthless and pursue a lie?"* Despite his suffering, he could see their deeper dilemma—ignoring God. Affliction has a way of doing that—bringing clarity to what matters and doesn't matter. So keep persevering as you climb higher . . . in reveration!

Inspiration ✝✝✝

Your maximum heart rate declines steadily over time, regardless of how active you are. —Chris Crowley & Henry Lodge in *Younger Next Year*

Jupiter

March 8

Psalm 8:3,4—When I observe Your heavens, the work of Your fingers, the moon and the stars, which You set in place, what is man that You remember him, the son of man that You look after him?

Scientist Palmer Bailey, "the stars and rocks guy" airs a heavenly radio segment each week called *The Northern Sky*. In a fresh broadcast he shared that the planet Venus, after the Moon, is the brightest natural object in the night sky and is referred to as the "evening star." Normally we see it in the southwest. However, as Palmer tells us, recently the brightest star in the sky has not been Venus but rather Jupiter. Once every thirteen months the earth passes Jupiter in its slower larger orbit, an event called "opposition" because Jupiter appears in the eastern sky exactly the opposite direction from the setting sun.

Jupiter is eleven times the diameter of earth and its mass is 317 times greater. This king of planets has 63 moons, the four largest of which were discovered by Galileo. When it rotates closest to our planet, we get a beautiful bright light in a dark sky and that fits nicely to the point Palmer makes from Scripture.

Most people for a multitude of reasons will not notice Jupiter. Sadly, how many will also not perceive the greatest Light ever sent to earth, God's Son? King David noted in Psalm 19:1, "*The heavens declare the glory of God, and the sky proclaims the work of His hands.*" God put in spin the planets and as Max Lucado wrote in *3:16 The Numbers of Hope*, "Our universe is God's preeminent missionary." Looking above, Israel's poet wondered why God should remember and look after us. I suspect when David peered into the heavens and saw the Milky Way, the moon, and countless constellations, he was more than a bit inspired by the love of his Creator.

Should you observe the brightest of stars shining opposite a vanishing sun, thank God for the reminder of His handiwork! Sing with the glory chorus that is all around us. Ask the Father for the opportunity to share with someone who may have seen Jupiter but has yet to see Jesus—the One who says about Himself, "*I am the Root and the Offspring of David, the Bright Morning Star*" (Rev. 22:16).

Inspiration † † †

To say that the universe was created by chance is to say that it came from nothing. That is intellectual madness.—RC Sproul in *The Holiness of God*

Scheming

March 9

When I read newspaper and internet stories and listen to the radio and television, one word leaps to mind—*scheming*! Republicans accused the President and the Democratic-controlled Congress of trying to impose socialism. Democrats accused Republicans of fear mongering and not caring about the American people. Special interest groups accused Supreme Court justices for not holding to the Constitution. Radio talk hosts accused the media of sensationalism and distortion. There is no happiness. Unity is as easy to find as a unicorn. Perhaps we would do well to pause and to consider the nature of man.

Psalm 10:4—In all his scheming, the wicked arrogantly thinks: "There is no accountability, since God does not exist."

I suspect rebellion was the first recorded sin in history. Two essential ingredients fuel an evil rebellion: pride and scheming. Satan turned against his Lord. Then he incited Adam and Eve to disobey. Absent pride, there was no reason for Satan to usurp God. Minus scheming, there would be no action. From the time of Eden to the last words of John, the Bible is sated with pride and scheming.

A man without God is a man who lives for himself. Even a generous atheist at heart gives to make himself feel good. Scheming is the natural byproduct of a man or woman's attempt to get what he or she wants. Thus, it is asinine for us to act surprised at the selfishness we see in actors and leaders across societal spectrums. Even those in the presence of Jesus were natural schemers—just look at the twelve apostles! Too often, I am concerned with my own agenda. It is only by grace and the merciful help of a loving Counselor that I can set my heart to do what God wants!

Impious people will plot; they cannot help it. We do not have to stew and let the actions of the arrogant upset us. We are responsible to do what is right, to pray, and to seek the will of the Father. Our confidence comes when we remember, *"But You Yourself have seen trouble and grief, observing it in order to take the matter into Your hands. The helpless entrusts himself to You; You are a helper of the fatherless"* (Psa. 10:14).

Inspiration †††

The vision of socialism is magnificent; there are benedictions and blessings for mankind on the line of socialism which have never been yet; but if once the root is cut from redemption, it will be one of the most frantic forms of despotic tyranny the human race has ever known. It looks like the lamb, but when the big crisis comes, it gives life to the beast.—Oswald Chambers in *The Shadow of an Agony*

# Liberty Lowered Her Torch	March 10

Psalms 17:3—You have tested my heart; you have examined me at night; You have tried me and found nothing evil; I have determined that my mouth will not sin.
Matthew 12:36b—I tell you that on the day of judgment people will have to account for every careless word they speak.

It was in part what the President* wouldn't say that disturbed a nation. Liberty lowered her torch and sat on her pedestal of stone weeping from the bitter blow his pride struck. She cried because he lied. She sobbed because he robbed—he stole the trust of a nation to enjoy forbidden pleasures. Tomorrow she will rise and light her torch. But it will not burn as bright. Around her base swirls water blackened with the slick oil of deceit. It's mixture runs downstream leaching through soil at an alarming rate. Her children are poisoned by this hazardous waste of rationalization that dares to call evil good and good evil.

When the thunder of judgment claps from clouds of condemnation, Liberty will not raise her voice with rush. She will not shake her clenched hand in anger. She knows that he is not the first to commit a sin. He is the exposed and vulnerable chief of a mixed tribe in which not one member can fire an arrow from an unrepaired bow.

She will cover her eyes and mourn because his conduct is a brazen blow to the cause of integrity. While dishonesty burns like acid indigestion what hurts her most is that so many don't care. Her spirit sags against this growing tide of apathy. The loss of character hastens the death of trust. People, who no longer see fit to honor God by saying "no" to selfish desires, will no longer honor one another.

God said to King Solomon in 1 Kings 9:4,5:
As for you, if you walk before Me as your father David walked, with a heart of integrity and in what is right, doing everything I have commanded you, and if you keep My statutes and ordinances, I will establish your royal throne over Israel forever, as I promised your father David: You will never fail to have a man on the throne of Israel.

Why should the same God who allowed His people to be conquered because they abandoned morality, allow us to prosper if we mortgage our integrity on whatever our hearts covet? Abraham Lincoln said that for a man to train up a child in the way he or she should go, he must walk that way himself. If ever there was a time to be walking, the bells toll now! May God make us whole again that we might bring Him glory and shine before a world desperately trapped in the dark.

*(Multiple U.S. presidents have been accused of lying.)

Inspiration † † †

A little lie is like a little pregnancy it does not take long before everyone knows.—C.S. Lewis

Despair

Psalm 17:15—But I will see Your face in righteousness; when I awake, I will be satisfied with Your presence.

Aside from Jesus, Job is perhaps history's most famous man associated with suffering. Messengers report to him one fateful day of: enemies stealing his oxen, donkeys, camels and killing his servants; lightning destroying his sheep and shepherds; and, a powerful wind that wipes out all ten of his children. The poor man stood up, tore his robe and shaved his head and then fell on the ground in worship saying, *"Naked I came from my mother's womb, and naked I will leave this life. The LORD gives, and the LORD takes away. Praise the name of Yahweh"* (Job 1:21).

It was bad enough to lose what he loved, but then Job was afflicted with *"incurable boils from the sole of his foot to the top of his head"* (2:7b). His wife counsels him to curse God and die. In constant pain, his spirit caves to the convulsing of his soul and it is not hard to understand why he uttered the following words. *"Remember that my life is but a breath. My eye will never again see anything good"* (Job 7:7).

Despair is like a tornado. The sky darkens ominously, the winds roar in fury while fear grabs you by the throat. It may crush your world and destroy all you hold dear replacing structure with debris.

Despair is like a flood. The waters rise unmercifully tossing aside sandbags so frantically placed and breaching walls with the grim force that knows no restraint. High ground brings safety but cannot hide disaster. It is when we reach our lowest point—exhaust all our human means of gaining relief—that we discover the limit of anguish. For the child of God, misery need never prevail. Through it all, Job remained faithful and God restored his property, doubled his possessions and gave him seven sons and three daughters who exceeded all other women for beauty in the land. He lived to see his great, great grandchildren (42:10,13,15,16).

Oswald Chambers wrote in *Baffled to Fight Better*:

When we get to despair we know that all our thinking will never get us out; we will only get out by the sheer creative effort of God, consequently we are in the right attitude to receive from God that which we cannot gain for ourselves.

God's salvation is our solution. You may encounter the worst of disasters, fail miserably, and give up on hoping. Remember who you worship. Take your distress to your Savior. Even the worst nightmare will end and you will find in Him the reality of blessing.

Inspiration ✝✝✝

The more you despair of self, the more you trust in God.—Jeanne Guyon in *Final Steps in Christian Maturity*

Pathway

March 12

There is a very challenging obstacle at Fort Lewis that ROTC cadets are required to negotiate during their summer training. One at a time each student climbs up a metal staircase, stands up on a narrow beam about 6 inches in width and must walk to the middle to negotiate a step. Next, the student must grab a rope, swing the legs over the rope and slide out to the center, hang and wait for a command to drop about 20 feet down to the lake below. It is amazing how hard it is to walk up and over that centrally placed step so high above the water without falling or succumbing to fear.

Psalm 18:36—You widen a place beneath me for my steps, and my ankles do not give way.

Occasionally God may ask us to traverse narrow walkways. High above our comfort zone, He tests us to see if we are willing to trust Him. He asks us to do what we would normally avoid and takes us where we do not want to go. Without challenges, how would our faith grow? However, some believe that God purposely makes life demanding and does not care that they suffer. For them, He is an unfair Lord bent on making their life like that of Job. Perhaps you have gone through a hard time and felt like God was intentionally out to make you squirm. Yet, while it is true that He does test us, far more often, He is actually making life better for us. He removes those things that would work to our ruin creating a safer path for our journey.

One songwriter wrote in Psalm 66:9, *"He keeps us alive and does not allow our feet to slip."* In Psalm 94:18 we read, *"If I say, 'My foot is slipping,' Your faithful love will support me, LORD.'"* Again, in Psalm 121:3, it says, *"He will not allow your foot to slip; your Protector will not slumber."* Clearly, those who followed God thousands of years ago recognized that He was their Benefactor, alert, loving, and dedicated to helping them.

Friend, today would be a great day to pause from what you are doing and take inventory. Ask God to remind you of incidents where you have seen His hand of protection at work in your life. You might inquire if there were times you took for granted and failed to see Him at work behind the scenes on your behalf. Do not be a sleepwalker and take divine protection for granted! I am certain you will be amazed to discover in God's presence, how oblivious you were to His working to better your life. If we would even slightly believe that our Father cares enough to broaden our pathway and protect our journey, we would have much greater reason to step out in faith!

Inspiration †††

The property of power is to protect.—Blaise Pascal

Mold

March 13

My sinuses filled and it became ridiculous trying to breathe at night. Slowly I found my energy ebbing while my frustration grew at constantly being stuffed. Most of the summer was like this. I went to the doctor and she prescribed medication. It did not help. I went back and she gave me a stronger prescription which worked wonderfully until it ran out. Again my head felt like a piñata. I've never had allergies and I didn't think I was allergic to Wisconsin but something clearly was wrong.

To make things worse there was a persistent odor in the bathroom of the house I was renting. At the end of my six weeks at Fort McCoy, I sent a note to the Installation Commander. I thanked him for the use of the cottage but also noted that they should have it checked for possible mold. He acknowledged my email and promised to have an inspector examine it. Sure enough, they found a broken pipe behind a wall that was not properly repaired causing all kinds of mold to grow. Mold—a four lettered word with hidden meaning: **M**aking **O**ur **L**iving **D**ifficult. No wonder I was sick!

Psalm 19:12—Who perceives his unintentional sins? Cleanse me from my hidden faults.

There are sins of omission and sins of commission. Sometimes it is the ones we miss by oversight that can be more damaging. For example, if someone is talking to me and I pretend to be listening but my thoughts are really engaged in something else (like reading emails on a Blackberry), the message I send is that I'm not really interested in what the speaker has to say. The unintentional sin is deficient caring—rooted in self-centeredness. If this misbehavior is not corrected, a child may grow up concluding her father doesn't care about her; the coworker may quit coming for help; the spouse may despair of ever having meaningful conversation; and the list of unintended consequences grows.

Hidden mold kept me sick. Until I left the environment I could not properly heal. Unintentional sins can be just as bad. This might be a good time to pray, "Lord, is there anything in my life that is causing others to be sick and is disturbing You? If so, Lord, please bring it to my attention, purge it from my life and forgive me. I'm sorry for causing harm. Make my life a pleasing aroma for Your glory! Amen."

Next go and confess to the person(s) and ask their forgiveness. This is what makes us truly fragrant to the world and pleasing to God.

Inspiration ✝✝✝

It is time we awaken to the fact that conformity to a sick society is to be sick.—Richard J. Foster in *Celebration of Discipline*

Fallen

March 14

Shock is what happens when we hear the news that someone we admired or respected as a spiritual leader is caught in some disgusting sexually immoral behavior. The root of the problem is much deeper than sex. History is long in examples of clergy who strayed from vows—whether vows of celibacy or vows to be faithful to one's spouse. A man can wear the cloth or collar that identifies him as a follower of God. But if his heart is intent on pleasing himself, then his true allegiance is exposed.

Sadly, many people will use the unfaithfulness of clergymen to prove the unreliability of Christianity. They will conjure the Crusades to contest the Gospel. They will trump hypocrisy as license for godlessness. But to do this is to err spiritually. It is not Christianity or Christian leaders that we worship and neither saves sinners. Nor should we find God derelict for the actions of those who follow their own misguided causes under the guise of religion. Nowhere does the Bible call us to pick up our cross and follow Father Clancy. It is holy Jesus, the cross-hanging, grave-departing Savior, who calls us to follow Him. God will not absolve me of sin because I was turned off by the sins of others. He will judge me on whether or not I obeyed Him.

Psalm 19:13—Moreover, keep your servant from willful sins; do not let them rule over me. Then will I be innocent and cleansed from blatant rebellion.

Oswald Chambers wrote in *Disciples Indeed*, "Sin is the outcome of a relationship God never ordained, a relationship that maintains itself by means of a wrong disposition, namely, my claim to my right to myself." Max Lucado noted, "Sin is not an unfortunate slip or a regrettable act; it is a posture of defiance against a holy God."[15] I hope in these days where wickedness seems to be the plant most watered in the garden, we will fall to our knees and beg God to keep our eyes on Christ. Let us not give in to evil and let us not fail to pray for those who have fallen. There are many good servants of the Lord—leaders who work hard to honor their Lord and keep Him first. But there is only One perfect Savior.

Inspiration †††

Sin is the outcome of a relationship God never ordained, a relationship that maintains itself by means of a wrong disposition, namely, my claim to my right to myself. That is the essence of sin.—Oswald Chambers in *Disciples Indeed*

Bowling

March 15

The difference between a strike and a split is but a matter of inches. If the bowling ball hits the center pocket correctly, all ten pins fall down. But if the ball veers just slightly off its intended course, all kinds of crazy formations can appear to include the dreaded split where pins are left standing on opposite sides of the lane. I had my share of splits last night as the bowling ball just missed the strike zone time and again!

Psalm 25:4-5—Make Your ways known to me, LORD; teach me Your paths. Guide me in Your truth and teach me, for You are the God of my salvation; I wait for You all day long.

When I try to live life on my terms, I have a great idea of what needs to happen. Unfortunately, the result of self-determination is truth deviation. My path leads to problems. To negotiate life correctly, I need to be on God's path. King David was probably not a bowler, but he knew all about center pocket living. Here's what he reveals in Psalm 25:

1. We need the Lord to show us His ways. His ways are perfect! This calls for prayer on our part—asking for God's help.
2. We need to be teachable so we can learn God's paths. This calls for humility.
3. We have to be malleable so that God is able to guide us in His truth. This calls for flexibility and a willingness to be directed.
4. Our eyes have to look to God for His direction at all times. This calls for patience and eyes that look not to the world but to God for instruction.

Psalm 25 offers more great news.

The LORD is good and upright; therefore He shows sinners the way. He leads the humble in what is right and teaches them His way. All the LORD's ways show faithful love and truth to those who keep His covenant and decrees... Who is the man who fears the LORD? He will show him the way he should choose (vv. 8-10,12)

Despite our tendency to find the gutter, God is willing to show us His way. He honors the humble by revealing His leading will. His mannerisms are full of love as we do our part to obey Him. When we revere Him, He reveals for us. Given what God offers, isn't it amazing how quick we are to ignore Him or miss His instruction and try and negotiate life by our own stubborn will! Let's remember where our salvation comes from and live accordingly!

Inspiration ✝✝✝

As I abide in the presence of my King, a holy instinct guides my steps.—Eric & Leslie Ludy in *When God Writes Your Life Story*

Terrified

March 16

I received an email that tore my gut in two. A friend from seminary wrote to those on his mailing list. He was back in his home city with his children, no longer in the Asian country where God led him and his wife to minister. Their work was vital in a place restricted and fraught with danger. He knew what it meant to serve God through opposition. But he never expected his wife to fall in love with someone she met on the internet. She left her family devastated. As if confused and heartbroken was not bad enough, his mission organization requested his resignation. Now what does he do? Who can he trust? His children struggle mightily to adjust to a new culture. They wrestle with the reality their mother is living in immorality. He wonders what more could go wrong.

Psalm 30:7—LORD, when You showed Your favor, You made me stand like a strong mountain; when You hid Your face, I was terrified.

Friends, there are times in life when we know God's favor is on us. We are like a strong mountain, impervious to any and all threats. Times of favor are seasons filled with joy. But what about those periods when God cannot be found? Suddenly, life makes no sense. Pain is as present and real as a deep cut or a serious burn. Our worst fear or nightmare becomes a wretched reality. Those we trusted abandon us, we fall to sickness or become victim to some abrupt calamity. When God vanishes, terror screams her offbeat note and her chorus makes even the brave shudder.

David was a heroic lover of God. Nevertheless, he faced horrific dangers. David knew the real and present shock of betrayal—his own king and later one of his sons tried to kill him. David understood the sting of rejection—his wife, Michal, mocked his joyous dancing. His friends were murdered and his life often hung on the verge of elimination. If ever there was a man to quit, to put away the harp, to bathe in the water of bitterness, to turn away from His Lord, or to yield to his enemies, it was Judah's singer-warrior.

Yet, this handsome man clothed in grief also wrote, "*LORD my God, I cried to You for help, and You healed me . . . You turned my lament into dancing; You removed my sackcloth and clothed me with gladness*" (Psa. 30: 2,11). David emerged safe and died old. He remained blessed because he knew the One who hid His face would always reemerge. Can you hear him exhorting his warriors, "Terror may come in the morning, but don't give up! Pain may suck at the very marrow of your bone but don't stop believing in God's love. Forget about trying to understand the whys, just believe in the who."

Inspiration ✝✝✝

God honors faith and faith honors God.—OE Smith

Water on the Head   March 17

I was standing on the sideline of a pick-up soccer game after subbing out so another player could reenter the game. It was a hot afternoon. My buddy, Dan, took his plastic water jug and poured it over my head. Unlike the unsuspecting football coach doused with iced Gatorade after winning a cold winter game, this shower was reviving!

My wife took blueberries from our backyard and mixed them with a bread concoction that was mouth-wateringly delicious. She made two batches for me to take for my co-workers. It was a boost to their morale and they were thankful for her thoughtfulness.

Whether pouring cool water on a friend's hot head or taking the time to bake food for others, the effect of goodness is spirit-lifting. David, the popular, handsome, contemplative warrior-lover of God was bothered by wicked people. He was so troubled that he asked God to shame them and silence their lying lips. But then, instead of dwelling on troublemakers, he turned to his great Friend and uttered the words below.

Psalm 31:19—How great is Your goodness that You have stored up for those who fear You and accomplished in the sight of everyone for those who take refuge in You.

David recalled the times God rescued and sustained him. His heart turned from distress to praising His Lord. Who dominates your thoughts—troublemakers or your mighty Father? Have you thought much lately of the goodness God has stored up for you? It is so easy to fixate on problems and enemies that we forget that God exercises goodness to us. First, He sustains and provides for us on earth when we trust in Him for our protection and respect His awesomeness. Second, some day in our great heaven homecoming, He will shower on us eternal goodness as a reward for our faithfulness in following Jesus. There is <u>nothing</u> on earth that comes even remotely close to the goodness God has in store for us.

Inspiration †††

How excellent is your lovingkindness, Oh God! I am not worthy of the least of your benefits. Oh, the depths of the love and goodness of the Lord.—Charles Haddon Spurgeon

Should've Been

March 18

Psalm 32:5,10—Then I acknowledged my sin to You and did not conceal my iniquity. I said, "I will confess my transgressions to the LORD," and You took away the guilt of my sin. Selah ... Many pains come to the wicked, but the one who trusts in the LORD will have faithful love surrounding him.

Should've Been

Will You open up Your arms when You know I've fallen down;
When I've stumbled and I've hurt You once again?
Though I said that I would follow I've waited for tomorrow
I'm tired of having to say, "I should've been ...

I should've been a faithful witness not a coward.
I should've been an honest man to make You proud.
I should've come when You first called;
I should've done just what You said.
I should've died to all the things that make me dead.
I should have loved the ones right here I know as neighbors!
I should have listened instead of opening up my mouth.
I should've come when You first called;
I should've done just what You said.
Lord, it's time to put this selfish man to bed.

Will You open up my eyes so I have You in my sight?
Will You give me strength to live the way I should?
Will You help me die to self and take me off the shelf.
I'm so tired of having to say, "I should've been ...

Will You take me to the cross, where You suffered for my gain
Will You break my heart and make it whole again?
Lord, I truly am persuaded that You alone are able,
To change my heart until the words are said ...

I am a faithful, standing witness to Your power.
I am an honest man whose word is sure as gold.
I come running when You call me; I will do just what You say.
I'm the living light that honors You each day.
I put my neighbor's needs above my own obsessions.
I'm known as wise now, for listening very well.
I come running when You call me; and I do just what You say.
I'm alive to You and dead to should've been.
©2006 Daniel York Evidence CD ARR

Delivered

March 19

Psalm 34:4—I sought the LORD, and He answered me and delivered me from all my fears.

At the age of one month, he was dedicated to be a witch doctor and to one day replace his grandfather. But as a ten year-old, he ran away mad because the ancestral spirits wanted him to start practicing divination. Consequently, this young boy grew up rejected by both his paternal and maternal family.

In 1987, while living in Nairobi, he used to eat from a garbage pit. A year later, while staying with the wife of his mother's brother, he was mistreated and his clothes were filled with lice. For an entire year, he had only one pair of shorts and a T-shirt to wear. At the age of 12, he suffered from whooping cough and runny nose. He developed wounds on his lungs which caused him to cough heavily for twelve more years.

In 1992, he went to a soccer stadium to watch a scheduled match. At 6:00 p.m. when the contest ended, a crusade commenced and he listened intently to the visiting preacher. The only words he remembers were, "Those who would like to accept Jesus . . ." and then he moved forward. He recalls John 1:12, *"But to all who did receive Him, He gave them the right to be children of God, to those who believe in His name."* That night, May 14, Daniel Mugeni gave his heart to Jesus at the age of 13.

Eleven years later, Daniel slept on a dusty mat in a church. In the course of praying, God healed him from his cough and chest pains and relieved his severe stammering. Increasingly he received joy, peace and the unmistakable reality of God's love for him. Now his stammering is gone. Delivered from the pit of rejection and abuse he now ministers the gospel sharing his story to any who will listen in his land of Uganda.

One of the beautiful aspects of the internet is that it helps shrink our world so that we who love Jesus can meet new brothers and sisters and communicate with one another. Through our journey and ministry in Kenya we met Joseph. Later, he and Brian traveled into Uganda. Providentially, God connected our First Cause family to Daniel and Joy and others with whom they serve. Though physically they have never met, today my Dad has the privilege of helping Daniel grow spiritually by sending him instruction via email. This is what it means to know Christ. He delivers us from Satan and his insidious attacks and links us together to thrive under grace. Jesus sets us free! Are you living delivered?

Inspiration ✝✝✝

The Christian way to solve the problem is not by removing the thing, but by delivering the heart from the grip of that thing.—Watchman Nee in *Love not the World*

Coaching Eighth-Grade Boys

March 20

Oswald Chamber stated in *Shade of His Hand,* "Very few of us are sensitive; we are all impressionable."

Nine young men sat on the hardwood court as I read to them a short sport story and then gave two applications. They listened attentively to the lesson on courage. After sharing I handed them each a copy to put in their notebooks. The practice was over but one player lingered to read the story on his own. Another stood silent as his dad animatedly discussed the paper with him. One of the mothers came and commented on how much she appreciated the character lessons.

I volunteered to serve as the assistant coach for an eighth grade boys' basketball team. My son, Stephen, is on the team and it seemed like a great opportunity to be with him and hopefully minister to the lives of young men. But it's not just basketball skills I hope they will learn but even more so, I want them to learn about the game of life. Joe eagerly agreed to let me close each practice with a lesson. For the next several months on Monday and Wednesday evenings from 8:55-9:00 p.m., I get to share valuable lessons with impressionable minds.

Psalm 34:11—Come, children, listen to me; I will teach you the fear of the LORD.

Because it is not considered politically correct to tell collegians what is right and wrong, many prestigious colleges and universities in our land do not even offer courses on ethics. Yet, there is a growing awareness in businesses around the country that something is desperately wrong. Young adults are taking jobs with little appreciation for integrity and lack fundamental convictions of what is right and wrong. Is relativism winning the war of mind-shaping?

Young minds are always impressionable; the question is what content will fill their brains? If we don't teach ethical principles when people are young, should we be surprised if they age preferring immorality? Let's pray that God would give us opportunities to minister to impressionable minds. The days are growing short and evil is not shrinking so we should be climbing higher . . . in reveration.

Inspiration † † †

If you look to lead, invest at least 40% of your time managing yourself - your ethics, character, principles, purpose, motivation, and conduct. Invest at least 30% managing those with authority over you, and 15% managing your peers.—Dee Hock

Storm Power

It's hard to sleep at night with the realization that you may wake up with your house tumbling into the ocean. Such is the case of many Oregonian coast dwellers watching in apprehension each winter as Pacific waves continue to steadily devour beaches and sand dunes. The persistent cries of desperate homeowners have reached lawmakers who must decide whether to allow the emplacement of huge boulders that would form a wall against the water.

Psalm 40:2—He brought me up from a desolate pit, out of the muddy clay, and set my feet on a rock, making my steps secure.

The destructive power of storms is like the harshness of sin. Psalm forty is David's prayer for God's mercy. *"For troubles without number have surrounded me; my sins have overtaken me; I am unable to see. They are more than the hairs of my head, and my courage leaves me."* (40:12) Yet in the midst of adversity, David realized the saving power of His heavenly Father. As a man who personally experienced divine safeguarding, he becomes a singing testimony to others of his awesome Deliverer (40:3).

Andrew Murray wrote in *With Christ in the School of Prayer* "Faith is the one condition on which all Divine power can enter into man and work thorough him."[6] Without God, life is like trying to climb out of a clay-soaked cavern. Each attempt to climb higher is matched by a slide downward. But when we place our trust in Jesus, God pulls us from the slimy sin-lined hole whose bottom is forever separated from His presence, to place us on the solid rock—His Son. Only Jesus can say "HELL NO!" The hammering of Satan cannot split this Rock. The drilling bit of every enemy breaks upon this Stone. No power on earth or force beyond can overcome those whose foundation is laid in Christ. Blessed is the person whose confidence is in the Rock that knows not the taste of erosion. Jesus is our safeguarding Savior. And you can rest assured on that.

Unwelcome Visitors

In the course of life, I've learned that my mind daily receives an unwelcome visitor. On some days he keeps to himself and is hardly noticeable. On other days he's obnoxious, devious and overbearing. Sometimes he boasts while at other times he is smooth and spellbinding. The mind's manager, Will, knows not to underestimate his ploys. Even still he inexplicably will entertain this unsavory fellow or give him the room with the largest view. Until the Owner returns, he cannot throw him out for he retains his own hidden pass key.

He goes wherever I go. In some ways he's more persistent than a shadow. His name is Temptation. His goal is to pulverize my Will and yours as well, for he also lives inside you.

There is within us a persistent urge to be good. We want God to take pleasure in our thoughts and actions, conduct and attitude. However, when we are not pleasing Him, it is incredibly simple to manufacture excuses. Self-denial is not easy. But our Will cannot be overcome by temptation unless we give in. The Bible encourages us with this truth:

No temptation has overtaken you except what is common to humanity. God is faithful, and He will not allow you to be tempted beyond what you are able, but with the temptation He will also provide a way of escape, so that you are able to bear it. (1 Co. 10:13)

If what you are doing is wrong, don't blame God. Don't fasten the fault on how you were raised. Don't hide behind circumstances or suggest that others are responsible for your behavior. Get off the sin-stained couch of rationalization and take responsibility for that which shapes your every decision—your Will! Are you sleeping with someone to whom you are not married? Are you stealing to make ends meet? Are you cheating to get ahead? Are you lying so others think of you more favorably? Do you gossip because it feels good? Do you ignore meeting with God because you are too busy?

Psalm 40:8—I delight to do Your will, my God; Your instruction lives within me.

King David knew what sins he was capable of committing. He wisely prayed, *"Teach me to do Your will, for You are my God. May Your gracious Spirit lead me on level ground"* (Psa. 143:10). Are you weary of climbing the carnal mountain range? Seek God's will. Let Him lead you to level ground. If your will is to do His will, His will is to help you. Perhaps the way to level ground is to start down the path of confession.

Inspiration † † †

I was in my thirteenth year when I heard a voice from God to help me govern my conduct. And the first time I was very much afraid.—Joan of Arc

Longing for You March 23

How do I know when I am growing spiritually? One sure way to tell is to evaluate my desires. Jesus said, *"For where your treasure is, there your heart will be also"* (Mat. 6:21). Treasures do not have to be tangible possessions. Our thoughts our often our treasures.

Where do your thoughts take you? What does your heart linger after in the palace of your mind? Stop dreaming of being noticed! Jesus loves you! You already possess a heavenly fan club. May your focus be on your loving Lord. Give up lusting over food—let your appetite be for God's Word.

Desires—we are a people consumed with desires. Will you allow the Holy Spirit at this moment to bring before your inner eyes those desires that you battle on a daily, sometimes moment-by-moment basis. May I offer a word of encouragement? Strip your mind of those desires that pull you inward and instead seek God. Be a thirsty child who finds and drinks Living Water. The definition of joy is spiritual longing satisfied. May our joy be full because our cup is Jesus.

Psalm 42:1—As a deer longs for streams of water, so I long for You, God.
1 John 2:15-17—Do not love the world or the things that belong to the world. If anyone loves the world, love for the Father is not in him. For everything that belongs to the world—the lust of the flesh, the lust of the eyes, and the pride in one's lifestyle—is not from the Father, but is from the world. And the world with its lust is passing away, but the one who does God's will remains forever.

Inspiration †††

I want deliberately to encourage this mighty longing after God. The lack of it has brought us to our present low estate.—A.W. Tozer in *The Pursuit of God*

We walk ever day on the razor edge between these two incredible possibilities. Apparently, then, our lifelong nostalgia, our longing to be reunited with something in the universe from which we now feel cut off, to be on the inside of some door which we have always seen from the outside, is no mere neurotic fancy, but the truest index of our real situation. —C.S. Lewis in *The Weight of Glory*

Down the Tennessee River   March 24

Greg is an avid kayaker. Along with his two sons, they decided to take a trip on the Tennessee River. Together they had a great day paddling until they hit a section where five-foot swells continually pounded them. His boys were in larger kayaks and had little difficulty cutting through the waves. Soon they were far away from Greg. But then Greg hit a portion in the middle of the river where he could no longer cut through the waves and he began to take on water. With only a water bottle to bail he continued to sink. Calmly recognizing that his life was in serious danger, he prayed, "God, I need Your help. There is nothing I can do."

Almost immediately after praying, his son Shawn pulled alongside of him. "Dad, are you alright? I heard you call me." Greg was stunned to see his son and said, "Son, I didn't call you."

"Yes, you did, I clearly heard you call my name." Shawn then pulled out a bilge pump and was able to empty the water out of his dad's kayak and help him get to shore.

Psalm 46:1—God is our refuge and strength, a helper who is always found in times of trouble.

Our ministry team enjoyed our brief stay with Greg and Helena Garcia as we crossed the country. God used Greg to open up a filming opportunity in Clarksville, Tennessee with Harold Witmore that will give First Cause television exposure and, Lord willing, help us raise the $44,000 we need to open a training center in Nigeria. But what encouraged me more than Greg's help was reflecting on the growth in his life as he faithfully lives to serve God. His river rescue story is both amazing and a great reminder of how blessed we are to have a Savior we can call on at anytime for help.

Panic is the natural response to danger. Greg did not panic when it looked hopeless. He knew his life belonged to God and therefore he sought his Father's help. Calmness in calamity is the supernatural response that comes from faith. When the sons of Korah wrote the verse of meditation above, they shared from experience a timeless truth. In times of trouble, God is here to be found. When your next time of adversity comes, remember that and you will be able to sing with the writers the next verses, *"Therefore we will not be afraid, though the earth trembles and the mountains topple into the depths of the seas, though its waters roar and foam and the mountains quake with its turmoil. Selah."*

Inspiration † † †

Courage is resistance to fear, mastery of fear—not absence of fear.—Mark Twain

No Referees

March 25

For ten years, I led an adult coed soccer league in the city of Tigard, Oregon. For two years we operated the league without referees. The first season we tried it there were complaints and it was a rocky transition. It was clear that some players preferred refs because they could cheat. They could bend the rules to their advantage. If the official didn't see the infraction, then that was part of the game.

Without referees the peer pressure to be honest was phenomenal. Suddenly, cheating came with a steep price—people agitatedly addressed any player who ignored the rules. It was encouraging to see adults work through conflict via their team captains. No longer did we have to listen to the incessant whining of those attracted to whistle-laden judges. The league was never perfect but we did become a more trustworthy community. Hallelujah!

Psalm 51:6—But you desire honesty from the heart, so you can teach me to be wise in my inmost being. (NLT)

King David penned, *"The mouth of the righteous utters wisdom; his tongue speaks what is just. The instruction of his God is in his heart; his steps do not falter"* (Psa.37:30,31). If we stumble morally, it's because God's truth is not operative in our hearts. Honesty requires a clean interior. Honesty cannot live with these statements:

- *"I'm not really hurting anyone, so what I'm doing is okay."* The words "not really" give away the reality that deep inside we know the contemplated action is wrong.
- *"Everyone else does it!"* or *"Cheating is a cultural norm here."* This renders God's laws subservient to whatever the norm is.
- *"Tit for tat!"* Retaliation does not excuse falsehoods, leave revenge in God's hands.
- *"But if I tell him the truth he might be hurt."* Proverbs 12:19—*"Truthful lips endure forever, but a lying tongue, only a moment."*

By speaking falsehoods to gain temporary peace we presume to be junior holy spirits and to know what is best. If we assume that sparing someone from hurt is always better, then we misunderstand pain and how God can use it to bring about growth. Sometimes the most truthful thing to do is to say nothing.

In the gospels, 78 times Jesus uttered the phrase "I tell you the truth," before imparting lessons to His listeners. The people recognized His divine wisdom. May it be so with us! May God's wisdom permeate our speech because we make the conscious choice to be honest!

From the Roof

March 26

I had the privilege for several weeks of working with four Army generals. In discussing the importance of a good reputation, several of them shared the vitality of avoiding any appearance of impropriety. Their conduct was measured by standards but also the perception of those standards. Aside from their own moral and spiritual convictions what they were willing to do or not do was tied directly to the people they served. I was encouraged that powerful men modeled integrity with humility.

Psalm 51:12,13—Restore the joy of Your salvation to me, and give me a willing spirit. Then I will teach the rebellious Your ways, and sinners will return to You.

Why did King David watch a naked woman bathe, get her pregnant, show duplicity, murder her husband and act like nothing ever happened? What made this heroic king dive into a pond of filth? How did he get so fouled up? Let's examine his life and see if we can discover what caused such horrendous moral failure.

Before Bathsheba, David set himself up for adultery by marrying many wives in direct violation to God's instruction for kings in Deu. 17:17a: *"He must not acquire many wives for himself so that his heart won't go astray."* The more women he took for himself, the easier he rationalized, "I can have anyone I want. I'm the king!" A man single-minded for God does not build female condominiums in his heart.

In 2 Samuel 11:1a we read, *"In the spring when kings march out to war, David sent Joab with his officers and all Israel."* Did you catch that? David sent his general to do what he should have done. When the ground is replaced by the featherbed, cause is made for carousing. Further on we read, *"From the roof he saw a woman bathing—a very beautiful woman. So David sent someone to inquire about her . . ."* (2 Sa. 11:2b,3a) Stop! Nothing good ever comes from naked woman investigations. The moment David began his inquiry he set in motion desire that should have been squelched by immediately leaving the roof.

"David sent messengers to get her, and when she came to him, he slept with her." (2 Sa. 11:4a) By sending messengers, David involved others in his crime. I think they knew what "get" meant. Why didn't any of them warn him that he was breaking God's law? Either they were moral cowards or they feared a king unafraid of God. And why didn't Bathsheba refuse his advances? Her man was out in battle! She was more flattered by the attention of her king and the possibilities of a life with him than she was concerned about faithfulness to her Lord and to her husband. And where were the priests during all this time? And why did every other wife keep silent? Can we see what happens when power is the order of the day?

Lest we think that we could never duplicate David's crimes let's take personal inventory, a *willing test*. Here are questions I ask myself that you might find helpful:

1. How spiritually fit am I? Do I faithfully study the Bible? Is the Holy Spirit able to speak to my life? Do I consistently meet with the Father in prayer?
2. How socially fit am I? Am I accountable to someone who is spiritually mature and willing to check up on my conduct, thought-life, and overall state on a regular basis? Am I engaged in meaningful fellowship where believers have freedom to observe and speak to my life?
3. How emotionally fit am I? Am I feeling sorry for myself? Do I feel entitled to do something I normally would not do because I am prideful? Or am I strong in the Lord?
4. How intellectually fit am I? Am I bored and therefore misusing the free time I have? Is my life absorbed in pursuing activities that have no redeeming value?

Self-evaluation can assist a better understanding of where I may be spiritually weak. But I have to go a step further and recognize that I cannot create a willing spirit to do what God wants me to do. The moment I think my spiritual condition is dependent on me, I am in trouble and pride is lurking. Let's be honest, because of a sin nature, my character is permanently cracked. Yes, temptations will come and God will always provide the way of escape, but the choice will always be ours—God's will or mine.

A careful reading of Psalm 51 reveals the crux of David's moral failure. The king who *willingly* abided by God's will at some point in his reign decided *his will* was more important. This is why David's prayer for God to give him a willing spirit after Nathan confronted him for his sin, is so profound. David knew what was wrong. Without a willing spirit, he was done—spiritually dead! The journey away from God's will rarely consists of one step. It occurs over time and is almost always paved by the stones of lust, compromise, indifference and pride. So, like David, I need God's help to be obedient to His will. Fortunately, I have a Father who understands, forgives, heals and provides!

Inspiration †††

There is impurity in you. More than you could ever conceive. And it is fatal to union with God.—Jeanne Guyon in *Experiencing the Depths of Jesus Christ*

Jungle Prisoner

March 27

Psalm 56:4—In God, whose word I praise, in God I trust; I will not fear. What can man do to me?
Psalm 86:12—I will praise You with all my heart, Lord my God, and will honor Your name forever.

Martin (Bernie) Burnham attended and graduated from Faith Academy, a K-12 school established for the children of missionaries in the Philippines and surrounding Asian countries. His dream was to serve God by becoming a missionary pilot. God honored his desire. Martin flew planes. Following in his parent's footsteps, he and his family served as missionaries in the Philippines. He and his wife were in the right place at the right time to be kidnapped. Yes—the right place at the right time. You see, anyone who has the courage to set aside concern for his own life to praise God in the midst of a terrifying situation must have been hand-picked by God.

In a remote Philippine island, Martin sat with his wife and over a dozen other captives. A story circulated by a former captive is that while the hostages prayed to God to be rescued, Bernie praised God. He was content to trust in the sovereign power of his Heavenly Father. He was content despite the fact he and his wife were separated from their three children. When the Philippine military finally located their captors and attempted to free the Burnhams, a firefight broke out and Bernie was accidentally shot and killed.

My hunch is that Martin looked for opportunities to share his faith with his captors. I'm certain he prayed for their salvation daily because he realized that the real prisoners are those who do not know Jesus Christ as their Lord and Savior. The reason he could praise God was because he knew that no matter what happened, his life and the lives of his family were secure in the hands of the Almighty.

Martin and I were high school classmates. I'm so proud of his faith and the powerful testimony he maintained. We can learn much from his example! I hope that when you and I face adversity, we will have the courage and maturity to focus our attention on praising God!

Inspiration † † †

Genuine praise has a way of changing our focus from self to God, from problem to solution, from disappointment to great expectation, from depression to joy, from despair to hope. The result does not come from our efforts but from God's interaction with our heart, soul, mind and spirit.—Tom Capps in *Pray and Plan*

Peruvian Concert   March 28

We walked into a large meeting hall at a nursing technological university in Huancayo at about 3:30 p.m. on March 28th. I was asked to give a concert. Mentally I questioned the value of singing songs in English to a group of Spanish-speaking students. Yet this was our last day of ministry in Peru and clearly some effort and expense had gone into making arrangements for me to sing.

About 200 people filled the room. We did not have time to translate the songs and put them on transparencies to project on an overhead. So I asked Viki, our translator, to sit on the stage with me and explain the songs to the audience before I sung them. Without the benefit of an accompanying band and sound system I played on a borrowed classical guitar and sang. Something quite amazing happened. The Holy Spirit began moving marvelously on the hearts of that audience. Over sixty people responded with a firm commitment to follow Christ. So far as we could tell, these were not students saying "yes" to God to be polite to me. Nor were they responding to some emotional moment. These were people hungry to know the Savior and it showed in the way they sought help.

I've always believed that God-glorifying music bypasses the brain to massage the heart. Perhaps it's because I've rarely had someone come up to me six months or more after preaching and say, "You know that message you spoke is really ministering to me." Yet, countless times people have shared how a song sung long ago continues to bring encouragement. The Holy Spirit often seems to profoundly move upon hearts through the medium of worship. Whether it be through music, message, or by godly conduct, when we live so as to glorify God, He uses us to bring those in search of truth into contact with Himself.

Psalm 96:2—Sing to Yahweh, praise His name; proclaim His salvation from day to day.

Jesus said, *"For this is the will of My Father: that everyone who sees the Son and believes in Him may have eternal life, and I will raise him up on the last day"* (John 6:40). Oswald Chambers noted in *As He Walked*, "Personal contact with Jesus alters everything." In a crowded hall many Peruvians met for the first time the King of kings and Lord of lords. Will you pray that they would hold to Jesus' teaching and faithfully follow Him? And let us pray for each other that our first cause would always be to love God.

Inspiration ☩☩☩

Personal contact with Jesus alters everything. He meets our sins, our sorrows, and our difficulties with the one word—"Come."—Oswald Chambers in *As He Walked*

Heritage

March 29

The Honorable Sid Jones, former Assistant Secretary of Treasury gave his "Somewhere Over the Rainbow" lecture to over 55 senior leaders from industry, the military and the government. His address punctuated the bleakness of the U.S. economy, future dangers and possible remedies. He foresaw an economic collapse for America given the great number of aging adults and the demands they place on social security. In describing U.S. assets and priorities one of his statements grabbed my attention. "We spend as much on security as the rest of the world combined." Those words reminded me of Psalm 61:5.

Psalm 61:5—God, You have heard my vows; You have given a heritage to those who fear Your name.

What we view as security says much about our spiritual maturity. Perhaps you own land or possessions passed on to you by your family. You could spend your whole life earning and putting money into savings or investments to pass on to your children as a heritage. But the reality is our world is temporary. There is no guarantee that you or your children will keep what is possessed. Wars, sickness, graft, theft, failed ventures and a host of other unknowns can easily destroy what we value. Therefore, while we should certainly appreciate what we inherit on earth we must never lose sight of a better heritage.

- Without salvation, there is no heritage; therefore, life is the ultimate heritage! Jesus told His followers, *"I am going away to prepare a place for you"* (John 14:2b).
- God's Word is an eternal heritage. The writer of Psalm 119 wrote in verse 111, *"I have Your decrees as a heritage forever; indeed, they are the joy of my heart."*
- The love of Jesus is a heritage to all who keep His commands. *"If you keep My commands you will remain in My love"* (John 15:10a).
- Jesus taught that after He returned to heaven the Holy Spirit would come upon His followers (Acts 1:8). Incredibly, God makes Himself our heritage. *"Don't you yourselves know that you are God's sanctuary and that the Spirit of God lives in you?"* (1 Co. 3:16).

Do we understand what God offers us? Let's not worry over what will eventually burn when we should passionately glow in what can never be taken away! King David wrote, *"But as for me, LORD, my prayer to You is for a time of favor. In Your abundant, faithful love, God, answer me with Your sure salvation"* (Psa. 69:13). David got it right. He knew the best heritage was salvation. How about you, do you get it?

Inspiration † † †

Christ is not simply preparing a place for us; He is preparing us for that place. —Randy Alcorn in *Heaven*

Rendering Judgment   March 30

Jonathan Justice is elected Mayor of Reckless City. Immediately upon assumption of office he determines to instill law and order. He fires the corrupt police chief and sacks the city administrator. He appoints a special commission to go after organized crime bosses. His new district attorney is armed with the full cooperation of municipal government to nab criminals with effective passion. A weary city sighs in relief.

Psalm 64:9,10—Then everyone will fear and will tell about God's work, for they will understand what He has done. The righteous one rejoices in the LORD and takes refuge in Him; all those who are upright in heart will offer praise.

King David astutely noticed that when God rendered judgment by punishing the evil, six good things occurred—three in the nations surrounding Israel and three in the lives of his own people. First, those nations who witnessed the power and authority God exercised held Him in awe. Second, they shared what He had done with others. Third, they pondered His actions. What god or person can do what the Hebrew God does?

For the Jews, rejoicing took place that God punished wrongdoers and rescued them. Second, they realized their safety was found in Him. Third, they praised God! What a beautiful thing it is to be safe from one's enemies.

A great mayor can restore civility to a crime-ravaged city for a time. An awesome God renders judgment to a sin-ridden world that lasts for eternity. When He exercises justice, the effect is magnetic. The same Heavenly Father who exercised His providential power on earth thousands of years ago is still at work today. He leads. He saves. He convicts. He disciplines. He loves.

If we fellowship with God our attitude, thought and action are revealed and judged by His holiness. Though it is painful to fall short of His standard, it is comforting to know that ultimately when we stand before Him, we will be represented by the Lord of Grace in whom we trust! To be freed from sin, to be forgiven, to be given a new perfect body, to behold God in His glory, to soar in the sweetness of salvation will be exhilarating!

Inspiration †††

Nordstrom's Employee Handbook One Rule: Use good judgment in all situations.

Colonel R

March 31

Here's a nightmare! If we don't spiritually invest in the generations that follow us, who will rise up willing to carry the torch of Christ? A self-centered spiritual body is an embarrassment to the throne of the One who so loved THE WORLD—past, present and future!

Psalm 71:18—Even when I am old and gray, God, do not abandon me. Then I will proclaim Your power to another generation, Your strength to all who are to come.

Colonel R inspires me. He has an uncommon passion in an occupation that can easily become self-serving. He identifies those under his command who show promise two or more ranks below him and then works with diligence to groom them for greater responsibility and reward. Conceptually we call this mentoring. Col. R is passionate about the future—one in which he will be retired. Why? Because he cares about his nation and he wants to leave a legacy that surpasses his own name.

Good fruit never occurs haphazardly. It comes intentionally. You and I have the opportunity to bear fruit! Some God-followers shirk the responsibility of passing what they've learned to others. The excuses range from fear of ineptitude to busyness. But you and I cannot afford to find reason not to invest spiritually in the lives of the generations that follow us. Just as I dare not neglect the spiritual training of my children so you too, whether you are married or single, cannot afford to let those lessons the Holy Spirit has engraved on your heart die like some forgotten blackboard lesson in a boarded up schoolhouse.

Let us declare with motivation, truth and simplicity all that we can about our awesome God to those who are younger. To bear good fruit takes more than leading someone through some check-the-block six-week instructional program. It is more than once-a-week coffee get-togethers with the gang. It requires deed, character, attitude, word and faithfulness that naturally teaches and models what it means to follow Jesus in this day-to-day living we call LIFE.

The test of effective fruit-bearing is that the generation we invest in invests in the next generation . . . *"And what you have heard from me in the presence of many witnesses, commit to faithful men who will be able to teach others also"* (2Ti. 2:2). Are you bearing fruit or hardening on the vine?

Inspiration † † †

And so the believer has but one reason for his being a branch—but *one reason for his existence on earth*—that the heavenly Vine may through him bring forth His fruit.—Andrew Murray in *The True Vine*

Home

April 1

I was born in Colorado Springs. I can't remember the event but my birth certificate proves the date and location. Whenever I return to the Springs I feel like my batteries are getting recharged. Does that make any sense? Somehow, being in Colorado rejuvenates my spirit and I always look forward to a visit to that state. Yet, as beautiful as the state is, if I try to get in a workout by running at that high elevation with its lack of oxygen, I am quickly winded. After just a few days, my sinuses are affected and my lips quickly chap in the dry air.

Psalm 73:24,25—You guide me with Your counsel, and afterward You will take me up in glory. Who do I have in heaven but You? And I desire nothing on earth but You.

In Philippians 3:19-21, the Apostle Paul describes the enemies of the cross by stating:

Their end is destruction; their god is their stomach; their glory is in their shame. They are focused on earthly things, but our citizenship is in heaven, from which we also eagerly wait for a Savior, the Lord Jesus Christ. He will transform the body of our humble condition into the likeness of His glorious body, by the power that enables Him to subject everything to Himself.

We live on earth in a temporary home. If Jesus is our Lord, our longing should be to live with Him. Our best dwelling will be the place He creates for us in our redeemed bodies. If there is a lack of yearning for Him, a reluctant pining to reach *home*, we have a serious problem. This is not to say we cannot enjoy where we live or visit but certainly that our pleasure for any earthly place should pale in comparison to our desire to reach our permanent address. *There* trumps *here* or our love is corrupted with a spoiling of contaminated earth.

If our focus is on earthly things, we have a sick contentment and a mouth disinclined to proclaim Christ. *If* our eagerness is to unite with Jesus, our conversation should be expectant, pregnant with hope and shared with those whom we would never wish to miss eternal glory. Ambassadors work on behalf of their true homeland and represent the intent of their appointed leader. May those who are around us see our true allegiance and long to reach the home where He is present!

Inspiration ✝✝✝

By listening to the music of the earth, birds find their way home. — Wayne Muller in *Sabbath*

Wise Sayings

April 2

Scott is a professional bowler. After a victory in 2012, he openly kissed his "husband." ESPN waited until the end of the year to air the footage. For those who believe that homosexuality is a sin, it seems like there is a never-ending onslaught to redefine the institution of marriage, to reeducate children to accept same-sex relationships, and to cast anyone who opposes such behavior as "haters" or intolerant.

Homosexuality has been around for a very long time. Some societies like Rome, embraced it as normative while many other cultural groups have never accepted it. God forbid such behavior to the Israelites in Scripture thousands of years ago. His moral laws were defended and taught by Jesus' Apostles after the Son of God ascended. So what should we as Christians do with a media determined to push the boundaries in presenting alternative lifestyles? Perhaps we might learn something from Asaph. This man watched the moral decay of his countrymen. He saw the cost of rejecting God's will. But rather than despair he challenged his listeners with the best antidote possible.

Psalm 78:2-4,7—I will declare wise sayings; I will speak mysteries from the past— things we have heard and known and that our fathers have passed down to us. We must not hide them from their children, but must tell a future generation the praises of the LORD, His might, and the wonderful works He has performed . . . so that they might put their confidence in God and not forget God's works, but keep His commands.

We ought to be more focused on declaring wise sayings. Our children and their children need to hear us sharing what God did in our forefathers and what He is doing in us. We can get so focused on *sin* that we lose sight of the Savior. Our society will never get better when it is flesh-focused. It will only change as people in the presence of a holy Lord repent of their deviant behavior.

If we are to impact the next generation and see them walk in holiness, then we must be in love with our Father now and be active in serving Him. Our children are far more likely to put their confidence in God if we are confident in God! As they serve Him, He will through His magnificent Holy Spirit validate our Biblical convictions and lead them as to what is wrong or right. *"Make Your ways known to me, LORD; teach me Your paths. Guide me in Your truth and teach me, for You are the God of my salvation; I wait for You all day long"* (Psa. 25:4,5).

Inspiration † † †

God grant me the serenity to accept the things I cannot change; the courage to change the things I can; and the wisdom to know the difference.— The Serenity Prayer

Restoration

April 3

When we bought our house, the floor was covered with an ugly, soiled green '70s-style carpet. To the owner, the carpet was special and no doubt held some sentimental value. We could not replace it fast enough! To our amazement, when we pulled up the carpet, we discovered a beautiful hardwood floor. Friends came over and lovingly applied the proper finish to reveal the wood's texture in all its beauty. When the carpet was new, it looked good. No one would have thought much about what was underneath. Slowly it began to wear and fray and soil. Eventually it became an eyesore. Finally, it was so bad it was fit only to be destroyed.

The story of the carpet is the parable of mankind. Jesus sees us in our true condition. He longs to pull up and remove the filthy old nature that covers our souls. He, alone knows how to give us a new nature—to restore us to be holy as He is holy. Restoration is not pleasant. It hurts to be sanded, to have old embedded tack strips removed. But the deep grain of holiness that shines in breathtaking beauty only comes out when we submit ourselves to the Master's hands.

Psalm 80:3—Restore us, God; look on us with favor, and we will be saved.

> Oswald Chambers wrote in *The Shadow of An Agony*:
> There are three facts of our personal life that are restored by Jesus Christ to their pristine vigor. We get into real definite communion with God through Jesus Christ; we get to right relationship with our fellow-men and with the world outside; and we get into a right relationship with ourselves. We become Christ-centered instead of self-centered.

Are you ready for salvation? Let go of the carpet! Does the grain of your character need polishing? Let God do His work. "Restore us, God; look on us with favor, and we will be saved."

Inspiration † † †

All the operations of God in your interior are toward two things: One is to deliver the soul from wickedness and from the malignity of its fallen nature. The second is to restore the interior—the soul itself—to God; to restore it, as fair and pure as can be rendered this side of the fall.—Jeanne Guyon in *Final Steps in Christian Maturity*

Seven Themes Regarding Truth   April 4

In reading through the Bible in 2009, my selected theme was truth.

Psalm 85:11—Truth will spring up from the earth, and righteousness will look down from heaven.

There are seven themes regarding truth. The first and most common theme deals with the veracity of our words. Approximately 115 times in 40 books, the Bible illustrates importance in the accuracy of what we speak from our mouths.

The second major theme ties truth directly to God as an attribute and expression of His words and nature. In Exodus 34:6 we read, *"Then the LORD passed in front of him and proclaimed: Yahweh—Yahweh is a compassionate and gracious God, slow to anger and rich in faithful love and truth."* At least 78 times in 21 books of the Bible truth describes God, and His Word. Jesus and the Holy Spirit are also equated with truth.

The third major truth theme has to do with integrity and pertains to the character and actions of people. This is illustrated aptly by the description Jesus gives Nathaniel in John 1:47—*"Here is a true Israelite; no deceit is in him."* Fifty-nine times in sixteen books truth is illustrated primarily as an issue of integrity where there is total congruence in one's walk and one's talk.

The fourth major truth theme is particularly relevant to us because it describes the benefits of living truthfully. Because this list is so encouraging I am going to share at least 25 benefits we gain from truth:

1. God's truth guides us in how we should live and what we should do.
2. God's truth guards us and He becomes our shield.
3. We are sanctified by truth.
4. God does not withhold good from those who live with integrity.
5. People of integrity will remain in the land and dwell on the heights
6. Job notes how painful honest words can be. Truth forces us to examine issues we might rather avoid or set aside.
7. God does not reject a person of integrity.
8. Living honestly allows us to dwell in God's presence
9. The LORD is near to those who call on Him with integrity.
10. The one who follows the way of integrity can serve God.
11. Integrity helps us wait on God whereas living in the flesh pulls us away.
12. Because of our integrity, God supports us.
13. Truth endures forever!
14. An honest witness does not deceive others.
15. A truthful witness rescues lives.
16. The king loves one who speaks honestly.
17. The children of a parent with integrity will be happy
18. An honest answer refreshes people.

19. The one who lives with integrity will be helped.
20. The nations will be blessed by the one who speaks God's truth
21. The one who lives by truth, comes to the light.
22. The truth will set us free.
23. People of the truth listen to the words of Jesus.
24. Truth leads to godliness and makes us pure in God's sight
25. Whoever lives with integrity fears the Lord.

The fifth theme reveals truth corrupted or attacked and the consequences that come from not walking in the truth. In sixteen books, we see truth undermined 31 times.

The sixth theme clearly reveals that God expects us to live and speak truthfully. The Old Testament prophets often reminded the people that they were only to speak God's words. The Apostle Paul reminded the Ephesian church, *"Since you put away lying, Speak the truth, each one to his neighbor, because we are members of one another"* (Eph. 4:25). At least 16 books illustrate 27 times that truth is expected.

The least mentioned theme shows how truth is applied to material objects (honest scales, true tabernacle, the book of truth, etc.).

Let us resolve to walk in truth for the glory of the Father of Truth. Our hope in reaching people with the gospel is to walk with integrity thereby gaining God's favor and help.

This Awesome Affirmation   April 5

I was driving down the road recently asking God to forgive me for a persistent sin in my life when I was overcome with the realization of how much God loves me. There is no greater feeling in the world than to be loved. Consider and reflect on this awesome affirmation—God loves you! He loves you with a permanent, immeasurable, all-understanding, beautifully-sculpted, cross-bearing, resurrection-resounding love!

Now pause with this succeeding thought. There will be someone near me today who needs to hear a poignant message, "I don't know how your week is going but with certainty I can tell you, God loves you!"

Brennan Manning in *The Ragamuffin Gospel*, writes, "Do you really accept the message that God is head over heels in love with you? I believe that this question is at the core of our ability to mature and grow spiritually."[17]

Psalm 89:1—I will sing about the LORD's faithful love forever; I will proclaim Your faithfulness to all generations with my mouth.

Ethan the Ezrahite was so blessed by God's love He would sing of it forever. Friends, there is no time to embrace: the pettiness of holding grudges; feeling ignored; wallowing in the swamp of self-pity; believing no one cares; thinking life is not worth living; or, despairing that problems can ever be overcome. Add to Ethan's song your own harmony to the symphonic truth that gives hope today—"God loves you!"

Inspiration ✝✝✝

The evidence that we are in love with God is that we identify ourselves with His interests in others, and other people are the exact expression of what we ourselves are, that is the most humiliating thing!—Oswald Chambers in *The Psychology of Redemption*

Kneeling

April 6

Ken and Brenda and their sons joined me for dinner in Virginia. They told me about all the people who have lost jobs in Richmond and how thankful they are Ken still has his job. Ken said it hasn't been this bad in this area since the early 70's.

I'm sure you have noticed there are lots of people looking for work. Companies are laying off employees by the droves or completely going out of business. Houses are in foreclosure at record numbers.

Psalm 95:6,7—Come, let us worship and bow down; let us kneel before the LORD our Maker. For He is our God, and we are the people of His pasture, the sheep under His care.

I'd like to start a kneeling campaign. What if at noon tomorrow, everyone of you reading this found a private place to kneel or if you are with Christian friends you invited them to join you! What if we did this for a week, or a month, or a year! Why we'd have people in India, Israel, Japan, Kenya, Malawi, Uganda, Nigeria, Ghana, New Zealand, Singapore, the Philippines, Cambodia, Guatemala, Nicaragua, Peru, Scotland, Sweden, Germany, Ukraine, the United States and who knows where else all kneeling whenever noon arrived.

Focus on kneeling before the Lord, the Creator, the One who loves us with an eternal care plan. He IS our God. The antidote to every crisis is worship. The attitude that beats discouragement is one of humility before the King—recognizing that He is above all our problems and He is worthy of our focus.

Knowing he faced an enemy out to take his life, Daniel, God's mighty man of faith, did not fear to pray.

When Daniel learned that the document had been signed, he went into his house. The windows in its upper room opened toward Jerusalem, and three times a day he got down on his knees, prayed, and gave thanks to his God, just as he had done before. (Dan. 6:10)

If Daniel could do this three times a day, every day, can we handle once a day setting aside everything to privately come before God in prayer?

Are you too busy to kneel? Are you too proud to bow down? I didn't think so! I'm not either. So let's do it. When your next noon arrives, kneel before the Lord and thank Him for His leadership. Let's tell the world that we have a Savior we trust.

Destitute

April 7

She stood by the side of the road in the face of a steady rain as cars streamed by her in both directions. Across her waist was a cardboard sign with large letters pleading, "I need work for food. Have two kids. Please God." Hers was not the ordinary sign of the typical person waiting at strategic intersections for someone to feel guilty, stop and give money--the kind of person whose demeanor actually begs the question "Why don't you go get a job and work instead of standing here all day." This woman was sobbing. Her eyes cried the pain that emanates from a broken spirit. Her trembling transcended wet-induced cold to a dark hopelessness. Her plight evoked deep compassion in me not because she needed food or money. Her sign was more profound than that. Her real cry was—"Please God!" This woman knew that her deepest needs went far beyond what caring strangers could offer.

We don't like the reality behind destitution do we? Typically we respond to the indigent in one of three ways.

1. We do all we can to protect the one hurting from crashing. In our haste to avoid pain, we would save Lazarus from dying and therefore we miss God's resurrecting power. Before we attempt to be saviors we should listen to the voice of the One who saves and follow His promptings. He may allow a person to experience utter hopelessness so that repentance and a willingness to trust Him can occur. This is a deeper love than we often understand.

2. We ignore the one hurting and move on. Our callousness betrays our own impoverished state.

3. We rationalize that what looks like one hurting is not what it seems, justifying our right to not get involved. Strangely, we respond in similar fashion to God's commands by finding ways not to obey Him.

Psalm 102:17—He will pay attention to the prayer of the destitute and will not despise their prayer.

> Oswald Chambers wrote in *My Utmost For His Highest*:
> We have to realize that we cannot earn or win anything from God; we must either receive it as a gift or do without it. The greatest blessing spiritually is the knowledge that we are destitute; until we get there Our Lord is powerless.

Despair is the gateway to salvation. *"Please God,"* is the right place to start. *Please God, hear her prayer and surround her with Your awesome love.*

Inspiration † † †

If we are to see the poor as God sees them, we first have us repent of our judgmental attitudes and feelings of superiority. —Richard Stearns in *The Hole in our Gospel*

Gloom

April 8

When cadets return to West Point in January, they enter what is called *the gloom period*. The buildings are gray, the skies are dreary and a feeling of "I wish I could just take a long, extended nap" settles upon the Corps. I lived through four years of that gloom period. Imagine my surprise when I moved to San Diego and discovered that June was called the same thing! The ever-present sun gave way to incessant fog and a chilly air. So what were we thinking when we moved to western Oregon, a place famous for what can often be eight months of drizzle and fog?

In the midst of rain, I had to put Bear to sleep, the best dog I ever owned. My good friend Brian put the gun to the head of a four legged companion too impacted by cancerous tumors to continue living.

Psalm 107:13,14—Then they cried out to the LORD in their trouble; He saved them from their distress. He brought them out of darkness and gloom and broke their chains apart.

Do you know what the formula for overcoming gloom is? The Bible gives us the solution. It consists of at least four components:

1. Admit going through trouble. The key to escaping gloom is to first recognize it exists. Pretending that everything is fine when it isn't is a sure recipe for breakdown. It is dishonest to act like gray is green. It is phony to be optimistically cheery when your clothes are on fire.

2. Cry out to the Lord. Asking the Lord for help is a key admittance that we can't solve everything. It gives God glory by noting His power and Him as our Champion who delights when we put our trust in Him. Crying out to God also takes our eyes off the problem and shifts them to the Problem Solver.

3. Praise the Lord. Try being gloomy and praising God at the same time. It doesn't work. It's like riding a roller coaster and muttering "what a drag." Praising God changes our attitude and helps us reclaim joy ground.

4. Wait for His deliverance. Gloom doesn't always vanish in a night; it may linger for a season depending on the severity of our murk. But if we cry out to God and praise Him, we WILL see victory. He guarantees it. He is our chain-breaking, dimness-brightening, life-replenishing, hope-making King. The sooner we get that through the haze in our heads the faster our hearts will rejoice!

The Road to Wisdom   April 9

In 2010 my Bible-reading theme was *wisdom* along with sixteen base words key to examining this topic: wise, teach, instruct, advise, know, learn, understand, counsel, reveal, discern, insight, intelligence, guide, perceive, realize, and revelation.

Psalm 111:10—The fear of the LORD is the beginning of wisdom; all who follow His instructions have good insight. His praise endures forever.

There are two kinds of wisdom: secular and spiritual. The *World English Dictionary* defines secular wisdom as "the ability . . . to think and act utilizing knowledge, experience, understanding, common sense, and insight."[18] We might define spiritual wisdom as simply knowing and following God! Whereas secular wisdom is dependent upon our effort and ability, spiritual wisdom comes through full dependence upon God.

Whenever the Bible repeats a proposition multiple times—we would do well to listen. At least *three* times (Psa. 111:10, Pro. 1:7, 9:10) Scripture emphasizes that wisdom <u>begins</u> with fearing God! By respecting God, we gain His willingness to teach us. For example, this summer I was asked with very little advance notice, to speak to a group of college educators who traveled from across the country to observe their students training at Fort Lewis. It was an intimidating assignment. I had *no idea* what to say to them! So I asked several key friends to pray for me and approached God from a position of humility, recognizing my need for His help. The Lord gave me ideas that enabled me to connect on far more than just an academic level—the speech became a spiritual event where God ministered to people listening who were deeply hurting.

Where do you get your instructions for living? Secular wisdom is aptly described by the Dutch poet, Piet Hein who wrote, "The road to wisdom?—Well, it's plain and simple to express: Err and err and err again but less and less and less." We should not be surprised if this approach leaves us miserable! Fear God and obey His plan and love Him with the right attitude and suddenly wisdom thrills us like viewing objects through a kaleidoscope!

> *Now if any of you lacks wisdom, he should ask God, who gives to all generously and without criticizing, and it will be given to him . . . But the wisdom from above is first pure, then peace-loving, gentle, compliant, full of mercy and good fruits, without favoritism and hypocrisy.* (James 1:5,3:17)

Inspiration ✝✝✝

I do not feel obliged to believe that the same God who has endowed us with sense, reason, and intellect has intended us to forgo their use.—Galileo Galilei

Our Compassionate God   April 10

Psalm 116:5—The LORD is gracious and righteous; our God is compassionate.

Another day of silence . . . what sickness quells my mind and muzzles my voice when it should thunder like a waterfall the roaring news of God's eternal love? Why do I languish far behind the Master's call and command? Where is the compassion in my heart for those groping to find the Light? How can I shun spreading the antidote to sin to those whose eyes wear its unmistakable mark? Have I forgotten so quickly the One who willingly hung there abandoned and abused to take my sin?

I cannot bear another stare . . . a child asks, "Why do you cry?" If only they were tears of faithfulness instead of self-centeredness! Shame breaks out upon my face like some unholy rash. Where are the tears that ought to flow for rebellious lives rejecting God's holy gift? What makes my callused eyes unable to see the race of Adam God sees? What madness propels me forward too busy to notice opportunities all around me?

He stumbled beneath a crossbeam He should not have had to shoulder. I am weighted down beneath the I-beam of my own making. My neck bends so that I see only myself. How could I chew the food of complacency when He whose entire body was racked in agony refused pain-killing gall! Do I not see the brutal war for souls?

It is finished. O God, I cannot march through these motions any longer. I've read Your Word and bent my knee. I've encircled myself with those who know You like some magic bracelet. But I've not yet made it my ambition to put others before myself. My heart is not broken for the world. I am not desperate for You. My feeble love is like a blaring radio. I don't have Your compassion. No more Lord! Make caring my robe. Renew my spirit. Take me to the cross. Raise me from my tomb. Help me ascend above the plains of mediocrity. May the honor of Your Son be the focus of my heart for Your eternal glory. "Lord I lift Your Name on high! Lord I love to sing Your praises . . ."

> When He saw the crowds, He felt compassion for them, because they were weary and worn out, like sheep without a shepherd. Then He said to His disciples, "The harvest is abundant, but the workers are few. Therefore, pray to the Lord of the harvest to send out workers into His harvest." (Mat. 9:36-38)

Inspiration † † †

I am sorry for the man who can't feel the whip when it is laid on the other man's back.—President Abraham Lincoln

Empty Tomb

April 11

Like most Christians, we went to church on Easter Sunday. The pastor gave a message from John 20. His sermon was thoughtful and true to the Word but I left feeling something profound was missing.

John 20:1,2—On the first day of the week Mary Magdalene came to the tomb early, while it was still dark. She saw that the stone had been removed from the tomb. So she ran to Simon Peter and to the other disciple, the one Jesus loved, and said to them, "They have taken the Lord out of the tomb, and we don't know where they have put Him!"

When Jesus rose from the tomb, He changed history forever. When He commissioned the disciples to go and share the gospel, it was in the context of what they experienced. The same holds true for us—the idea is not to go and tell what the disciples experienced we are to go and share what we are experiencing. That is what makes the empty tomb relevant! What makes the Easter story complete is what God is writing upon us and those who know Him now! Think about it—Jesus' resurrection and our subsequent faith in Him as Savior, changes our lives radically!

As I write this, I write full of hope—why? Death has no sting! When I die, I go to be with the Lord who deeply loves me. Pain is temporal! No matter what I endure on earth, there is an end to distress in heaven. Sin is defeated! Regardless of my mistakes, shortcomings and errors, Jesus offers me forgiveness and stands as my Advocate before God on the day I am judged.

When we tell people only the historical account of Jesus' resurrection, we have just shared part of the story. Our neighbors are less than likely to find hope in history. Where they find hope is in history *fulfilled*. When you and I tell our neighbors, friends, coworkers and family what an awesome difference Jesus is making in our lives, that's when the empty tomb truly takes on meaning. Otherwise people are left trying to find His body—because like Mary, they don't get it.

Don't just tell people about what God did, show them what He is doing <u>now</u> in <u>your</u> life! What we need to hear is the stories of those who have found the Messiah and who believing without seeing are blessed. Mary finally saw her resurrected Lord. That glorious meeting led to an excited pronouncement, *"I have seen the Lord!"* (v. 18). How about you? Have you seen the Lord? How has the empty tomb brought you a full life and who will hear your story?

Inspiration † † †

Faith is a compound of knowing, trusting, hoping, and stubbornly persisting in trustful hope against all odds.—J.I. Packer in *Rediscovering Holiness*

Real Freedom   April 12

Just because we live in a free country does not mean we have freedom. In fact there are many indicators that suggest that all kinds of cords entwine us. A graph of the stock market looks like some anchor tossed in water that only grows deeper. Those who wear sweaters of worry, whose fortunes are tied to investments, live with the chill of anxiety. Companies lay off employees to keep their profits. Lights go out from city to city across the state whose economy may be the sixth largest in the world, but who cannot create the energy to prevent brownouts. If our hopes are based on the strength of a nation, our dreams will one day be nightmares. The prevalence of fear is a sure sign of the absence of freedom.

Psalm 119:45—I will walk freely in an open place because I seek Your precepts.

When we trust in God, nothing can take us down. Even in death we are moved to a redeemed life with Him forever! True freedom comes by loving God and submitting to His law which brings liberty! When of our own volition we seek to bring Him glory, our hearts sing praises in notes unflattened by trying circumstances. The Apostle Paul proclaimed:
> Christ has liberated us to be free. Stand firm then and don't submit again to a yoke of slavery... but whenever a person turns to the Lord, the veil is removed. Now the Lord is the Spirit, and where the Spirit of the Lord is, there is freedom. (Gal. 5:1, 2 Co 3:16,17)

Dull minds and veiled hearts are the traits of those whose eyes do not look to God.

By the power and holiness of Jesus Christ, you have the right to live with joy! By the grace of your Savior you are set free! Don't get tied up by those who teach self-worship. Do you truly believe your work, your boss, your brains, your luck, your spouse, or your popularity dictate your joy? Real freedom dances in the embrace of the omnipotent Father. "How happy is everyone who fears the LORD, who walks in His ways!" (Psa. 128:1). I pray you will be blessed.

Inspiration † † †

The freedom humanity has is not that of power but of choice, consequently we are accountable for choosing the course we take.—Oswald Chambers in *The Moral Foundations of Life*

Kelcy's Rescue

April 13

Marvin Alan Klegman was an eleven-year old Jewish boy who lived in a small two-bedroom home in Tacoma, Washington with his mom and dad and his younger brother Kerry. Marvin was a motivated Cub Scout and honor roll student. At Lowell Elementary School he served as a crossing-guard. Marvin also worked as a paperboy. He won a Schwinn bicycle in a citywide contest by selling the most Tacoma News Tribune newspaper subscriptions.

On Wednesday, April 13th, 1949, at 11:55 a.m., a 7.1 magnitude earthquake struck the Puget Sound area. While the earth shook, streets buckled, windows shattered, and chimneys toppled, the school emergency siren blared full-blast. Teachers and students quickly escaped their trembling brick structure. For some reason, Marvin re-entered the school and went to the ground-level basement where he spotted Kelcy Allen. Marvin yelled at him, "Hey, we've got to get out of here!" Then he grabbed Kelcy's hand and led him out onto the school ground.

Bricks from a crumbling, overhead cornice began falling on them. Marvin cried, "Look out!" and then, instead of running, pulled the young six-year old under his own body protecting him from the falling bricks. Two days later Marvin was laid to rest at the Home of Peace cemetery in Tacoma. Fifty-one years later, triggered by another earthquake near Seattle, Kelcy did some investigating and found the forgotten name of his rescuer. He was shocked to discover that no one knew of Martin's heroic sacrifice. So Kelcy shared with community leaders what happened that fateful day and two years later, thanks to great work by Mrs. Babe Lehrer, a statue was created and unveiled in front of Lowell Elementary memorializing Marvin's heroism.

Hebrews 10:12—But this man, after offering one sacrifice for sins forever, sat down at the right hand of God.

Marvin gave his life for Kelcy and in so doing instilled in him a motivation to live well; to make that boy's cost worth the price. Kelcy's story of a young man's sacrifice reminds me that bricks of envy, lust, rage, impatience, gossip, theft, gambling, murder, rudeness, lying, cheating, immorality fall from the sky. Some have your name or my name on them. But Jesus, the faultless One, heard our cry for help and sacrificially threw His body over yours and mine. He took our bricks and died. But unlike Marvin, death could not keep Him. His victory over His stone tomb defines our divine rescue.

If we haven't had the motivation to share our story how God saved us into eternal life, then it begs the question of whether we truly understand and appreciate the cost and reality of our rescue!

Covenant

April 14

Psalms 119:50—This is my comfort in my affliction: Your promise has given me life.

We live in an age of broken words. I once participated in a wedding for a man entering his third marriage to a woman who had never married before. As might be expected, there was some underlying concern that this marriage would last. This gave me the opportunity to share with this couple about a certainty that is infinitely greater than the likelihood that their marriage will last. It is the certainty that God has made an awesome promise to us. *"Believe on the Lord Jesus, and you will be saved"* (Acts 16:31).

Oswald Chambers shared in *My Utmost For His Highest*, "All the great blessings of God are finished and complete, but they are not mine until I enter into relationship with Him on the basis of His covenant." I pray this couple will hear the notes of a different wedding song, the melody of God's voice inviting them to receive Him in their hearts.

When we stand for the first time with Jesus at the altar of faith, He shares a promise of salvation that will never be broken! He will not divorce us. Though we suffer the indignity of broken dreams and shattered promises, His Word bursts through the darkness in permanent brilliance proclaiming, *"And everyone who has left houses, brothers or sisters, father or mother, children, or fields because of My name will receive 100 times more and will inherit eternal life"* (Mat. 19:29).

Eternal life with Jesus is beyond what we can fathom. How does a mortal mind grasp an immortal heritage? How do we who are infected with sin conceive of a future holy marriage? The soiled church becomes the spotless bride. What an exciting future we are promised!

Inspiration ✝✝✝

No Christian should be a pessimist. We should be realists—focused on the *reality* that we serve a sovereign and gracious God. Because of the *reality* of Christ's atoning sacrifice and His promises, biblical realism is *optimism*.
—Randy Alcorn in *Heaven*

Walking on Ice

April 15

Have you ever walked on ice? The Japanese have developed a nifty invention for dealing with slippery surfaces. They designed a small rubber sole that can be attached to the bottom of boots. On the rubber sole are two rows of steel teeth which bite the snow and ice when one walks. When I traveled without this device, it was very difficult not to slip and slide. Once these grippers were stretched over my boots walking on frozen ground was much easier.

Life can be filled with ice-covered pathways. Often we encounter circumstances which require care in negotiating. If we try to overcome them in our own power, we may be in for a fall. For example, someone offers me the opportunity to cheat on exam which may raise my grade point average. If I take the time to study the Bible, I discover that it condemns cheating. Someone else asks me to use foul language to be a more effective leader. The Bible says we are to abstain from such language. Someone else is rude and treats me poorly. I want to retaliate but the Bible says I am not to take revenge. Do you see how God's Word is like a gripper sole? It gives us the wisdom and guidance we need to successfully negotiate life.

The Holy Spirit uses Scripture to help us walk treacherous terrain--to bite whatever could cause us to slide with His enabling power. The Bible gives us a steady cleat to cling when others around who are not so equipped slip and fall. If you need to get a grip, get into God's Word. How many times must we fall down before we understand this?

Psalm 119:104,105—I gain understanding from Your precepts; therefore I hate every false way. Your word is a lamp for my feet and a light on my path.

Inspiration † † †

The river of the Spirit of God overcomes all obstacles. Never get your eyes on the obstacle or on the difficulty . . . Never allow anything to come between yourself and Jesus Christ, no emotion, or experience; nothing must keep you from the one great sovereign Source.—Oswald Chambers in *My Utmost For His Highest*

Fencing Sadie April 16

Our neighbors have a new puppy, Sadie. She is a lovable pit bull full of energy and eager for attention. To keep her from getting lost or running away, it was necessary to finish fencing their yard. So, with help from family members, holes were dug, cement was poured, and metal posts for a chain-link fence were sealed into the ground. That fence is not going anywhere; Sadie is quite secure.

Psalm 119:112—I am resolved to obey Your statutes to the very end.

To be steadfast, as defined by the dictionary, means to be fixed or unchanging, firmly loyal and constant; unswerving. Like a cemented fence post, a steadfast person is secure. The question is to what are we committed? For example, a person devoted to having a good time and not becoming locked into rules or regulations is steadfastly free-spirited—like Sadie, the pit bull without a fence. We determine what defines steadfast by finding what a person is locked into doing or being.

Psalm 119 is a devotional on the importance of the word of God. Appropriately, it is the longest chapter in the Bible. Interestingly, it is very close to Psalm 117, the shortest chapter and the middle chapter in the Bible. The theme of Psalm 119 might best be captured by the meditation verse above. The psalmist recognizes the value of God's word and therefore commits to a lifetime of obeying His commands.

What are you steadfastly pursuing? How would those who know you define what you live for; what values and convictions have you cemented into the ground? How does God see you? He judges us according to our willingness to obey and follow after His Son, Jesus. He promises us that when we set His Word highest and pursue Christ first, we will be blessed! It's not easy to be steadfast, but it is essential! The world will mock and label you as a legalist, a fundamentalist, and intolerant for choosing to obey God's Word. But the world holds no authority over your soul, cannot give you eternal life, and has only its false pledge to bring you happiness and fulfillment in place of God's commands. Forget about the world. Quit pursuing what is ultimately useless. Take up the psalmist's cry, *"Turn my eyes from looking at what is worthless; give me life in Your ways . . . If only my ways were committed to keeping Your statutes!"* (119:37,5).

Inspiration ✝✝✝

Are we willing to commit ourselves to a goal of obedience without exception? Such a commitment is necessary if we are to make progress in the pursuit of holiness.—Jerry Bridges in *The Discipline of Grace*

Maria

April 17

1 Samuel 2:6-8—The LORD brings death and gives life; He sends some to Sheol, and He raises others up. The LORD brings poverty and gives wealth; He humbles and He exalts. He raises the poor from the dust and lifts the needy from the garbage pile. He seats them with noblemen and gives them a throne of honor. For the foundations of the earth are the LORD's; He has set the world on them.

Every person has a story. Command Sergeant Major Loera and I walked beneath the famous Arch in St. Louis. We were in uniform and looking around at the different venues when a woman walked up and invited us inside the theater where she worked. As soon as the movie about making the Arch finished, she slipped us two free tickets and sent us to watch the Lewis and Clark film. She repeatedly thanked us for our service.

The next day, I returned to the Arch from our hotel to give Maria a small gift to thank her for her kindness. Later I asked her to tell me her story. She protested that her life was boring but thankfully shared anyway. Maria was born in Red Bud, Illinois, on November 19, 1954. At the age of sixteen, she was forced to leave home to find work and a place of her own. In 1974, she married a man who sadly turned out to be an abusive alcoholic. The day after her husband hit her son in a drunken rage and sent him flying across the room, Maria escaped with her children to stay three months with her pastor and his wife in a room they prepared for her. Her marriage lasted just under ten years.

On April 17, 1995, while at work Maria received a call from the hospital—the call every parent dreads. A nurse told her that her youngest son Tim was admitted for treatment but that he was okay. But each time she asked about her daughter the nurse would not answer. Maria knew her seventeen year-old Angela was with Tim and had a bad premonition. Just three months earlier, Angela told her mom about a reoccurring dream about a black truck, a hill, and a glowing hand that reached out to her. She was afraid to see what was beyond the hill and to take the hand for fear she would not see her mom again. Maria told her if the hand was offered and she wanted to go, she should take it.

A sovereign Father prepared His children for a difficult time. Angela and her brother Tim were passengers in a black truck. The driver was young and foolishly speeding on a country road when he lost control. His pickup launched off a hill and rolled three times killing him and Angela. Somehow, both Tim and Angela's boyfriend survived. Tim held his sister's arm as her pulse expired.

When Maria notified her boss of her daughter's death, he told her if she missed a day of work, she would be absent without leave (AWOL). Incredulous, she responded that she would be gone all week regardless of what he did. Fortunately, another employee heard the conversation and reported it to the supervisor who immediately called and apologized to Maria. Then he gave her a month off with pay! This incident seems to capture her life—Maria suffers adversity, responds with courage and receives grace from God to continue! Her joy meter stays lit. She is a woman who makes everyone around her better.

Inspiration ✝ ✝ ✝

Love sweetens pains. And when a Christian loves God, he can suffer for His sake, joyfully and courageously.—Brother Lawrence & Frank Laubach in *Practicing His Presence*

Word from God   April 18

Have you ever asked the question, "How do I know when God is speaking to me?" I remember vividly, as if it were this very day, a choice I had to make decades ago. The decision involved where I was to go in serving God with an organization called The Navigators. Some of my closest friends and counselors advised me to stay in the region where I had lived for the past four years. Other close friends and family advised me to leave and serve in a region to which I had been invited. It was a very difficult time because people's emotions were stirred and strong rational thoughts were presented by both sides. I chose to go to the latter for two reasons: 1. Throughout the process I had a persistent sense that that's where God wanted me to go. 2. God confirmed His direction for me through a Bible passage in the book of Isaiah. Looking back, it is clear that going was the right decision.

It is incredibly important that we discern when God is speaking to us. Yet, it is not often easy to hear Him! Our own personal preference, the opinions of others, varying circumstances and our own character flaws-impatience, pride, fear, etc., all stand in the way of our listening. I recall many times when I have been spiritually deaf to the Holy Spirit's leading. As I grow in my relationship with the Lord, I am becoming more cognizant of how He speaks. He is persistent and the leading does not go away. He talks quietly and firmly, devoid of fanfare and hype. What He asks me to do, say, or be, always leads to His glory. When He speaks, He also provides (Php. 4:19), so that His will is accomplished and my faith is strengthened in the process.

Make it a priority to hear and discern what the Lord has to say to you. Don't let life's traffic jams and the unceasing roar of activity cause you to miss the quiet voice of your Counselor. He is faithful to share with us if we will be faithful to listen!

Psalm 119:130,133—The revelation of Your words brings light and gives understanding to the inexperienced . . . Make my steps steady through Your promise; don't let any sin dominate me.

God has a word for you. When you hear what He has to say, obey quickly and be blessed as you become a blessing to others.

Inspiration † † †

I know when the proposition comes from God because of its quiet persistence: When I have to weigh the pros and cons and doubt and debate come in, I am bringing in an element that is not of God, and I come to the conclusion that the suggestion was not a right one.—Oswald Chambers in *My Utmost For His Highest*

Check Engine   April 19

I was driving down Lombard Street when a red light illuminated my dashboard with the words "Check Engine." Now I'd be the first to admit I'm a mechanical dummy but I know that when that light comes on, it doesn't mean to pop the hood and check to see if there is still an engine in there! That reddish glow is an unsubtle directive to get to a mechanic who can run a diagnostic test and hopefully discover why the warning message is activated without charging me an elbow and a thigh.

Wouldn't it be nice if God placed a little red light in the upper left portion of our chest that flashed the words, "Check Heart" whenever something inside us is amiss? It's not a good idea to ignore warning messages in cars. To do so can lead to a mechanical breakdown. Neither is it a good idea to ignore distress, hoping it will just go away. Our manufacturer's warranty says God made us. And God says that when we are in trouble, we are to go to Him. He knows if we need an attitude adjustment, character alignment, or spiritual tune-up. He will equip us to negotiate the road hazards we'll encounter on life's highways.

Psalm 120:1—In my distress I called to the LORD, and He answered me.

If you're filled with angst, schedule an appointment with God. Follow His guidance. Don't perspire over the price. He's paid your tab. Trust in His Word and obey His will, believing that the Holy Spirit intercedes on your behalf!

For much of his senior years, my dad has made and protected time to call on God. He does this at least five days a week by hiking up the mountain behind his house. While he climbs he prays. As he prays he also listens. Often God gives him the encouraging word he needs to make a life correction or to help someone else. Often he has an encouraging word to pass on to me and to my sisters and brother. I know that God blesses my life because my father daily is praying for me. When I have concerns, I call him. Better yet, I am reminded of how critical it is for me when I am under stress or out of sorts, to pray!

Inspiration † † †

If I am a child of God, distress will lead me to Him for direction.—Oswald Chambers in *The Pilgrim's Song Book*

Casa de Niños

April 20

Psalm 121:1-3,5,7-8—I lift my eyes toward the mountains. Where will my help come from? My help comes from the LORD, the Maker of heaven and earth. He will not allow your foot to slip; your Protector will not slumber . . . The LORD protects you; the LORD is a shelter right by your side . . . The LORD will protect you from all harm; He will protect your life. The LORD will protect your coming and going both now and forever.

They live in the hills and the valleys surrounding Malacatan. Orphans, children with only a mother, or some with parents too poor to provide adequate food and clothing. Juan Carlos and Nivea already care for 14 youngsters in Solace's children's home but that does not account for the ones they cannot help, still waiting to receive assistance.

"*My help comes from the LORD.*" Boys and girls learn firsthand from Juan that God loves them and it is life changing to come to a personal relationship with the Protector. They learn that God hears and answers prayers. God is their protector. When He is the One we turn to, there is no problem that cannot be overcome.

- "*He will not allow your foot to slip.*" What about those times when all the Tilapia die in their pond because of contaminated water? When the chicks perish because they got wet and now a second source of income is gone, what does Juan do? He prays and He trusts that God means what He says. Never underestimate the creativity or power of God in getting us back on solid footing.

- "*The LORD protects you; the LORD is a shelter right by your side.*" When prayers uttered each day and night do not vanish into the humid Guatemalan sky, but are heard by the Preserver who lives in the midst of chaos. He makes His presence known by touching hearts and healing wounds. Daily, the Lord is right by their side sheltering them. His omnipresence is more than comforting, it is life sustaining.

- "*The LORD will protect you from all harm.*" There are those times when God allows no evil or disaster to befall His children. We pray and God brings instant and complete deliverance. But some of us know and carry deeply the marks of hurt. How do we learn to trust our Father when bad things happen? The reality of valley dwelling is suffering and death but the Maker of mountains brings life beyond evil, disease and disaster. Harm is averted, harm is absorbed, but ultimately harm is destroyed by the Deliverer who forever banishes sin, sickness, and death.

- "*He will protect your life . . . your coming and going both now and forever.*" Beware of blaming God for the loss of transient things. It is not what is passing and will burn that God guards. It is the security of our lives for eternal fellowship the Creator sustains.

● *"I lift my eyes towards the mountains."* In the shadow of a great volcano, the kids at Casa De Niño's are learning much about their Keeper. We valley dwellers would do well to look up more often. Our Preserver and Protector, Yahweh, is mighty.

Immanent

April 21

Her Asian face stares at me with a confident look that belies the caption blazoned across her neck. It reads, "I'm everywhere." Microsoft advertised its Windows 2000 Professional preinstalled on the "highly reliable, wireless-enabled Dell Latitude® C6000 notebook and you can get total mobility." That's what we want isn't it—the ability to go anywhere and take what we need with us?

Psalm 139:8-10—If I go up to heaven, You are there; if I make my bed in Sheol, You are there. If I live at the eastern horizon or settle at the western limits, even there Your hand will lead me; Your right hand will hold on to me.
Proverbs 15:3—The eyes of the LORD are everywhere, observing the wicked and the good.

I'm not everywhere. I can only be where I am, one place at a time. And yet wherever I am, He is. And wherever you are, He is. I make no moves that His eyes do not see, no thoughts or actions escape His notice. If the clouds are gray and my heart is unsettled, I need only look up and call His name and know that He hears. If my spirit soars like some unleashed falcon, He climbs with me to the glory of His name.

Despite awesome technology and a world that shrinks with every microchip, we occupy infinitesimal space. I will not place my laptop on some carefully arranged embroidered cloth and burn incense to it! It may allow me the privilege of taking information wherever I go but what is that compared to the One who gives me breath and saves my soul? Wherever I go, He is there. He's everywhere. "Don't you yourselves know that you are God's sanctuary and that the Spirit of God lives in you?" (1 Co. 3:16).

How can He reside in so many temples? How can He decipher the thoughts of millions of His children simultaneously? What a magnificent Father we have! God, You are near! In Your nearness may our love please You. In our nearness may Your Spirit lift our hearts to worship You. May those who feel alone find You and know the comfort that comes from hands that hold the world.

Inspiration † † †

An atheist and a Christian were engaged in an intense public debate. On the blackboard behind the podium the atheist printed in large capital letters, "GOD IS NOWHERE." When the Christian rose to offer his rebuttal, he rubbed out the W at the beginning of where and added that letter to the preceding word no. Then the statement read, "GOD IS NOW HERE."—Vernon Grounds in *Radical Commitment:*

Two Words to Avoid   April 22

Two words in the English language frequently reveal conceit—"I can't." Whenever I say "I can't" in the context of not doing what should be done, I'm really saying "I won't!" I profess to know myself and my limitations and therefore to pronounce what *I* will not do. Of course I have the right to state what I am unwilling to do. But it is not a question of rights when conceit is exposed, rather it is a question of will. God sees me for who and what I really am.

Check your language. Are you missing God's best for you because it is easier to be staked to your own pronouncements? Unless directed towards refraining from what is wrong, "I can't" is a statement of will that reveals distrust, lack of confidence, push-back, or laziness.

Psalm 139:23,24—Search me, God, and know my heart; test me and know my concerns. See if there is any offensive way in me; lead me in the everlasting way.

I remember an occasion as a young man when my girlfriend broke up with me. She sent me a "Dear John" letter during my fall semester as a plebe at West Point. When I went back to stay with my uncle and aunt in Idaho for Christmas vacation, I needed to spend a significant amount of time studying for the calculus exam I faced when I returned to New York. But my heart was so crushed by a broken relationship that I had no motivation to study. I said, "I can't." I gave up trying to review my textbook and notes. When I ended up taking the final, I had the lowest score I'm sure in my class and badly failed the course. I ended up having to go to summer school. I learned a powerful lesson about giving up.

All the most clever observations I utter about myself and even the most thoughtful pronouncements fall infinitely short of God's understanding of who I am. The ease with which I can fabricate excuses if I want my own way or prefer a certain course by hiding behind "can't" in no way glorifies God. Therefore in order to expunge my own conceit I must declare with King David, *"Search me, God . . ."*

You truly know what lies in my heart. You know all my thoughts. You see that which needs repairing. Forgive me for pretending to suggest I know what's best for me. Repair what's broken in me. Lead me in Your way, the way that lasts forever!

Inspiration †††

I've found that God usually wants to do something in us before he can do something through us.—Doug Pollock in *God Space*

Finding Answers   April 23

How often do you seek answers from the Bible so as to know what to do? For years, Kathleen and I were not able to sell our home and because of this our equity was tied up. Not having the ability to free up that money was frustrating. I wonder how many hours I spent trying to identify a solution to our situation. Recently, I read in Psalm 16:5, *"The LORD is my chosen portion and my cup; you hold my lot"* (ESV). What a great reminder that He is in control of my *lot* (in context lot refers to the future but here it makes a nice property statement)! He will resolve our housing situation when the time is right. Occasionally finding answers is not the issue. What I need is to be at peace with the Answer.

Unfortunately, often our action or expectation can prevent us from finding God's solution. It can be quite annoying to wait. Where we go wrong is by impatiently setting course by our own reasoning. We run on hunches or draw from the library of our own experience. We dance to the beat of worldly composition only to discover later we are profoundly off key. Maybe you have waded into the Bible expecting to find solutions without success. You won't be the first to have had such experience. Sometimes reading the Bible may feel like a drive through the desert.

It is precisely when we least feel like searching the Scripture that we need the most to be immersed in it. Why? Because God often reveals His will outside of our time schedule. If I will be patient, He will unveil His perfect plan. When the rain comes, the sand yields flowers from seeds we had no idea were even there. The Scripture we read yesterday that seemed pointless may point our way tomorrow.

Proverbs 1:5; 2:1-6—A wise man will listen and increase his learning, and a discerning man will obtain guidance . . . My son, if you accept my words and store up my commands within you, listening closely to wisdom and directing your heart to understanding; furthermore, if you call out to insight and lift your voice to understanding, if you seek it like silver and search for it like hidden treasure, then you will understand the fear of the LORD and discover the knowledge of God. For the LORD gives wisdom; from His mouth come knowledge and understanding.

How much better it is to prepare our hearts to wait for God's leading. Finding answers comes from listening, learning and obtaining guidance; but always we must do the work of preparing our hearts.

Inspiration   † † †

The Christian lives, and is guided, not by rules specifying just how far he may mix with men, but by these inward qualities which are mediated to him by God's Holy Spirit.—Watchman Nee in *Love Not the World*

Against My Wife's Better Judgment April 24

Have you ever had a period in life where you felt like an idiot and wish you could crawl in a hole and hide? I know what it is like to emerge from the hole! Against my wife's better judgment, we put a man I trusted in our vacant house to lead a ministry to homeless people. It was to be a sanctuary where folks could get their lives back in order. We gave clear guidance on how the home was to operate—so much for good intentions. The man running the home refused to be accountable. He began insisting I gave him the house and quit paying "mortgage assistance." We gave all the occupants a 30-day eviction notice and they refused to leave. Finally, after securing an attorney and going through several sessions in court, we got our house back. The renegade leader promised before the judge to pay us a sum of money and to turn the premises over with everything moved out and "broom clean." He reneged on paying us and left the place a mess. Instead of vandalized we felt *Randalized*.

Proverbs 1:23—If you respond to my warning, then I will pour out my spirit on you and teach you my words.

- Wisdom grows through the discipline of unity. *"Can two walk together without agreeing to meet?"* (Amos 3:3). My wife was never at peace with the decision to use our house in the manner it was run. She sensed there would be problems. My optimistic compassion was founded on a floor of sand. Her practical compassion looked for a solid floor of accountability.
- Wisdom grows through the discipline of obedience. There were countless signs that the policies we established in the beginning were violated. Instead of correcting the problems early on, I chose to be gracious and give the director every chance to succeed. By allowing him to disregard standards a hill of discontent became a volcano of rebellion. *"The one who keeps a command will not experience anything harmful, and a wise heart knows the right time and procedure"* (Ecc. 8:5).
- Wisdom grows through the discipline of rest. We saw that the director was often overwhelmed by the problems of those in the home and that in reality it was far too big a ministry for him to handle. We should have extracted him from the mess and used a different leadership approach. Relief is sometimes the best answer.

Wisdom is not grown by hoping problems will go away, by avoiding confrontation, by naïve kindness, or by lowering standards. She offers her counsel to those willing to listen, and that takes discipline. I hope you learn from my mistakes and I hope you remember what I'm reminded of—God's love and grace is always deeper than our misfortune.

Delnora's Life

April 25

Delnora Erickson left the earth. She was 91 years old when she completed her race to meet Jesus at the finish line. She was an inspiring example of what it means to be a follower of Jesus. This amazing woman never lost her thirst to grow closer to her Heavenly Father. Even as an octogenarian her creative mind would not find a hammock to gracefully swing on old lessons. She launched a fresh study of the Old Testament to identify every reference to Christ. Often she would gleefully share her findings oblivious to the fact she was repeating herself, and what did it matter she was excited! I recall many times talking with her and she would ask, "Do you think Jesus will return before we die?" Then with sparkling eyes she'd exclaim, "Oh, I think He's coming soon!"

This beloved artist and writer possessed an insatiable appetite for the Bible. Who but God knows how many lives she touched through her long life as a Sunday School teacher, Bible Study leader, published author of children's stories and devoted sharer of Christ.

Most amazing was the quality of life she led. She was hardly ever ill. Despite the deaths of two of her daughters one to diabetes and the other to cancer, and the wretched suffering of her pastor-husband in his final years, her own health remained vibrant. She shunned evil. She was not perfect. Yet, she feared the Lord and like a child sought to live a life pleasing in her Father's eyes. To be physically healthy the body must effectively resist germs and disease. To be spiritually healthy, the spirit must withstand and overcome sin. One may take vitamins, antioxidants and other vital supplements to keep the body sound, but the key to attaining spiritual health is to fellowship with Jesus—the Living Water, the Bread of life. Though the body will eventually fail us, the spirit in love with Christ will never see decay. She knew this.

Today her spirit soars in the presence of the One to whom her life was devoted. I am glad my children could learn and be blessed by the godly heritage of their great-grandmother. Grandma, we will miss you. We love you. Thank you for your example of what it means to be healthy. Hug my mom for me. And yes, we'll be home soon! Won't it be great to all be there together with Jesus.

Proverbs 3:7,8—Don't consider yourself to be wise; fear the LORD and turn away from evil. This will be healing for your body and strengthening for your bones.

Inspiration ✝✝✝

Grandmas are moms with lots of frosting.—Author Unknown

A grandmother is a little bit parent, a little bit teacher, and a little bit best friend.—Author Unknown

Critters

April 26

Tuesday morning I was sitting next to two students in a van as we headed off towards our classes. I couldn't help but overhear their conversation. The guy shared with the gal about how he was staying in a motel in Hawaii one time and saw a centipede in his room. He was told that they can bite and cause quite an infection and so it concerned him. That night as he was ready to go to sleep, he saw a gecko, an indigenous lizard. He did not realize that it is a good thing to have a lizard in his room (they eat bugs). Unnerved and unable to sleep, he had the person at the front desk move him to another room.

Wednesday night, while reading email, a centipede walked across the air conditioning unit in my room. I'm used to growing up around cockroaches, ants, bees and spiders so it didn't bother me. But at three in the morning, something ran across my chest, jumped on to the nightstand and then scampered towards the far wall. Now that woke me up and was rather freaky! I got up, turned on the light but saw no critters. I realized the bedspread was touching the floor making it very easy for anything to crawl into or across my bed, so I pulled the bedspread up and *tried* to go back to sleep. The next morning I asked the front desk what creatures they had in their place—mice, cockroaches, etc. The gal said she didn't know of any mice or big bug problems, but she felt terrible I had such an unpleasant experience. She volunteered that she would move me if only she had a free room! I told her it was okay and I'd stay where I was.

Proverbs 3:24—When you lie down, you will not be afraid; you will lie down, and your sleep will be pleasant.

Could I sleep Thursday night not knowing what might come out or be lurking in the shadows? Proverbs 3:24 provided the solution. God gives me the right perspective, strength and sleep. I don't have to fear what I can't see or catch, I have to trust the Replenisher.

How can He lead us in the right direction if He doesn't know or care where we are? Life is full of things that can "bug" us. So we have to make a choice—we either lose sleep over what concerns us, or we trust God and rest. The test for rest is trust. Could it be that God allowed me to overhear a man's bad hotel experience to measure my attitude? I don't know the answer to that, but I do know that to complain about the room or lay awake wondering, might be to question the path.

Lord, thanks for renewal. Please keep me You-focused.

Knecht the Dots

April 27

In *Something to Think About . . . in Reveration*, I shared the story of David Knecht, a West Point classmate who suffered a horrifying injury while on a military exercise that left him partially paralyzed and blind in his right eye. The name of that reveration was *Glory*. Five years after writing that account I was able to visit Dave and Annette in their home in Tampa, Florida.

At the time of Dave's accident, the Knecht's had five young children. Dave was relocated from California to Tampa's brain trauma center. Annette moved with five young children to a city where she knew no one to somehow reestablish family life and care as much as possible for her recovering husband. With no facilities for dependents, she often slept in her car. Children were not allowed inside the center. Knowing Dave needed to see his kids and vice versa, Annette insisted on bringing them in and was arrested! She and other suffering spouses were appalled at the lack of support and resources.

So often, when we face a difficult situation, it is easy to give up. Annette refused to feel sorry for herself. Instead of suing an unresponsive institution, she organized the hurting into an effective group committed to reform. Now, each Saturday morning Annette volunteers to help those in rehab and meets with an ongoing support group. They helped initiate a Fisher House that provides free lodging for as long as is needed for family members. The Clarion Inn in Tampa, also provides rooms for people to stay. Food and cell phone vouchers are available for dependents in need of assistance. What was once a bleak situation is now an effective ministry of helping hands.

Proverbs 3:27—When it is in your power, don't withhold good from the one it belongs to.

Annette and David are people of grace. This family now of twelve draws upon God's love, trusts Him to provide and thrives. They are making a difference in Tampa for God's glory. How about you, are you so discouraged by difficult challenges that you feel like giving up? Don't! Trust the Lord to do you good. He will bring you through the valley to the place He wants you. And if you have opportunity and the power to help others, don't hold back. The child of God aflame in hope brings help to hearts who cannot cope! Like Mother Theresa, we may say, "I don't do big things. I do small things with big love."

Milestone   April 28

April 28th is a milestone in the York household. Bryan was diagnosed with a brain-stem tumor on February 14, 1991. His doctor told us he had zero chance of survival; his tumor was a ticking time bomb. At the age of three Bryan endured 72 radiation treatments that shrunk his tumor, damaged his hearing, impaired his mobility, and degraded his ability to process information. In June of that same year, a group of young-married couples gathered with Kathleen, Bryan, and me to weep, pray for him, and worship in song our awesome God. The Holy Spirit descended into our midst and healed our son. Today there is no trace of his tumor.

God profoundly taught me the power and hope that come from worship. How long we will live on earth is a mystery. So we have the sober responsibility of living each day with purpose. I cannot imagine life devoid of God. The reality of death and living a meaningless existence would be overwhelming were it not for the hope of eternal life and direction that comes with a personal friendship with Jesus Christ. True joy flows in the grace and mercy that abound in the love of our Father who made us to know us and so He would be known.

I cannot answer why God chose to extend the life of my son. Only He knows why He chooses to heal or withhold healing. What I do know is that Bryan's quiet spirit and deep love for God and people inspire all of us privileged to be around him. He never complains about his limitations nor does he focus on what he cannot do. He is obedient, kind, and exceedingly patient.

Oh God, I want to live my life for You. How true those words are. Is it the amount of our days that is important or is it what we do with what we have that matters? We are so easily preoccupied with trivial things. We are so easily consumed by what ultimately fades into oblivion. Consequently we miss so many opportunities to invest in what is eternal. Days rightly lived are not about coveting wealth, popularity, or power. Such things will not impress our Creator. Good days are measured by faith, obedience, and a simple, pure love for God reflected in our worship. Through them, we gain wisdom.

On this milestone I give thanks for Bryan and pray that his numbered days will lead to millions finding the joy he has in Jesus—for the glory of our Maker.

Psalm 90:12—Teach us to number our days carefully so that we may develop wisdom in our hearts.

What's Wrong With You? April 29

Irish Proverb: "Don't let your tongue cut your throat."

"What's wrong with you?" The question stung. Bryan replied from the safety of a carpeted banister, "Hey, this is my first time and I don't have very good balance." "So? It's easy," the boy retorted. Then with a look that said, "You're incompetent!" he took off. A friend skated to Bryan who then shared what the kid had said. He was appalled at the boy's rudeness. He went over to some of their mutual friends and reported the insult. They devised a plan to body check the smart aleck. Not a godly response—but humorous. For Bryan, the balm of supportive friends covered the sting of criticism.

Proverbs 12:16—A fool's displeasure is known at once, but whoever ignores an insult is sensible.

If we understood the source of insults, I suspect our need to defend ourselves would evaporate. Insults come from insecurity. A person who is not confident in his own standing for a multitude of reasons needs to belittle the character or status of another. Our difficulty stems from our own insecurity. Thus, when we get ripped, every pore in our body screams, "Get even!" If we were secure in the Lord, the comments of derogatory people would be like eggs sliding off a new Teflon pan.

Did you ever stop to consider that an insult affords you an opportunity? A sinful world teaches that the best response to derogation is a better put-down. But that only escalates the process of wounding. Listen to what the Scripture teaches us. *"Do not repay evil with evil or insult with insult. On the contrary, repay evil with blessing, because to this you were called so that you may inherit a blessing"* (1 Pe. 3:9, NIV).

Are you discouraged because someone you know continuously puts you down? Is your joy depleted by the attacks of others? Turn the verbal poison away by committing to pray for the offender. Look for the source of insecurity in the one spewing and heap kindness upon evil. This will strengthen you and bring honor to God. If you are being insulted for your walk with Christ, listen to what Jesus said:

You are blessed when they insult and persecute you and falsely say every kind of evil against you because of Me. Be glad and rejoice, because your reward is great in heaven. For that is how they persecuted the prophets who were before you. (Mat. 5:11,12)

Inspiration † † †

A tongue is the only tool that grows sharper even after constant use.— Washington Irvin

The Power of Language — April 30

Here's a great word for you—logorrhea. It literally means excessive use of words.

Proverbs 12:18—There is one who speaks rashly, like a piercing sword; but the tongue of the wise brings healing.

Language represents power. The better we are able to communicate, the more effective we will be in accomplishing our goals, edifying others, and minimizing confusion and misunderstanding. The *American Heritage Dictionary* gives us helpful insight into types of speech we often use:

These nouns refer to concise verbal expressions setting forth wisdom or a truth. A *saying* is an often repeated and familiar expression . . . *Maxim* denotes particularly an expression of a general truth or a rule of conduct . . . *Adage* applies to a saying that has gained credit through long use . . . *Saw* often refers to a familiar saying that has become trite through frequent repetition . . . A *motto* is a maxim that expresses the aims, character, or guiding principles of a person, a group, or an institution . . . An *epigram* is a terse, witty expression, often paradoxical or satirical and neatly or brilliantly phrased . . . *Proverb* refers to an old and popular saying that illustrates something such as a basic truth or a practical precept . . . *Aphorism*, a concise expression of a truth or principle, implies depth of content and stylistic distinction.[19]

Have you ever said "hang in there" to a person you know who is going through a tough period in life or, "Cheer up, things will get better!"? Unfortunately, these expressions are saws. Saws can be symptomatic of laziness on the part of the speaker, insensitivity, confusion over what to really say, or, embarrassment because of the awkwardness of what the other person is enduring. We don't want to be trite! What we say and how we say things does matter. Another overused saw today is *"That's cool."*

When I see someone in need, my goal is to be an agent of healing. I must decide if it is best to remain silent or to share. The next time you see someone who could use encouragement, avoid verbalizing a cheap platitude. *"Listen, for I speak of noble things, and what my lips say is right"* **(Pro. 8:6)**. Our language matters!

Inspiration †††

A bird that you set free may be caught again, but a word that escapes your lips will not return.—Jewish Proverb

Initiative

May 1

"Go for it" is a common slogan in an uncommon age. We live in the swift-enhanced decade where innovation in the realm of technology is stunning. Purchase a computer and in just a few years it will be obsolete. The slogan for our age seems to be "UPGRADE."

I don't think I've ever needed someone to encourage me in the area of taking initiative. Ideas flow through my veins like electricity—only it's usually others that get shocked! Ideas are the necessary spark plugs that fire initiative. They can be fruitful or they can be fruitless. Initiative that is not God-ordained has the potential of hurting people, leading one down a track God never intended and chewing up valuable resources. Initiative that is in response to God's leading bears divine results.

So how do we know when "going for it" is self-promoted versus Spirit-led? Perhaps the answer to that question involves asking questions.

- "God, what is it You desire me to do today?"
- "Lord, am I chasing my own dreams or following Your will?"
- "Father, I'm going to be quiet and listen for Your leading. Would You enable me to hear Your voice and obey Your will?"

Proverbs 16:1—We humans make plans, but the LORD has the final word. (CEV)

> Oswald Chambers taught in *The Devotion of Following*:
> In the natural world everything depends upon our taking the initiative, but if we are followers of God, we cannot take the initiative, we cannot choose our own work or say what we will do; we do not have to find out at all, we just have to follow.

Initiative isn't worth all the diamonds in South Africa if it sidetracks us from following God. Jesus was proud of His disciples when they demonstrated spiritual initiative. But He didn't teach them to sit in the lotus position and trust their inner voice. He taught them to pray, *"Thy will be done."* So when is initiative ordained by God? It has His blessing when it is in response to His leading.

Inspiration †††

You cannot follow God in neutral.—Erwin Raphael McManus in *Chasing Daylight*

Work in Progress   May 2

If a child sees a butterfly struggling to free itself from its cocoon, the natural tendency is to help it escape. But those who know about these beautiful insects, understand that to prematurely help the butterfly is to give it the death sentence. The butterfly must struggle to gain the strength it needs to later fly and survive.

If you were to look real closely at certain people you would find that God has hung a sign just above the heart that says, "Don't touch—Character work in progress." Unfortunately many of us have a savior complex. We don't take the time to pray and ask God *if* we should intervene with help because our 9-1-1 spiritual pager is beeping. We assume that if someone we know is in trouble, it is our God-assigned task to step in and problem-solve. Beware, to intervene without God's approval is presumptuous.

Proverbs 16:23—A wise heart instructs its mouth and increases learning with its speech.

When my children entered college, Kathleen and I both struggled with the desire to pay their tuition. We did not want them to amass debt. We chose to pay only part of their costs. By doing this we taught them several principles. First, they learned the importance of finding work that paid so they could pay down their debt. Second, they learned to appreciate the education they were receiving because it cost them something. Third, it made them more appreciative of the help we gave rather than taking it for granted.

Wisdom is trusting that God knows best what a person needs and that best may not include our services or resources. Wisdom is a willing heart wed to a discerning mind. If the Holy Spirit authenticates our good Samaritan impulse, wonderful. If not, don't get in the way of His work—He's never made a mistake.

Inspiration ✝✝✝

There are times when a person needs to be handled by God, not by his fellow man, and part of the gift of human wisdom is to know how to be reverent with what he does not understand.—Oswald Chambers in *Conformed to His Image*

Opinions

May 3

Man's perceptions are often not in line with God's intentions. Had Jesus chosen to heed the opinions of his key men, the dynamic dozen when they:

- Said, "*Send the crowds away so they can go into the villages and buy food for themselves*" (Mat. 14:15b). There wouldn't have been a miraculous feeding of the 5000 with 5 loaves of bread and 2 fishes.
- Rebuked the people who brought children to see the Lord. We would have missed the lesson that God loves little children and doesn't want them hindered from coming to Him because the kingdom of heaven belongs to them and those like them.
- Became indignant because a woman poured expensive perfume on Jesus' head. "'*Why this waste?' they asked. 'This might have been sold for a great deal and given to the poor'*" (Mat.26:8b,9). We would have lost the truth that God delights in special acts of sacrifice meant to honor Him.

Those who are leaders especially need to be careful before expressing opinions. It is too easy for those in positions of responsibility to become enamored with their own authority and to make recommendations without going to God first for His advice. Remember when Jesus explained to His disciples that He must go to Jerusalem and suffer and eventually be killed? Peter, an impetuous follower with strong leading skills said emphatically: "*Oh no, Lord! This will never happen to You!*" (Mat. 16:22b).

We can gain valuable insight from Jesus' response to Peter. "*Get behind Me, Satan! You are an offense to Me because you're not thinking about God's concerns, but man's*" (Mat. 16:23). Those words may seem overly harsh but they were uttered for a purpose--to illustrate how quickly one with good intentions can subvert God's plan!

Oswald Chambers wrote in *My Utmost For His Highest*:

Be careful to see that you never bind a yoke on others that is not placed by Jesus Christ. It takes God a long time to get us out of the way of thinking that unless everyone sees as we do, they must be wrong. That is never God's view . . . Jesus said, "*Go and make disciples,*" not make converts to your opinions.

Words make a difference. Choose them wisely. Use them judiciously for the glory of God.

Proverbs 18:2—A fool does not delight in understanding, but only wants to show off his opinions.

Inspiration ✝ ✝ ✝

Does not our preaching contain too much of our own opinions and convictions, and too little of Jesus Christ?—Dietrich Bonhoeffer in *The Cost of Discipleship*

The Balance of Justice   May 4

Tragedy has a way of releasing the inner ideologies of people that normally would go unstated. After terrorists attacks we often hear cries for "Revenge!" Wounded victims seethe with anger. "Blow away the enemy! Make sure he never strikes us again."

There are many problems with advocating revenge. First, it is often based in pride—I'm going to take action in my power to fix the problem. God hates pride. The Apostle Paul wrote: *"Friends, do not avenge yourselves; instead, leave room for His wrath. For it is written: Vengeance belongs to Me; I will repay, says the Lord"* (Rom. 12:19). Second, it easily becomes misguided because its main purpose is to satiate personal injury. Stirred by a bitter brew, many will needlessly suffer. Rather than wait until the terrorists are punished, anyone suspicious is targeted. Third, revenge begs the question, "When is enough, enough?"

Another voice passionately rises from the chair of contemplation. Palms extend outward symbolizing the need for tolerance. "Don't let any more people die! We must exhaust all means aside from force to achieve peace." Those who refuse the application of force cite Paul's admonition not to take revenge, as well as Jesus' words: *"But I tell you, don't resist an evildoer. On the contrary, if anyone slaps you on your right cheek, turn the other to him also"* (Mat. 5:39). The case for mercy and grace seems strong.

Yet, the voice of tolerance also is problematic. First, in my opinion, pacifists have taken Mat. 5:39 out of context. They use a verse that Jesus applies to the individual who would follow Him and make it into a formula for national policy. Jesus clearly teaches that the reason we are to endure persecution, insult and injury is connected to our love for Him. Likewise while Paul admonishes us not to repay evil with evil, he further teaches us in Rom. 13:1-3 that we are to submit to our governing authorities. Implied in this instruction is the centrality of the law.

The law remains in effect (because of man's sinful condition—see Mat. 5:17). Our authorities prescribe upholding the law through punishing by necessary force those who engage in evil actions. Tolerance that excludes punishing wickedness invites anarchy! Proponents of nonviolence damage the real meaning of godly love by divorcing behavior from consequences! Consider that God in His mercy for us as sinners still exacted punishment for our sins by allowing His Son to brutally die on a cross for us. Our loving God does not ignore sin. From His justness comes forth justice.

Thankfully, there are voices calling for justice—upholding what is morally right and valid according to the law. Until Jesus returns and establishes His universally effective authority, rulers will govern according to laws established for self-preservation. Therefore, if a country is attacked and its innocent people are murdered, that country is morally obligated to defend its citizens using the appropriate force necessary to punish the enemy and keep him from committing further atrocities.

We are not a Christian nation. If we were, we could all willingly lay down our lives before terrorist attacks knowing we would all go to heaven. We could nationally proclaim, "For us to live is Christ to die is gain!" We are a secular nation that contains Christians. We need justice to preserve moral living and accountability:

> *We know that the law is not meant for a righteous person, but for the lawless and rebellious, for the ungodly and sinful, for the unholy and irreverent, for those who kill their fathers and mothers, for murderers, for the sexually immoral and homosexuals, for kidnappers, liars, perjurers, and for whatever else is contrary to the sound teaching based on the glorious gospel of the blessed God that was entrusted to me.* (1Ti. 1:9-11)

"Now we know that whatever the law says speaks to those who are subject to the law, so that every mouth may be shut and the whole world may become subject to God's judgment" (Rom. 3:19). May God help us to act in accordance with His just will!

Proverbs 18:5—It is not good to show partiality to the guilty by perverting the justice due the innocent.

Scientism

Have you ever met a scientist who was an agnostic or atheist? Chances are high that such a person may have seemed intimidating when it came to sharing faith in God because in this person's view, religion is essentially unverifiable superstition. Scientific naturalists who suppose "science is the paradigm of truth and rationality," believe in scientism.*

There are basically two kinds of scientism—strong and weak. Those who believe in strong scientism advocate that something is true only if it is a scientific claim that was successfully tested and used in compliance with correct scientific methodology. Therefore, apart from scientific truths, there are no truths. Weak scientism postulates that truths can exist apart from science but gives science the overall position of authority in determining learning.

Proverbs 20:12—The hearing ear and the seeing eye—the LORD made them both.

We may not be able to *prove* scientifically that God made us, offered a miraculous solution to our sin and is able to provide us eternal life in His presence. But that is insufficient basis to doubt what we believe. *"Now faith is the reality of what is hoped for, the proof of what is not seen"* (Heb. 11:1). Furthermore, scientism is self-refuting.

Strong scientism's claim that only scientific propositions are true and valid is not scientific but rather a philosophical proposition *about* science. As J.P. Moreland notes, "Propositions that are self-refuting do not just happen to be false; they are necessarily false—it is not possible for them to be true." Similarly, weak scientism's position that scientific propositions have "greater intellectual authority than those of other fields" is rendered bogus by the simple fact that this would mean scientific conclusions are more certain than the philosophical presuppositions used to validate them. The existence of truth by itself is a philosophical and not scientific presupposition.

We know that there are true beliefs in fields outside of science. Just ask a strong scientist if she believes that it is wrong to torture her so she cannot practice her craft! I heard a scientist say "there is no God" but just exactly what science does he base that on? Lord Kelvin noted, "There is nothing in science which teaches the origin of anything at all."

The proof is not in the science, the science is in the proof. The question is, "who *really* understands the truth about Truth?" Could it be the best explanation is a Creator who should be appreciated best by science AND theology!

Dan's Letter to Cole

May 6

Recently I read from 1 Samuel 24 for my quiet time. It records the story of King Saul in pursuit of David whom he viewed as a threat to his throne. In God's providence, David was hiding with his men deep in a cave that Saul entered alone. David had an easy opportunity to kill Saul and was encouraged to do so by his men but he refrained from killing the ruler the Lord anointed. After Saul left the cave, David followed and shouted, *"My lord the king!"* (v. 8). Getting Saul's attention, he alerted him to the fact that God had put him in his hands and yet he spared his life. David strongly challenged King Saul even reminding him of an old proverb, *"Wickedness comes from wicked people."* (v. 13) Saul was so stricken by David's words, that he ended up crying. He confessed that David was the better man and pronounced a blessing upon him as well as recognition that David would indeed be given the throne and would be a successful leader. Shortly thereafter, the king departed with his army for home but David and his men returned to hiding out.

After securing blessing from the king why didn't David follow him and go back home? I believe David knew Saul's heart inclined toward evil and that he could not be trusted. Sure enough, in 1 Samuel 26, Saul and his troops again went hunting after David to kill him.

Proverbs 21:2—All a man's ways seem right to him, but the LORD evaluates the motives.

Our hearts represent who we are. David had a good heart and went on to become Israel's most famous and powerful king. Sadly, Saul did not give his heart to God causing the Lord to grieve that He ever made him king. Perhaps this is why Solomon, David's son, penned the proverb above—he knew the reason he inherited the throne was because of the strong moral principles of his God-fearing dad.

Dan Berg emailed me a letter he mailed to his daughter Cole, who had joined the Marines. I've edited it slightly to reduce the length. Let me invite you to read and profit from Dan's insight. His words speak about prayer and the heart.

Cole, I went fishing with Dana and it was cold. As we were out on the lake in his raft it started to snow but we kept at it. After four hours I had pulled in seven big trout and Dana caught one small one. As we sat there in his raft with the snow coming down Dana started to get discouraged, so he began to ask me how it was I was catching all these fish. I told him I started praying more when Gabe went into the Marines and even more so when you went in and I find myself praying about everything—even catching fish. Dana shared that he had not been praying as much as he used to and so he looked up and prayed. Then he changed the fishing pole he was using and on his second cast he pulled *in a trophy trout! It got me thinking that <u>sometimes prayer first must change the way we do things so it can change the things we do</u> . . . Cole I have to ask the Lord often to change my heart so I can see better what He wants me to say or do.*

Inspiration ✝✝✝
Man's motive power is his moral code.—Ayn Rand in *Atlas Shrugged*

Consideration

May 7

Between leading First Cause and serving in the Army Reserves, I average about two weeks of travel each month. Consequently, I have many opportunities to meet new people as I experience the ups and downs of flying. Recently, as I was in an airport and feeling hungry, I purchased a large smoothie (a blended and chilled, sweet beverage made from fruit) before boarding the plane. I placed the drink on the side of my seat and then put my luggage in the compartment. Unfortunately, in the act of sitting down I knocked the cup over. Horror of horrors—dark, red liquid poured all over the carpeted floor.

Exceedingly embarrassed, I asked the flight attendant for napkins and advice to best clean up the mess. She gave me a cactus-withering look and told me it was not her problem. But she did bring me napkins (not enough) and after much sponging with reinforcements from other attendants, I was able to dry up the surface until only the huge stain was left to remind me of my clumsiness. For the rest of the trip home, that flight attendant would not look me in the eye and even when she handed me peanuts, I felt like an outcast before her aloof demeanor.

As the plane descended, I tried to think of something I could say to that woman. Should I ask her if she knew the meaning of kindness and forgiveness? Should I quietly whisper an apology and note that I felt sufficiently scolded? In the end, I just kept my mouth shut. I figured she was having a bad day and I was just one more reason why.

Proverbs 21:10—A wicked person desires evil; he has no consideration for his neighbor.

A self-absorbed person does not feel for others except when it is personally advantageous. Kindness requires setting aside my opinion and feelings to help others. To be understanding towards one who is the source of need or the cause of inconvenience or discomfort requires effort.

Paul wrote in Philippians 2:25,26:

But I considered it necessary to send you Epaphroditus—my brother, co-worker, and fellow soldier, as well as your messenger and minister to my need—since he has been longing for all of you and was distressed because you heard that he was sick.

Paul needed Epaphroditus. He was a vital friend and helper. But Paul looked beyond his needs to those of the Philippians. That's what consideration is all about—looking past my needs to the needs of others.

God help me to be kind when it's my carpet that is stained by someone else's mess.

Peruvian Patriarch   May 8

In 1937, Pastor Rubio Beltazar challenged young men in his church to take missions seriously. The Holy Spirit used his words particularly to inspire Juan Cueva with the task of taking the gospel to the world.

Celestina Cueva gave birth to thirteen children. Ten of them survived and live today in the United States, Sweden, Peru, and Great Britain. Of the ten, three are pastors and all but one are serving God in some capacity. Each of them grew up listening to Senior Juan's passion. His vision led to the formation of Iglesia Misionera Evangelica (I.M.E.), an organization with six churches in three nations. In the last five months, I have met Señor Cueva and seven of his children. I have spoken with Pastor Samuel by telephone in the U.K. It is absolutely inspiring to see the passion for God that radiates from this family. Watching 93 year-old Señor Cueva smile and sing worship songs to God, one cannot help but praise the Lord for His hand of power at work through this humble man of faith.

Proverbs 27:19—As the water reflects the face, so the heart reflects the person.
Hebrews 13:7—Remember your leaders who have spoken God's word to you. As you carefully observe the outcome of their lives, imitate their faith.

Señor Juan Cueva ran a business making and selling hats. But his legacy will not be human head coverings. His reward will be a crown of eternal jewels for the men and women around the world who found Jesus because he would not stop asking, "What can we do for preaching the gospel?" When I.M.E. asked for volunteers to go to Spain and no one stepped forward, Señor Cueva led by example at the young age of 83. At the airport in Barcelona, he shared with a security guard, "You conquered our land for your country, we are going to conquer your country for the Lord."

Now the same Lord who inspired this wonderful man, may be speaking to your heart. The globe that Juan Cueva yearns to see reached still rotates around its axis. God wants to use you to take the saving knowledge of Jesus to those who are lost in sin. Are you ready to go? Are you willing to walk by faith? Don't surround your life with "can'ts." Don't fear the Holy Spirit's promptings. You may be the one through whom nations may be touched to the glory of God and the advance of His kingdom!

Inspiration †††

[Emmy] Werner observed that resilient children—the ones who grew up to be productive, emotionally healthy adults—had at least one person in their lives who truly supported them and served as an admired role model (Werner, 1993; Werner & Smith, 1992).—Steven M. Southwick & Dennis S. Charney in *Resilience*

Time

May 9

On the bottom floor of a cheap motel near Fort Leonard Wood, Missouri, a bespectacled man works late into the night cleaning piles of laundry. His eyes reveal his loneliness. Room 111 tells the story of a directionless life. On the table beside an old television sits a black Bible underneath a plate, a notepad, dust and her descendants. In the chaos of the surroundings a parable is born of a man whose dial is stuck in the shadow of futility.

How many people wear the pain of frustration from their daily execution of this thing we call life? Worn out by conflict, illness, and the stressful myriad of events, circumstances and self-centered focus too lengthy to enumerate, the end result is a disheveled existence.

Time is neither merciful to those who suffer or a benefactor to those who celebrate. She merely marches hourly hand by hand across the vision of a race marked by birth and death. Yet like the Russian proverb says, "Every day is a messenger of God." C.S. Lewis wrote, "Where, except in the present, can the eternal be met?"[21] *"Night will no longer exist, and people will not need lamplight or sunlight, because the Lord God will give them light. And they will reign forever and ever"* (Rev. 22:5).

Yesterday, today, and perhaps tomorrow are shaped by a 24-hour period centered on the earth's sun. But the quality of our days is determined by our relationship to God's Son. Charles Haddon Spurgeon wrote, "A man's heart has only enough life in it to pursue one object fully."[22] If your life is unbalanced, what is your heart pursuing? If we desire to know the One who made us, we should give Him our prized time—not our spare moments.

So spend your time:
- with zeal in His Word to know Him;
- with prayer that listens and conveys truth;
- with honor in conduct free of regrets;
- with wisdom for that which brings blessing;
- with love for the perfect Lover . . . all to His glory, all for His praise—forever!

Ecclesiastes 3:11—He has made everything appropriate in its time. He has also put eternity in their hearts, but man cannot discover the work God has done from beginning to end.

Inspiration ✝✝✝

It is not little time that we have to avail of, it is much time that we do not make use of.—Roman philosopher Seneca (4 bc to 65 ad)

Comradeship

May 10

Ecclesiastes 4:9,10—Two are better than one because they have a good reward for their efforts. For if either falls, his companion can lift him up; but pity the one who falls without another to lift him up.

Before I agreed to start a new church, one of the stipulations was that God would have to provide me a ministry partner. I don't mean to suggest that I was telling God what He had to do. Rather, I was reflecting a principle He firmly established in my heart.

Ministry is tough. I empathize deeply with pastors. Too much is expected of them. Most work too hard and are unappreciated. Many have few close friends and yet must shoulder an incredibly heavy load placed on their shoulders by people who expect: a shepherd, CEO, polished speaker, 24/7 attendant, super dad with awesome children, Bible-expositor, humility-radiator, husband to a piano-playing-sweet-singing woman of incredible beauty, and a willingness to live on the budget of a fast-food worker. Now there is a whole lot of realism!

Fortunately, God answered my prayer and gave me a great ministry partner also named Dan. On Saturday evenings Dan and I prayed for Sunday, the lost we might encounter, our precious body, our families and whatever else the Lord led. We had fun competing on the soccer field. We wept together as God broke our hearts. We disagreed on issues. We were completely different in some respects and incredibly joined at the hip in others. When it came to spiritual growth and serving God, I'm blessed to know Dan. He is always there for me and vice-versa. It's a great thing to be able to serve knowing God provided a man who deeply loves Him, who dispenses wise counsel, who is not afraid to be vulnerable and who most of all is REAL.

Whether you're a man or a woman, I hope you are not swayed into thinking you can go your way alone. Trust me, you won't grow correctly on your own. You are less than God intended if you operate without letting Christian brothers and sisters have a place in your heart. So be willing to be vulnerable. Sure, you may get hurt. Friends will let you down. But if your eyes stay fixed on Jesus, you'll find that God-fearing friends are invaluable. Just remember, to find a friend you have to *be* a friend. Hmmm. It's time to give my buddies a call!

Inspiration †††

The comradeship of God is made up out of men who know their poverty.—Oswald Chambers in *My Utmost For His Highest*

Annie's Grief

May 11

I remember Michael Bennett as a man who truly loved God and it showed in the way he treated people. Mike was funny, kind and a quick wit. He was totally in his niche as a children's pastor. When he unexpectedly died last year, he left a hole in a lot of people's hearts and a grieving wife and four children. I wasn't able to attend Mike's funeral. And I didn't do a good job of connecting with Annie, his wife, always missing her with phone calls or procrastinating. But last week, prompted by the Holy Spirit, I knew I needed to talk to her. In the sovereign kindness of the Lord it was the night of their wedding anniversary.

Sorrow is an amazing emotion. You can feel it in the air. Sometimes it is heavy and almost overpowering. Other times it is subtle like some light mist. But talking to Annie I experienced a different kind of sorrow—a dignified grief that conveys the unmistakable signature of wisdom.

Ecclesiastes 7:3—Sorrow is better than laughter, for sadness has a refining influence on us. (NLT)

Annie reflected on how her journey with grief has taught her many things. I'd like to share some of the lessons she conveyed with the hope that it might encourage some of you who are going through difficult times. Sorrow can often make us question God. But what Annie is learning through grieving is that God's character does not change. He remains faithful and loving and trustworthy despite her pain. She has grown spiritually through the valley of the shadow of death and found that God meets her through people and through His Word.

Annie attended a women's retreat located near a grove of California Redwoods—towering majestic cedar trees. Near the conference center there was a circle of trees that formed a natural chapel. In the midst of seeking the Lord and soul-searching, God led her to that special place in the forest. There she saw Michael with the Lord. He communicated to her, "You don't have need for me anymore, what you need is Jesus." He then took her hand and placed it in the hand of Jesus. It was an incredible moment of closure and understanding that her sufficiency truly is in Christ. Renewed by God's kindness, she found strength to move on. "If God can use my pain, I will be happy. . ."

Pain and happy can only go in the same sentence when Jesus is the One holding our hand. Who is holding your hand?

Inspiration ✝✝✝

If we try to evade sorrow and refuse to lay our account with it, we are foolish, for sorrow is one of the biggest facts in life, and there is no use saying it ought not to be, it is.—Oswald Chambers in *The Place of Help*

Unflappable

May 12

Admiral Yi Sun-Shin (1545–98) was one of the most famous military heroes in Korean history. He was born into a poor family but through hard work and effort rose to become a brilliant strategist and admiral. At the age of 28 he took the government examination to become an officer but during the practical portion fell off his horse and failed. Shamed by his failure he worked harder and four years later he retook the exam and passed. Eventually his persistence and wisdom convinced his superiors to give him command of a naval station in Cholla province.

Anticipating a Japanese invasion in 1592 under the direction of their great conqueror, Toyotomi Hideyoshi, Yi Sun-Shin designed and constructed the Turtle Ship, an ironclad warship shaped like its namesake. The first Turtle Ship was about 65 feet long, 15 feet high and built with portholes through which cannons fired. Thick iron plates with iron spikes were mounted on the deck to keep the enemy from boarding. At the bow was a fearsome dragon's head and by burning a combination of sulfur and saltpeter, clouds of smoke came through the head creating a smoke screen. Admiral Sun-Shin's turtle ships sank 26 of the 30 invading ships. Five years later the Japanese attacked and lost 300 more vessels.[23]

Ecclesiastes 9:17—The calm words of the wise are heeded more than the shouts of a ruler over fools.

We don't know what Admiral Sun-Shin's spiritual condition was but we do know that an unflappable person is one who is "not easily upset or confused, especially in a crisis."[24] Despite overwhelming forces arrayed against him, Korea's military hero remained calm. His courage inspired his countrymen to fight for their freedom. Unfortunately a stray bullet killed the Admiral.[25]

It is easy to lose our composure when things don't go our way or circumstances seem hopeless. King David prayed *"Vindicate me, LORD, because I have lived with integrity and have trusted in the LORD without wavering"* (Psa. 26:1). Our key to calmness is trust in the Lord. When we place our faith in Him, there is no danger too great to overcome. If you want unwavering courage in the den of adversity, look to Jesus, the unflappable Savior. He braved the screaming mob, wore the crown of thorns, felt the spikes of hate, and, instead of falling apart, prayed, *"Father, forgive them, because they do not know what they are doing"* (Luke 23:34).

Hero Hit a Jetta

Here's a fantastic way to test your life pace. How long can you wait without uttering derogatory words or pressing your hands against the wheel, behind a car that is not moving when the traffic light turns green? Today, on my way to a function, the red light changed but the car to my left did not move. In less than four seconds, horns were blowing. At the next light I did not move fast enough and again there was honking. I guess the drivers in Houston have even less patience than the drivers in Portland. So what's the big hurry?

Solomon writes of the bride who is awakened to the sound of her beloved knocking at her door. Unfortunately, she takes too long to answer.

Song of Solomon 5:6—I opened to my love, but my love had turned and gone away. I was crushed that he had left. I sought him, but did not find him. I called him, but he did not answer.

Instead of waiting, she chose to hurry after her man, but at a time when it was unsafe for a woman to be wandering the streets. "*The guards who go about the city found me. They beat and wounded me; they took my cloak from me—the guardians of the walls*" (v. 7). She should have waited until morning. The cost of her need to hurry was a beating.

The next time we attack the day like there is no tomorrow, perhaps we would do well to remember who made today and knows tomorrow. Often frenetic activity has unintended consequences. Our dog Hero was swatted by a cat while running with me on a trail. Not liking the cat's rude move, the big lab chased her—out into the road, right into a car! Hero survived his hasty pursuit but not without severe bruising and putting a dent in a Volkswagen Jetta. The "guardians of the wall" charged us over a thousand dollars to fix the damage. Categorically, the cat causing the *cat*astrophe emerged uns*cat*hed!

Could it be the opposite of hurried is deliberate? Oswald Chambers wrote in *Not Knowing Where*, "God is never in a hurry." Let's take an intentional time out and thank Him that He does not act impulsively.

Perhaps you will join me in praying. *"O Lord, forgive me for all the times I rush in the flight of my own doing. Forgive me for failing to plan wisely; for acting hastily in the heat of emotion, thus hurting others and myself. You know the plans You have for me. Help me to act at the speed that brings You glory!"*

Inspiration † † †

We don't wait well. We're into microwaving; God, on the other hand, is usually into marinating.—Dutch Sheets in *Intercessory Prayer*

Snow in May

May 14

Outside it fell, but until Tom called, I was oblivious. My children cheer at the rare sight of large white flakes gracefully tumbling earthward. Gone are the raindrops plopping their melancholic harmony. Silence. New measures of rest bring dramatic change.

I'm reminded of the One the prophet Daniel described in his vision, *"As I kept watching, thrones were set in place, and the Ancient of Days took His seat. His clothing was white like snow, and the hair of His head like whitest wool. His throne was flaming fire; its wheels were blazing fire"* (Dan. 7:9). Snow is bestowed theological meaning. Scripture compares God's clothing to its maximum lightness.

My thoughts find a broken-hearted but relieved David who sang, *"Purify me with hyssop, and I will be clean; wash me, and I will be whiter than snow"* (Psa. 51:7). Can you feel the gratitude of a man who knows that a divine shower not only removes the grit and cake of sin but leaves him glowing more brilliantly than a colored earth blanketed in white?!

I think of those flakes born of frigidity, how, when molded together, they provide a structure that decreases the cold and the sting of hostile winds. God is my shelter. How many caught in the grip of ferocious storms have lived to praise Him because they had the good sense to shape a cave, to build an igloo?

I consider tomorrow where the accumulation of tons of snow on steep-sloped mountains may descend with a roar upon any unfortunate ones to lie in the path of its cascading fury. Just the wrong amount of noise can create an avalanche! What tragedy do we create when we yell without thinking, when we speak without consideration?

A child-voice climbs from my mind's cellar, "Find gloves and warm socks. Hurry!" I race out and make snowballs to fling at scattering boys. "My cap! You've knocked off my cap—good shot son!" Wet snow forms nicely! How many flakes make a snowman? What would the world see if we'd allow the Holy Spirit to sculpt us together in holy unity to proclaim the joy of knowing Jesus?

Snow. We don't see much snow here—especially in May! But when it comes, I'm thankful.

Isaiah 1:18—"Come, let us discuss this," says the LORD. "Though your sins are like scarlet they will be as white as snow; though they are as red as crimson, they will be like wool."

Under the Flight Path

May 15

I once lived in Point Loma, a beautiful community in San Diego. The condominium my family lived in was located below the flight path of airplanes taking off from the San Diego Airport. Often during the day we had to stop all conversation and wait. It was useless to talk because of the explosive roar of jets fighting to gain elevation. Pausing became a necessity for effective communication.

Honda once ran a commercial of a man besieged by one problem after another who found his escape by climbing into his car. The great enemy of peace is often clamor. The method of escape may be to slump mindlessly before the television, spend hours in computer games, go shopping, compete in sports, or engage in some hobby. But will these supplements bring true relief? Is not the enemy of the best, the good things we find to do?

If you are serious about wanting peace in your life, set your mind to steadfastly following after God. Give Him part of your day for fellowship. Resist the false notion that you don't have time! You can't afford not to invest time with God—if you really want peace. If your day looks to be incredibly busy, or your emotions swirl in frenzy, spend MORE time with Him. Then watch as He intervenes on your behalf.

If you will faithfully study the Bible, make time for prayer and be willing to listen to the Holy Spirit—you will gain peace. Will your problems go away? Probably not—life is full of challenges. Will everything work out? Not necessarily the way you planned. But peace does not mean the absence of conflict--or that we ski and never fall down. Peace is a resting condition of the heart. It is an attitude that says, "Come on world give me your best shot. You can't shake me because my confidence is in my Father who loves me and knows what is best for me—He is in control." When my mind is devoted to Him, my heart is placid regardless of what storms swirl around me.

Isaiah 26:3,4—You will keep the mind that is dependent on You in perfect peace, for it is trusting in You. Trust in the LORD forever, because in Yah, the LORD, is an everlasting rock!

John 16:33—*I have told you these things so that in Me you may have peace. You will have suffering in this world. Be courageous! I have conquered the world.*

In the roar of right now, pause and proclaim, "*Oh God, may You restore me to Your rest, the comfort of Your calm, so that I might gain Your peace that surpasses all understanding.*"

Certain

May 16

Oswald Chambers wrote in *Not Knowing Where*, "Always beware when you are perfectly certain you are right, so certain that you do not dream of asking God's counsel. Our confidence rests not with our wits, but with God."

Every four years the U.S. elects its president. Election years are fraught with polarized citizens who seem to either adore or disdain the candidates running for office. It is surprising how passionate people can be in the certainty of their choice. Men and women will staunchly defend their politician with a force of conviction that can at times be unsettling. Perhaps in the tempest it is wise to remember the temptation to lean on our own understanding sets us up for failure. If our hope for the future is pinned on a man or a party, we are destined for an overdose of pain. As Dr. John George noted, "Should every Christian vote for the person believed to best fit the description? Yes, but the position is an office, not a Savior!"

Isaiah 28:16—Therefore the Lord GOD said: "Look, I have laid a stone in Zion, a tested stone, a precious cornerstone, a sure foundation; the one who believes will be unshakable."

God made His Stone of flesh and blood, but of a kind not seen in the sons of Adam. Jesus grew up a Jew in an Israel seeking a political hero, an emancipator, and dashed their hopes. He was not out to free them from Rome, He came to save them from sin and ensured the "them" included all nationalities.

God laid a Stone that was tested. Satan offered Jesus the world. The Son of God rebuked Him with Scripture. Religious leaders debated with Him and tried trapping Him into making mistakes. He exposed their hypocrisy and chastised their blatant phoniness. His closest followers offered what looked like good advice to strengthen His campaign only to be rebuked for not understanding God's will. In following that will, Jesus ended up spiked to a cross, betrayed, battered and mocked. He lost at the polls and died on a pole. He arose with His holiness intact.

God gave an undeserving world a Cornerstone of incalculable value and indispensable worth. God promises that if we trust in Jesus, we will never have our courage destroyed or our joy defeated. It is our moral responsibility to vote. But who we entrust our future with transcends the ballot box. If you want to be certain, be certain in Jesus.

Inspiration ✝✝✝

To know Christ is life's greatest achievement.—L.B. Cowman

Gracious

May 17

Isaiah 30 contains a stern message from God to a nation consistently at odds with His will. Judah was rebellious and unwilling to listen to His instruction (v. 9). The people told the prophets to stop telling them what was right. They asked them to speak pleasant things and to share illusions (v. 10). I'm reminded of Paul's word to Timothy when he foretold, *"For the time will come when they will not tolerate sound doctrine, but according to their own desires, will multiply teachers for themselves because they have an itch to hear something new"* (2 Ti. 4:3).

God warned Judah that her sin would collapse upon her like a high wall falling down (v. 13). But in verse 15, He stated four keys that could save them. *"This is what the Sovereign LORD, the Holy One of Israel, says: 'In repentance and rest is your salvation, in quietness and trust is your strength, but you would have none of it'"* (NIV). Even though God knew that they would reject His advice, Isaiah wrote, *"Therefore the LORD is waiting to show you mercy, and is rising up to show you compassion, for the LORD is a just God. All who wait patiently for Him are happy"* (v. 18).

It is no different today. People race headlong to disprove God's existence, to denounce His Word, to glorify what is wrong, and to pronounce as sinister what is right. Still, God longs to be gracious and rises to show us compassion. The ingredients of graciousness are mercy, kindness, and compassion stirred in elegant justice. God's sense of fairness reaches down to us to draw us to Himself, to give us opportunity to do what is right, and to fear Him. Were we gods for a season and treated to the scummy sin that fouls the earth, most of us would be quick to call fire from heaven as punishment. God remains gracious. However, one day His patience will reach the line of enough. He will have to judge all who rejected His extended favor. The Bible says *"It is a terrifying thing to fall into the hands of the living God!"* (Heb. 10:31).

Never take God's graciousness for granted! Psalm 67:1, *"May God be gracious to us and bless us; look on us with favor,"* is incomplete without verse 2. *"So that Your way may be known on earth, Your salvation among all nations."* God's graciousness to His people is meant to accomplish salvation throughout the earth! Now, while His hand of mercy has not yet drawn back, it is not the time to seek comfortable lives, to insulate ourselves with religious activity that leaves us too busy to share the truth with those in darkness, or to pretend that life is good when we know so much is not right. To do so would be to miss the whole salvific intent behind God's graciousness! His cordial treatment of an incorrigible race transformed many of us. With that transformation comes the responsibility that we will reflect His grace.

Afraid to Share   May 18

Isaiah 35:3,4—Strengthen the weak hands, steady the shaking knees! Say to the cowardly: "Be strong; do not fear! Here is your God; vengeance is coming. God's retribution is coming; He will save you."

Recently, a barber cutting my hair shared that unless he knew a customer was a Christian, he was afraid to share about Jesus. He said if he shared the gospel, he might lose his business because people would stop coming to him. He decided that when he retired, he would boldly share his faith. I went away troubled by his comments.

In truth, he might be right. Perhaps he would lose his business. But is that really the issue? Jesus emphatically promises in Matthew 6 that His Father is quite capable of taking care of us. We are not to worry. The real issue is if we trust God. To be fainthearted or fearful, is an indicator that we do not have the confidence to rely upon Him. We would rather trust our own plans, knowledge and abilities. Therefore, we acknowledge Christ privately yet refrain from publicly offending anyone with His name. Is there any wonder why our land is increasingly becoming godless? If we saw a person's house was on fire, we would not hesitate to warn them. Yet people's very souls are headed to hell and we remain mute because they might get angry with us for caring enough to share fire-quenching, life-blessing Living Water. God help us.

Paul challenged Timothy, the young man he was training, *"So don't be ashamed of the testimony about our Lord, or of me His prisoner. Instead, share in suffering for the gospel, relying on the power of God"* (2 Ti. 1:8). It is not an accident that Paul references the power of God. Whenever we willfully obey Him and share the gospel, we entrust ourselves to His power. It is not our job to convince people that Jesus is the Savior. Only the Holy Spirit can do that. But we <u>all</u> our commanded by Jesus to share our faith! When prompted by the Lord to testify, we need to be brave and share our hearts, not quiver behind a wall of excuses.

Yes, we might lose our job. Is it more important to keep a job than to obey the Holy Spirit? We might be persecuted and ridiculed. Excellent! God will reward us in heaven because we stood confident in Christ. We might die for what we believe. Well, if we are not willing to be slain for the very Lord who brutally suffered and died for us, what good is our faith? I'll pray for courage for you! Will you do the same for me?

Inspiration † † †

My business is to preach the gospel. I repair shoes to pay the expenses—William Carey

Cross Country Racing   May 19

Isaiah 40:31—But those who trust in the LORD will renew their strength; they will soar on wings like eagles; they will run and not grow weary; they will walk and not faint.

As a sophomore in high school, Isaiah 40:31 became my favorite verse for cross-country. There is nothing quite like running up mountainous terrain in the humidity and heat of the Philippines. My hope was definitely that the Lord would provide me renewed strength! I look back on those days with fond memories. God was teaching me lessons I would need for life which in many ways is like a cross-country race. It is full of ups and downs. Just when it feels good to coast, a hill looms ahead. At the point of sheer exhaustion peaks give way to plains and the weary spirit rejoices.

Wednesday night, a saint fell. My special friend, Georgia Drake, tripped and broke her femur despite the presence of a steel rod and an artificial hip. Osteoporoses leaves her susceptible to serious injury. Arthritis has turned her race into a daily battle with affliction. If her strength resided in her Greek ancestral roots, even her gutsy spirit would cave in to the merciless attacks of pain. But her hope is in Jesus. Not even a hospital bed can rob her of the power to walk and not be faint. Her gait is not measured by gravity because her soul is not tethered to dirt. She soars where eagles can only dream of flying. She's a remarkable woman who wears the robe of grace.

Do you know how wonderful it is to hope? Life for the follower of Christ, is a journey in joy. Do accidents occur? Certainly! Do we always get what we want? No! Can life be unfair? Yes! So what?

For I am persuaded that not even death or life, angels or rulers, things present or things to come, hostile powers, height or depth, or any other created thing will have the power to separate us from the love of God that is in Christ Jesus our Lord! (Rom. 8:38,39)

Are you discouraged? Take heart—have hope. Get back in the race! Run in the strength of Jesus. God loves you so much He gave you your very own Savior! That's reason to climb higher . . . in reveration.

Inspiration ✝✝✝

Hope without faith loses itself in vague speculation, but the hope of the saints transfigured by faith grows not faint, but endures "as seeing Him who is invisible." Oswald Chambers in *Christian Disciplines*

Consider These Thoughts   May 20

Isaiah 42:13—The LORD advances like a warrior; He stirs up His zeal like a soldier. He shouts, He roars aloud, He prevails over His enemies.

For those who believe the military is an evil profession or who decry the wearing of a uniform and the responsibility that comes with it, please consider these thoughts.
1. The prophet Isaiah uses a warrior, a soldier, to provide an analogy for God's actions.
2. The man Jesus most admired for faith during His ministry on earth was not a Jew but rather a Roman centurion (Mat. 8:5-10).
3. When Jesus died upon the cross, betrayed, beaten horribly and abandoned by His own followers, it was a centurion with fellow soldiers who truly recognized Him as God's Son (Mat. 27:53,54).
4. When God revealed to Peter that the gospel was to be preached not just to Jews but to the Gentiles, it was to a centurion named Cornelius that he was sent. Cornelius and his family were mightily filled with the Holy Spirit to the astonishment of Peter (Acts 10).
5. The Apostle Paul, when mentoring Timothy, used the soldier as the model by which to teach Timothy about suffering and keeping free of worldly entanglements (2 Ti. 2:3,4).
6. Before sending out His disciples a second time to minister, He instructed each without a sword to sell his robe in order to buy one (Luke 22:35,36).
7. Nowhere in Scripture does God forbid serving in the military. Not once in the gospels do we find Jesus speaking against the Romans that occupied Israel, or forbidding believers from serving in the military. The reason for this is clear—so long as we live in a fallen world where evil is committed, we will need armies, police forces and civil defenders.

Perhaps the reason the Bible portrays soldiers favorably is because a soldier knows that he must be honorable and be willing to lay down his life for his nation if he is to be successful. Is it not true for followers of Christ, that we must be willing to live holy lives and to die if necessary to be true to our faith and allegiance to God? Perhaps it would be good to remember about warriors:

They are not dead—they are alive. Men and women still serving—an ongoing expression of duty and devotion to the United States and the constitutional principles written in its foundation. Some are recently retired and look back with mixed emotions on a career that demanded sacrifice, created a "band of brothers" and wrought pain, joy, wisdom, and a cascading range of feelings born beneath a uniform. Some are aged and think back to their time when much was different and sacrifice was measured often by an entire nation gripped with war. They don't understand so many of the values and thoughts espoused today but they stand ever tall to those hallowed words, duty, honor, country.

They are not dead—they are wounded. Some carry the hidden demons of horror and know the sweat-stained sheets of nights rolled in restless nightmare. Theirs is the burden of explosions, ambushes, the searing pain of bullets tearing flesh and the ever-present fear, "I might not make it." Some have fought these memories of yesterday for decades, scarred as well by the shameful treatment they received by thoughtless citizens upon returning to the very people for whom they fought. Some are more recent returnees, mostly from deserts of searing heat and an enemy whose concept of life is as twisted as the metal fragments blown outward by their ideological hatred. These veterans left spouses and children, jobs and friends countless times to serve an overstretched military. They are the new faces of Post Traumatic Stress Disorder (PTSD), the amazing heroes who sacrificed limbs and measured loss and yet still press forward to serve and to matter.

They are dead. They lie in ground known and unknown—silent testaments to sacrifice; souls in the hands of God. Some will rise to reward, all will rise for judgment. Male and female, they paid the ultimate price—laying down their lives for their comrades, their families, their friends, their countrymen and strangers in the very land they fought or worked. They no longer march but their ranks still pass us by. Their lineage is that of patriots.

These are your veterans—Army, Air Force, Coast Guard, Navy and Marines. They deserve your moment of silent recognition. They appreciate deeply your thanks. Gratitude matters.

To all of you who serve, may God bless you and keep you safe and may you look always to Him.

Anodyne

May 21

On my flight to Minneapolis I sat next to a fascinating gentleman. He is a successful economist who asked if I would be interested in reading his paper on solving our nation's current economic woes. I read it with interest and afterwards as our conversation turned to things more personal, he shared his story. It was obvious that Walt* lived most of his six plus decades working through much physical pain and challenge. Forced to take an assortment of medicines and constantly in need of relief I asked him if he had God in his gut (which meant, in the context of the conversation, "Do you have the Lord to help you through your stomach issues?"). He said "no" but that he did believe there was a higher power.

Isaiah 45:12—I made the earth, and created man on it. It was My hands that stretched out the heavens, and I commanded all their host.
Psalm 139:13—For it was You who created my inward parts; You knit me together in my mother's womb.

So many people believe in "the Man upstairs" but resist accepting He is personally concerned about them. It is within their scope of reason to conceptualize a Designer but somehow presumptuous or far-fetched to conclude the Designer might have deep personal concern over their condition and fate. Walt is seeking anodyne. God sent Anodyne. I took the opportunity to relate my own personal experience of Him coming into a room with myself and gathered friends to heal my son. Had the flight been longer I could have shared many more stories of God's personal involvement.

As we deplaned we exchanged business cards and I hope to have made a new friend. He asked me multiple times to email him. I pray the man of faithless dying meets the Father of grace and living. Believing there is a higher power is a first step. But the best step is the faith to agree with King David, *"But I trust in You, LORD; I say, 'You are my God.' The course of my life is in Your power"* (Psa. 31:14,15a). Hmm. How incredible the blessing to know God.

Do you take your faith for granted or do you grant your faith opportunities to proclaim God's reality? But it is our privilege to share our stories of God's special interest—in rescuing us from sin, healing our diseases, and leading us to eternal joyous living! Jesus told us, *"Indeed, the hairs of your head are all counted. Don't be afraid; you are worth more than many sparrows!"* (Luke 12:7).

*Not his real name

Forgetting

May 22

Not long ago a woman walked up to me and said, "Do you remember me?" Her face looked familiar but I was at a complete loss as to her name or where I had served with her! The Indians have a proverb, "A good memory is fine—but the ability to forget is the true test of greatness."[26] Obviously the writer was not thinking about forgetting someone's name unless he knew something we don't!

Isaiah 49:14-16—Zion says, "The LORD has abandoned me; The Lord has forgotten me!" "Can a woman forget her nursing child, or lack compassion for the child of her womb? Even if these forget, yet I will not forget you. Look, I have inscribed you on the palms of My hands; your walls are continually before Me."

Dan was over visiting and shared that his grandmother in an assisted living home forgets each day that she is home and asks, "Do I have a room here?" Truly that is an insightful picture of what can happen to us as we get older. So how blessed we are to commit to memory two things about God:

- He will never forget us. He did not make us to abandon us. He loves us with a permanent love—promising to abide forever with us who choose to trust in Him for our salvation!
- He will forget our sins. Hebrews 8:12 says, *"For I will be merciful to their wrongdoing, and I will never again remember their sins."*

As humans, it is easy to forget names yet to remember the injustice committed by another against us. So quick we are to make commitments and then forget to do what we said we would do. We are so unlike God! Os Guinness reminds us in *The Call*, "Ingratitude and forgetfulness are ultimately moral rather than mental; they are the direct expression of sin."[27]

Dear Lord, please fortify my mind to retain what will honor you and edify others and let go of what would dishonor You or cause another to stumble. Thank You for never forgetting me, for forgiveness and for not holding my sins against me. Amen.

Inspiration † † †

Forgetting in the Divine mind is an attribute, in the human mind it is a defect, consequently God never illustrates His Divine forgetfulness by human pictures, but by pictures taken from His own creation.—Oswald Chambers in *Run Today's Race*

Lean on His God   May 23

Isaiah 50:10—Who among you fears the LORD, listening to the voice of His Servant? Who among you walks in darkness, and has no light? Let him trust in the name of Yahweh; let him lean on his God.

There comes a time in life when we must decide if we believe in God or not. The four words *"lean on his God"* ought to be sealed permanently on the hearts of all who know God's name and seek Him. They are not the casual words of a sober prophet. They are the bedrock conviction of a lover of God. They are syllables that form absolute conviction, not relative words like "Gee, I hope so." Isaiah offered his countrymen words of great encouragement. They were words he knew to be true from his own experience trusting God.

David wrote, *"Even when I go through the darkest valley, I fear no danger, for You are with me; Your rod and Your staff—they comfort me"* (Psa. 23:4). Isaiah and David are terrific examples of godly men who chose to lean on Yahweh! How about you? Are you able to lean on your Master?

Trust is not established by lack of preparation. Indeed, that is the stuff of folly. Solomon said to observe the ant. The ant is diligent and hard working. The danger comes when our trust is in our preparation and not in God. The best-stocked house can be instantly destroyed by a tornado—then what? Can God be trusted still? If the economy collapses, does God lose His chair in heaven? If our rights to worship should be taken away, is the Holy Spirit paralyzed? If society turns its apathetic back on morality, is Jesus no longer sovereign?

Trust is our firm reliance on the integrity, ability, and character of God. He is able! Maybe that's why the letter 't' is the shape of the cross. Take away the 't' and all that's left is rust. Therefore, no matter what comes tomorrow, no matter how bad today seems, we can joyfully look upward and know with confidence that Jesus loves us and is perfectly in control. He will never leave or forsake us! We need not fear our earthly future if we trust our forever Savior.

Inspiration ✝✝✝

It is not our trust that keeps us, but the God in whom we trust who keeps us. We are always in danger of trusting in our trust, believing our belief, having faith in our faith. All these things can be shaken; we have to base our faith on those things which cannot be shaken.—Oswald Chambers in *The Pilgrim's Song Book*

Liberty

May 24

There is a Kenyan proverb that states "A satisfied man does not know another one is hungry." Imagine spending seventy years of life under the oppressive hand of communism. The shackles of tyranny were so severe that today in the nation of Georgia the majority of those who hold leadership positions are under the age of forty. Those who are over forty were so impacted by Soviet rule that the ability to think freely or take decisive actions is just too difficult.

In 2011 there were five communist countries with a combined population of over 1.4 billion people—over 20% of the world's total inhabitants living in Cuba, China, Laos, North Korea, and Vietnam.[28] To that list we could add the 29 nations ruled by strong dictators and those nations like Mexico that are wracked with violence. It should be clear to us who live in liberty that we are indeed fortunate.

George Bernard Shaw, the Irish playwright stated that "Liberty means responsibility, that is why most men dread it." Liberty is not some cheap attainment. It must be nourished, fed and appreciated by sage people. If we take it for granted we will surely lose it to those whose god is control.

Isaiah 61:1-3—The Spirit of the Lord GOD is on Me, because the LORD has anointed Me to bring good news to the poor. He has sent Me to heal the brokenhearted, to proclaim liberty to the captives and freedom to the prisoners; to proclaim the year of the LORD's favor, and the day of our God's vengeance; to comfort all who mourn, to provide for those who mourn in Zion; to give them a crown of beauty instead of ashes, festive oil instead of mourning, and splendid clothes instead of despair. And they will be called righteous trees, planted by the LORD to glorify Him.

Thanksgiving must be more than symbols and tradition, for even those eloquent expressions fade with time into rote dancing to music few are left to understand. Thanksgiving is made rich by recognition. We have what we have because of God's grand generosity. Finally, thanksgiving is completed by humility. We don't deserve our spiritual liberty any more than we do our physical, emotional, and social liberty.

Thanksgiving is a daily proclamation of the Lord's favor—never taken for granted, always to bring hope. Thomas Jefferson warned that "The tree of liberty must be refreshed from time to time with the blood of patriots and tyrants." Our tree of liberty was more than refreshed, it was eternally guaranteed by the Son of Heaven whose blood ran pure bringing forth a power never before seen—sin-cleansing power. For that we are grateful!

Contrite

Isaiah 66:1,2—This is what the LORD says: "Heaven is my throne, and the earth is my footstool. Where is the house you will build for me? Where will my resting place be? Has not my hand made all these things, and so they came into being?" declares the LORD. "These are the ones I look on with favor: those who are humble and contrite in spirit, and who tremble at my word." (NIV)

When God has to remind His children that He is the Creator and King, the context normally reflects His displeasure. Imagine how you would feel if you were the leader and you called, and no one answered; you spoke, and no one listened; and you established standards of conduct which were ignored and blatantly disobeyed (66:4).

People ask what it takes to gain God's favor and in truth the answer is straightforward. Obey what He commands and keep a contrite spirit. Someone says, "Obey the Bible? Why, that is just man's dated interpretation." They determine their own courses of action, their own relevancy and then wonder why life is a mess. Others dispute the notion of remorse as an unnecessary symptom of weakness or sign of fear. So they do whatever they want to do, and treat those of differing conviction with disdain. Prideful living reaps enemies and feeds discontent.

The world would have us think that compliance with God's dictums only proves we are misguided fools. How absurd. Check out the world's ways and measure for yourself how successful they are. Who is the real fool, the one who listens to a sovereign God or the one who listens to a selfish flesh?

God did not establish commands and ask us to live humble, morally righteous lives to make us miserable. He communicated principles to help us succeed. He knows that if we approach Him contritely, we are teachable, respectful, and capable of growth. If we revere His Word, He has our attention and we are focused on making correct application. Obedient living is not stifling. Contriteness is not demeaning. It shows remorse for our sin condition with an accompanying desire to do and be what is right.

This very day I had to reprimand a leader who erred in judgment. He took reckless action that hurt others and caused embarrassment to our command. When I corrected him, his voice was subdued. He felt bad and owned up to his error. Then he corrected his action and reconciled with those who were offended. This is a leader who can be trusted, a man with whom it is an honor to serve. We look with favor on those who choose humility because they are trustworthy. We learned this from God.

Inspiration † † †

God looks first for contrite hearts in the worshipers.—Jack Hayford, John Killinger and Howard Stevenson in *Mastering Worship*

I Don't Know How to Speak!   May 26

Yesterday an eleven year old boy rode his bicycle for the first time without training wheels. "Well what's so great about that, most eleven year-old kids ride bikes." Well this boy was different. He knew what it meant to fall down repeatedly because of poor balance. He feared getting hurt. He was afraid to go too fast. His physical therapist recommended he ride a special three wheel bike that would compensate for his deficiencies. He tried riding on two wheels but gave up--it was too tough. He didn't believe he could do it so he ceased striving.

So what made the difference? His six-year old brother. You see, his little brother learned to ride unsupported on his second day of trying. Bryan, my son, decided that if Stephen could do it, so could he. He left the couch for the track and accomplished what no one believed he could. We had a 7-11 celebration complete with a full round of Slurpees. It was a joyous occasion, a rare victory over real doubts.

Jeremiah 1:6,7—But I protested, "Oh no, Lord, GOD! Look, I don't know how to speak since I am only a youth." Then the LORD said to me: "Do not say, 'I am only a youth,' for you will go to everyone I send you to and speak whatever I tell you."

Jeremiah lacked confidence in himself. But his insecurity also revealed a failure to appreciate God's strength. It was easier to disqualify himself and resist God's selection and calling for his life. God appointed this son of a priest to be a prophet to the nations. Fortunately, he obeyed and though the weeping prophet would suffer much, he was greatly used by his Father.

Is your life stationary? Have you stopped growing because you've quit trying? Is it too hard to move on because it's not worth the pain? Perhaps it's time. Time to ask God to give you the faith to do what you know needs to be done. Are you willing to ask God to provide the inspiration you need to grow? He may surprise you. Sure, you may fall down and get hurt. Your pride may take a beating. That's okay. Get back up and try again. Ask Bryan. He will proudly show you his scrapes and bruises—they've become badges of honor.

Is your life in motion? Are you thrilled at what God is teaching you? Great!!! Ask your awesome Savior to give you the privilege of encouraging someone else who is stuck in the immobilizing mud of doubt and fear.

Inspiration † † †

Beware of being stationary! God grant that we may be going on with Him continually so that we can disciple all we come in contact with.—Oswald Chambers in *Workmen of God*

Deception

May 27

Deception is a technique employed by the military on occasion to help win campaigns or to influence the battlefield so that the enemy is confused as to our real intent. In the battle of Normandy in World War II, a large deception campaign was orchestrated which utilized fake machinery, misleading radio traffic and a mock buildup of troops to confuse the Germans as to the real landing sites where the allied forces would land in France. Throughout many wars, psychological operations have played a key role in helping influence the enemy and the population of a country where forces operate.

For four years I served in a Psychological Operations (PSYOP) Company. Our leaders taught us that it is always the best policy to operate by the truth. The reason for this is simple. If what we communicate to an audience is a lie, we lose our credibility. Thus, the best means to win the hearts and minds of people is to tell the truth. A good PSYOP company is adept at spotting the deception the enemy uses and then exposing those lies so that a population can discern what is really happening.

Jeremiah 9:6—You live in a world of deception. In their deception they refuse to know Me. This is the LORD's declaration.

Deception is nothing new. The prophet Jeremiah, speaking for the Lord, challenged his own people, the Israelites, with the reality that they were deceiving each other on a regular basis by: spreading slander, betrayal, speaking lies, and doing wrong. What brought a people whose history was rich with the active hand of a loving Father to a place of sham?

First, they collectively had poor eyesight. When God liberated them from Egypt and took them towards Canaan, they continually looked back with a myopic lust for their former condition. Once in the Promised Land, they could not take their eyes off the practices of their enemies—they rejected God's leadership so as to have their own king (see 1 Sa. 8:4-8). Their eyes constantly focused on their surroundings and not their Leader.

Second, they had hard hearts. Consistently, Israel gave up God's gold for fools' gold. He gave them His Word; they preferred the laws of their neighbors. He asked for their loyalty, they chose to lust after manmade idols. He demanded their obedience; they chose to do whatever they pleased. They were ripe for deception because they disdained His truth.

We judge them as a foolish people but in truth are we much different? We say God is our first cause but are our priorities really fashioned after possessions, feeding our amusements or building whatever suits our needs? Do we make worship into a Sunday gathering formatted into a controlled segment while our weeks are mostly devoid of God? Do we give the appearance that all is fine when, in reality, we wonder where God is and if He really loves us? If so, deception has as firm a grip on us as it did them.

Lest we think that we would never compromise our integrity, consider this. We live in an age of deception. Increasingly, our media, our courts and our leaders redefine what we once knew to be true as now untrue. Institutions such as marriage and family are under constant attack by those committed to their undoing. Men revise history to suit present values. Sexual perversion is made out to be a civil right. Adherence to moral principles is labeled fanaticism. Those who speak according to their convictions are called haters. Those who point out misconduct are labeled racist or intolerant. A daily, steady assault persists to label good as evil and evil as good. This is nothing more than a psychological campaign led by Satan himself—that great hater of Truth and master of deception. He lied in the Garden of Eden and continues to spin misinformation.

God promised Jeremiah that the Israelites would be soundly tested and punished for giving in to deception. *"Should I not punish them for these things? This is the LORD's declaration. Should I not avenge Myself on such a nation as this?"* (Jer. 9:9). He is doing the same to our nation. He will not idly condone illicit behavior and corrupted truth. If we are to be God's people, we must repent of all that violates His law and pursue His clearly communicated truth. To do anything less is to live a lie and that is not worth the consequences.

Knowing God

May 28

There is a strong tendency in Christianity to measure our relationship with God by our circumstances. God encourages us not to be proud over our brains, our muscles, or our money. His advice implies that if we are to be proud, it should be in knowing Him. It isn't easy to be content with God when we are in control or we feel secure about tomorrow! Yet when the hurricane unexpectedly turns and twists our serene plans to chaos, then what do we think of God?

Whether life is good or tough, pleasant or demanding, fair or unfair, just or unjust, predictable or chaotic am I pointed true north? Do I seek to understand God—not what He will do, not what others say about Him, not what I suspect is true but rather a running to His presence to be with Him. I remember when Stephen was seven. He would spring from bed, run down the stairs and pounce on my back. He wanted to be with his dad. As you can guess, I relished this attention.

Jeremiah 9:23,24—This is what the LORD says: The wise man must not boast in his wisdom; the strong man must not boast in his strength; the wealthy man must not boast in his wealth. But the one who boasts should boast in this, that he understands and knows Me—that I am Yahweh, showing faithful love, justice, and righteousness on the earth, for I delight in these things. This is the LORD's declaration.

Oswald Chambers noted, "God does not tell you what He is going to do; He reveals to you who He is."[29] Knowing is one thing, knowing God is everything!

Oh God help me to run to You. If I am to have wisdom let it be to find You and listen to what You have to say. If I am to have might may it be the power to blow through any obstacles that might come between us. If I am to have wealth, let it be the riches of dining in Your presence—forever.

Customs

May 29

Warm Indian air enveloped me as I walked towards the last gate that separated me from the Cochin airport and Silas and Sam who stood ready to greet me. Just as I thought the long journey was about to end, a customs official motioned me to his table. "Please open your suitcase," he said. So I complied. Immediately the inspector's eyes locked on the contents of a large cardboard box. "What are these?" he asked.

"These are my CD's," I replied.

He looked at me skeptically and was quickly joined by more curious officials. "These are commercial products, and you will have to pay a duty tax."

"Oh Lord," I uttered a silent prayer. "You know these CDs are to further Your kingdom. Please help me."

I showed the official the picture on the *Choices* album and he could see that it was truly my face. Next I explained that I was a singer here in India to do concerts and these were my own products. I was ready to refuse to pay and just leave the box with them—at least anyone who took them would hear the gospel! But their demeanor changed. Suddenly, they wanted to shake my hand. I offered each of them a CD and two men awkwardly accepted. They asked what was in my other suitcase. When they found that my description matched the contents inside, they waved me on. I was free to go with no tax to be paid. Thank You, Lord!

Thus began what would be an incredible three weeks of ministry. God continued to bless each step of the journey. It was obvious that many people were praying for our team! God miraculously worked in the lives of people because a great number were praying.

Jeremiah 17:10—I, Yahweh, examine the mind, I test the heart to give to each according to his way, according to what his actions deserve.

When we enter any nation, all we own and have is subject to being examined. Customs is the procedure for inspecting goods and baggage. For most of us it is an unpleasant reality to be subjected to inspection. But in truth it is a good reminder. Every day we go through a spiritual customs. It is God who examines us. He sees the very motives that dwell in our hearts and knows the thoughts that wind through our minds. Are we clean? Is our Father pleased with what He sees? *"May the words of my mouth and the meditation of my heart be acceptable to You, LORD, my rock and my Redeemer"* (Psa. 19:14).

Inspiration ✝✝✝

. . . an unexamined belief system is not worth holding.—Jan David Hettinga in *Follow Me*

I Will Listen to You   May 30

In planning for a mission trip to Peru, one of the inevitable questions that arose in my mind was, "How do I know this is *really* what God wants me to do?" Do you experience similar feelings when deciding whether to engage in some activity or pursuit? So how do we know what course of action to take or refrain from taking?

Before launching any major initiative, we need to follow the example of King Jehosphaphat who prior to agreeing to go into battle with King Ahab, said, *"First, please ask what the LORD's will is"* (2 Ch. 18:4). We can obtain God's counsel through studying the Bible, prayerfully listening to the Holy Spirit, and through seeking counsel from God-fearing sages. It is presumptuous and foolhardy to act without first seeking God's will.

Second, we ought to examine our motivation. The reason God blessed the prophet Daniel is made clear in the following passage. *"Then he said, 'Don't be afraid, Daniel. Since the first day you began to pray for understanding and to humble yourself before your God, your request has been heard in heaven. I have come in answer to your prayer'"* (Dan. 10:12 NLT). Jesus said that we are to make the Kingdom of God and what has His approval our primary concern (Mat. 6:33). Am I acting in humility before God and is my heart's intent the furtherance of His will!

Third, God is more interested in our character and our relationship with Him than He is in our activity. He calls me to love Him with all my heart, soul, and strength (Deu. 6:5). If my first priority is to love Him, it follows that my actions will result in obedience to His leading. If He does not lead, then I need not feel any pressure to go. What is most important is not the activity I engage in, but rather that my heart is right with my Lord.

Fourth, nothing happens by chance under the watchful eye of an Almighty Father. I received an e-mail message from a good friend. It turned out that he and another friend would be in Lima, Peru, the exact days I was scheduled to be there. He expressed a desire to help with our mission work. Now what are the chances of two personal friends spending the exact days in the precise city in the same country without any advance knowledge? As we pursue Him, we begin to see more clearly His hand at work. Therefore, circumstances often help us see more clearly what God desires we do.

Jeremiah 29:12,13—You will call to Me and come and pray to Me, and I will listen to you. You will seek Me and find Me when you search for Me with all your heart.

Inspiration   † † †

A life lived listening to the decisive call of God is a life lived before one audience that trumps all others—the Audience of One.—Os Guinness in *The Call*

Faithfulness

May 31

The nation of Israel excelled in angering and alienating God. They exceeded the sins of the evil nations He commanded them to destroy. Repeatedly they quit following Him. They broke His heart and deserved annihilation as seen in the following words of Jeremiah.

Jeremiah 31:37—This is what the LORD says: If the heavens above can be measured and the foundations of the earth below explored, I will reject all of Israel's descendants because of all they have done—this is the LORD's declaration.

God is giving us a formula through His prophet Jeremiah: If A (heaven can be measured) and B (earth's foundations can be explored), then C (Israel's descendants will be rejected). Scientists with all their amazing technology and brilliance are incapable of measuring the heavens or exploring earth's foundations. Since man is incapable of fulfilling A or B, God will not reject Israel's descendants. What we have is the formula of faithfulness stated inversely to what we would expect, and with a touch of brilliance, a quick reading misses. God is the epitome of faithfulness to His children—the embodiment of unfaithfulness—what a paradox! Seven times the Lord's faithfulness is extolled in Psalm 89. Notice in verse 1 the extent of it: *"I will sing about the LORD's faithful love forever; I will proclaim Your faithfulness to all generations with my mouth."*

What does this mean to us? Do you ever wonder if your salvation is secure because of sin you've committed? Do you ever struggle with the thought that God might not let you into heaven? I imagine there is not an honest Christian who has not lived with such doubt. But consider this. In John 10:28, Jesus states, *"I give them eternal life, and they will never perish—ever! No one will snatch them out of My hand."* This is not a wishy-washy commitment God is making but rather an absolute promise to anyone who has placed faith in Jesus as Lord and Savior! *"For this is the will of My Father: that everyone who sees the Son and believes in Him may have eternal life, and I will raise him up on the last day"* (John 6:40).

In 1 Corinthians 1:8,9, Paul teaches, *"He will also strengthen you to the end, so that you will be blameless in the day of our Lord Jesus Christ. God is faithful; you were called by Him into fellowship with His Son, Jesus Christ our Lord."* Notice that our salvation is not tied to our ability but rather to God's faithfulness which is a follow-up to His calling us to Himself! To be discouraged and to fear for our salvation, if we are Jesus-followers, is really to question His word and His capability of delivering what He promised. Don't go there!

Inspiration † † †

Often times God demonstrates His faithfulness in adversity by providing for us what we need to survive.—Pastor Charles Stanley

Motivation

June 1

I once met with a man whose marriage was tottering towards collapse. He felt alone and unwanted in his own household. His wife was more devoted to his children than to him. He could not do enough to please her and he was ready to quit. When I asked how his relationship with God was doing, he shared that it was anemic. He grew up without a loving father which effected how he related to his Heavenly Father.

Jeremiah 32:39,40—I will give them one heart and one way so that for their good and for the good of their descendants after them, they will fear Me always. "I will make with them an everlasting covenant with them: I will never turn away from doing good to them, and I will put fear of Me in their hearts so they will never again turn away from Me.

We cannot summon the enduring motivation to overcome our problems if we do not have a right relationship with the One from whom pure motivation comes. If our walk with God is flawed, we should not be surprised if we struggle in marriage, work, finances, self-esteem, or our relationships with others. To focus on problem-solving without restoring communion with God is like throwing coins into the air hoping they will somehow fall into the parking meter and buy us more time.

By working to keep my relationship with God strong He gives me unceasing motivation. Otherwise I wouldn't have a chance—life's struggles would tear me up. Without Him I would naturally rely upon myself and that would be a sure formula for frustration and ineptitude.

God promised the Israelites that He would give them singleness of heart and action so that they would always revere Him. Jesus prayed for those who would believe in Him, "*May they all be one, as You, Father, are in Me and I am in You. May they also be one in Us, so the world may believe You sent Me*" (John 17:21). Unity with God brings capability to overcome any difficulty. Singleness of heart moves our eyes off problems so we can focus on the Lord. Honoring our Lord empowers us to see our sinful condition, enables us to appropriate divine forgiveness and encourages us to do what is right! "*I will give them a heart to know Me, that I am Yahweh. They will be My people, and I will be their God because they will return to Me with all their heart*" (Jer.24:7).

When God inspires His people to fear Him, He is motivating! He is our galvanizer. He gives us hope, purpose and meaning. He promises that our earthly existence will be transformed into an awesome eternal abiding with Him. Now that's exciting! Don't let the trials and troubles spoil your incentive to live for Christ. By living for Him, You are an overcomer!

Hidden

June 2

Jeremiah 36:26—Then the king commanded Jerahmeel the king's son, Seraiah son of Azriel, and Shelemiah son of Abdeel to seize Baruch the scribe and Jeremiah the prophet, but the LORD had hidden them.

God told the prophet Jeremiah to take a scroll and write on it. His purpose was to communicate all the disasters He planned to inflict on Israel, Judah and other nations. His concern was that the people of Judah would repent when they heard what He was going to do and receive forgiveness. So Jeremiah dictated God's words to Baruch, his helper, who wrote them on a scroll. Then, because he was restricted from going to the temple, he sent Baruch to read to the people. Word of the scroll's contents reached Judean officials and they had Baruch read the scroll to them. Concerned how their evil king would react and afraid of the message, they told Baruch to go and hide with Jeremiah. Then they took the scroll and had it read to King Jehoiakim who instead of repenting burned the scroll and issued the command above.

There are some very significant lessons we can extract from this story. When God asks us to do something, we are not to question the risk of the task; find excuses, modify the command or recommend someone else; or, fear that we might suffer. Our job is to obey God. He is quite capable of using us to deliver the truth and then protecting us from those who react violently. Just as God hid Jeremiah and Baruch, He is capable of hiding us.

Francois Rabelais, a major French Renaissance writer, said, "I place no hope in my strength, nor in my works: but all my confidence is in God my protector, who never abandons those who have put all their hope and thought in him."[30] Is it possible we waste time worrying what enemies might do to us? Alternatively, do we smugly embrace our eternal inheritance yet ignore the reality that we have a temporal mission? Do we live as undercover Christians hoping to be left alone and unpersecuted?

It may seem like what God asked Jeremiah to do was a waste of time and energy. The king did not fear Him. The people did not repent. What was the point? Here is where we go astray. Quit looking for the point. Listen to God and trust that He knows what He is doing. If He wants to, He can hide us. He may allow us to suffer and perish—many a prophet died a horrific death. Our responsibility is not to worry about our condition but to condition ourselves to obey. Praise God, we will always be hidden under His eternal wings. No one can take what Jesus won for us and that's why we stay encouraged!

Inspiration ✝✝✝

When we submit to God, He doesn't suppress who we are. He frees us to become who we're made to be, within the boundaries of His protection.—Stormie Omartian in *The Power of a Praying Husband*

Hasty Words

June 3

A white policeman arrested a prominent black professor, and eager journalists needled the president to answer before he knew all the facts. He misspoke. Perhaps a lingering frustration birthed unfortunate vetting. Our society is sensitive to racial harmony. Should we be surprised when our melting pot is a degree away from a boiling kettle?!

Jeremiah 37:11-14—When the Chaldean army withdrew from Jerusalem because of Pharaoh's army, Jeremiah started to leave Jerusalem to go to the land of Benjamin to claim his portion there among the people. But when he was at the Benjamin Gate, an officer of the guard was there, whose name was Irijah son of Shelemiah, son of Hananiah, and he apprehended Jeremiah the prophet, saying, "You are deserting to the Chaldeans." "That's a lie," Jeremiah replied. "I am not deserting to the Chaldeans!" Irijah would not listen to him but apprehended Jeremiah and took him to the officials.

All he was trying to do was claim property he bought in Anathoth from his cousin Hanamel; land he spent 17 shekels of silver to buy. But Irijah was convinced that Jeremiah, the prophet of doom, was making an opportune break to join the Chaldean enemy. Despite Jeremiah's pleas of innocence, he was beaten and thrown in the dungeon.

Scandals are either real or falsely perceived. We assign fault and rather than search for the underlying truth or cause of the problem, we look for ropes and cry for a hanging. We see disgrace and disregard grace. We interpret facts through human lens often marked as nearsighted.

Note what Jesus did when the religious leaders brought before Him a woman caught in the act of committing adultery. She was dripping in scandal. But this was an outrage of opportunity. The scribes and Pharisees cleverly hoped the Messiah would collaborate with Moses and issue the call for rocks. They really didn't care to stone the woman—adultery was fairly common. They knew it was against the Roman law for a Jew to put a person to death. No, this was their opportunity to spread dishonor from a loose lady to the Son of Man they hoped to tarnish. All they needed was for Him to issue a decree. Instead, He stood up and uttered those famous words, *"The one without sin among you should be the first to throw a stone at her"* (John 8:7).

Find the truth before you grab your gun. Let time elapse before you hastily speak words that may ring in the sky like some rapacious thunder. Pray and then pray some more—for the accused and for discernment. Scandal is not the sister of prudence. There is plenty of sin to go around, may God help us behave like saints for a change.

Hesitant

June 4

Have you ever gone through periods in your life where you knew what God wanted you to do but were afraid to obey because of circumstances? I have a friend whose marriage is going badly. He knows from the counsel he has received and from God's Word that divorce is wrong and, in his situation, not an option. But his wife treats him badly and he is tired of trying to improve their relationship. He is reluctant to apply any advice he receives. He says it is time he took care of himself and was free to do what he wants to do. So he filed for divorce and bought a new car thinking now his problems should end.

King Zedekiah was the weak ruler of Judah. After hundreds of years of Judah's rebelliousness, God finally had enough and led King Nebuchadnezzar and the Babylonian army to attack His wayward people. It was during this period that the prophet Jeremiah ministered. Many times Zedekiah called the prophet into his presence to hear the Word of the Lord. Faithfully, Jeremiah relayed God's will and plan. Finally in Jeremiah 38:15, *"Jeremiah replied to Zedekiah, 'If I tell you, you will kill me, won't you? Besides, if I give you advice, you won't listen to me anyway.'"*

All the king had to do was follow God's instruction to surrender! Instead, he hesitated for two and a half years, while Jerusalem was under siege. In verse 19 of chapter 38, we learn the source of Zedekiah's unwillingness to obey God. *"I am worried about the Judeans who have deserted to the Chaldeans. They may hand me over to the Judeans to abuse me."* Despite God's assurances of protection, the king wavered and wobbled. In the end, he fled and was captured. In the town of Riblah in the land of Hamath, King Nebuchadnezzar pronounced sentence, putting Zedekiah's sons to death in the sight of their father and then putting out the eyes of Zedekiah before binding him with bronze shackles and sending him to Babylon. The worst nightmare of a hesitant king was fulfilled.

There is a saying, "He who hesitates is lost." But what makes us vacillate and refrain from doing what God asks? Perhaps it is fear that God cannot deliver what He promises or that we will not obtain what we want if we do God's will. Further distilled, our hesitancy reflects a flawed understanding of eternity. We see time through distorted lens and act or refrain from acting to please our fleeting needs. In contrast, our timeless Father knows what is best for us.

My friend's divorce and new car did not cure his troubles. Until he chooses to obey God he will continue to struggle. If you know what God wants you to do, do it! Never sacrifice obedience with its eternal blessings for temporary desires that in the end will not matter! May the God who makes all things possible give you the strength to trust and obey.

Inspiration † † †

On the Plains of Hesitation bleach the bones of countless millions, who, at the Dawn of Victory, sat down to wait, and waiting—died.—George W. Cecil

A Deeper Kindness

June 5

The prophet Jeremiah foretold disaster for his countrymen and they felt he was a traitor. Powerful officials talked King Zedekiah into having him killed because his words weakened the resolve of their soldiers. So they took the old man and threw him into a cistern where he sank into the mud. Ironically, Ebed-melech, an Ethiopian eunuch who served the king, interceded on Jeremiah's behalf. The king had a change of heart and ordered Ebed to take thirty men and rescue Jeremiah before he died. The wise eunuch threw rags down to him to put under his armpits and then with ropes pulled him out. God was pleased with the Ethiopian and through Jeremiah He promised to preserve his life.

Jeremiah 39:18—"Indeed, I will certainly deliver you so that you do not fall by the sword. Because you have trusted in Me, you will keep your life like the spoils of war." This is the LORD's declaration.

Isn't it interesting that God commends Ebed-melech's trust in Him when the context would clearly suggest it was his kindness to Jeremiah that was significant? Could it be that true kindness finds its essence in faith? The Ethiopian went against the crowd and put his foreign life on the line to save the man who spoke doom when his fellow prophets promised deliverance. Kindness was important but God recognized a deeper quality—courageous trust. Ebed-melech believed God spoke through Jeremiah and it was that belief that fueled his conviction to save the seer.

Kindness that flows from our own strength is unlikely to rise to the occasion of unpopular need. It is when we look to God, relying on Him, that we find the ability to render help that goes against the very roar and vanity of society. A crowd ready to stone an adulteress woman missed compassion by trusting the law. Jesus refused to condemn her and by His empathy showed a deeper truth—trust in the will of His Father's forgiveness. A crowd cried "crucify" defying consideration because their trust was in power. God let His Son die because His trust was in Himself and kindness was the natural expression of divine love.

The fact that our Creator offers eternal kindness to a species seeded with rebellion reveals a power far beyond our comprehension. Knowing this ought to fill us with joy and fortify us with a potent resolve to help those in need even when doing so puts us at risk. It took an Ethiopian to free a holy prophet. What will it take for us to trust our Lord enough to be His thoughtful instruments?

Inspiration ✝✝✝

The end result of kindness is that it draws people to you.—Anita Roddick, Founder and CEO, The Body Shop

Consequences

June 6

In 586 B.C., King Nebuchadnezzar was the most powerful king in the world. During this time, the city of Riblah (located in Syria) served as a base of operation for the Babylonian King. In Riblah, Nebuchadnezzar watched the execution of the sons of Judah's King Zedekiah, and all the Jewish nobles. Then, in one of the lowest points in the history of Judah, he blinded Zedekiah and put him in chains for deportation to Babylon.

Nebuzaradan was a Babylonian captain of the guard of Nebuchadnezzar. Under the king's explicit orders, he released the prophet Jeremiah from his chains. In Jeremiah 40:2,3 we read:

> The captain of the guard took Jeremiah and said to him, "The LORD your God decreed this disaster on this place, and the LORD has fulfilled it. He has done just what He decreed. Because you people have sinned against the LORD and have not obeyed Him, this thing has happened."

Then Nebuzaradan gave Jeremiah a ration of food and a gift before sending him home.

Does it strike you as amazing that a pagan captain understood and attributed the fall of Judah to their sin? Notice he did not link their defeat to Babylon's superior military, brilliant strategy, or economic might. He was obviously familiar with the prophecies Jeremiah uttered against his countrymen for their rebelliousness. Furthermore, it appears he ascribed to the validity of God's sovereign power. He understood why *"this thing has happened."*

Is it possible that many of the people who surround us and who do not worship God, actually know more about Him than we think? Could they both believe in His existence and understand *why things have happened*? Our conduct validates God's work in our life. Our misconduct can do the same. The former is seen as blessing, the latter as punishment.

Scripture validates that God holds us accountable for our actions. A pagan world understood who Israel was expected to worship and perversely enjoyed her demise. I suspect our pagan world knows the same for most who claim to be Christians. There will always be consequences. The challenge is where we sit on that final day before the King of kings, when *"this thing has happened!"*

Lord, may we do what is right because we love You. May our conduct lead people to recognize Your glory. May those who understand what we should do, understand what they should also do so that when this life has happened we all may know Your embrace and hear, "Well done my good and faithful servant!" Amen.

Inspiration † † †

To the distinguished character of a Patriot, it should be our highest glory to add the more distinguished character of a Christian.—President George Washington

Lamenting

June 7

Watching the news is as about as fun as playing Frisbee with a cat. Between the stock market plunging over 500 points in one day, Syrian rioting, Mexican gang violence, Texas drought, and political bickering, lamenting seems to be a worldwide sport. Listening to a Christian radio station in Wisconsin, I heard the DJ ask if it seemed like God was angry. That seemed ironic since I had just read from my quiet time in Psalm 85:5, *"Will You be angry with us forever? Will You prolong Your anger for all generations?"* Moses observed in Psa. 90:7, *"For we are brought to an end by your anger; by your wrath we are dismayed"* (ESV). Jeremiah warned, *"Come out from among her, My people! Save your lives, each of you, from the LORD's burning anger"*(51:45). What people in what century have not experienced pain and attributed it to God's wrath?

Lamentations 1:12—Is this nothing to you, all you who pass by? Look and see! Is there any pain like mine, which was dealt out to me, which the LORD made me suffer on the day of His burning anger?

Is God angry? Certainly the actions of rebellious people provoke Him. Scripture establishes that He is not limited in ways or means to punish. He is not a disinterested Creator. So what are we to do when times are tough and blessings seem removed?

God may not tell us if He is angry or targeting us with punishment. Nor is He offended when we question Him. Sorrow is a natural emotion and response to hard times. But when we know that God is displeased, it is especially wise to lament. Jeremiah was broken up by the realization of his own sin and the sorry condition of his countrymen. *"My soul has been deprived of peace; I have forgotten what happiness is"* (Lam. 3:17).

If we cannot lament sin the condition of our heart is seriously in question. Genuine mourning leads to true repentance—a condition God expects if we are really willing to obey Him. Perhaps this is why Solomon wrote in Ecclesiastes, *"Grief is better than laughter, for when a face is sad, a heart may be glad. The heart of the wise is in a house of mourning, but the heart of fools is in a house of pleasure"* (Ecc. 7:3,4). Finally, while the Jews had a heightened sense of God's anger in the Old Testament, they also understood the vastness of His love. *"Because of the LORD's faithful love we do not perish, for His mercies never end. They are new every morning; great is Your faithfulness"* (Lam. 3:22,23)! The hope in lamenting is the surety of God's love. What could be more tragic than to have no expectation beyond sorrow? What can be more triumphant than to know grief is resolved by Christ's blood?!

Inspection in Ranks   June 8

The military has a formal practice known as "Inspection in Ranks" where a commander examines each soldier standing at attention in formation. I never enjoyed these reviews when I was the inspectee. The long period of sustaining a rigid posture only made my back and thighs ache. Yet, I did learn some interesting lessons. Formal inspections serve a necessary purpose but they do not always give a commander an accurate assessment of a soldier. A warrior may look good in uniform but be incompetent in battle.

The test of genuineness is often gauged by what goes unseen. We may smile and give the impression that all is well while our mind is full of anger and our spirit is critical. We may say nice things but think mean thoughts. The Bible states:

> For those who live according to the flesh think about the things of the flesh, but those who live are according to the Spirit, about the things of the Spirit. For the mind-set of the flesh is death, but the mind-set of the Spirit is life and peace. For the mind-set of the flesh is hostile to God because it does not submit itself to God's law, for it is unable to do so. Those whose lives are in the flesh cannot please God. (Rom. 8:5-8)

Ezekiel 11:5—*Then the Spirit of the LORD came on me, and He told me, "You are to say: This is what the LORD says: That is what you are thinking, house of Israel; and I know the thoughts that arise in your mind."*
Jeremiah 17:10—*I, Yahweh, examine the mind, I test the heart to give to each according to his way, according to what his actions deserve.*

Oswald Chambers taught in *Studies in the Sermon on the Mount*:
> The test Jesus gives is not the truth of our manner but the temper of our mind. Many of us are wonderfully truthful in manner but our temper of mind is rotten in God's sight. The thing Jesus alters is the temper of mind.

Did you know that we are inspected daily by our Heavenly Father without our ever having to line up on cement slabs in our best clothing? The One who knows how many hairs we have on our head also knows our thoughts. In truth, there are many times when I wish this were not so. It's pretty embarrassing to have God scrutinizing my mind when my focus is selfish. This is why I find King David to be such a remarkable man. He had the guts to say, "*Test me, LORD, and try me; examine my heart and mind*" (Psa. 26:2).

Inspiration † † †

In fact, it's doubtful that I can know myself adequately or accurately without reflection from others.—Dick Foth in *When the Giant Lies Down*

Lenience

June 9

Thank God we are not a heap of ashes! 1. Do you know people who believe the Old Testament God is exceedingly harsh but not the same New Testament God? 2. Have you ever done something so bad there was just no way you thought God would forgive you? 3. Do you know someone who has committed some disgusting sin and Christians will have nothing to do with that person despite his or her repentance?

Ezekiel 18:21-22—Now if the wicked person turns from all the sins he has committed, keeps all My statutes, and does what is just and right, he will certainly live; he will not die. None of the transgressions he has committed will be held against him. He will live because of the righteousness he has practiced.

The Hebrew word *rasha* translates *guilty one* or *one hostile to God*.[31] One deserves to be smoked who blows sin in His face. God told Ezekiel that he would spare a *rasha* person if that person stopped sinning and lived righteously. Ezekiel is chocked full of pronouncements of punishment for depraved people, yet here is a passage of amazing grace. It is this merciful Lover of humanity who appears throughout the writings of the poets, priests, and prophets. For an inconsistent human to label his Creator mutable is like the fool defining wisdom.

If you answered the second question above with a "yes," this passage should jolt your thinking. 1 John 1:9 says, *"If we confess our sins, He is faithful and righteous to forgive us our sins and to cleanse us from all unrighteousness."* Don't let Satan beat you up with guilt. Stop dissolving grace with the acid of disbelief. God's intent is to extend grace, not fire. If this were not the case, Adam and Eve would be the tiniest footnotes in history for their unhealthy fruit selection. God is full of compassion. If you committed the unpardonable sin, you wouldn't be reading this. Only if you are not confessing should you be trembling. Only if you hold on to evil should you be afraid.

For question three, if a believer will not forgive a recovering stumbler, a most troubling paradox arises: his tainted flag of legalism flies higher than God's flag of leniency.

Ezekiel reveals a Father who wants to grant His children life. Some may say, "But no one could keep all of God's statues and do what is just and right, so God is setting us up for failure." But to say this is to miss Jesus. God's Son did what we cannot do and because of His faithful righteousness we have a Savior-Redeemer!

Saber's Annoying Habit

June 10

I apologize in advance for this crude illustration but I want to make a crucial point. When Saber our Sheltie was a young pup, he had an extremely annoying habit. As I walked him with Hero, our Labrador retriever, if he encountered dung from another animal (I'm guessing raccoon) before I could stop him, he would literally take an in-the-air rollover dive into the mess and slide his chest and back all over it! This action really made me mad because with his thick long hair, it was quite difficult to clean him up!

Ezekiel 36:23-28—"I will honor the holiness of My great name, which has been profaned among the nations—the name you have profaned among them. The nations will know that I am Yahweh"—the declaration of the Lord GOD—"when I demonstrate My holiness through you in their sight. For I will take you from the nations and gather you from all the countries, and will bring you into your own land. I will also sprinkle clean water on you, and you will be clean. I will cleanse you from all your impurities and all your idols. I will give you a new heart and put a new spirit within you; I will remove your heart of stone and give you a heart of flesh. I will place My Spirit within you and cause you to follow My statutes and carefully observe My ordinances. Then you will live in the land that I gave your fathers; you will be My people, and I will be your God."

God led the Israelites to Canaan, the land He promised to Abraham and his descendants. He expected them to live righteously in contrast to the heathen nations that occupied that territory. Instead, they jumped and rolled in the sin of the residents they failed to remove and brought such a stench upon themselves that God in disgust, forcibly removed and scattered them through the armies of Assyria and later Babylon. I think we tend to be hard on the Jews and to judge them for turning their backs on God and walking in wicked behavior. I wonder, are we so different? How many people do you know who wear the name *Christian* yet live identical to their Christ-disdaining neighbors? How many Jesus followers wear the odor of the world because the aroma is powerfully attractive? If you and I do not carefully watch ourselves, we can easily find ourselves guilty of doing and being the very things God forbids.

Here's the good news: God is a forgiving, loving Father. Rather than abandon His people and start over with a "new breed," He promised to bring them back to their own land, clean them up, place His Spirit within them, and cause them to obey His laws and to be His children. God demonstrates His holiness through people. He honors His holy great name by helping us be holy. May God be forever praised for His faithful commitment to our well-being! We don't deserve it. So, the next time you see a fellow believer engage in sinful behavior, remind him or her whose Name they represent. And before you are tempted to do evil, think of the consequences of your action. Remember that God wants to work His holiness through us so that every nation can see what clean and pure looks like to His glory! Robert Coleman observed in *The Master Plan of Discipleship*, "The demonstration of holiness has always been at the heart of God's strategy of world evangelization."

Dear Lord, I am so sorry for thoughts and actions that caused You to hold Your nose and look away. Thank You for loving me enough to cleanse me. May I walk in holiness each day to the betterment of our relationship and so those around me see Your holiness at work!

Inspiration †††

For the first time I examined myself with a seriously practical purpose. And there I found what appalled me; a zoo of lusts, a bedlam of ambitions, a nursery of fears, a harem of fondled hatreds. My name was legion.—C.S. Lewis in *Surprised By Joy*

Abundant Compassion

June 11

Sandy sits on the iron bench bolted to the sidewalk by Prink Avenue and finishes her cell phone conversation. Unhesitatingly, she stands and moves into the crosswalk practically daring the cars to not stop. The yellow *Walk* light has not yet flashed but she doesn't care, she is an important person and she knows the drivers will wait. Her spiritual life is much the same. Sandy approaches God and expects that He will listen to her because she is a *good* person and her list of accomplishments warrants in her mind, His favor.

Daniel 9:18—Listen, my God, and hear. Open Your eyes and see our desolations and the city called by Your name. For we are not presenting our petitions before You based on our righteous acts, but based on Your abundant compassion.

At a time in history of national shame, the Jews desperately needed God's kindness. Daniel understood how to appeal to his Father. He knew that petitions backed by moral accomplishments could never repair the damage done by centuries of blatant spiritual rebellion. If cedar tabernacles filled with chanted psalms could undue sin, God would not have resorted to a crude cross. Daniel based his request for help on divine compassion—the Hebrew script bearing witness to its abundance.

We fool ourselves if we think that we somehow earn God's blessing. Desolation is not removed by demonstration. Certainly many Biblical characters like David appealed to God's mercy based on personal righteousness. But do we ever read God replying "You are right, I owe you favor because you have been so good." Instead, He reveals His grandeur and in the process, the one appealing comes to the humble recognition that it is His mercy and compassion that are awe-inspiring.

God's compassion is the sweetest nectar known to man. It calms the anxious mind. It mends sin with a stitchery of golden thread that cannot be broken. It soothes the soul of sorrow with notes of grace. It clears the clots of a plugged heart with the redeeming blood of the holiest Lamb. Seventy-seven times Scripture specifically mentions God's compassion to His people.

Inspiration †††

If you really want to be used in a healing ministry, ask your heavenly Father to let you feel his compassion for the hurting.—Jack Deere in *Surprised By The Power Of The Spirit*

Promiscuous

June 12

One of the reasons I love to study the Bible is the amazing way God speaks to the times in which we live. Read what the prophet Hosea wrote to his countrymen sometime between 755 and 722 B.C. and see if his words speak to your nation.

Hosea 4:1-4,6,10,11,12,14—Hear the word of the LORD, people of Israel, for the LORD has a case against the inhabitants of the land: There is no truth, no faithful love, and no knowledge of God in the land! Cursing, lying, murder, stealing, and adultery are rampant; one act of bloodshed follows another. For this reason the land mourns, and everyone who lives in it languishes, along with the wild animals and the birds of the sky; even the fish of the sea disappear . . . My people are destroyed for lack of knowledge . . . They will eat but not be satisfied; they will be promiscuous but not multiply. For they have abandoned their devotion to the LORD. Promiscuity, wine, and new wine take away one's understanding . . . For a spirit of promiscuity leads them astray; they act promiscuously in disobedience to their God . . . People without discernment are doomed.

At the root of our national decline is our lack of knowledge of God. We have abandoned a thirst to know Him with a craving to please our flesh. The result of this plunge into pleasure is the replacement of truth with lies and the betrayal of fidelity for unabated lust. Cursing, lying, murder, stealing and adultery paint the walls of our cities. Degenerate people cause the land and all who live in it to suffer. Instead of the proliferation of evil driving people to return to God, the opposite occurs—an insatiable appetite screams for worse. The liturgy of promiscuity worships with two key words, "Please me!" For flesh to be gratified, anything based on truth must be discredited and labeled as intolerant and wrong. The Creator is disobeyed and sinners seem to flourish.

So what do we do when society manifests all the signs of a freefall to hell? Certainly, this is not the time for isolation. Hosea did not hide in the hills when Israel was dying; he took God's message to the streets. Certainly, this is not the time to fear, cowardice only reaps defeat. This is not the time to doubt. God's omnipresence is not earth-exclusive nor is His power muted by fools. This is not the time for brotherly backbiting! Unity is essential wherever ignorance and wickedness speak. This is the time to run after God, to seek His presence and in living for Him enable others to see Him. This is the time to know God. Anything that scorns or disdains pursuing Him is promiscuous.

Get Your Own Dirt!

June 13

One day a group of scientists assembled and decided that by virtue of mankind's tremendous accomplishments, God was no longer needed. A spokesperson was selected to inform God that they were done with Him. The scientist, not knowing exactly how to reach God, walked into the nearest church and in a loud voice exclaimed, "God, we've decided that we no longer need you. We're to the point that we can clone people and do many miraculous things by our own brilliance."

After a moment of silence, a quiet voice replied, "Very well, let us have a man-making contest." The somewhat surprised scientist replied, "OK, great! What are the rules of the contest?" The Lord answered, "We will make man just as I once made Adam." The scientist, somewhat familiar with the Genesis account said, "Sure, no problem." He walked outside bent over and grabbed himself a handful of dirt. But before he could even straighten, God said, "No, no, no. You go get your own dirt!"[32]

Hosea 13:6—When they had pasture, they became satisfied; they were satisfied, and their hearts became proud. Therefore they forgot Me.

A self-sufficient world mocks the notion of God's existence and worth. Therefore should it surprise us when a governor used to pinning men with his brawny muscles scoffs as weak any who are religious? As technology improves, and human pride in accomplishment ascends so will the volume of disdain for a holy Father and His imperfect followers.

That anyone would dismisses God as obsolete ought to rally us to stand up and proclaim His profound relevance. Paul once cried, "For *I am not ashamed of the gospel . . .*" (Rom. 1:16). Peter admonished his listeners to be prepared to give those who ask, an answer for their hope (1 Pe. 3:15).

These are not days to cower behind walls protecting holy huddles. While freedom still exists, we must stand up under the guidance of the powerful Holy Spirit to proclaim in the clear manner of one redeemed, that our God reigns and He is indeed an awesome God. Is it cowardice or a disturbing lack of regard for the call of Christ who bids us to go and tell, that we mute our voices? Get off the couch, turn off the tube, treat the cancer of complacency and shine your light. The world desperately needs GOD! The surgical miracle He worked in our hearts was not so the angels could marvel, but so men and women, boys and girls could fall on their knees, repent and find salvation in the One who saved us—GOD—the greatest word our language knows.

Word Pictures

June 14

Located in Belgium, Supreme Headquarters Allied Powers Europe (SHAPE) is the Headquarters of Allied Command Operations (ACO), one of NATO's two strategic military commands. While visiting SHAPE headquarters a group of about twenty of us received a briefing from Admiral James Stravidus. Unlike any other meeting we attended over a five-week period Admiral Stravidus used only pictures on his PowerPoint slides. His presentation was spell-binding. By telling stories through the use of pictures he captured our attention and held our interest.

Joel 2:31—The sun will be turned to darkness and the moon to blood before the great and awe-inspiring Day of the LORD comes.

To get the attention of His people, God often spoke to His prophets by using word pictures. In warning of God's impending Day of Judgment, Joel warned his countrymen, "*A fire destroys in front of them, and behind them a flame devours. The land in front of them is like the Garden of Eden, but behind them, it is like a desert wasteland; there is no escape from them*" (2:3). Imagine the thoughts that must have gripped Israelites as they who were familiar with disasters, contemplated great fires and devastation. Raging fires, a wasteland, a sun-less day and a red moon were all images they could understand and no doubt stuck in their minds. Word pictures and real pictures are effective ways to bring understanding.

Too often when we have important things to say, we can be lazy and choose words and means to convey ideas that are overused or irrelevant to the life of the one listening. For example, if a person is struggling with sin and needs Jesus' grace, instead of drawing a bridge and putting a divide between the person and heaven, why not use a graphic image with which they can better relate? My friend Brian asks his secular friends, "Have you ever put together a jig-saw puzzle?" If the person nods yes, he says, "Imagine if you were trying to put together a puzzle and some of the pieces were missing." Anyone who has ever put together a puzzle immediately grasps the problem. Brian clarifies with his listener that anyone who engages in sin destroys the pieces God intended to be intact for life to form the right picture.

If a picture is worth a thousand words, what is a video worth? If we care about people, let's make the time and effort to be creative in sharing! There is a reason Jesus taught using parables. The value of a well-communicated story is priceless!

Revealer

June 15

Curiosity is a powerful thing. If you are in a group and happen to notice two people whispering to each other, don't you have an urge to know what they are saying? We don't typically like it when people keep secrets from us. Nor do we appreciate it when those who are in charge withhold information we need to know. I remember the stress on Matt and Angie, our neighbors, when Nike was getting ready to lay off hundreds of employees. For weeks they were in suspense as to whether they would keep their jobs. Fortunately, they both did, but the stress of not knowing weighed heavily on them.

Amos 3:7; 4:13—Indeed, the Lord GOD does nothing without revealing His counsel to His servants the prophets . . . He is here: the One who forms the mountains, creates the wind, and reveals His thoughts to man, the One who makes the dawn out of darkness and strides on the heights of the earth. Yahweh, the God of Hosts, is His name.

Amos was a shepherd from the town of Tekoa which was about twelve miles from Jerusalem. God gave Him visions and burdened him to share what He revealed with the Israelites living to the north of Judah. We don't know much about Amos other than that he prophesied during the reigns of Israel's King Jeroboam II (782-753 B.C.) and Judah's King Uzziah (767-740 B.C.).

The fact that God called a sheep breeder to proclaim His message is profound in many ways. First, who more than a shepherd would relate simply to other people with plain and easily understood speech? We fuss about the technique, style, or preciseness of communication but what God is looking for is understanding. Second, that God would divulge His plan to a common man and not the king or someone wealthy or powerful suggests that His intent was for all of Israel to receive His warnings.

Amos reminds us of God's power and invokes His most sacred name—Yahweh. This is important, if for no other reason, because it gives us confidence that the Revealer is completely credible and worthy of trust. Do you believe that God loves you and wants to reveal His thoughts to you? If you will but stop your frenetic activity and make the time to be quiet and to ask Him for His thoughts, you will be greatly surprised that He indeed will speak to you. It is when I go to Him humbly and inquire from a genuine heart, that I often hear His voice. He speaks to my thoughts and touches my heart. It is exhilarating when God speaks, for we instantly know He cares. He is the Revealer and that He would speak to us is awesome!

Inspiration † † †

It is not *your* diligence, it is not *your* examination of yourself that will enlighten you concerning your sin. Instead, it is God who does all the revealing . . .—Jeanne Guyon in *Experiencing the Depths of Jesus Christ*

Gloating

June 16

In football, when a player taunts an opposing player after tackling him or completing an exceptional play, if the referee sees or hears the infraction, it often costs the team a fifteen yard penalty for unsportsmanlike conduct. Choosing to gloat is not very smart. Why give the other team momentum and the possibility of winning the game?

Gloating is taking excessive pleasure in another's adversity or misfortune. It reveals the ugly side of people's character. While Jesus hung on a cross:

> *Those who passed by were yelling insults at Him, shaking their heads, and saying, "Ha! The One who would demolish the sanctuary and build it in three days, save Yourself by coming down from the cross!" In the same way, the chief priests with the scribes were mocking Him to one another and saying, "He saved others; He cannot save Himself! Let the Messiah, the King of Israel, come down now form the cross, so that we may see and believe." Even those who were crucified with Him were taunting Him.* (Mark 15:29-32)

That a holy Messiah suffering in the most unimaginable manner could be mocked and taunted by His own countrymen, reveals the blackness of their wicked hearts.

Obadiah 12—Do not gloat over your brother in the day of his calamity; do not rejoice over the people of Judah in the day of their destruction; do not boastfully mock in the day of distress.

God raised up the prophet Obadiah to warn the nation of Edom of His impending judgment. He was angry with the descendants of Esau because they were related to the Israelites yet took no action to help Israel during her time of plight. They gloated at Israel's misfortune and were smug in their own security. Today, there is no Edom.

Do you take satisfaction seeing someone who is a rival or enemy suffer? Stop. Why bring God's hand against yourself? Do you observe others around you gloating? Remind them that it takes but a moment to die—we have no mocking ground, no taunting foundation or gloating rock to stand upon. More importantly, we are made in the image of God and we ought to act like it.

Lord, forgive me for taking pleasure in someone else's misfortune. Help me to see people the way You see them. May kindness cover my thoughts and actions. Amen.

Illogical

June 17

Have you ever wondered how astronauts fly up into space to rendezvous with a space station or other orbiting objects such as the Hubble space telescope? It is an incredibly difficult task. Let's listen in to scientist and retired Colonel Palmer Bailey as he articulates the challenge:

> The basic problem is that both of the rendezvousing objects are in individual orbits around the Earth. The shape and size of a spacecraft's orbit is determined by its velocity. Thus if you try to speed up to catch something travelling ahead of you in the same orbit, you change your orbit and then are no longer in the same orbit . . . Therefore, if you are in orbit behind your rendezvous target and try to speed up to catch it, what actually happens is that your increased speed is used up raising you into a higher and therefore slower orbit and you fall farther and farther behind. You must slow down, thus dropping into a lower but quicker orbit until you are ahead of your target, then speed up at just the right rate to go into the higher slower orbit as the target craft catches up to you. It's pretty tricky to get that timing just right.

Jonah 1:12—He answered them, "Pick me up and throw me into the sea so it may quiet down for you, for I know that I'm to blame for this violent storm that is against you."

God told Jonah to go to Ninevah—it was an illogical order to the prophet because the Assyrians were a wicked people and did not merit God's mercy. So Jonah fled in a boat headed in the opposite direction to Tarshish. God, who sees all, sent a storm to capsize his wayward servant. Recognizing his sin, Jonah then gave an illogical command to the sailors as seen in the verse above. Throwing someone into the sea does not make a storm go away! Hmm. But it did in Jonah's case.

By logic when Jonah entered the stormy sea, he should have drowned. But God calmed the waters and illogically saved him by having a great fish swallow him. Logically, a man dies inside a fish, but God illogically kept him alive for three days and nights and then had the fish spit him out alive onto dry ground. Now here is the really fun part: It is illogical to believe the book of Jonah really happened and is not just an allegory! But if we vote for logic, we then consistently must hold anything in Scripture that is miraculous to be allegorical and by doing so we negate the resurrection and logically must reject Christ's claim to be our hope for salvation. Do you see why man left to his own thinking is never able to rendezvous with God?

Jesus said in Mark 8:35, *"For whoever wants to save his life will lose it, but whoever loses his life because of Me and the gospel will save it."* It is illogical to die in order to live! Yet to fulfill God's orbit for my life I have to let go of my program, my speed, my control and let Him lead me. Logically, I have not figured this out yet, but, thankfully, I'm illogically learning!

Palmer gives us some great parting thoughts:

Just as the instructions for orbital rendezvous may seem wrong unless you understand orbital mechanics, so God's principles and plan for your life may seem illogical unless you can see things from God's perspective. Trust Him. He knows a lot more about your life and what is good for you that any of us know about orbital mechanics.

33

Taken for Granted   June 18

I once spoke on the subject of maintaining our spiritual house. At the end of the message I asked each person to fill out a form. On that form each individual rated what kind of personal devotion time he or she was getting with God. The scale ranged from nonexistent--'0' to consistent time with the Lord—'10.' Eighty-six percent of those who turned in response forms inconsistently set aside time to meet with the Lord. If that trend continues, there will come a day when it is very lonely following God. The question begs to be asked, "How can people grow in their relationship with their Father if they are unwilling to spend any time reading what He has communicated?"

Micah 7:1,2—How sad for me! For I am like one who—when the summer fruit has been gathered after the gleaning of the grape harvest—finds no grape cluster to eat, no early fig, which I crave. Godly people have vanished from the land; there is no one upright among the people. All of them wait in ambush to shed blood; they hunt each other with a net.

Can you feel the sadness in Micah's words? He felt like a man alone. He followed God steadfastly yet suffered immensely by countrymen who scorned him for his faith. On top of the opposition he faced for daring to speak God's Word, was the intense loneliness of not having other like-minded believers to fellowship with and find encouragement.

Knowing God does not come naturally or easily because our flesh's proclivity is to resist the Holy Spirit. It's much easier to do what I want to do than to obey God. Rather than take our relationship with Him for granted we must encourage each other to pay the cost of saying "no!" to self and "yes!" to spending time with God. Incredibly, as we say "yes" to God many of those distractions that kept us from Him in the first place, disappear.

Inspiration † † †

What we take for granted is never ours until we have bought it by pain. A thing is worth just what it costs.—Oswald Chamber in *Approved Unto God*

Contemptible

June 19

Do you ever wonder what the point is for reading books of the Bible that primarily contain prophecies of God's impending judgment against certain people and nations? Jonah, Nahum and Zephaniah all prophesied against the Assyrian empire. When Nahum predicted the impending destruction of the capital city, Nineveh, Assur-bani-pal was its evil king. Nineveh was full of bloodshed, deceit, plundering and constant warring against others (3:1).

We don't know much about Nahum. His name means "comforter," and he was an Elkoshite from the town of Alqosh which may have been in the area of Capharnaum in northern Galilee.[34] What we do know is that he wrote strong words of warning from God, who was very angry with the behavior of Assyria. Nahum's words to Assur-bani-pal were hardly comforting!

Nahum 1:14—The LORD has issued an order concerning you: There will be no offspring to carry on your name. I will eliminate the carved idol and cast image from the house of your gods; I will prepare your grave, for you are contemptible.

There are multiple things we learn about God from reading Nahum.
1. *"The LORD is a jealous and avenging God"* who punishes His enemies (1:2). If the Lord was not jealous for His people, we could rightfully question the depth of His love. If God did not take action against evildoers, then what is to be gained by living righteously?
2. God is *"slow to anger but great in power"* (1:3). We ought to be encouraged that God is not hasty in taking action—He is deliberate. He considers what He is going to do and when He acts, it is for the right reason.
3. *"The LORD is good, a stronghold in a day of distress; He cares for those who take refuge in Him"* (1:7).
4. God knows exactly what is happening on earth, cares about what He sees and acts when He needs to act. A contemptible person reaches the point where he or she has exhausted God's patience and angered Him greatly through unceasing wickedness. The end result of loathsome behavior is eternal judgment.

After Jonah warned Nineveh of God's impending wrath, the city repented. Later, when Nahum delivered his warning, the Assyrians ignored God's messenger and continued their despicable behavior. Nineveh was destroyed by fire and a corrupt empire came to an end.

John Calvin noted, "All wickedness flows from a disregard of God . . ."[35] Since the fear of God is the bridle by which our wickedness is held in check, its removal frees us to indulge in every kind of licentious conduct." Do you know someone who personifies wickedness? Be courageous and warn of God's hatred of evil. Offer the truth of God's grace and kindness and pray the contemptible individual will repent. God's judgment of eternal separation is the fruit of a contemptible life.

Inspiration † † †
Evil is easy, and has infinite forms.—Blaise Pascal

What Makes a Good Father? June 20

A recent study "*A Tale of Two Fathers*," found that "married fathers are far more involved today in rearing children compared to their counterparts 40 years ago. However, the percentage of fathers living apart from the kids more than doubled in the last half-century." Statistics show almost 50% of men less than 45 years old admit to having children out of wedlock. President Barack Obama stated, "Father's Day reminds us parents that we have no more solemn obligation than to care for our children. But far too many young people in America grow up without their dads, and our families and communities are challenged as a result."

Proverbs 4:1-5—Listen, my sons, to a father's discipline, and pay attention so that you may gain understanding, for I am giving you good instruction. Don't abandon my teaching. When I was a son with my father, tender and precious to my mother, he taught me and said: "Your heart must hold on to my words. Keep my commands and live. Get wisdom, get understanding; don't forget or turn away from the words of my mouth.

So what makes a good father? In looking at Proverbs and thinking about what my own dad modeled, here are five things I hope my children will say about me:

1. *My dad loves God and he loves me*. Dads who love God foremost have their priorities straight. Loving God creates a spiritual foundation and helps a father recognize the value of investing in his children, enjoying them, praying for them, and helping them develop healthy self-images so they know they are valued. In essence they bestow blessing. Harmon Killebrew relates, "'My father used to play with my brother and me in the yard. Mother would come out and say, 'You're tearing up the grass.' 'We're not raising grass,' Dad would reply. 'We're raising boys.'"

2. *My dad teaches me*. Dads who want their children to succeed in life make the time to inform them, to provide insight and counsel. Wise fathers communicate the value and importance of acquiring wisdom. British author George Herbert shares from his 17th Century *Outlandish Proverbs*, "One father is more than a hundred Schoolemasters."

3. *My dad has high standards*. Dads have to give commands and establish absolutes. Clear boundaries provide protection and safety. Dads who model what "right looks like" help their children form strong convictions and choose wise behavior.

4. *My dad is not afraid to discipline me*. When children violate absolutes (tell the truth, respect your elders, etc.), they must be corrected and if necessary punished. Hebrews 12:9 states, "*Furthermore, we had natural fathers discipline us, and we respected them. Shouldn't we submit even more to the Father of spirits and live?*" A father who is wishy-washy, compromises

on truth, or who lets his children do whatever they want, sets them up for pain not success.

5. *My dad is humble.* Good fathers are always learners. Not only do they not have all the answers, they also recognize and admit when they make mistakes. They depend upon God and are not afraid to rely on others. Humility establishes trust and creates an enduring relationship of respect.

Inspiration ✝✝✝

I watched through blinding tears, till his form faded from my gaze; and then, hastening on my way, vowed deeply and oft, by the help of God, to live and act so as never to grieve or dishonour such a father and mother as He had given me.—John G. Paton

Made a Spectacle

June 21

Nahum 3:3,5,6—Charging horseman, flashing sword, shining spear; heaps of slain, mounds of corpses, dead bodies without end—they stumble over their dead ... I am against you. This is the declaration of the LORD of Hosts. I will lift your skirts over your face and display your nakedness to nations, your shame to kingdoms. I will throw filth on you and treat you with contempt; I will make a spectacle of you.

You may remember the contorted body images flashed across the television screen. Daily, protestors fell slain in streets before the bullets of tyrants. Cries for freedom were met by ruthless rockets. In 2012, Syrian President Bashar al-Assad refused to listen to the protests of his people. Iran's President, Mahmoud Ahmadinejad, threatened to build nuclear weapons to destroy Israel. Iran supplied weapons and trained fighters to kill and terrorize any who opposed her agenda.

Whenever a nation embraces wickedness know with certainty that God is against her. The main theme of the book of Nahum is God's impending judgment of Nineveh—the powerful Assyrian capital. God paid her back for her ruthless treatment of her enemies and for mocking Him. His past hand of judgment is not presently asleep. God does not let evil run completely unrestrained.

To be made a spectacle, to be treated with contempt by heaven, is a sure indicator that God is provoked. He does not destroy righteous nations. Countries beset with strife and ablaze with chaos reflect the shame that comes from feeding evil. There is no such thing as an enduring immoral empire—the cost of iniquity is eventually paid by the blood of its perpetrators.

But what nation on earth <u>is</u> righteous? The problem so often with those of us who love God is that we like to cheer when the bad guy gets what is coming to him. Would the charging horseman God hates have begun riding if there had been fasting saints alert to manifest His love? Whenever there is a spectacle, there is always a story behind it. Over a hundred years before Nahum, Jonah shared with Nineveh of God's impending judgment and the people repented. What happened? Were there no righteous people to continue speaking? Nahum wrote, *"The LORD is good, a stronghold in a day of distress; He cares for those who take refuge in Him"* (1:7). Too bad the Assyrians lost that truth. May we fear God's hand and pray that before any are shamed, they might be saved. Spectacles are nothing to celebrate.

What Constitutes Security? June 22

Beware the dreaded Babylonians! Habakkuk, a contemporary of the prophet Jeremiah, was a man of profound faith who complained to God from a troubled heart. His world (605 B.C.?) abounded with injustice. His nation, Judah, was awash in sin and about to be conquered by a godless enemy. *"How long, LORD, must I call for help and You do not listen or cry out to You about violence and You do not save? . . Why are You silent while one who is wicked swallows up one who is more righteous than himself?"* (Hab. 1:2,13b). Have you ever felt that way towards God? Have you ever wondered amidst evil-dominated headlines if God was off on some celestial sabbatical?

Habakkuk 3:19—Yahweh my Lord is my strength; He makes my feet like those of a deer and enables me to walk on mountain heights!

The three short chapters of Habakkuk located near the end of the Old Testament provide us invaluable insight into the value of faith. Read God's perspective and response to the universal pride, greed, theft, extortion, murder, injustice, drugs, idolatry and their root cause—the desire to please self that left the godly feeling abandoned and insecure.

If I go to bed feeling safe because my nation's military might is greater than any other land on earth, I rest on a pillow filled with radioactive reasoning. Does materialism and the prestige of a good name secure my place in eternity? Is plenty the blanket that covers fear or money the means to achieve peace? In the best of times what constitutes security?

If the stock market flops and the economy melts is God dead? If natural disasters rip the land, is divine mercy hollow? If prejudice mocks my color and discrimination chains my bones, who owns my soul? If disease wracks my body, can I still hope? In the dungeon of darkness where does one find joy? In the worst of times what constitutes security?

Habakkuk heard the Lord, took a deep breath and reached the following conclusion:

Though the fig tree does not bud and there is no fruit on the vines, though the olive crop fails and the fields produce no food, though there are no sheep in the pen and no cattle in the stalls, yet I will triumph in Yahweh; I will rejoice in the God of my salvation! (3:17,18)

Inspiration † † †

How difficult it is to grow spiritually if our security is based upon the stability of outward things! Our security must come from God, not circumstances, nor even relationships.—Francis Frangipane in *Holiness, Truth and the Presence of God*

Jenny

June 23

Jenny wears a smile as pure as mountain spring water. She does not understand the girls sarcastically mocking her bowl-cut hairstyle because for her, there is no sarcasm. But she does know pain. When the teams are picked for kick ball, she wonders why they don't want her to play. When she drops her tray of food at lunch and they laugh and point their fingers, her spirit droops. When the 4th grade bully rubs mud on her new jacket and calls her "stupid," it takes a small box of tissues to dry her tears. Yet, when he breaks his hand playing football, she will be the one who brings him flowers from her mother's garden.

Jeff and Candace wonder why their child had to be different. Their dreams for their firstborn girl were thrashed against the cold rocks of reality. There is no pill or exercise or magic word to end Down Syndrome. Yes, they fiercely love their brown-haired girl with the crooked smile and almond-shaped eyes—whose undying quest is to please them. They laugh when she giggles and ache when she suffers. Aside from the wallet-draining trips to the doctor, their big challenge is dismissing the questions. What if she had been "normal"? Why are people mean and insensitive? Does anyone truly understand our world? Why did God let this happen? . . .

Zephaniah 3:19—Yes, at that time I will deal with all who afflict you. I will save the lame and gather the scattered; I will make those who were disgraced throughout the earth receive praise and fame.

Unless Jesus returns first, the day will come when Jenny dies. Then she will face the greatest Lover of all time. He will fill her new body with unspeakable joy and wrap her in a hug that takes away the breath of the nearest angels. She will take His hand and walk the gold streets to the applause of an inspired multitude. She will give voice to the words she knew in her heart and now can sing with the choir, *"Great and awe-inspiring are Your works, Lord God, the Almighty; righteous and true are Your ways, King of the Nations"* (Rev. 15:3).

Who is afflicted? Who is lame in walk, dogged with ridicule every step? Look up! The Lord who understands will deal with the afflicters. He will gather the scattered because He can. Don't let faith waver. Don't drink the cup filled with pity's tears. Drink deeply from the Living Water. Faith in the Lion finds in His glory the eternal antidote to affliction. Walking with Jesus is walking to peace and happiness.

Inspiration ✝✝✝

God's wrath arises from His intense, settled hatred of all sin and is the tangible expression of His inflexible determination to punish it.—Jerry Bridges in *The Gospel for Real Life*

Self-Centered

June 24

Sometimes Scripture jumps from the pages and slaps me. Such was the case recently when reflecting on 1 John 2:3,4.

This is how we are sure that we have come to know Him: by keeping His commands. The one who says, "I have come to know Him," without keeping His commands, is a liar, and the truth is not in him.

If I know God, why don't I keep His commands? If I have a love relationship with Him, why, then, do I *still* have a lust relationship with the world? If I'm reading John correctly, lust of the flesh and lust of the eyes and boastful pride of life cannot cohabit with love for God. *"If anyone loves the world, love for the Father is not in him"* (2:15b). This profoundly disturbs me. Obviously, I don't know and love God very well. Too often, my thoughts cruise down Self-Centered River. My boat seems inexorably caught in currents that flow away from His presence. The intimacy I crave with Him is sabotaged by *into-me-see*, my desire to please myself.

Haggai 1:9—"You expected much, but then it amounted to little. When you brought the harvest to your house, I ruined it. Why?" This is the declaration of the LORD of Hosts. "Because My house still lies in ruins, while each of you is busy with his own house."

Haggai relayed to his countrymen God's displeasure with them. Instead of rebuilding His temple and worshiping Him, they were preoccupied with their own things. While the temple sat in ruins, the Israelites looked after personal needs. Because of their self-centered attitude, God kept them from experiencing blessing.

The paradox of spiritual blessing is that it comes at the cost of personal indulgence. Jesus stated clearly that if we want to pursue Him, we must deny self-wants (Luke 9:23). The mark of spiritual intimacy is the disappearance of self-gratifying love. God's command is *"Do not love the world."* How do we know what worldly love is? Extended to its conclusion it is meaningless. Possessions wear out and leave us unfulfilled. The best lust ends in death. Feelings lead to failings. Nature fades, the planet burns. Anything pulling us away from God is pointless.

God is not saying we cannot experience pleasure—that would contradict His purpose in creating us. What displeases Him is when we are so busy with our own house that we neglect His house (Him). Disobedience is intimacy's cancer. Our kingdom must never displace His Kingdom. So how do I remove my self-centered bent? I need God's help.

Fow Diow

June 25

Ken shared with me a great thought from AF Trekker that I pass along to you. In Thailand, Christians say, "Fow Diow."

It means to have a personal, private audience with the King. Thais have a great respect and understanding of living under a King who rules them in love but who is quite distant in life experience from them. Very few Thais ever see the King; much less have a private audience with him. Those who do come into his presence enter on their knees far below his high throne.

Zechariah 8:20-22—The LORD of Hosts says this: "Peoples will yet come, the residents of many cities; the residents of one city will go to another, saying: Let's go at once to plead for the LORD's favor and to seek the LORD of Hosts. I am also going. Many peoples and strong nations will come to seek the LORD of Hosts in Jerusalem and to plead for the LORD's favor."

I fear too many Christians have lost their awe for God. They treat Him casually and use His name carelessly. For those unfamiliar with royalty, I guess it is not surprising that holy fear is an uncommon virtue. The prophet Zechariah speaks of a time when the world recognizes the ruling power of the Lord and with a sense of urgency seeks His holy presence. Why should people go to Jerusalem? Zechariah gives us the answer in verse 23. "*. . . Let us go with you, for we have heard that God is with you.*'"

God told Moses in Exodus 33:19,20:

"*I will cause all My goodness to pass in front of you, and I will proclaim the name Yahweh before you. I will be gracious to whom I will be gracious, and I will have compassion on whom I will have compassion.*"

But He answered, "*You cannot see My face, for no one can see Me and live.*"

His face is too great to be seen by our mortal eyes! Yet His love is so astounding that He bids us to come and worship Him. Fow diow! Our Father gives us private audience. When we kneel before Him and share our hearts, He hears and responds.

We are the most privileged people in existence to know and serve such an incredible God. To bow before a king who cannot own our souls is an act of respect. To bow before the King who made us is unending adoration. E.B. Browning wrote, "Earth's crammed with Heaven and every common bush is afire with God, but only he who sees takes off his shoes." Fow diow!

Inspiration ✝✝✝

We make ourselves what we are by the way we address God.—Thomas Merton

Immutable

June 26

People change. They are fickle like the weather and predictably unpredictable. Two people pledge to be faithful to each other until death yet divorce. Companies promise employees pensions but if they go out of business, the hope of a secure future is dashed. Governments make pledges to their citizens yet renege when circumstances turn unfavorable, newly elected officials reverse policies, or whole administrations are overthrown. My assertion that people change is believable because you change and you've seen others change.

But how can I believe that God does not change? How can I state that His nature is pure; that when He gives His word, He keeps it; and, that His attributes are unblemished by error? My mutability casts doubt on the permanence of anything I suggest. If I recommend you believe the Bible when it asserts that God is immutable, you rightly can respond that the book was written by people. Eventually, you and I must test Scripture and reach our own conclusion if God inspired its writers. His permanence for us can only rest on trust—unchanging faith. If He is not immutable, we have great reason to fear!

Scripture teaches that Abraham received the following promise from God. *"I will keep My covenant between Me and you, and your future offspring throughout their generations, as an everlasting covenant to be your God and the God of your offspring after you"* (Gen. 17:7). Countless times, the children of Abraham broke God's covenant by chasing after other gods. Repeatedly He punished them and the wicked nations that surrounded them. Yet, at no time did He break His promise.

Malachi 3:6—Because I, Yahweh, have not changed, you descendants of Jacob have not been destroyed.

The Old Testament's depiction of God constantly judging and punishing Israel is in stark contrast to the loving manner He is portrayed in the New Testament. For this and many other reasons, people accuse Him of changing and therefore do not trust Him. But we should understand that His promise to Abraham was modified and expanded not because He changed His mind but because His chosen people so frequently refused to follow Him! In Hebrews 8:7-10 we read:

> *For if that first covenant had been faultless, there would have been no occasion for a second one. But finding fault with His people, He says: Look, the days are coming, says the Lord, when I will make a new covenant with the house of Israel and with the house of Judah—not like the covenant that I made with their ancestors on the day I took them by their hands to lead them out of the land of Egypt. I disregarded them, says the Lord, because they did not continue in My covenant. But this is the covenant that I will make with the house of Israel after those days, says*

the Lord: I will put My laws into their minds and write them on their hearts. I will be their God, and they will be My people.

In Ephesians 2:12,13 we learn that God kept His word to Abraham's descendants, and further provided through Jesus a promise for all people!

At that time you were without the Messiah, excluded from the citizenship of Israel, and foreigners to the covenants of the promise, without hope and without God in the world. But now in Christ Jesus, you who were far away have been brought near by the blood of the Messiah.

The angry God who punished a rebellious people was truly a loving God unwilling to eradicate them (and us) from the face of the earth! *"For God loved the world in this way: He gave His One and Only Son, so that everyone who believes in Him will not perish but have eternal life"* (John 3:16). That same Son, promised, *"I am the way, the truth, and the life. No one comes to the Father except through Me"* (John 14:6).

To question and ultimately reject God's permanence and, with that, His offer and ability to deliver to us eternal life is to put our faith in what is temporary. We trust the untrustable and decay to meaninglessness. Only an unchanging Father could offer an unchanging Son to bring salvation to a changing people. All other solutions rest on no permanent solution.

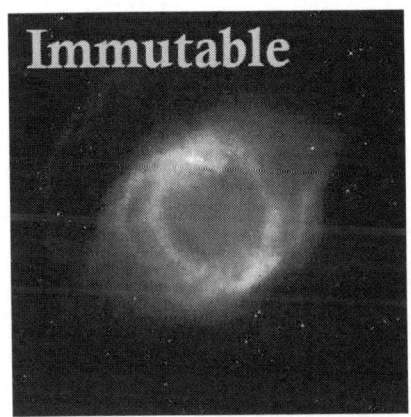

Genealogy

June 27

Matthew 1:1—The historical record of Jesus Christ, the Son of David, the Son of Abraham.

Whenever I come to a section of Scripture that is a genealogy or a long list of names, my tendency is to quickly skim through it and move on. After all, why spend time reading a list of names? One year for my daily quiet time I decided to read through Scripture and include the study notes in my Holman Study Bible. I was quite blessed by what I learned about Matthew 1:1-17 which is the genealogy of Jesus Christ.

1. The phrase, *"the historical record of Jesus Christ,"* is unusual. Usually a genealogy is named after the oldest ancestor whom the Jews would have considered most important since all were derived from that person. That Matthew names his genealogy after Jesus implies that He is more important than Abraham. That he writes Jesus Christ further substantiates Him as the Messiah.

2. Matthew identifies Jesus as the Son of David which immediately validated all the Old Testament prophecies concerning the Messiah descending from the line of King David (2 Sa. 7:16; Isa. 9:2-7).

3. Matthew identifies Jesus as the Son of Abraham which "implies that just as Abraham was the father of national Israel, Jesus will be the founder of a new spiritual Israel."

4. Four Gentile women are mentioned in Matthew's genealogy. The inclusion of Tamar, a Canaanite; Rahab from Jericho; Ruth, a Moabitess; and Bathsheba, who was most likely a Hittite; is remarkable! We discern that it was God's intention to redeem not just the Jews but also Gentile men and women.

5. Matthew's work coincides remarkably well with 1 Chronicles 1-3 and Luke 3:23-38 from the generation of Abraham to David. Given that genealogies could follow either legal or biological progression, the discrepancies between the different lists can be explained and are remarkably well preserved. The Jews took special pride in recording their descendents especially with respect to the line of David since the Messiah was prophesied to come through his line.

6. Matthew identified a human mother but not a human father of Jesus, implying His virginal conception.

7. The arrangement of Jesus' genealogy into three sets of 14 generations was probably an example of gematria. Gematria is a system which gives a numerical value to alphabetical letters (A=1, B=2, etc). If Matthew wrote in Hebrew, which many scholars contend, then the numerical value of the letters which make up David is 14! Matthew may actually be artistically highlighting Jesus' Davidic lineage.[37]

In essence, even a list in Scripture can reveal much to us if we will just take the time to study it carefully. That God is so intentional about history ought to encourage us with both the depth of His sovereign planning and the breadth of

His love for humanity. Therefore, even a list can strengthen our faith and give us pause to worship afresh, our Awesome Savior!

Ron and Dan York, Mark and Jadon Tegtmeier

Inspiration ✝ ✝ ✝

People will not look forward to posterity, who never look backward to their ancestors.—Edmund Burke

One Star

June 28

Coffee Cottage is a popular coffee shop near George Fox University in Newberg, Oregon. One of their draws for students is the free wireless service. Often I come in to find tables occupied with folks writing papers or working projects on their laptops. But unless a person knew that wireless was free and available, they could work on their computer and have no idea they could access internet connection capability simply by asking for the password.

Matthew 2:1-3—After Jesus was born in Bethlehem of Judea in the days of King Herod, wise men from the east arrived unexpectedly in Jerusalem, saying, "Where is He who has been born King of the Jews? For we saw His star in the east and have come to worship Him." When King Herod heard this, he was deeply disturbed, and all Jerusalem with him.

It more than amazes me that wise men, after careful examination of the heavens, would observe a special star, interpret its meaning and follow it so as to worship a baby king. But as I began to meditate on the Magi and their special trek, several thoughts came to mind.

That star was not just available to their eyes; anyone with a clear view of the heavens could see it. Yet, they were the only ones who understood its significance. Why? Was it because they faithfully studied the stars and when this new amazing light showed up, they were ready because they were looking for it? These Magi were not even Jews for all we know. The Jewish religious leaders would have considered them as heathens. Certainly, it must have offended them to hear that these men foresaw a king to be born for their own people and they knew nothing of it. The mere fact that they came to worship further reveals a relationship with God that must have flabbergasted the Jews.

Is it possible that God wants to lead me today and the star is in plain sight but I don't see it? Am I so occupied with myself and my own things that I miss His word, His prompting? Like Herod, do I become so concerned with my kingdom that anyone with a new word is a threat? I think God communicates with us in many ways. Romans 1:20 records, *"From the creation of the world His invisible attributes, that is, His eternal power and divine nature, have been clearly seen, being understood through what He has made. As a result, people are without excuse."* The star is there but we don't see it. The star is there and we see it but don't understand and therefore ignore it.

Oh Lord, am I so in love with You that I see what You want me to see? Do I hear Your whispering voice? Help me Lord, to be like the Magi!

Where's the Excitement?! June 29

Have you ever made an exciting discovery? You go and share your new found information with those who should be interested and their response is unenthusiastic. Instead of them celebrating with you or wanting to learn more, you are met with disinterested head nodding. The test of whether someone really cares about what you care about is their genuine willingness to get involved.

Matthew 2:3-5—When King Herod heard this, he was deeply disturbed, and all Jerusalem with him. So he assembled all the chief priests and scribes of the people and asked them where the Messiah would be born. "In Bethlehem of Judea," they told him, "because this is what was written by the prophet."

Herod was disturbed because his reign was threatened by the emergence of the unexpected King. All he wanted was for the wise men to reveal the location of Jesus so he could destroy Him.

Does anything strike you as odd about the religious leaders? First, unlike Herod, why didn't they join in the excitement of the wise men? As the nation's religious leaders supposedly waiting for the coming Messiah, shouldn't they have been the first to jump with joy? Why didn't they join the search for the One Micah prophesied over 700 years earlier? Unlike the Magi who traveled over 800 difficult miles, all they needed was at most a two hour walk of six miles![38] The fact that they knew Scripture yet were uninterested in accompanying foreign worshipers is quite telling. Either they were skeptical of the reported Savior, or they were smug in their own religiosity. Their actions foreshadowed what Jesus would experience thirty years later.

Never let what God reveals in your heart to be dampened by the skepticism, apathy or opposition of others. If the Lord reveals something new or important, revel in your discovery. Too often we take our cue from the response of people and in the process lose the joy of what the Holy Spirit inspires. Don't be surprised when the people you would expect to support you are the least helpful. If God reveals to you a star, follow it! Thank God the wise men did not take a survey before they decided to mount their camels! You may face ridicule and scorn but your quest is to worship not to be popular. Beware of those with false agendas and those who quote Scripture but have no intent of following it. Take your joy in Jesus and enjoy the journey!

Inspiration ✝✝✝

The word *joy* is in the Bible 182 times.—Beni Johnson in *the Happy Intercessor*

Leadership

June 30

James Kouzes and Barry Posner spent five years investigating the perceptions that followers had of leaders. In every survey they conducted, honesty was the most sought after leader characteristic. Similarly, a leader's trust in others was the single most important behavior. In essence, the best leaders are trustworthy and lead by modeling trust in those who work for them. Competence, forward-looking, and inspirational were the other predominant qualities people look for in their leaders. But what I found most amazing in reading their article, "Leadership Is in the Eye of the Follower," were the following statements:

Successful leadership depends far more on the followers perception of the leader than on the leader's abilities. Followers, not the leader, determine when someone possesses the qualities of leadership. In other words, leadership is in the eye of the follower.

Matthew 4:19,20—"Follow Me," He told them, "and I will make you fish for people!" Immediately they left their nets and followed Him.

What caused Andrew and Peter to leave their livelihood as fisherman to follow Jesus? They saw something in Him that was profoundly credible. Perhaps it was His teaching. Maybe they saw something unique in His disposition and manner. Whatever caught their eye and touched their heart remained forever with them. These men would not just follow Jesus, they would one day willingly and joyfully lay down their lives for Him.

When it comes to leaders, Jesus is the highest point of excellence. The law-obsessed religious leaders vainly tried to find fault in Him. He was perfectly honest. If ever there was a leader who held the right to do everything himself, it was God's Son. Yet, He chose to entrust His life and mission to imperfect followers. He trusted His disciples by giving them authority and then sending them away to drive out evil spirits and to heal every disease and sickness (Mat. 10:1). Before He left for heaven, He formally commissioned His followers to go and make disciples (Mat. 28:19,20). In essence, God trusted His children to carry out His will.

Jesus' ability to teach is unsurpassed. He teaches us how we are to live. He gives us a vision of a permanently restored relationship with God in heaven as a result of the grace He offers us—sin squelching grace! To say He is inspirational would be a huge understatement. Today, all around the globe, people's lives are literally transformed as they place their faith in the Messiah. If leadership is in the eye of the follower, Jesus is unquestionably the greatest leader of all time.

Inspiration † † †

I think Christ is awesome and wants us to be "awesomites."—Dutch Sheets in *Intercessory Prayer*

Billboards

July 1

Matthew 5:16—In the same way, let your light shine before men, so that they may see your good works and give glory to your Father in heaven.

Tigard, Oregon—HOME! Our Plymouth Voyager rolled up 8153 miles drinking over 341 gallons of gas as we traversed 25 states, Washington D.C. and parts of Canada. We weren't able to visit everyone we hoped to see, we got sick and at times I think our three children reached the travel saturation point. But it can be a great thing to be stretched beyond our comfort zone. God was gracious to us and we experienced an unforgettable month visiting relatives and friends and learning more about our nation and its people.

There are many memories that five Yorks will collectively carry from our adventure. One lingering thought pulsates through my mind. One cannot drive across America and not see billboards. They are everywhere. They proclaim a myriad of messages all created with the intent to entice: Visit the famous Wall Drugstore, SD; Fireworks—next exit; Shopper's Paradise; Comfort Inn—24 miles ahead, free HBO, continental breakfast; Drink Miller Lite; Barbie Dolls—adult entertainment; McDonalds; etc.; etc.

Imagine if you were a billboard. What message would people see as they drove by you? It is a challenging thought that people form their opinion of us largely by what they see. If my action consistently broadcasts love for God and for people, then am I not an enticement for God's kingdom? Conversely, if my life is devoted to pleasing my carnal cravings, then am I not a sign promoting ME? The former leads to peace, joy and fulfillment, the latter perpetuates a lifelong quest for meaning.

Hopefully within every town there are people devoted to Jesus. If we all shine for Him, what effect, what influence might we have in a nation of billboards mostly calling for that which will burn?

> *Every day they devoted themselves to meeting together in the temple complex, and broke bread from house to house. They ate their food with a joyful and humble attitude, praising God and having favor with all the people. And every day the Lord added to them those who were being saved. (Acts 2:46,47)*

Inspiration †††

Nothing hinders more the effective witness of the church than inconsistency in the lives of her members.—Robert Coleman in *The Master Plan of Discipleship*

Practice Secret Acts of Kindness

July 2

Matthew 6:1—Be careful not to practice your righteousness in front of people, to be seen by them. Otherwise, you will have no reward from your Father in heaven.

Have you seen the bumper sticker, *Practice Random Acts of Kindness*? Random means there is no specific pattern, purpose, or objective. There is a kernel of profoundness to that pithy saying. The idea is to work at being kind spontaneously. A friend was describing a book to me that he enjoyed. Then, spontaneously, he handed it to me and said, "Please take this. I know you will find it beneficial."

Jesus, knowing the hearts of people, goes even deeper. He tells us in Matthew 6:3,4, to give without our left hand knowing what our right hand is doing. Many randomly give but in such a way that others will notice. Try being good without being observed. There is a covert goodness God sees and rewards. He wants our bumper sticker to read, "Practice Secret Acts of Kindness."

Oswald Chambers noted in *Studies in the Sermon on the Mount*:

Get into the habit of having such a relationship to God that you do good without knowing you do it, then you will no longer trust your own impulse, or your own judgment, you will trust only the inspiration of the Spirit of God. The mainspring of your motives will be the Father's heart, not your own; the Father's understanding, not your own. When once you are rightly related to God, He will use you as a channel through which His disposition will flow.

Inspiration †††

The end result of kindness is that it draws people to you.—Anita Roddick, Founder and CEO, The Body Shop

The Narrow Gate

July 3

Imagine if an angel came to you and said, "I'm giving you ownership of this car lot. You may drive any vehicle you want. There is just one restriction. You must never get behind the wheel of a Saturn LS2. That car is off limits. The day you drive it you will ruin your driving privileges."

Life is great and you enjoy driving a wide variety of cars and trucks. One day, a creature you have never seen before shows up and invites you to test drive the Saturn. You relay to this stranger that the LS2 is off limits. But this creature is persistent. He says you were misinformed, that what the angel meant to say is once you drive the Saturn, nothing else will seem the same, you will be thoroughly enlightened. So what do you do?

Matthew 7:13,14—Enter through the narrow gate. For the gate is wide and the road is broad that leads to destruction, and there are many who go through it. How narrow is the gate and difficult the road that leads to life, and few find it.

In Gen. 2:16,17, God gave Adam and Eve jurisdiction over the entire garden. The only stipulation was that they could not eat from the tree of the knowledge of good and evil. They chose to disobey God and every human since was infected with a sin nature.

Moses challenged the Israelites at Mt. Ebal in Deuteronomy 30:19,20 to choose life by following after God or death by rebelling against Him. They consistently rebelled. Joshua before passing away, called on his promised land kinsman to either fear the Lord and serve Him faithfully or worship the idols of their forefathers or the idols of the Amorites (Jos. 24:14,15). After he died they rapidly embraced idol-worship.

Jeremiah passed on God's instructions to those in Judah to surrender to the Babylonians and live, or resist and die (Jer. 21:8,9). They fought and fell to disease and the sword.

We can make some clear observations about people.
1. People resist absolutes. Rather than prosper by following God's guidance we wilt inside the prison of our own relativism. We despair at the hole in our soul and prefer to fill it with the dirt of our own choosing.
2. Pride to our own detriment is at the core of our resistance. "I don't like being told what I have to do." We focus on the forbidden at the expense of the fabulous so rather than enjoy the forest we obsess on one forbidden tree.

Isn't it amazing that God knowing what He does about us, persists in allowing us the right of choice! He will not take away our free will nor will He coerce obedience. He purposely sacrifices His holy Son to rescue us from our evil state. Enter the small gate. Follow the narrow road—the way marked by persecution and opposition.

We can fault God's way from our ever-present pride and drive down our self-made freeways to hell. Or we can celebrate His awesome love and be redeemed. We can blast God for what is off-limits or praise Him for His grace. Eternal condemnation is a sad outcome when a permanent celebration was clearly available. Open the narrow gate!

Inspiration † † †

Beware of turning your back on what you know is true because you do not want it to be real. Jesus Christ never says that a man is damned because he is a sinner; the condemnation is when a man sees what Jesus Christ came to do and will not let Him do it.—Oswald Chambers in *The Servant As His Lord*

Insecurity

July 4

National holidays provide a natural period for introspection. As we approach another celebration of our nation's independence, I think this year of the word insecurity. In the 1770's when our forefathers fought for the freedom we celebrate today, they lived in a time of great tumult. Consider this: they faced an opponent far superior in wealth and military might; they knew starvation, harsh weather and disease; they lacked basic supplies in armament, clothing and food; and they did not always know who was truly for or against them. But in the midst of great challenges the trumpet call for liberty persisted. Men and women strove mightily to protect their foundation of freedom. For self-determination, insecure lives bled nobly; though pained, pilgrims refused to give up; trepidation clung to truth and the right to dispel tyranny.

The stock market dropped over 220 points in reaction to news of the highest unemployment rate (9.4%) in 26 years. The Labor Department reported that employers cut 467,000 jobs in June, on top of the 322,000 jobs lost in May. Many wonder if the recent swine flu pandemic is the precursor to a global health disaster. Televisions display bizarre weather patterns as states battle prolonged drought, tornadoes and flooding. While our challenges are different in some ways from those of America's first citizens on July 4, 1776, they are also eerily familiar. Insecurity is not confined to one generation it is passed forward without regard to race, position or creed.

Psalm 4:8—I will both lie down and sleep in peace, for You alone, LORD, make me live in safety.
7:10—My shield is with God, who saves the upright in heart.
18:2—The LORD is my rock, my fortress, and my deliverer, my God, my mountain where I seek refuge, my shield and the horn of my salvation, my stronghold.

On this day celebrating independence, let us be certain that while we face challenges, we are also *uncommonly* blessed. Even in the midst of oppression which rages like some uncontrolled forest fire, we have a future through Jesus that is permanent and safe. We are able to worship God. We are adorned with hope and mostly able to sleep in the peace that surpasses understanding. In the soil of insecurity, our roots remain fed by grace. Don't let the times fool you and don't fool with the times—stay secure in Jesus. Happy Fourth of July!

Inspiration † † †

Search the organization for an alert, aggressive, gifted young man who could someday step into my shoes. And when you find him, fire him!"— Memo from a Company President from *Leaders Who Last* by Dave Kraft

Getting Away

July 5

Matthew 14:13—When Jesus heard about it, He withdrew from there by boat to a remote place to be alone. When the crowds heard this, they followed Him on foot from the towns.

John the Baptist was beheaded, and his disciples, after recovering his body for burial, came and reported his death to Jesus. Matthew's gospel gives us some insight into the fact that this news weighed heavily on Jesus and He felt the immediate need to get away. Imagine how He must have felt when the boat comes to shore and there is a crowd waiting for Him! Have you ever had the flu and had unexpected company arrive the same day? Have you ever lost your job only to receive a call from your children that you are needed to chaperone a party that night for a hundred kids?

Because Jesus was wholeheartedly committed to reaching people, when He saw the huge crowd, He felt compassion for them. Instead of feeling sorry for His own inability to be left alone to grieve, He healed their sick and in one of His most famous miracles, fed over 5000 people from five loaves of bread and two fish. This is where most preachers end the story—they laud Jesus for His incredible love for people at a time when He was emotionally fatigued.

But the story is not over. After dismissing the crowds, Jesus did not jump in the boat with His disciples and return with them home. Instead of giving up on personal time, *"He went up on the mountain by Himself to pray"* (14:23). He spent hours with His Father decompressing, perhaps unburdening His heart or shedding tears for John. The perfect Minister needed a break and took it.

Beware of making ministry more important than spending time alone with God. There will never be a shortage of sick or hungry people. When the Holy Spirit leads you, help them; just remember that dismissal is also a part of ministry. All of us need time to get away to be alone with God. Refreshment, strengthening, wisdom and peace come from His presence. Don't be afraid to climb the mountain to meet with God and miss the boat.

Prayer Walks

July 6

The idea came to life on a mountain in northern Idaho. Dad's high blood pressure meant he either took prescribed drugs or exercised. He chose the latter. So, five days a week he hikes trails and roads that at points are ridiculously steep but altogether invigorating! One day while walking the Lord whispered that he might also pray!

Matthew 18:19,20—Again, I assure you: If two of you on earth agree about any matter that you pray for, it will be done for you by My Father in heaven. For where two or three are gathered together in My name, I am there among them.

What began in Idaho spread to India. Dad awoke early each morning and walked around a nearby field to pray. He invited men from Cochin to join him. In groups of three they walked and interceded. The man in the middle prayed (so each person could hear) for a minute or two and then moved to the side to be replaced by another prayer warrior. As more people came to pray, new lines formed and then shifted in composition so that men could pray with different men but always in little groups of two or three.

Prayer walking spread to Kenya, Uganda, Benin and Nigeria. Pastor Shikokoti in Eldoret and Pastor Joel in Jos sent us wonderful reports of people praying! Whenever our **First Cause** team enters a new land we will initiate and model prayer walks. The idea is to establish a habit that will endure after we leave.

God delights in answering prayer! He promises that where we are gathered together in His name, He walks with us! Prayer walks keep us focused on our objective—raising up mature followers of Jesus. And because each person has different thoughts, many topics and needs are brought before the Lord as well as praise, adoration and confession. We are mutually encouraged as we lift our hearts to heaven. We grow more sensitive to the needs around us. We find our bonds of love are strengthened. We put the enemy to flight and build faith in the process. The community is encouraged by our example. Even our bodies are strengthened physically by exercising.

The key to building strong Jesus-followers begins, continues and extends through prayer. Why not encourage others to join you in the same exercise? You won't regret it and who knows what God might do in your life as you ask Him!

Inspiration † † †

Prayer was the means by which the power of Satan can be overthrown and the kingdom of God advanced.—John Calvin

Creeds

July 7

A boy, frustrated with all the rules he had to follow, asked his father, "Dad, how soon will I be old enough to do as I please?"

The father answered immediately, "I don't know. Nobody has lived that long yet."[39]

Matthew 23:23,24—Woe to you, scribes and Pharisees, hypocrites! You pay a tenth of mint, dill, and cumin, yet you have neglected the more important matters of the law—justice, mercy, and faith. These things should have been done without neglecting the others. Blind guides! You strain out a gnat, yet gulp down a camel!

The *American Heritage Dictionary* defines a creed as "1. A formal statement of religious belief; a confession of faith. 2. A system of belief, principles, or opinions." It is not the first definition that causes us trouble—we need to know and stand true to what we believe. It is the second definition that invites trouble. Bruxy Cavey wrote in *The End Of Religion*, "Religion uses *rules* to force our steps, *guilt* to keep us in line, and *rituals* to remind us of our failure to live up to those rules. In doing this, religion adds more weight to those who are already burdened with life's hardships."[40]

Jesus blasted the religious leaders of His day. They were more concerned with their beliefs, principles and opinions than in leading people to God. Jeanne Guyon noted in *Experiencing the Depths of Jesus Christ*, "Burdening the new Christian with countless rules and all sorts of standards does not help him grow in Christ."[41]

Find a person absorbed with petty rules and most likely you see a curmudgeon. True joy comes in worshiping Jesus, not one's religious views. By following Him we become runway lights marking for seekers the way to a safe landing. By following creeds we become bug lights—instruments not of grace but of zapping. In addition as Jack Deere points out in *Surprised By The Power Of The Spirit*, "If the essence of the Christian life becomes conformity to rules, we will always be led into self-righteousness." Let's get wrapped around Jesus!

Inspiration † † †

A Christian is to be consistent only to the life of the Son of God in him, not consistent to hard and fast creeds. Men pour themselves into creeds, and God Almighty has to blast them out of their prejudices before they become devoted to Jesus Christ.—Oswald Chambers in *Studies on the Sermon on the Mount*.

Living off Small Strips

July 8

My friend Brian shared an interesting vignette about a Romanian village. Thousands of fertile acres surround the town yet the people cultivate only small strips to grow what they can eat. Decades of communist oppression and the lack of modern farm equipment rob these wonderful people of vision. Their concept of what they can attain in the future is shaped by what they could not do in the past.

I wonder how many of us have a false estimate of what God can do in our lives. We look at sin that seems unbeatable. We think of hardships that occur when we've tried to follow God or the unfair treatment we've received at the hands of those who misrepresent His authority. Our Father wants to bless us with abundant fruit but we only give Him a small strip on which to plant.

Matthew 25:24,25—Then the man who had received one talent also approached and said, "Master, I know you. You're a difficult man, reaping where you haven't sown and gathering where you haven't scattered seed. So I was afraid and went off and hid your talent in the ground. Look, you have what is yours.

The man who hid his talent was probably not a bad guy. He was most likely an ordinary person like you or I. But somewhere along the way of life he got lost. He set his eyes on the perceived hardness of his master and let fear become his guiding plight. Just as the villagers cannot see the possibility of plantations, he could not see the reality of succeeding in business. Consequently, he lost the blessing.

Friend, Jesus said, *"You did not choose Me, but I chose you. I appointed you that you should go out and produce fruit and that your fruit should remain, so that whatever you ask the Father in My name, He will give you"* (John 15:16). God's estimate of you is not based on what you can or cannot do but on what He has already done. He chose you. He loves you. He's waiting for you to follow His lead. Your capacity is to be carved in faith not in flesh. The Apostle Paul wrote, *"I am able to do all things through Him who strengthens me"* (Php. 4:13). Paul based his estimate on what he could accomplish by the power of Christ!

Inspiration † † †

We estimate by what a man possesses; God's only concern is what a man is.—Oswald Chambers in *Notes On Isaiah*

Jed July 9

Jed* is disturbed by the actions and beliefs of people who call themselves Christians. He disdains the notion of putting his faith in the Lord. Yet, as argumentative as he is, he loves to engage in conversation about God and what the Bible says. Jed is sort of an odd bird. People don't tend to get along with him. I found early on that his mouth goes far beyond where my ears want to go and he doesn't take hints real well. But the Lord began to convict me for my lack of patience with Jed. Rather than engage him in conversation, I was too quick to try and avoid him. I had to learn to put aside my agenda and listen. Gradually, he began to open up about things that caused him pain. Because I took time to befriend him, he went out of his way to help me in my job. The day will come when I believe Jed will give his heart to Jesus. I suspect most of his arguing is a smokescreen to avoid having to yield his life to the Lord.

Mark 6:19,20—So Herodias held a grudge against him and wanted to kill him. But she could not, because Herod was in awe of John and was protecting him, knowing he was a righteous and holy man. When Herod heard him he would be very disturbed, yet would hear him gladly.

I wonder what John the Baptist thought of King Herod? Herod threw him in prison because Herod's wife Herodias wanted John dead. This was because John told Herod, "*It is not lawful for you to have your brother's wife!*" (6:18). Yet the sinner admired the saint and took the time to engage him in conversation. Who knows what the two of them talked about behind cell walls? Even though the truth greatly bothered him, Herod evidently looked forward to his talks with the prophet.

George Barna in *Growing True Disciples*, wrote:
Indisputably, evangelism is not a priority to most Christians. Less than one out of ten said that they have ever intentionally built a relationship with someone in the hope of being able to lead the person to Christ. Fewer than one of every five believers claimed to know a non-Christian well enough to share their faith with that individual in a context of trust and credibility.[42]

Do we go out of our away to avoid sharing truth with those who disturb us or seem bent on sinning? As best we can tell, Herod rejected John's message but that did not stop Jesus' cousin from sharing. If we neglect sharing with spiritual antagonists, we may avoid losing our head, but for sure we will not gain any hearts. Better to be jailed for telling the truth than to be free and to say nothing.

*Not his real name

The Ghost   July 10

When I look back on my life, one of the scariest memories I have was the time I was rock climbing. Somehow I got into a position where I was stuck. I was frozen to a giant slab of granite knowing I had to move but scared that if I lost my grip, I would plummet far enough that my chances of getting badly hurt were considerable. I still remember asking for God's help and for the immediate peace that came over me as He answered.

Mark 6:49,50—When they saw Him walking on the sea, they thought it was a ghost and cried out; for they all saw Him and were terrified. Immediately He spoke with them and said, "Have courage! It is I. Don't be afraid."

It is easy to question the disciples' mettle as we read about them from our sophisticated twenty-first century perch. We wonder how they could be terrified; after all, who really believes in ghosts? But think for a second. How would you feel at three in the morning rowing against battering waves if a figure came walking towards you on waves? I suspect there would be some screaming.

Never be afraid of fear. Fear is a natural first response to the unnatural. For example, a warrior being shot at *should* feel a certain amount of alarm. That surge of adrenalin that pulsates in the face of danger quickens the mind. Luke does not write that Jesus rebuked the disciples for being afraid or lectured them on the absurdity of ghosts. He identified Himself. He gave them courage.

God understands when you are afraid. The question is what will you let fear do in you? If it immobilizes you or causes panic, by all means cry out to Him. Remaining on the path of fright, clinging to apprehension will not bring victory. Saints walk in the assured trust that they can always cry out to the Lord. In times of quavering we need to ask God to reveal Himself. What we fear may be Him, what we cannot see He can reveal. In Him we find our courage.

Inspiration ✝✝✝

Courage never takes away fear; courage simply redistributes fear to get the job done.—Dan Allender in *Leading With A Limp*

Interference

July 11

We are watching the big game and all of a sudden the screen gets blotchy and the picture is terrible. Something is interfering with the signal. I hate it when that happens!

God is doing a wonderful work in the life of one of His children. He is allowing suffering to take place because He is building character. But we in our humanness miss what He is doing. We assume that we know best. So we step in to "fix" whatever is going wrong. In the process we hinder what God is trying to do. I wonder if the angels "hate it when that happens".

Mark 10:14—When Jesus saw it, He was indignant and said to them, "Let the little children come to Me. Don't stop them, for the kingdom of God belongs to such as these."

Before you or I go interfering in the lives of those around us we must be certain that we are led by the Holy Spirit and not our own overweighed sense of mercy or duty. If the chrysalis is prematurely opened, the butterfly will die. It will never fly for its wings will not have attained the strength God meant the cocoon to develop. Likewise, if we attempt surgery on the lives of people we love to help them, we may in fact harm them. God did not make us Holy spirits but Homo sapiens. There is a difference.

Do you know someone struggling? Offer to pray. Extend as much love and kindness as you can. But only take action in accordance with the leading and blessing of the Holy Spirit. I thank God as I look back in my life, for those people who were wise enough to let me struggle, who refused to prematurely bail me out.

Are you struggling? Are you tempted to fabricate some shortcut to alleviate your circumstances? What we see as bad, God may see for our good. Trust in the One who will never leave you or forsake you.

Inspiration † † †

The fear of the Lord will keep us from compromising God's truth for the pursuit of personal gain.—John Bevere in *The Fear of the Lord*

Generous Peruvians   July 12

Felipe dresses up as a clown. Each Sunday, he and his team of fellow youth workers from Iglesia Misionera Evangelica (I.M.E.), go to the poorest sections of Cerro de Pasco to minister to the children. As many as 40-60 kids come out to watch the antics of Bomba the clown, to sing and dance to Christian music and hear Bible stories. Wonderful boys and girls glow with expectant smiles. Their lungs produce hearty cheers and sweet melodies. They held on to us with forever-loving grips. In truth, they ministered to our team more than we did to them.

Underlying each I.M.E. church is a strong commitment to missions. I have rarely encountered a group of churches as zealous about reaching the world with the gospel as I witnessed in each I.M.E. congregation. In Cerro de Pasco, even the poorest of the poor passionately understand God's command to share the saving news of Jesus globally. Youngsters find ways to save money and then bring what they have to the church to support missionaries most have never met. They prove Mother Teresa's words, "The more you have the less you can give, and the less you have the more you can give."

Mark 12:42-44—And a poor widow came and dropped in two tiny coins worth very little. Summoning His disciples, He said to them, "I assure you: This poor widow has put in more than all those giving to the temple treasury. For they all gave out of their surplus, but she out of her poverty has put in everything she possessed—all she had to live on."

Little boys and girls gladly give what they have to further God's work. I can just see Jesus pointing to His angels and saying, "Look friends what my sons and daughters in Cerro de Pasco are doing!" Generous hearts reveal faith, humility and selflessness. It was your generosity that sent us to Peru. It is the giving hearts of Peruvian children that are making a difference around the world. God takes their small gifts and multiplies them like Jesus breaking five loaves and two fishes to feed thousands. Whenever you give to further God's kingdom, you make an eternal investment. In heaven you will be rewarded beyond your wildest dreams.

Inspiration ✝✝✝

Giving with glad and generous hearts has a way of routing out the tough old miser within us. Even the poor need to know that they can give. Just the very act of letting go of money, or some other treasure, does something within us. It destroys the demon greed.—Richard J. Foster in *Money, Sex & Power*

Prove Yourself! — July 13

Sergeant Major Cedric Moore shared with me his story as we sat in his car at Fort Monroe, Virginia. Raised in a black community in Huntsville, Alabama, he often attended church and had uncles who were pastors. But what these men preached was not what they lived. Watching "spiritual" men engage in adultery, robbery, lying and other sinful behavior caused Cedric to conclude that God must not be real.

While attending college in Birmingham, Cedric was exposed to Black Muslims who gave him literature and tapes in order to recruit him. At first he was interested but the more he investigated them the more he realized that they were just as racist as the KKK. Two years into his education but out of money, he had to drop out. He did not want his mother to have to go to work to pay for his education so he joined the Army. On his dog tags he listed, "No Religious Preference."

Stationed at Fort Bragg, several people asked Cedric to go with them to church. Most often he brushed them off wanting nothing to do with Christians. One day, frustrated and wondering what even gave people the desire to live, he said, "God, if you are real, You have to prove yourself to me." Later that day, a white stranger invited him to church. Cedric told him he would not go to church with him. But then, convicted by his rudeness, he called after the man, "If you have a service tonight, I will go with you." To his surprise, the man turned, smiled and said, "Great, we have a service at 7:30 and I'll pick you up at 7:00." Because he was a man of his word, Cedric went to church.

That night, for the first time, Cedric experienced interracial worship. He watched a white preacher whose face reddened as he spoke with intensity. As he listened, the pastor said, "Some of you here tonight have told God that to believe in Him He must prove Himself real to you. But if you want to know God, you must prove yourself real to Him!" Stunned by the words he knew were from heaven, he walked down the aisle and gave his life to Christ.

Mark 15:39—When the centurion, who was standing opposite Him, saw the way He breathed His last, he said, "This man really was God's Son!"

A Roman centurion experienced an earthquake and saw inexplicable things associated with Jesus' crucifixion. He watched the way Jesus died and concluded the Son of Man really was the Son of God. He had to come to his own conclusion. God gave him all the evidence He needed.

Inspiration † † †

Faith is not believing in spite of the evidence; it is obeying in spite of the consequences.—Chuck Missler

A Mother's Milk

July 14

Did you know that God designed a formula that no one has ever replicated? Dr. Marianne Neifert writes, "Human milk is nature's perfect design for helping your baby's body and brain grow and develop. No formula can be made exactly the same as human milk because we do not know all the ingredients of human milk."[43] Of course we know it is God and not nature who designed the perfect beverage! He also created a formula with hidden benefits. Nursing causes the body to release a hormone called oxytocin which enables the uterus to return to its normal size after delivery. Nursing burns calories which help moms shed the extra pounds gained during pregnancy. Nursing also creates a strong psychological bond which emotionally strengthens both the mother and her infant.

Luke 1:46-49—And Mary said: My soul proclaims the greatness of the Lord, and my spirit has rejoiced in God my Savior, because He has looked with favor on the humble condition of His slave. Surely, from now on all generations will call me blessed, because the Mighty One has done great things for me, and His name is holy.

God provided the means for a mother to give milk to physically help her baby and to recover from a fairly traumatic exercise called labor. Aside from His infant formula, He has given us many prescriptions to help us grow. In Luke 1:46-55 we find Mary's song, called the Magnificat, or what I call the Glorifying Formula. Let's take note of the pattern in Mary's song and the benefits we obtain when we follow her example.

Glorifying Formula
1. Mary glorified God recognizing His attributes—a holy name, mercy, power, compassion and faithfulness to His promises—vv. 46, 49-55. By giving credit to God we take our focus off our problems, promote humility and align our heart with heaven. We look forward to receiving the reward He gives to those who reverence His name (Rev. 11:18).
2. Mary's spirit rejoiced in God her Savior—v. 47. To rejoice means to be delighted! As laughter is medicine to the soul so rejoicing is a powerful blessing to us and to God.
3. Mary recognized what God did for her—vv. 48, 49. Gratitude is a reflective process that appreciates God's actions on our behalf. Thankful reflecting draws us closer to Him and puts life in the right perspective.

Are you nourished by the One who loves you? Join Mary in giving Him the glory and let Him fill your hunger with good things.

Overwhelmed   July 15

"I want to know You. Let Your Spirit overwhelm me. Let Your presence take over my heart." Repeatedly the worship leader led us in singing those 17 words that, if analyzed, meant far more than we could imagine.

"I want to know You." Ayn Rand wrote in *Atlas Shrugged*, "To live, man must hold three things as the supreme and ruling values of his life: Reason—Purpose—Self Esteem."[44] Ayn's god was the mind and she had no place for God. I've seen enough of what man does with reason, purpose and self esteem—without God the recipe creates disaster. I want to know God, the Maker of the Universe and mind Designer. Knowing anything else is inadequate and unfulfilling.

"Let Your Spirit overwhelm me." Typically, when we use the word *overwhelm*, the context is negative. The origin of this word traces to England in the 1520s or earlier. *Whelm* means to submerge; engulf or to overcome utterly. To overwhelm is to turn upside down. Picture a boat washed over by a large wave.[45] To ask the Holy Spirit to overwhelm me, is to request that He turn me upside down—empty me of what I hold to or whatever distracts me.

Let "Your presence take over my heart." No hurting business looks forward to a hostile takeover. But what human, hurting or healthy, would not stand up and cheer if he or she truly knew what it meant to have the heart be taken over and Lord-led.

Luke 1:57,58—Now the time had come for Elizabeth to give birth, and she had a son. Then her neighbors and relatives heard that the Lord had shown her His great mercy, and they rejoiced with her.

The phrase "*had shown her His great mercy*," literally means *the Lord magnified His mercy with her,*[46] He overwhelmed her! Discontented in her own barrenness, Elizabeth watched God turn her old life upside down and bless her with a child. "*The Lord has done this for me. He has looked with favor in these days to take away my disgrace among the people*" (1:25). God's wave of mercy to Elizabeth in giving her a son-messenger was an improbable blessing which prepared the way for His tidal wave of grace—the gift of His Son, our Savior! Overwhelmed? *God, let it be so—with You, with You, with You!*

Inspiration ✝✝✝

I offer to a merciful God at the close of this year my humble tribute of gratitude for the blessings with which He has, in the course of it, favored me and those dear to me . . . —John Quincy Adams

I Will Be Yours   July 16

Luke 2:29-32—Now, Master, You can dismiss Your slave in peace, as You promised. For my eyes have seen Your salvation. You have prepared it in the presence of all peoples—a light for revelation to the Gentiles and glory to Your people Israel.

    Simeon was an old man to whom the Holy Spirit promised that he would not die before seeing the Lord's Messiah (v. 26). Imagine the welling joy that traversed his veins as he beheld baby Jesus. What great tenderness and love must have flowed from his hands to the perfect child he held.
    Missionary Jim Elliot prayed, "God, I pray light up these idle sticks of my life and may I burn up for Thee. Consume my life, My God, for it is Thine. I seek not a long life but a full one like yours, Lord Jesus."[47] Simeon lived a long life waiting to see the Savior. Jim's life was tragically cut short attempting to share his Savior with the Waodani people of Ecuador.[48] Yet it is not the length of our life that matters so much as the consecration. When I think of these two men's zeal to follow God, I am inspired to pray to God, "*I Will Be Yours.*"

You are my God, You are my Lord, and I will be Yours, I will be Yours.

When I rise in the morning, I will search for Your face.
You are more than a longing, every breath that I take.
You're the Maker of mountains and the highest of lore,
You're the Song of the silence, You're the Praise in the roar!

When I stand in Your presence with my hands full of grace,
From my soul comes this worship for You in this place.
You're the healing Redeemer, You're the Truth and the Call
You're the Word and the Promise and I give You my all!

You are my God, You are my Lord, and I will be Yours, I will be Yours.

Inspiration ✝✝✝
    Praise is the honey of life which a devout heart extracts from every bloom of providence and grace.—Charles H. Spurgeon

Watching Him Closely   July 17

Whenever Lee takes a new job, one of his first acts is to publically share with those he will be serving his faith in Jesus as his Savior and the priority He holds in his life. There are several reasons Lee does this. First, Jesus said in Matthew 10:32, *"Therefore, everyone who will acknowledge Me before men, I will also acknowledge him before My Father in heaven."* Second, by stating his conviction upfront, Lee makes himself accountable. If he acts or speaks in a way incongruent with Jesus, those who work for him are quick to point out his error. This also helps kill the temptation for him to do anything that might discredit God. Third, by sharing his faith, opportunities arise for Lee to help those who are struggling and who would like prayer, counsel, or information how they too can follow Christ.

Some employees do not like it that Lee makes public his testimony. They will look for ways to discredit him or to accuse him of proselytizing as he lives out his convictions. The challenge for Lee is to maintain his composure and not retaliate or be discouraged by those who question his every move.

Luke 6:7—The scribes and Pharisees were watching Him closely, to see if He would heal on the Sabbath, so that they could find a charge against Him.

Imagine how frustrated Jesus must have felt with the religious leaders. Instead of cheering when He healed a man's paralyzed hand, they got angry! They were so concerned with their picky laws they could not celebrate miracles. They did not spend time with Jesus to learn from Him. They followed Him so as to scrutinize His every action and charge Him for any wrong move. They watched without learning and observed without caring. Their problem was their allegiance—they spent time with the Savior serving Satan's agenda.

Robert Coleman wrote in *The Master Plan of Evangelism*, "People are looking for a demonstration, not an explanation."[49] Are you willing, like Lee, to let your every move be watched knowing that some simply hope you will err so they can harm you? Often it is those we would think would appreciate our values who are the first to cast stones. Don't despair. Jesus did not stop ministering because He did not have the approval of the religious elite. He was following His Father's agenda. Nor did He take on a martyr's complex. We can become so proud of the fact that we are picked on, that we make our reputation more important than our mission. Jesus did not let this happen. When we identify with Christ, He blesses us. We may find opposition and trouble on earth, but in heaven we will reap the reward of an approving Father!

Inspiration ☨ ☨ ☨

God forbid that I should travel with anybody a quarter of an hour without speaking of Christ to them.—Jack Wyrtzen

Meet Manasseh   July 18

Meet Manasseh Wakawa. He is one of the most fruitful men I have ever met and his heart for the Lord is expansive. He is a powerful example of why spiritual trainers are so vital to the Kingdom of God.

Manasseh ran away from home to find a new life in a bigger city. In 1971, he happened to be in a large church when a Nigerian government official spoke about those who had departed from following Jesus. Manasseh's dad was a pastor and his family full of Christians so he thought the speaker was talking directly to him. After the message he approached him and said, "It seemed you were talking about me." The speaker asked him why he felt this way and upon hearing Manasseh's activities, told him to repent. Wakawa began going to the official's home to talk. One day the official showed him the *Four Spiritual Laws*. He realized his spiritual bankruptcy and in 1972, he asked the Lord to become his Savior. Manasseh was so hungry he devoured Scripture and prayed and soon the Lord blessed him with a solid assurance of salvation.

God called Wakawa to preach the gospel in Nigeria. He did not have much education and felt inferior. So, he argued with God that he was not capable of preaching. Still the persistent voice of the Holy Spirit told him to write down his calling and to take it to his spiritual father. Manasseh obeyed and the government official with joy affirmed his new direction.

As Manasseh actively shared his faith countless people came to Christ, many of whom he then trained. During this time, a friend introduced him to Campus Crusade for Christ in Jos and he ended up serving on staff with them for five years. Later he attended Lexington Baptist College in Kentucky, where he received a B.A. in Biblical Studies. After graduating, he returned to minister in Maiduguri of Borno State, a dangerous Muslim area where he grew up. God blessed his efforts there and then called him to further his education. So he earned a double Masters Degree in Biblical studies and in Christian Education at Ashland Theological Seminary in Ashland Ohio. Manasseh returned to Nigeria in 1997. Since then, he has faithfully led people to the Lord and ministered to them.

Luke 6:39-40—He also told them a parable: "Can the blind guide the blind? Won't they both fall into a pit? A disciple is not above his teacher, but everyone who is fully trained will be like his teacher."

The mark of a *great* trainer is to raise up students who not only learn but are capable of in turn replicating what they have learned. While ministering in Jos, our team was impressed by the number of spiritual leaders we met who were trained by one legendary figure called Wakawa. This humble, 56 year-old man has over a 100-trained people serving Jesus in Africa and in the U.S. It was no surprise to us that his favorite Bible passage is 2 Timothy 2:2—*"And what you have heard from me in the presence of many witnesses, commit to faithful men who will be able to teach others also."*

Inspiration † † †

Highly trained men in extraordinarily dangerous circumstances are less likely to break down than untrained men in little danger.—Sebastian Junger in *War*

Building the Foundation   July 19

Luke 6:47,48—I will show you what someone is like who comes to Me, hears My words, and acts on them: He is like a man building a house, who dug deep and laid the foundation on the rock. When the flood came, the river crashed against that house and couldn't shake it, because it was well built.

No doubt you have heard the parable of the wise and foolish builders. I remember as a child singing the song "The wise man built his house upon the rock . . ." Most messages I have heard on this parable focus on the comparison between the two builders and the obvious need to build our foundation on Jesus the Rock. But what is often missed in the passage above is the first sentence. To build a successful foundation one must apply three critical steps.

First, we must come to Jesus. Watchman Nee in his book, *Spiritual Authority*, wrote:

> The acts of God issue from His throne, and His throne is established on His authority . . . Authority is a tremendous thing in the universe—nothing overshadows it. It is therefore imperative for us who desire to serve God to know the authority of God.[50]

We disobey God's authority if we don't come to His Son. Left to our own devices our nature takes over and we immediately head to trouble. Some of you are trying to live life on your terms, by your own strength. It won't work—the moment you leave or ignore Jesus you replace rock with sand and you should not be surprised when every wind of adversity and rain of testing blows you down and dampens your joy. Jesus showed us what we should do by His own example. In John 12:50, He said, *"I know that His command is eternal life. So the things that I speak, I speak just as the Father has told Me."* Jesus came to the Father; we are to come to Him.

Second, we must hear His words. Jesus' expectation is that we <u>value</u> what He says. Any good builder will tell us that if we want to put together a sound structure, we must follow a blueprint. God's Word is our blueprint for building! He has the perfect plan. Do we take it for granted and haphazardly pay attention, or do we take it for granite and build a holy monument?

Finally, we put God's word into practice. *"But be doers of the word and not hearers only, deceiving yourselves"* (Jam. 1:22). Hearing is not the same thing as doing. Scripture finds meaning when we hear, read, study, memorize, and reflect so as to apply its wisdom and nourishment. *"Even more, those who hear the word of God and keep it are blessed!"* (Luke 11:28). *"If you know these things, you are blessed if you do them"* (John 13:17). When the floods come and torrents strike, be gratefully unshakeable!

Proclaiming

July 20

John Thornbury wrote about David Brainerd in *Five Pioneer Missionaries*, "The few women and children who formed his first congregations were so much interested that they travelled as far as fifteen miles in a day to tell others of the white man who spoke of Jesus the Savior."[51]

Luke 8:1—After this, Jesus traveled about from one town and village to another, proclaiming the good news of the kingdom of God. (NIV)

The word *proclaiming* in the verse above comes from the Greek word, *evangelizo* from which we get the word *evangelize*. The Bible is replete with proclamation. Over 86 times the English word *proclaim* in some form recognizes God, His works, His Word, His attributes and most incredibly for us, the good news of Jesus Christ and the salvation He brings us. Prophets proclaimed Jesus' coming. Kings shared God's endearing qualities. Leaders like Moses and Joshua testified to the power of God's word. The Bible is truly a book of proclamations thus it was natural for Jesus to travel throughout Israel proclaiming the good news of God's kingdom. After all, the Word was modeling the word.

You and I cannot be reminded enough of our sacred responsibility to proclaim what we know and have experienced. Good news was never meant to be stored in jars of clay. God did not make us to be vases. He made us to be candles. We are to burn every day the light of Jesus; fragrant aromas of salvation from eternal wicks fashioned joyfully by the Father of all. Too often we extinguish our wicks because we don't feel like shining. But God's plan was never fashioned upon our feelings but rather His will. It is interesting that when we shine in obedience, we also experience deeper joy.

Too often we don't proclaim because we are not sure what to say. But the greatest truth we have to share is the truth of what God is doing in our lives. If we will share our story, we have ample opportunity to proclaim His glory. The power of the gospel is our Father working our sanctification. If we are obeying Him, our lives are being transformed, we have purpose in living and we have a story to tell. Unless we speak how will a hungry world hear?

Inspiration † † †

Indisputably, evangelism is not a priority to most Christians . . . Fewer than one of every five believers claimed to know a non-Christian well enough to share their faith with that individual in a context of trust and credibility.— George Barna in *Growing True Disciples*

Down to Hades

Luke 10:15—And you, Capernaum, will you be exalted to heaven? No, you will go down to Hades!

"Jesus spent more time in ministry in Capernaum than anywhere else in Galilee. Yet, in their arrogance, the people of this city rejected Jesus and, as a result of their unbelief, would be sent to Hades,"[52] that site of death and punishment beyond the tomb. How remarkable that the perfect Minister suffered such imperfect results. How disturbing that the One with astounding miraculous powers would find among His countrymen skeptical hearts. How sick that the seeing were blind and the hearers were deaf to the Deliverer of grace and His message of life. The Messiah must have shaken His head in disbelief at their rigid hearts. Yet there are many lessons to glean from the Master's warning to the unrepentant.

Jesus did not proclaim hope for the town He understood so well. He knew their hearts. To proclaim goodness to those who refuse grace and to pronounce blessing to those who prefer sin is like giving doughnuts to a diabetic. If a man will not stomach Jesus, don't feed him platitudes, warn him of dire consequences.

Jesus did not hesitate to pronounce doom. He would be followed by His disciples who would be further armed with the great news of His resurrection. Yet they too experienced rebuff. Capernaum rejected the Son of God thereby scorning His Father who sent Him (vv. 13-16).

Jesus invested in that seaside town in Naphtali with anemic results. We ought not to be so discouraged when fruit does not follow our sweat, tears and love. Believe Jesus' words, *"How narrow is the gate and difficult the road that leads to life, and few find it"* (Mat. 7:14). Stop pouring water in a cup the Lord reveals to be cracked. Does this mean we leave Capernaum? Ask God. Do what He says and leave the results to Him.

We spend too much time fearing sorry results and the harm it may bring our reputation when our strength and purpose should be in the Lord. It is a tragic thing to live among the unrepentant. It is terrible to watch those we care about snub their Savior. This ought to make us mourn and be devoted to prayer. The wide road down to Hades is built on the stones of rebellion. Plead with Jesus that your town will not be one of its mileposts.

Inspiration † † †

I willingly believe that the damned are, in one sense, successful rebels to the end; that the doors of hell are locked on the inside.—C.S. Lewis in *The Problem of Pain*

Panya

July 22

In the early fall of 1976, homesick Panya Sawan walked the streets of Newberg, Oregon. While his feet moved, his mind questioned if he made a big mistake. Yet, as much as he missed his family, the thought of returning to his Thailand home was equally painful. Would his family consider him a failure?

Panya was invited to the U.S. by his American English teacher. At the age of twenty-one he left his country to attend George Fox University. But he had no friends in this quaint Quaker town and his English was too weak to understand much of what his instructors taught.

One October day, he walked into a small bank to open an account. A woman named Mary asked him why he looked so sad. He must have sensed genuineness in her voice for he proceeded to share with her his circumstances. Then the bank worker did a most amazing thing. She invited him to her home. Mary, and her husband Peter, gave Panya his own room. This childless couple asked him to be their son. They loved him and helped him persevere through his studies.

Peter is no longer alive. Mary recently lost a leg to cancer. But once a month, Panya flew from California to stay with his 82 year-old adopted mother. This Oakland policeman, husband, and father of two daughters, has not forgotten the kindness of a woman who after observing his need, reached out and helped him. Now he cares for her.

Luke 10:33,34—But a Samaritan on his journey came up to him, and when he saw the man, he had compassion. He went over to him and bandaged his wounds, pouring on olive oil and wine. Then he put him on his own animal, brought him to an inn, and took care of him.

Have you ever studied the word *observant*? The prefix *ob* is Latin, meaning "to turn toward." The Latin suffix *ant* means to promote or cause an action. To be observant implies turning towards performing an action. Mary, like the Good Samaritan in Jesus' parable, observed a man's condition and took action. She didn't just create a bank account for Panya, she opened a heart account. Be observant! God wants to use you to make a tangible difference in people's lives. The question is—what are you seeing?

Inspiration ✝✝✝

The way we treat our neighbor is the way we treat God.—Author Unknown

Crystallize

July 23

When we think of crystals, we usually think of beautiful clear objects. The process of crystallizing according to *The American Heritage Dictionary* means "to take on a definite, precise, and usually permanent form."

Luke 11:34—Your eye is the lamp of the body. When your eye is good, your whole body is also full of light. But when it is bad, your body is also full of darkness.

How are you crystallizing? What definite, precise and permanent form are you becoming? Jesus told His listeners that the eye was the lamp to their body. What we focus our eyes upon helps determine what form we will assume. Now I'm not suggesting we go out and buy a westernized picture of Jesus and stare at it all day. But maybe we should evaluate what draws our attention and therefore impacts our spiritual condition. Maybe we should inventory what our eyes are focused upon.

I want my eyes to be on Christ. When I wake up, I want my thoughts to run to Him. I want His direction and His fellowship. When I encounter adversity, I want Him forming me with His counsel and not the acids of my own agitation. I want to resist the temptation to be amused by what has no eternal value and leaves me with a mediocre shape and dulled outlook. I don't want to make my own formation nor do I want others whose eyes are not on Christ defining me. I want to take on the definite, precise and permanent form that brilliantly reveals I am a child of God. I want the light of His Son radiating through me encouraging all those who are around me. I want my neck muscles so strong that there is no discomfort from constantly looking up. I want to see Jesus. How about you?

Inspiration ✝✝✝

The thing that tells in the long run for God and for men is the steady persevering work in the unseen, and the only way to keep the life uncrushed is to live looking to God. Ask God to keep the eyes of your spirit open to the Risen Christ, and it will be impossible for drudgery to damp you.—Oswald Chambers in *My Utmost For His Highest*

Ready for Service   July 24

My neighbor's yard is filled with trash and piles of materials he brought home from work. His house is literally falling apart and I feel bad for him because I know he is depressed and lonely. When I get back from this long trip, I look forward to meeting with him and offering to help him clean up his place. I suspect his long bouts of unemployment have stripped away his self-esteem and caused him to feel useless. His plight makes me wonder how many Christians are not employed serving Jesus because they feel unworthy, unneeded, or have an unrealistic concept of what it means to be useful.

Luke 12:35—Be ready for service and have your lamps lit.

It's funny how we idolize in our minds how, if we could just do something spectacular for God, everything would be great. The truth is God is more interested in our being faithful to serve Him throughout the day. Today I can be useful by being sensitive to the person working next to me who perhaps has a need. I can be useful by sharing an encouraging word. I can be useful by completing a task well that I have been assigned. I can be useful by listening to my children, and especially my wife! I can be useful by telling God right now I love Him and it is a pleasure to serve Him.

Don't be discouraged by the hum drum of daily activities. Don't discount being used by God just because circumstances are tough. Believe God can make you useful right where you are and have a great day in Jesus!

Inspiration ✝✝✝

If you want to be of use, get rightly related to Jesus Christ and He will make you of use unconsciously every moment you live; the condition is believing on Him.—Oswald Chambers in *Studies on the Sermon on the Mount*

Challenges July 25

Luke 14:26,27,33—If anyone comes to Me and does not hate his own father and mother, wife and children, brothers and sisters—yes, and even his own life—he cannot be My disciple. Whoever does not bear his own cross and come after Me cannot be My disciple . . . In the same way, therefore, every one of you who does not say good-bye to all his possessions cannot be My disciple.

Jesus asks a hard thing, doesn't He? The terms He sets for those who would be His followers are neither simple nor linear and address our behavior, attitude and beliefs. A person may have the right thinking about what it means to follow Jesus yet behave poorly. We should also note that one's vocation does not prove spiritual worthiness. A nun may have splendid behavior and yet possess a negative attitude.

The Messiah challenges us to carefully count the cost of following Him. First, relationally, no one is to come before Him in importance. He is not asking us to hate our relatives or to hate ourselves! The Greek word, μισει does not mean hate, as if to abhor someone, but rather to love less. Jesus is establishing that when it comes to following Him, He must be first.

I once asked a girl I was in love with if she loved me more than God. When she answered "yes," I was stunned and, shortly thereafter, concluded I could not marry her. If I love even myself more than Jesus, my ability to follow Him is compromised. Calculation is involved in obeying God. We have to reckon the asking price! He demands our loyalty and by implication our time, our energy and our actions. The reason the world is so skeptical of Christians, is too many claim Son affiliation yet live with dimmed lights.

To be a follower of Jesus means nothing else may own us. Again, Jesus is not literally demanding each believer sell everything to prove loyalty. Rather, don't be owned or defined by what you have at the expense of obedient service!

So what keeps us from being fully committed to Christ? 1. Selfishness and self-preoccupation. 2. Fear. We suspect God might make us live with sacrifice and suffering if we truly serve Him. 3. Ignorance. We don't understand Jesus' teaching nor have we seen men or women who model what it means to be wholehearted followers.

Dietrich Bonhoeffer wrote in *The Cost of Discipleship*, "When Christ calls a man, he bids him come and die."[53] When we can dismiss anything that would come before Christ, we are meeting the Master's challenge. Nothing should hinder us in our desire to climb higher . . . in reveration.

Inspiration ✝✝✝

The ultimate measure of a man is not where he stands in moments of comfort and convenience, but where he stands at times of challenge and controversy.—Martin Luther King, Jr.

Stewardship   July 26

Luke 16:10-12—Whoever is faithful in very little is also faithful in much, and whoever is unrighteous in very little is also unrighteous in much. So if you have not been faithful with the unrighteous money, who will trust you with what is genuine? And if you have not been faithful with what belongs to someone else, who will give you what is your own?

According to my online dictionary, *stewardship* is defined as "a person who manages another's property or financial affairs; one who administers anything as the agent of another or others."[54] Did you know that we are responsible to God as His stewards? Everything that we have (including our lives) belongs to Him—our time, treasures and talents. Whether we have a lot or a little is irrelevant—what matters is what we are doing with what we have.

I find stewardship to be an exciting opportunity for several reasons. *"A person should consider us in this way: as servants of Christ and managers of God's mysteries. In this regard, it is expected of managers that each one of them be found faithful"* (1 Co. 4:1,2). We get to manage God's mysteries! By serving the Lord, we participate in His will and work—two areas that make no sense to those who refuse to trust Him.

"We always carry the death of Jesus in our body, so that the life of Jesus may also be revealed in our body. For we who live are always given over to death because of Jesus, so that Jesus' life may also be revealed in our mortal flesh" (2 Co. 4:10,11). The world sees the reality of Jesus through us when we die to ourselves to live as His ambassadors.

It is not a trivial matter to be a steward. *"For we must all appear before the tribunal of Christ, so that each may be repaid for what he has done in the body, whether good or bad"* (2 Co.5:10). God holds us accountable for our actions, our character and our attitudes. But instead of fearfully living afraid of His judgment, we have the great privilege to reap rewards that are literally out of this world! *"Look! I am coming quickly, and My reward is with Me to repay each person according to what he has done"* (Rev. 22:12).

If we spend our money on possessions, they will eventually burn. The greatest 401Ks, savings accounts, toys and property are worthless for us upon death. There is no moving van that drives to heaven. If we prayerfully invest as much of <u>God's money</u> as we can into advancing His kingdom, that investment pays an exponential, eternal dividend. Do we want to prepare for good living when we are old or prepare for awesome living when we are eternally young?

Donald Joiner wrote in *Creating a Climate for Giving*, "Christian stewardship begins not with an inventory of what we have, but from a recognition of whose we are."[55] Stewardship is a privilege and a blessing. God thinks highly enough of you to let you administer what He owns on this planet He created. Have you ever thought of carrying a business card that says, *Manager for God*? Come on, that's a lofty title you inherited when you

put your trust in the King. Give God the glory He deserves from the time, treasures and talents He invested in you. John Wesley said it so well:
Do all you can.
Do all the good you can,
By all the means you can,
In all the ways you can,
In all the places you can,
At all the times you can,
To all the people you can,
As long as ever you can.

Inspiration †††

Development projects that help people become employed should also include a spiritual emphasis on Christian stewardship. —Glenn Schwartz in *When Charity Destroys Dignity*

The Road Down to the City   July 27

Luke 19:35,36—Then they brought it to Jesus, and after throwing their robes on the donkey, they helped Jesus get on it. As He was going along, they were spreading their robes on the road.

They threw their robes across the curious donkey.
They took His hand and helped Him mount His ride.
And as took the road down to the city,
They spread their garments across the dusty path.

> The crowds of His disciples were all cheering.
> Remembering the miracles they'd seen.
> "Hosanna, hosanna Son of David
> The King who comes in God's own name is blessed."

As His eyes looked down the Mount of Olives.
He wept with tears of sorrow mixed with pain.
They couldn't see the trials that were coming.
Enemies who would crush them to the ground.

> The crowd of His disciples kept on cheering.
> They thought He'd come to sit upon a throne.
> They didn't know their hearts were what He wanted
> And that is why they'd crucify their Lord.

The road down to the city full of treason
They took His robe and nailed Him on two beams.
They couldn't see the Light inside their darkness.
For praise is sometimes not what it would seem.

> The crowd of His disciples fled in terror.
> They didn't understand He'd overcome.
> Until He rose alive and stood among them,
> And ever since Hosanna is our praise!

> The crowd of His disciples stand adoring.
> Remembering the miracles we've seen
> "Hosanna, hosanna Son of David
> The King who comes in God's own name is blessed."

Two Swords   July 28

Luke 22:36-38—Then He said to them, "But now, whoever has a money-bag should take it, and also a traveling bag. And whoever doesn't have a sword should sell his robe and buy one. For I tell you, what is written must be fulfilled in Me. And He was counted among the outlaws. Yes, what is written about Me is coming to its fulfillment."
"Lord," they said, "look, here are two swords."
"Enough of that!" He told them.

Jesus instructed His disciples in what they would need <u>after</u> He left them. Unlike the first time when He commissioned them and sent them out with nothing but the clothes on their back (10:3,4), this time He urged them to travel equipped. In the first instance He wanted to build their faith, now He was concerned with their ongoing survival. But not surprisingly, the disciples did not understand His guidance. They could not grasp the reality that He would be leaving them. This stemmed primarily to their belief that the Messiah came to be a liberator who would rescue Israel from Roman oppressors. Naturally it made sense to them to focus on the need for swords. If Jesus was to be counted among the outlaws, obviously they could look forward to upcoming battles!

Why did Jesus even mention the need to buy a sword? Could it be that He was testing the hearts of His followers? After five years of active duty in the Army, I heard the call of God to go into ministry. But before I left, I was offered the opportunity to earn my Master's Degree and return to West Point to teach. This was a dream job and the sweet chance to further my education at the government's expense. Certainly I felt the Lord giving me favor and could have remained on active duty. But to me, the test was turning down the secure job to follow the Lord's leading.

How often we miss the true meaning of God's instruction because we focus in on what we want to hear. Essentially, our agenda replaces the Lord's agenda and we gravitate towards that which will bring to fruition our goals. We offer up two swords not understanding Jesus has no intention of arming a force. The sword was for their protection not His.

Misinterpretation occurs when we fail to carefully listen to what the Master has said. If the disciples had asked Jesus to clarify His statement, they would have gained deeper insight into His advice. If we would ask more and listen better before making suggestions and taking action, we would be better saints. Doug Pollock wrote in God Space, "Listening requires us to die to ourselves and our agendas." The Russians have a proverb, "Don't hurry to reply, but hurry to listen." If God has to tell us, "Enough of that!" we have surely missed His meaning.

Blessing

July 29

I am continuously impressed with our Heavenly Father's desire to bless us. From Genesis to Revelation runs a consistent theme—God loves to give to His children. As a parent I understand some of what God feels. I look forward to giving my children gifts. There is something profoundly special about favorably touching lives.

When we live in obedience to God's will, we cannot help but experience His blessings. Does this mean that we will not suffer? Hardly! Some of the godliest people I know have endured tremendous hardships. Yet if you asked them if they knew God's blessings, they would joyfully nod affirmatively. The deepest blessing God can give us is knowledge of Himself. The more we grow in our understanding of Him, the deeper we appreciate life and recognize how wonderful His expressions of kindness are to us. Perhaps Jesus' death on the cross most emphatically demonstrates the length God will go to bless us—to give us that unquenchable, super-spectacular, eternal gift of life in His presence.

John 1:16—From the fullness of his grace we have all received one blessing after another. (NIV)

For over ten years Kathleen and I struggled with the heavy cost of health insurance. It was an expense we gladly shouldered because the life of our son far exceeded any premium a company could exact. In a sense, it is what we would call a mixed blessing. We realized how fortunate we were to even have insurance! At the end of that period our family was approved by an organization of Christians dedicated to sharing health costs. Our monthly rates dropped by over $400!

Imagine how thankful we were that God removed our financial burden through the assistance of believers committed to pooling their money for the good of each family. As I look back at that time of sacrifice and challenge, I'm grateful for my Lord who touches hearts to create generosity and unity resulting in His praise and glory. I'm thankful for you . . . that you desire to know God more deeply. I pray that you will be consumed with a growing hunger to know God; that you will experience His blessings; and that you will let Him know how much you love Him.

Inspiration ✝✝✝

Whenever God has given us a blessing, we must take time to meditate on the blessing and offer it back to God in a deliberate ecstasy of worship . . . If God has blessed you, erect an altar and give the blessing back to God as a love-gift.—Oswald Chambers in *Not Knowing Where*

Sin-Responsibility   July 30

Why is our civilization morally crumbling? Could it be that we are wearing excuses to hide our responsibility for sin? Pastor Joe Wright of the Wichita Central Christian Church gave an invocation for the Kansas state legislature. Joe's prayer was immediately denounced by the governor of Kansas and several legislators stormed out in anger. This prayer has much to say. I hope it will stir your heart as it stirred mine.

"Heavenly Father, we come before You today to ask Your forgiveness and to seek Your direction and guidance. We know that Your Words says, "Woe be to those who call evil as good," and that's exactly what we have done. We have lost our spiritual equilibrium, and we've inverted our values. We confess that we have ridiculed the absolute truth of Your Word in the name of moral pluralism. We have worshiped other gods and called it multi-culturalism, and we've endorsed perversion and called it alternative lifestyle. We have exploited the poor and called it a lottery. We have neglected the needy and called it self-preservation. We have rewarded laziness and called it welfare.

Father, in the name of choice, we've killed our unborn, and then in the name of right-to-life we've executed the abortionist. We have neglected to discipline our children and called it building esteem. We have abused power and called it political savvy. We have coveted our neighbor's possessions and called it taxes. We have polluted the air with profanity and pornography and called it freedom of expression.

We have ridiculed the time-honored values of our forefathers . . . Search us, O God. Know our hearts today. Try us, and show us any wickedness in us. And then cleanse us from every sin, and set us free!

Guide and bless these men and women who have been sent here by the people of Kansas and who have been ordained by You to govern this great state. Grant them Your wisdom to rule, and may their decisions direct us to the center of Your will. I ask it in the name of Your Son, the Living Savior, Jesus Christ. Amen."

John 3:19-21—This, then, is the judgment: The light has come into the world, and people loved darkness rather than the light because their deeds were evil. For everyone who practices wicked things hates the light and avoids it, so that his deeds may not be exposed. But anyone who lives by the truth comes to the light, so that his works may be shown to be accomplished by God."

Universalism

July 31

Texas A&M is one of the largest Reserve Officers' Training Corps (ROTC) programs in the U.S. Texas Aggies are known throughout the U.S. for their patriotism and high performance. So I was surprised to learn that despite spending four years engaged in military training, wearing military uniforms, and living in barracks steeped in military tradition 50% of the cadets decide to graduate as civilians.

John 3:36—The one who believes in the Son has eternal life, but the one who refuses to believe in the Son will not see life; instead, the wrath of God remains on Him.

How many people engage in church life, study their Bible, grow up in a spiritual culture, consider themselves Christians and on the day of graduation will miss out on heaven? There are people who believe that Jesus Christ died for everyone and therefore, eventually, all mankind will be saved. This theory is called universalism. A related doctrine, *apokatastasis*, teaches that all mortal beings will be reconciled to God, including Satan and his fallen angels.[56] When the Bible mentions eternal punishment, hell, or anything related, the universalist "interprets this to mean an inner sorrow due to loss of reward, and/or they maintain that the word 'eternal' does not mean "without end."[57] Scriptures such as 1Ti. 2:4, 4:10 and 2 Pe. 3:9 are manipulated to defend this doctrine.

Universalism is dangerous teaching. It absolves man of responsibility for his sin and his need to repent and live righteously by making Jesus' blood a universal solvent. It negates any need for faith! It violates a strong principle of hermeneutics never to build a doctrine around a few verses at the exclusion of looking at the whole of Scripture. Jesus *did* die for everyone, but not everyone goes to heaven. If such were the case, why would He warn people of eternal judgment or the unpardonable sin in passages such as Mat. 25:46, Mark 3:28,29 and John 3:36? Why command the disciples to go throughout the world and preach the gospel at the cost of their own lives, if everyone was already guaranteed salvation?! Clearly Rev. 20:10 teaches that the Devil receives eternal punishment.

Beware of assumptions. ROTC experience does not guarantee an Aggie cadet will become an officer. Because God is loving, don't think that everyone will enter heaven. The universal truth is that only God knows what is inside a person's heart and who is a true child of His.

Reported

August 1

John 5:15—The man went and reported to the Jews that it was Jesus who had made him well.

This poor man was sick for 38 years when Jesus first saw him. He asked him if he would like to get well. Instead of answering "Yes!" the man shared a pool of woes. You can read about it in John 5:1-7.

Jesus was not fazed by the challenges His immobilized listener shared. He told the man the best eight words he had heard in almost four decades. *"Get up! . . . Pick up your mat and walk!"* (v. 8). Instantly he was healed. Incredibly, those nearby missed the awesomeness of his healing and zeroed in on why he broke the Sabbath law by carrying his mat. The man explained what Jesus told him to do but he had no clue of Jesus' identity. Later the Lord found him and said, *"See, you are well. Do not sin anymore, so that something worse doesn't happen to you"* (v. 14)

What happened next is puzzling. Rather than follow the Messiah who just healed him, the man went to the same Jews who chastised him and informed them it was Jesus who led him to break the Sabbath rules. Why didn't he protect the identity of his benefactor? He could have celebrated his condition. Instead, his reporting caused the Lord direct persecution by the Jews. Was this what Jesus meant when He warned him not to sin anymore? It would seem the man was guilty of betrayal. It was also an eerie foreshadowing. When prodded by jealous religious leaders, the Jews (formerly blessed by Jesus' miracles and teaching), eagerly yelled, *"Crucify Him!"*

Welcome to a mysterious pool called Bethesda. Here we discover a disease worse and more widespread than blindness, lameness or paralysis. It is hardening of the arteries. It is what happens when a person is afraid of what people think instead of recognizing blessing.

The Bible tells us of days when children rise against their parents and vice versa. People will do what is in their self-interest in order to further their own reputation. If the authorities declare faith in Christ to be a crime, don't be surprised when the neighbor you helped reports you. Veins too clogged for faith whisper betrayal. It happened to Jesus and He was perfect.

Inspiration ☦☦☦

Clarity dissolves resistance. —Chip Heath & Dan Heath in *Switch*

The Work of God

August 2

John 6:27-29—Don't work for the food that perishes but for the food that lasts for eternal life, which the Son of Man will give you, because God the Father has set His seal of approval on Him. "What can we do to perform the works of God?" they asked. Jesus replied, "This is the work of God—that you believe in the One He has sent."

Jesus asks a hard thing. It makes much more sense to work for food that perishes. We need food to survive. We like food. Perishing food represents all that appeals to our senses. But God is not interested in the temporal at the expense of the eternal. Jesus came not to authenticate man's sinful aspirations, He came to fulfill God's will.

God is not so concerned with the cause, the methods, or needs. His concern is that we follow after Him. Our work is to build a strong personal relationship with Jesus Christ. Our responsibility is to obey the leading of the Holy Spirit who would have us follow the Father's agenda. Find a Christian who is steadfastly resolute in following Christ and you will discover a person of faith working for eternal food. Is there any reason why you and I should not be such a person?

Periodically it is good to reflect and ask "What am I working for? Am I focused on laboring for things that please me because I find it hard to trust God?" The reasons we work for perishing food are many. We may be insecure and feel work is up to us and we know best what our needs are. We may be tired. Fatigue causes us to make unwise decisions. We may be surrounded by people who don't walk by faith. Pressures of friends, coworkers and families not centered on Christ will unfavorably move us away from God's work.

Climbing higher requires faith. This is the work of God. Don't be discouraged—the Son of God will give you eternal food. He promised!

Inspiration † † †

Do we love the work God has given us to do at the expense of the Giver of it?—Watchman Nee in *Changed into His Likeness*

Skepticism

August 3

Paul* and I were together several times the past month. I discovered he loves billiards so I asked if I could join him when he went out at night to the local pool hall. I am a weak pool player but he is both a great teacher and a patient competitor. While conversing, Paul revealed that he is an agnostic. One evening the topic of death came up and I mentioned the emptiness of dying only to end up as worm food. He countered that life was still valuable if we contributed to the betterment of others—even if they too had nothing more than the grave to anticipate. I asked him if it wouldn't be much better to contribute to people's lives and then have eternal life with God to enjoy. He agreed and I felt led not to force the conversation further.

John 7:12—And there was a lot of discussion about Him among the crowds. Some were saying, "He's a good man." Others were saying, "No, on the contrary, He's deceiving the people."

Hypocrisy, rigidity, insecurity (viewed as controlling), and a failure to listen are four ingredients that hasten the emergence of skepticism. An agnostic prefers to camp on the ground of uncertainty. Since most of us dislike uncertainty, we try to force the doubter to leave what we see as unstable to enter our solid encampment. If we are not careful, our insistence that our ground is better while their soil is wrong, will only alienate them. There are a great number of people who do not appreciate being told where and how they should camp.

Truly only God can reach an agnostic since only He can reveal Himself. Since sin blinds men to truth and skepticism is a blind manifestation, our prayer should be for God's mercy to overcome man's hardness. My first responsibility is to love Paul and pray for his salvation. By loving him, I value who he is as a God-created man, treat him with dignity. I find with agnostics that if they see I am genuine, they open up with questions and trust that I will dialogue honestly not trying to force my views down their throats. Humility is a great damper to skepticism.

God does not call us to win arguments. He calls us to follow Jesus. Truth does not rely on force of persuasion; it stands on its own authenticity. This is why the fruit of truth is freedom. Therefore, those who disagree and resist what we espouse should not intimidate us or increase our vocal volume, but rather compel us to pray that the Lord of Light would shine His truth upon their darkness of doubt. I must make the time to know Paul. How can I hope to see him sing praises in the mansion if I am not first willing to shoot pool with him in the marsh!

*Not his real name

Sickness

Occasionally I meet Christians who profess that believers should never get sick. In their view, illness stems from either sin, or natural causes untouched by weak faith. You may have experienced sickness or prolonged disease and had someone imply your inability to get well was due to your lack of faith or unconfessed sin.

John 9:2,3—His disciples questioned Him: "Rabbi, who sinned, this man or his parents, that he was born blind?"
"Neither this man nor his parents sinned," Jesus answered. "This came about so that God's works might be displayed in him."

At least 44 times the New Testament references Jesus healing people whom He encountered. Sometimes the healing was so dramatic, like the man in John 9 who was born blind and recognized, *"Throughout history no one has ever heard of someone opening the eyes of a person born blind"* (9:32).

On at least two occasions Jesus taught that the sick needed a doctor and He used a hypothetical illustration of being sick to judge the actions of those who either helped Him or ignored Him (Mat. 9:12; 25:36-44). Twice Jesus revealed that sickness was part of God's plan either to reveal God's power, as in the case of the passage above, or to glorify Christ as in the raising of Lazarus from the dead (John 11:4-6). In at least two other instances, we discover that sickness at times can be directly attributed to God's discipline for sin (1 Co. 11:29,30 and Rev. 2:21,22).

Jesus delegated authority to the disciples to heal people who were sick (Mat. 10:1,8). This authority continued after He returned to heaven (Acts 8:7). Healing also served as a sign demonstrating the power of God at work by His followers (Mark 16:17-19). Unfortunately, some use this passage in Mark improperly as a proof text for people who engage in questionable behavior to prove their legitimacy. The Bible also reveals that authority to heal is validated by faith on the part of the one needing healing. The implication is that if one does not believe healing is possible, that unbelief may prevent God from working. Clearly faith is an important aspect to healing (see Mark 5:28 and Jam. 5:14,15).

However, just because someone remains sick does not prove insufficient faith. Not everyone ill in the Bible was healed as in the case of Timothy who was strong in faith yet suffered from stomach problems, and Trophimus, whom Paul left ill in Miletus (1 Ti.5:23; 2 Ti. 4:20). God may allow sickness in a believer for a number of reasons: to show His power through our weakness; because germs, illness, demonic attacks and injury are a natural part of living in a fallen world; or because of sin and possible judgment.

When I am sick, I pray for God to heal me, believing that His operational will is for me to function in good health. But I also am sensitive to discerning if it is possible that I am sick for a reason. I remember an instance in Thailand where after visiting a Buddhist Temple, I became so sick I was completely immobilized for a day. My teammates and family prayed for me and I recovered—but I believe that sickness was clearly a demonic attack brought on by my being in a place of spiritual darkness. My severe nearsightedness is a genetic reality and I need to wear contacts or glasses. While I would like the Lord to give me good eyesight, He has chosen to let me be legally blind. I have prayed for people to be healed and watched God miraculously heal them. I have prayed for people to be healed and yet as far as I could tell, nothing happened. In conclusion, there are many reasons for sickness. I believe our responsibility is to be humble, to believe that God can heal, to lay hands on and pray for those who are sick under the leading of the Holy Spirit, and to ensure what we believe is in line with what Scripture teaches. Never take one passage out of context from Scripture as a whole. Sickness happens. If you have Jesus, you have eternal healing.

Inspiration † † †

Simply to say prayers is not to pray; otherwise a team of properly trained parrots would serve as well as men for our experiment. You cannot pray for the recovery of the sick unless the end you have in view is their recovery.—C.S. Lewis in *The Joyful Christian*

To Live Each Day As if it Were My Last

August 5

There are certain memories as a parent that last a lifetime. Before going to sleep one night, Bryan asked his mom, about the seriousness of his brain-stem tumor. Through tears, he asked her, "Does this mean that I am going to die?" And so, we had the opportunity to share with our wonderful three-year old son the reality of death. He voiced the hope that Jesus would return before anything ever happened to his tumor. As best I could, I shared with him that even if his tumor were to grow, the reality is that he will be with Jesus and that is a wonderful thing to look forward to. Meanwhile, each day is a gift. As God would have it, Bryan was healed of his tumor in 1991 during a time of prayer and worship with several of our friends.

John 10:27,28—My sheep hear My voice, I know them, and they follow Me. I give them eternal life, and they will never perish—ever! No one will snatch them out of My hand.

David Widerski, a pastor and friend, wrote as one of his resolutions before starting a new year, "To live each day as if it were my last." I love Dave's desire. How comforting it is to know that given the temporal condition of this thing we know as earthly life Jesus offers a permanent solution. If we follow Him, no one can snatch us from His hand. This is not just security against people or Satan, this is security against any external contingency. Therefore to live each day as if it were my last is to live knowing that in Christ there is no last. We may die on earth but we will not perish—He gives us eternal life.

Life is challenging, dreams are not always realized and aspirations sometimes litter the highway as unfinished monuments. Our responsibility is not to fear what will happen or take time for granted. Our responsibility is to hear the voice of Jesus and follow after Him. He will give us eternal life and protect our souls.

We don't know how many more days we have on this planet. We should be careful not to chase selfish fantasies, or forsake following Jesus, for in doing so, we exalt meaninglessness. In climbing higher, let's resolve to *fix our eyes on Jesus*, the author and perfecter of our faith.

Inspiration ✝✝✝

Only when God takes a life in hand can there come deliverance from the blues, deliverance from fits of depression, discouragement, and all such moods.—Oswald Chambers in *Workmen of God*

Status

August 6

The air is heavy in Don's study. His youngest son is not happy with his tennis racquet. He wants a new one or to use his dad's oversized racquet for his upcoming tennis class. Don questions David repeatedly why the racquet he *has* is not good enough. Tears began to form and tumble down his son's cheeks. David wrestles with an inward battle his dad struggles to comprehend. "Son, if you won't tell me what is wrong, how can I meet your request?" David, with a quivering voice tells him that kids would make fun of his old racquet just like they make fun of him for being short. And then his father, also a short man, understands.

John 12:42,43—Nevertheless, many did believe in Him even among the rulers, but because of the Pharisees they did not confess Him, so they would not be banned from the synagogue. For they loved praise from men more than praise from God.

It would tear my heart up if my children grew up in age and grew out of faith. Each will move into a world that increasingly mocks anything that has to do with steadfast allegiance to Jesus Christ. They will encounter scorn for clinging to an "antiquated" belief in God and be pressured to become tolerant—that clever disguise for intolerance of absolutes. They will hear people state authoritatively that Jesus was a good man and splendid teacher but nothing more. They will listen to voices that dismiss Scripture they don't approve of as passages added by agenda-driven zealots. They will discover that lordship and obedience are direct threats to other's rights to live as they please. They will be told to forget Christ or to suffer the consequences.

It would tear my heart up if my children gave in to the lost to find acceptance. We grow up seeking human approval while our Father always offers His sufficiency. Status is a powerful drug to most of us and reveals our deep insecurity. For fear of ridicule, we compromise.

Don understands that the praise of man is a powerful stimulant that will not last. To pursue it is like grasping fog. If we are to be status hunters, let it be to please God! Like Don, I hope my children learn that when others make fun of them, they are in good company. I pray they will never let go of their Savior, regardless of the cost.

He was despised and rejected by men, a man of suffering who knew what sickness was. He was like someone people turned away from; He was despised, and we didn't value Him . . . But He was pierced because of our transgressions . . . punishment for our peace was on Him, and we are healed by His wounds. (Isa. 53:3,5)

Washing Feet

John 13:12-15—When Jesus had washed their feet and put on His robe, He reclined again and said to them, "Do you know what I have done for you? You call Me Teacher and Lord. This is well said, for I am. So if I, your Lord and Teacher, have washed your feet, you also ought to wash one another's feet. For I have given you an example that you also should do just as I have done for you."

If you believe that washing dishes is woman's work and refuse to set foot in the kitchen to help your wife, do you understand what Jesus did by washing His disciples feet? If you believe that sex is bothersome and refuse to meet your husband's needs because "you are tired," do you understand what Jesus did by washing His disciples feet?

Somehow we have glorified the foot-washing ceremony as deeply profound while at the same time shelving it as an antiquated demonstration that no longer pertains to our shoe-covered society. By doing so we have lost the dynamic truth that the very essence of ministering to people involves serving them at the most ordinary level.

Mowing a shut-in's lawn, changing the oil of one who is mechanically clueless, fixing a friend's computer, making coffee for tired co-workers--these are all simple foot-washing opportunities. Whenever we are adjacent to needs we are adjacent to ministry. It is the simple act of serving in the most mundane of places that enables us to communicate love to one another. How refreshing it is to encounter people who in humility think nothing of observing and seizing opportunities to assist those around them.

Would you stop what you are doing right now? Look around you with new eyes and ask, "Heavenly Father, who can I serve?" When the Holy Spirit speaks, don't hesitate. Give the cup of cold water to the thirsty soul beside you in Jesus' name and for His glory! And if, by chance, you are one of those discouraged souls who serves all the time without recognition, don't lose heart. God sees what you do. If your heart is right, your reward is in heaven!

Inspiration †††

Ministering as opportunity surrounds us does not mean selecting our surroundings, it means being very selectly God's in any haphazard surroundings which He engineers for us. The characteristics we manifest in our immediate surroundings are indications of what we will be like in other surroundings . . . Towels and dishes and sandals, all the ordinary sordid things of our lives, reveal more quickly than anything what we are made of.—Oswald Chambers in *My Utmost For His Highest*

Trinity

August 8

John 15:26—When the Counselor comes, the One I will send to you from the Father—the Spirit of truth who proceeds from the Father—He will testify about Me.

The last part of Matthew 28:19 reads, *". . . baptizing them in the name of the Father and of the Son and of the Holy Spirit."* Who is God? The Hebrew word *'elohim*, in the Old Testament is the plural form of the noun for God. The New Testament presents a powerful case for the deity of Jesus and His equality with His Father. The Gospel of John begins with the assertion of Jesus' deity by stating, *"In the beginning was the Word, and the Word was with God, and the Word was God"* (John 1:1). The Word was clearly Christ! In a similar manner, the author of Hebrews states that Jesus was the radiance of the glory of God and the exact representation of His nature. Paul wrote in Col. 1:15-20, 2:9 and Php. 2:6 that Jesus was the image (form) of the invisible God. He describes Christ's work as the Creator and the One who was before all things.

Though Christ never directly claimed, "I am God," He clearly established His deity. He spoke with the full authority of God. The Jews accused Him of blasphemy for claiming to forgive sins. Jesus mentioned angels, the kingdom of God and God's elect as His own. He claimed the power to judge the world. While on trial for claiming to be the Son of God, Jesus affirmed Caiaphas' statement that He was so (Mat. 26:64). In the same manner He did not correct His disciple Thomas, who stated, *"My Lord and my God!"* (John 20:28). Finally, He beat death and ascended into heaven fulfilling His purpose as God's Son to seek and to save the lost (Luke 19:10).

The Bible also identifies the Holy Spirit as God. Acts 5:3-4 illustrates that lying to the Holy Spirit was equated with lying to God. Numerous passages like 1 Co. 3, 2 Co. 13:14 and 1 Pe. 1:2 give the Holy Spirit equal billing with God. But how can three different Persons be one God?

It is this impalpable mystery which sets Christianity apart from all others. Attempts to illustrate the Trinity by the three-part egg or three properties of water are inadequate and unnecessary. What is required is not the perfect illustration but rather a humble faith expressed in consistent love. The Trinity is not ultimately what causes people to stumble. Jesus is the obstacle. The deeper issue man trips over is not how God could be three-in-one, but rather why he should surrender his life to the lordship of Christ. What draws people to salvation is not logic but the invisible working of the Holy Spirit sent by God to confirm in our hearts the authenticity of Jesus Christ.

Caution is necessary in attempting to explain what is inconceivable. Our attempt to offer a manmade solution to a God-sized mystery especially offends Muslims who frequently reject Christianity because of our callous presentation of the Trinity. Why not admit, "I don't understand, nor can I fully explain the Trinity." Why not share, "What I believe is that Jesus Christ came to earth, lived a sinless life, died on the cross and rose from the grave because God says in His word that He loves you and me. He _has_ changed my life and given me joy that overcomes all adversity. He _has_ filled my heart with peace and assurance so that I do not fear death or carry the guilt of my sins. His Holy Spirit not only guides me but also fills me with hope for the everlasting life I will experience with God in heaven. I know Jesus. The Holy Spirit resides in me. God sits enthroned in heaven. How they are all God is more than mystical—it's fantastic."

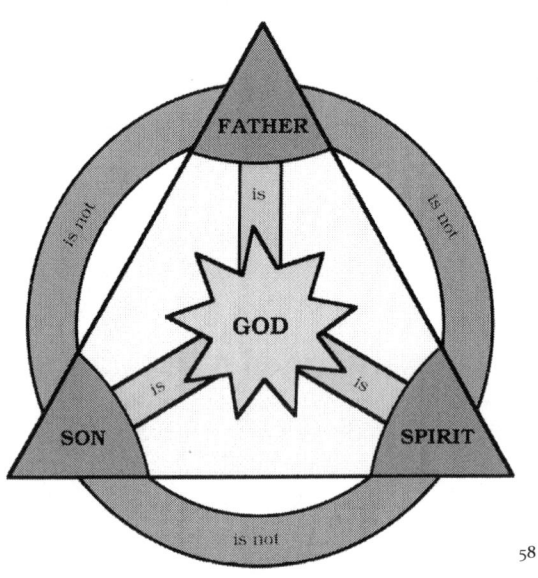

58

Slapped

August 9

Joan did everything they asked her. She studied the courses her managers recommended she take. She volunteered for the hard jobs and endured great stress because her leaders believed in her. She won awards for her speaking skills and was recognized by her peers as a superior performer with dynamic people skills. Besides loyalty to her organization, Joan invested much personal time and resources to make the company's work environment better. When it finally came time for a new human resources manager to be hired, she was sure the company would promote her to the position. But Joan didn't know that one of the applicants was the owner's niece.

John 18:22,23—When He had said these things, one of the temple police standing by slapped Jesus, saying, "Is this the way you answer the high priest?" "If I have spoken wrongly," Jesus answered him, "give evidence about the wrong; but if rightly, why do you hit Me?"

Imagine being perfect. Okay, I can't imagine that since I don't think I've ever even strung 24 faultless hours together! But God's Son lived perfectly. No mistakes. Every day He said the right things, thought the right things and did the right things. Not one moment of regret. No slips of the tongue. No caustic sarcasm from a bitter heart. He never woke up with a hangover or succumbed to a crabby attitude. He never overindulged the flesh or deceived anyone or even put His own will first; always submitting to His Father's plan—perfectly!

So what did it feel like getting slapped when what He said was right? How did God feel watching His holy Son get whacked by an overzealous jerk? He didn't fry the culprit with instant lightning. He absorbed the blow emotionally while His Son took the pain physically.

Are you one of those persons who did what you thought was right only to get punished unfairly? Have you put forward your best effort for God and then felt like He turned His back on you while ministry or work or your health suffered? Rather than get bitter or dwell on being wronged, remember Jesus got slapped. And that was just the start. He didn't get what He deserved. Instead He suffered for the undeserving—you and me. His Father let it all happen. You see the lesson is clear. Don't dwell on the setback—love the Lord. Don't try to figure out what doesn't make sense—trust the King. Sometimes God lets us take the blow to test our heart. Sometimes the slap is just the fruit of a sinful world. In the end, it doesn't matter. The sting will fade—will you? Or will you zealously carry your cross knowing that God has your back and your future!

Vasa

August 10

On August 10, 1628, King Gustav Adolf was away on business when the Vasa set sail. The warship was built to be a key asset for the Swedish Navy during its war with Poland. At the time of its commissioning the ship was ornately decorated and armed with the largest concentration of artillery in the world. Henrik Hybertsson supervised her construction but unfortunately was handicapped by the size and gun requirements King Adolf demanded. Unable to dissuade the king from rushing its production, the ship was precariously top heavy combined with insufficient ballast on its lowest deck. Unfortunately, Captain Söfring Hansson ordered its launch. The large craft sailed for less than a nautical mile before tipping and sinking. Historians believe 30-50 people drowned.

Because of the water condition and temperature the Vasa remained amazingly well preserved 105 feet below the surface. Three hundred and thirty-three years from its sinking, the Swedes were able to raise and treat it such that today it sits in a museum in Stockholm; the only warship of its era to ever be restored. The Vasa Museum is the most visited museum in Scandinavia with over 1,000,000 annual observers.[59]

Ezekiel 13:10-12—Since they have led My people astray saying, "Peace," when there is no peace, for when someone builds a wall they plaster it with whitewash, therefore, tell those who plaster it that it will fall. Torrential rain will come, and I will send hailstones plunging down, and a windstorm will be released. Now when the wall has fallen, will you not be asked, "Where is the coat of whitewash that you put on it?"

God was displeased with Israel's leaders in the time of the prophet Ezekiel because they proclaimed peace and portrayed strength when they were weak. Like the Vasa, they were doomed for destruction. But before we judge as incompetent those who design top-heavy ships or who cover weak walls with bright paint, we ought to consider our own vessels.

Too many of us build our lives according to our own design or the impatient and unrealistic demands of others. We work hard to be successful. Others may even consider us models to be emulated. But if our ballast is off, when adverse winds rise our imbalance will show. Our ballast is our spiritual foundation. Unless we are anchored in Christ and walk in obedience listening to the Holy Spirit, our equilibrium suffers. Never interpret appearance as a determinate of strength. Just because the Vasa was powerfully equipped and could float did not mean she was right.

Pardoned

August 11

Acts 2:20,21— The sun will be turned to darkness and the moon to blood before the great and remarkable Day of the Lord comes. Then everyone who calls on the name of the Lord will be saved.

J.I. Packer wrote in *Evangelism and the Sovereignty of God*, "While we must always remember that it is our responsibility to proclaim salvation, we must never forget that it is God who saves."[60]

Tuesday nights at half past eight he walks her to the door.
A kiss upon his forehead with a note she wrote at four.
He watches as she walks away her shadow on the yard
She turns around and waves and then she's gone.
        They lock the key behind him as he settles in his chair
        He pulls the ancient book out and reads the mystery there.
        And while he ponders heavily she waits to catch the train
        Folds her hands and prays he'll understand.
Eighteen years she raised him as best a mother could.
But eighteen years he added of raising hell instead.
Until one day too drunk to drive he struck and killed a boy
And now he only wishes he could die.
        Like lightning striking metal with fire-licking flames.
        He hears the demons calling thundering his name.
        He rolls his eyes in terror the nightmare never ends.
        Guilt is like a cut that cannot mend.
If you ever travel on the train to Gothenburg
You may have seen her sitting in the third car all alone.
She's reading from her Bible and talking to the Lord
She knows that He's the only hope he has.
        Then one day he reads in John that God so loved the world
        He sent His Son to save it—that none should go to hell.
        And while he ponders heavily she weeps in battle tears
        Praying on the train to Gothenburg.
She walks into the waiting room and looks into his eyes.
The twinkle in the blueness causes her to cry.
He holds her in his arms and says Mama I believe.
Jesus is the One who set me free!
        Like water falls in splendor washing through his pain
        He feels the peace of heaven coursing through his veins.
        He gives his sins to Jesus and puts his faith in Him
        Grace has sealed the cut that wouldn't mend.

Pierced to the Heart

August 12

Acts 2:36,37—"Therefore let all the house of Israel know with certainty that God has made this Jesus, whom you crucified, both Lord and Messiah!" When they heard this, they came under deep conviction and said to Peter and the rest of the apostles: "Brothers, what must we do?"

When I speak to my soldiers about safety, it is not hard for me to be passionate. I know firsthand what it is like to have one of my men decapitated because he drove his car right into a truck that he never saw pull out in front of him. I know what it is like to lose 248 men and women to a plane crash and be hampered in body identification because against regulations they carried their own dental records. I've seen what happens when people text and drive and die. So it's not hard to say the difficult things young people need to hear so they don't go out and do something stupid.

I can imagine how passionate Peter was when he stood in front of his countrymen and shared about Jesus. He heard them yelling "Crucify!" and approve His Lord's torture. He saw the hypocrisy that turned "hallelujah's" into murderous threats. He felt the lingering pain of knowing he had denied his own Master. His spirit was riled by the truth that lies were blinding his fellow Jews from understanding the certainty that Jesus was their Messiah. When he spoke, his words dripped with emotion. He cared.

Peter dared to declare truth with passion. He decided it did not matter whether he was killed or not, he would not be muzzled. His words boiled with authenticity. The result was that many of his listeners "came under deep conviction." Literally this means they were pierced to the heart.

Wesley Duewell says, "A passionless Christianity will not put out the fires of hell."[61] When was the last time your words sizzled with the fire of conviction? When was the last time you saw a heart pierced? If you are just living life and checking off each day as another boring marker, may I suggest a radical tune up? Read again what it cost God to reach you. Think again of the consequences for those who turn their back on heaven and trudge to hell. I pray to God someone will see in you and in me the eternal light of hope and ask with trembling voice, "*What must we do!*" If this has not been the case for a prolonged time, then brothers and sisters, we must wake up! If we slumber in apathy, we don't just miss the joy that comes from seeing pierced hearts saved by the pierced Savior, we are contributing to the very malaise that strangles our nation.

"Get Up and Walk!" August 13

Acts 3:6,16—But Peter said, "I don't have silver or gold, but what I have, I give you: In the name of Jesus Christ the Nazarene, get up and walk!" . . . By faith in His name, His name has made this man strong, whom y0u see and know. So the faith that comes through Him has given him this perfect health in front of all of you.

You've undoubtedly heard someone say, "Oh, I believe Christianity is just another path towards heaven. I'm glad it works for you but I've got my own path." Intellectually, it is quite rational to lump Christianity as another religion in a cosmos filled with man-made roads to meaning. After all, if someone has never come into a personal and meaningful relationship with Jesus Christ, then why shouldn't he or she see Christians any differently from the way he or she sees Buddhists, Muslims, Mormons, Hindus etc.?

The next time someone so easily dismisses what you consider invaluable, ask that person what he really knows about Jesus? Inquire if he has heard that Jesus offers something no one else can—eternal life. Find out if he knows the cost Jesus paid for him and the historicity of His resurrection from the dead. Ask if he has compared the truth claims of each religion to see what contradictions exist and what is offered by each.

If a person is truly searching for answers and meaning to life, then he will take the time and make the effort to conduct meaningful research to find the answers. If a person is unwilling to do this, then, in truth, that person is most likely closed or offended in some way by the absolute claims of Jesus. There is nothing we can do by wit or argument. Our responsibility is to model Christ-likeness and pray!

Peter knew with certainty that Jesus was the Messiah therefore in faith he watched God minister to the beggar. If our lives do not demonstrate the power of heaven to change sin natures, if our faith and obedience indicate no difference from any other person, then should we expect a passionate interest in Jesus? An irrelevant Christian is a terrible testimony to a relevant Savior. As we see needs we have the privilege of listening to the Holy Spirit, and if He so moves, speaking words of healing.

Inspiration †††

Christianity is personal, passionate devotion to Jesus Christ as God manifest in the flesh.—Oswald Chambers in *Approved Unto God*

"We are Unable to Stop Speaking"   August 14

We are apt to forget that the great reason for missionary enterprise is not first the elevation of the people; nor first the education of the people; nor even first the salvation of the people, but first and foremost the command of Jesus Christ—'Go ye therefore, and make disciples of all the nations.'[62]

Acts 4:18-20—So they called for them and ordered them not to preach or teach at all in the name of Jesus. But Peter and John answered them, "Whether it's right in the sight of God for us to listen to you rather than to God, you decide; for we are unable to stop speaking about what we have seen and heard."

Who Will Be The Answer?

There's a world of hurting people asking burning questions;
    facing a tomorrow without a hope today.
Who will go and show them Light to end their darkness,
    Who will hear His call and obey?
Who will be the answer, to a world with questions
    Who will be Your servants Lord?

Think of what a difference Jesus made inside you
    once your heart was empty, until you found the Lord.
Faith in God's own Son, changed your life forever
    You believed His Word and obeyed.
I will be Your answer, to a world of questions
    I will be Your servant Lord!

Nothing else must hinder, the race I run for God
    To share His holy message, to hear His holy call!

We will be Your answer to a world of questions
    We will be Your servants Lord!
©1999 Choices Dan York ARR

Inspiration ✝✝✝
    Mission is mediated through relationship.—Paul Sanders

His Power at Work   August 15

Acts 4 is a phenomenal chapter in the Bible. Basically, it contains the account of Peter and John appearing before the Jewish council of religious leaders to explain by whose power they acted to heal a man lame for over 40 years! The members of the council were amazed at the boldness and eloquence of two fishermen who had been with Jesus. After a day of deliberations the council commanded the apostles never again to speak or teach in the name of Jesus. Of course Peter and John refused to abide by their terms so the rulers threatened them but because of their fear of starting a riot, let the two men go. Peter and John reported to the church what happened and they went into a time of prayer that was so dynamic the Holy Spirit shook the place!

Acts 4:29,30—And now, O Lord, hear their threats, and give us, your servants, great boldness in preaching your word. Stretch out your hand with healing power; may miraculous signs and wonders be done through the name of your holy servant Jesus. (NLT)

Preaching Acts 4:23-31 on Sunday, I challenged our fellowship to expect bigger things of God, to increase our faith so that people in our community would see His power at work. I had no idea that God would put us to test in the process!

By Tuesday our son Bryan was into his fifth day of headaches and soreness on his neck (a particularly scary thing for us because of his brain-stem tumor). We took him into a doctor and a mass was discovered on Bryan's neck. He was immediately scheduled for a cat scan the next day. We prayed Acts 4:30 with our home group, and word went out to many people who also prayed for Bryan.

By late Wednesday afternoon the word came back, the cat scan detected no abnormalities. The doctors were perplexed and Bryan's headaches abated. We don't know what God is going to do when we pray. What we do know is that He delights when we come to Him in faith and trust Him in the midst of adversity. Our responsibility is to ask and trust that God will exert healing power and do amazing things.

We often look for immediate results—in our case, Bryan's healing. But the greatest result is not what happens in our temporary bodies but rather in God's eternal Kingdom. When we pray, the ultimate results that we seek should be the furtherance of the gospel. Unless our God is real and able to do far more than we can think or imagine, why should anyone put his or her trust in Him? Our faith is magnified. Our community is amazed. The important result is God gets all the glory.

Simplicity

Leaning against the gymnasium wall, Bob and I talked about our children and their involvement in sports. Between carting his kids to Cub Scouts, his work and everything else, his life sounded complex. Life in our land is like walking into Circuit City and seeing 15 different channels at the same time in the television section, while we talk on our cellular phones and wave at the sales clerk we know across the room. Isn't it comforting that no matter how fast the globe spins, no matter what level of activity we engage in, Jesus remains the same!

I don't need more activities to fill my life. I'm not looking to win some gold-plated plaque for juggling more balls on a motorized unicycle. I want to simplify. I want to give more attention, more effort to knowing God. My hunger grows to be with Him.

Acts 6:3,4—Therefore, brothers, select from among you seven men of good reputation, full of the Spirit and wisdom, whom we can appoint to this duty. But we will devote ourselves to prayer and to the preaching ministry.

Do we mistakenly think we look better if we are doing more? Are we missing the truth that what God wants most is not our activity? Listen to what He said to His faithful servant Moses about the Israelites, *"If only they had such a heart to fear Me and keep all My commands always, so that they and their children will prosper forever"* (Deu. 5:29). To the ever-sensitive prophet Jeremiah, He shared, *"I will give them one heart and one way so that for their good and for the good of their descendants after them, they will fear Me always"* (Jer. 32:39). What God wanted from the children of Israel, He wants from us—our hearts!

When we are able to relinquish the need to be busy, entertained or productive, we find that our Lord is near. Singleness of heart does not come about by crowding my life with MORE. If I cannot focus on Christ and walk after Him, I am headed for despair and trouble. Oh unchanging God, change me. Here's my heart. Let it beat the song of simplicity.

Inspiration †††

Now, as always, God [discloses] Himself to "babes" and hides Himself in thick darkness from the wise and the prudent. We must simplify our approach to Him. We must strip down to essentials (and they will be found to be blessedly few). We must put away all effort to impress, and come with the guileless candor of childhood. If We do this, without doubt God will quickly respond.—A. W. Tozer in *The Pursuit of God*

Crystal Elements   August 17

Just before 10:30 p.m. I found the cottage I would be staying in for the next 90 days. I unloaded the two large suitcases, my carry-on bag, and backpack from the Jeep and proceeded into the dark house. My aide-de-camp left a message on the table beside a container of fruit welcoming me to Fort McCoy. In the kitchen, the refrigerator was stocked with Powerades and Ginger Ale. On the coffee table was a bowl filled with what looked like gold hard candies. I thought to myself what a good job the aide had done and plopped one of the "candies" in my mouth.

Quickly I spit it out as it was not candy and it tasted horrible. I ran into the bathroom and flushed my mouth with cold Wisconsin water. Then I went back and discovered that my treat was actually a bowl of Crystal Elements—air freshening crystals scented with Amber Vanilla and definitely not to be touched or ingested! It took two days before I got the dire savor of that crystal out of my mouth. I assumed my aide was taking care of my sweet tooth, when, in fact, it was the environment that was the subject of attention.

Acts 7:24,25—When he saw one of them being mistreated, he came to his rescue and avenged the oppressed man by striking down the Egyptian. He assumed his brothers would understand that God would give them deliverance through him, but they did not understand.

Two words should grab our attention from Acts 7:25—"*He assumed.*" Moses thought he was God's solution to the suffering of his countrymen. But he intervened and killed an Egyptian without God's sanction or leading. Consequently he reaped scorn from his fellow Hebrews and anger from Pharaoh. Moses was forced to flee Egypt to live as a foreigner in the land of Midian.

Henry and Richard Blackaby wrote in *Spiritual Leadership*, "Too often, people assume that along with the role of leader comes the responsibility of determining what should be done." When we assume and take action without investigating, we invite trouble into our lives. Our guessing may be humorous with minor consequences like trying to eat crystals. But it may completely change the course of our lives as in Moses' case. All Moses had to do was to arrest the behavior of a cruel Egyptian. Instead he resorted to murder. Too often we get mad in our *rightness*, and miss God's way. Haste is the brother of assumption and both rarely lead us to the right solution. When confronted by wrongdoing, seek God's help. Crystal Elements are not made for eating and assumptions are a poor recipe for living.

Conversion

August 18

Acts 9:4-6—Falling to the ground, he heard a voice saying to him, "Saul, Saul, why are you persecuting Me?" "Who are You, Lord?" he said. "I am Jesus, whom you are persecuting," He replied. "But get up and go into the city, and you will be told what you must do."

He was trained by the great Gamaliel, thoroughly schooled in Judaism, and probably one of the most zealous religious men of his day. His spiritual pedigree was topnotch. Yet for some reason he was clueless to Jesus' identity. Despite listening to the impassioned speech of Stephen who willingly was martyred for his faith in Christ; despite hearing the marvelous accounts of Jesus' miracles and resurrection; despite knowing that simple fisherman, a hated tax-collector and various other men and women of questionable background were passionately on fire for the One they called the Messiah; Saul was undeterred in his quest to destroy followers of the Way.

It took an act of heaven to reach an earthly man. God had a special plan and ministry for Saul. Yet because his experience was dramatic, we should not think the hand of God is the exception—that the hand of believers is the norm in anyone else becoming a follower of Christ. This might lead us to think that it is up to *us* to save people. Our responsibility is to obey the Holy Spirit's leading and share our faith by our godly attitude, action and faith. Only God can bring about spiritual conversion.

The proof of true conversion is not emotion, not mental assent to proposed truth, but rather a life transformed that bears fruit (Mat. 7:20)! True conversion originates from the enabling work of God and it endures forever. John 16:8 informs us the Holy Spirit is the One who will convict the world of guilt in regard to sin. In John 6:44, Jesus says, *"No one can come to Me unless the Father who sent Me draws him..."* Why is this important? It frees us of guilt that people are not responding to the message we've shared. It liberates us from the pressure of trying to manipulate those who are unsaved to "accepting" Christ. It teaches us to truly depend upon God when we evangelize, for He, not us, is the One who saves!

Inspiration † † †

You cannot argue people into coming to Jesus or socialize them into coming; only one thing will do it, and that is the power of the Gospel drawing people by the constraint of God's grace.—Oswald Chambers in *God's Workmanship*

Hollow

August 19

Gray skies and cold temperatures framed my Sunday morning on the University of Syracuse campus. I walked to Hendricks Chapel in time to catch the 11:00 a.m. service. The building reminded me of a Roman cathedral with its large columns, balconies and great curtains. However, structural grandeur gave way to disappointment when I realized the student choir more than doubled the size of the few attendees.

Tomi*, stood up in her white robe and tennis shoes and delivered a message loosely tied to Acts 9:36-43. When she lifelessly described Tabitha's raising as an "environment of interdependent causal relationships," I realized why the place was empty. Later reading from Rev. 7:9-17, she questioned the intellect of John. How could he suggest robes could be made white by the blood of the Lamb or that a lamb could lead sheep? In her brightness the Word was made dim. Tomi offered suggestions of what we could glean in life from her lens of process theology. No wonder Hendricks was hollow.

Acts 9:40,41—Then Peter sent them all out of the room. He knelt down, prayed, and turning toward the body said, "Tabitha, get up!" She opened her eyes, saw Peter, and sat up. He gave her his hand and helped her stand up. Then he called the saints and widows and presented her alive.

Alfred North Whitehead (1861–1947) is the father of process theology, a school of thought influenced by his metaphysical process philosophy. Essentially it teaches:

- God is not omnipotent in power; He persuades rather than coerces.
- Panentheism—Essentially, everything past and present is in God.
- Free will by humans and creatures brings to the universe process and change. Self-determination defines everything in the universe, not just human beings.[63]
- Humans do not experience personal immortality, but rather *objective* immortality. Their experiences survive forever in God.[64]
- Jesus is not God, but rather fully identified with God. He is a created being.[65]
- God co-creates with all other creatures. "There is no beginning to creation; God and the universe are co-eternally creative." God incorporates all that happens into His own life.
- God does not know the future until it is actualized. He is not unchanging. He is dynamic absorbing new experience as the universe develops in creative transformation.[66]

Whenever people remove their confidence from the Word of God and place it in the teachings of man—beware. Process theology denies that God is the omnipotent, sole Creator. It disallows the Trinity and Biblical teaching that man will stand one day before God for judgment. It strips the Lord of His attributes and renders Him dependent on the world. Process theologian Robert Mellert admits, "God is in some sense dependent upon the world and that in that sense he is subject to the changes that take place in the world."[67]

Process theology neuters prayer because God is just a cooperative partner. *Pray* for those caught in this heresy for by making subjective claims about reality they render their pronouncements absurd in that they cannot be known by their own epistemology (The branch of philosophy concerned with the nature and origin of knowledge. Epistemology asks the question "How do we know what we know?"). For example, how does a finite philosopher suppose to observe God as being inside everyone? How does he who is measured in time decide an eternal God cannot know the future?

Decide your source of wisdom, choose your process, and live accordingly. If God is limited by man, you know the results will be hollow.

Inspiration † † †

If we let ourselves believe that man began with divine grace, that he forfeited this by sin, and that he can be redeemed only by divine grace through the crucified Christ, then we shall find peace of mind never granted to philosophers. He who cannot believe is cursed, for he reveals by his unbelief that God has not chosen to give him grace.—Blaise Pascal

*Not her real name

Off to the Jungle

August 20

Pete and Saul traveled from Lima, Peru to visit three Segadorian missionary families working in the distant Asheninka tribe. They journeyed seven hours by bus, six hours in the back of a pick-up over a rough road, then, finally, three hours in a motorized canoe in drizzling rain. Peter noted in his newsletter it was well worth the sacrifice. Why did these two men go to such lengths to visit these families? They went because they understood how important the value of encouragement is.

Acts 11:22-24—Then the report about them was heard by the church that was at Jerusalem, and they sent out Barnabas to travel as far as Antioch. When he arrived and saw the grace of God, he was glad and encouraged all of them to remain true to the Lord with a firm resolve of the heart, for he was a good man, full of the Holy Spirit and of faith. And large numbers of people were added to the Lord.

Antioch was about 300 miles north of Jerusalem. Whether Barnabas walked to a port city and took a boat to the port fifteen miles from Antioch or just walked overland, we can assume it took him at least a week to get to his destination. He either carried all he needed or paid to have his stuff transported. Chances are good he had never before met the people the church sent him to greet. From the passage above, we can assume that his presence was partly responsible for amazing church growth. Barnabas was so enthused by what God was doing in Antioch, that he went to Tarsus to find Saul and brought him back with him. For over a year they taught large numbers of believers—the first disciples to be called Christians.

Have you ever considered that one of the best helps to evangelism is encouragement? If I am discouraged and not doing so well in ministry and someone travels 16 hours just to visit and encourage me, is it possible that I will be reenergized to serve the Lord? If a total stranger travels over 300 miles to encourage my interest in learning about Jesus, is it possible I may conclude that the gospel is valid and indeed life changing!

Would you consider doing something with me? Stop and spend a few moments in prayer. Ask the Holy Spirit to reveal to you someone who needs encouraging. Then make the sacrifice to either travel to that person's location (if God so leads), or write a letter (don't email—that's too easy), or pick up the phone and call that person and build them up. Go the extra mile to make a difference in someone's life. Let God use you to be a soul-shiner. If we would spend more time encouraging saints, we would find a whole lot more people wanting to become saints.

Missionaries

August 21

Acts 13:2,3—As they were ministering to the Lord and fasting, the Holy Spirit said, "Set apart for Me Barnabas and Saul for the work I have called them to." Then after they had fasted, prayed, and laid hands on them, they sent them off.

How radical are you willing to be when it comes to supporting missionaries? It's nice to have an annual missions week in the church. It feels good to send a check periodically to those laboring overseas. But do you honestly understand what those you know as missionaries experience on a daily basis? Do you know what it means to leave your home country and live in a strange culture among people who speak a foreign language, eat different foods, and relate to one another with a different set of customs? Do you know what it is like to be homesick, vulnerable and inadequate?

Isn't love what makes the body of Christ unique in the world? Let's stoke the love that should flow in our hearts for one another. May I suggest you pray about exercising your love to those out on the frontlines of ministry! First, pray about planning a trip to spend a week or two with a missionary you know. Sacrificially begin setting aside the money you will need. Don't fall victim to the "can't syndrome." God can easily provide you the funds to go if you are willing. I suspect He would be immensely pleased you would even do such a thing. If you have children, take them with you. They will receive a greater education than a week in school could ever provide.

Second, get on the phone (check the time zone difference first ☺), and call a missionary you know. Ask how they are "really" doing and give them time to "really" respond. Tell them that you love them and are proud of what they are doing for the Kingdom. Be an encourager in Jesus' name! Your actions might just refresh a worn-out saint. You may bring tears of joy to a missionary who was beginning to wonder if God really cared. You might build a friendship that could change your own life. You will model caring! You will honor the Lord by serving those who serve!

One of the best ways to climb higher is to help others who are climbing. Be a kingdom builder!

Inspiration † † †

Unless the missionary is based on a right relationship to God, he will fizzle out in the passing of the years and become a negligible quantity from God's standpoint. The men and women who stand absolutely true to God's ideal are the ones who are telling for God. God has staked His honor on the work of Jesus Christ in the souls of those whom He has saved, and sanctified and sent.— Oswald Chambers in *So Send I You*

Mega Shift

August 22

Often I find Christians in the United States discouraged, wondering why it seems like there is little activity by God in our land. There is a sense that our nation is increasingly secular and a growing unease. I believe that materialism is a far greater threat to the growth of our faith than outright opposition. Why do I say this? My friends who face suffering, prison or the loss or rights because of their walk with God actually find renewal and supernatural strength in the testing of their faith. While those who live in comfort find it hard to die to self and actively proclaim truth. And contrary to what many of us may be thinking, there is a major work of God going on around much of the globe.

Acts 14:3—So they stayed there for some time and spoke boldly in reliance on the Lord, who testified to the message of His grace by granting that signs and wonders be performed through them.

We know because of the context and the reference that the passage above refers to Paul and his team. But did you know that this verse could easily describe countless places around the world where God is performing signs and wonders through His faithful servants? I highly encourage you to read the book *Mega Shift* by James Rutz. James' careful research shows that "most of the 'evangelism miracles' in China are healings, whereas in India they are more often power confrontations—demonic deliverances or spiritual 'turf battles' for a town or neighborhood under Satanic dominance."[68] James and his researchers estimate " that there are probably, at a guess, 350 Christians in India whom God has directly taught to read." Did you catch that?! Christians with no formal education or home schooling under the Holy Spirit's tutelage learned to read His Word.

Entire North African Muslim villages in Morocco, Tunisia, Algeria and closed nations in the Middle East are coming to faith in Jesus as a result of shared dreams and supernatural visions. Contrary to what we hear in our media, the fastest growing movement in the world by far is Christianity. "There has never been a time like this. The new spearhead of the kingdom is 707 million strong and adding two more each second. God is winning!" People are being raised from the dead, those with incurable diseases like AIDS are healed and prayers of God's children are answered in spectacular ways for the promotion of His Kingdom!

Are you willing to believe that God can still work miracles? Do you want to have your faith strengthened? Do you need a reminder about what priorities should really matter? I have seen what God can do when Christians engage in prayer walking. But that is a drop in the bucket compared to what I have not seen! He protects and preserves His people in the most dangerous settings. He frees adults and children from bondage so that they might know Christ. Read *Mega Shift* and share it with your friends. Be encouraged! Let's ask our Lord to wake up our nation and renew it with the only hope that matters—life in His name!

Inspiration † † †

I discovered that there are probably, at a guess, 350 Christians in India whom God has directly taught to read.—James Rutz in *Mega Shift*

James

August 23

Acts 15:13—After they stopped speaking, James responded: "Brothers, listen to me!"

    Does it surprise you that the leader in the church after Jesus returned to heaven was not one of the eleven apostles? Wouldn't it seem like the requirement for membership to the Jerusalem Council would be three years of faithful service under the Master? If Jesus said He would build His church upon the rock, and that rock was Peter (Mat. 16:18), why was James the one who rendered judgment as the leader of the Council (Acts 15:19-21)?

    James grew up with Jesus! He watched his older Brother closely. He never saw Jesus throw a temper tantrum, talk back to His parents disrespectfully, unmercifully tease him and his brothers and sisters, lust after hot girls, make shoddy furniture, complain about having to go to the synagogue, throw rocks at Romans, or refuse to eat what Mary prepared. He heard Jesus pray with depth and sincerity. He watched his Brother devour Scripture and seriously question the actions of those who should know better. Maybe he resented the fact that his Brother was the center of attention and the One with all the best answers. Consider, if he accused Jesus of always being right, He *was* always right! Perhaps he was jealous that Jesus could work miracles. Is it surprising that he doubted his Brother was God's Son (John 7:5)? After all, he lived with Him long enough to take His actions and attitudes for granted. Imperfect naturally misunderstands Perfect.

    Yet at some point the younger son of Mary and Joseph recognized truth. When he became his Brother's follower, he brought understanding to the team that even the apostles lacked. No doubt they often sat around and asked James what it was like growing up with the Messiah. When James spoke about Jesus, his words had the weight of time, close proximity and true brotherly love. The One who surely carved him toys eventually captured his heart.

    C.S. Lewis wrote in *The Weight of Glory* "Can anything be added to the conception of being with Christ?"[69] Why wouldn't God shepherd His church with the Shepherd's own brother! When James spoke, the church listened. I can't wait to meet him and get the inside edition of life growing up with the Savior!

[70]

Decision Making

August 24

The air is thick with smoke. Against the whizzing bullets of death a small patrol of rangers races up a desolate slope of carnage. Their mission is to take out a machine gun nest that has wasted the ranks of two squads previously attempting to seize the hill. Halfway through their inspiring charge, the patrol leader pauses. He rethinks his mission, reevaluates the situation and is overcome with the deafening voices of fear that permeate his head like some bewitching chorus. He tells his men to take cover behind the stones and wait. He cannot move forward.

"No!" you scream. You're the battle-hardened lieutenant and you understand that the cost of indecision will be catastrophic for these men you love. They must courageously assault using all the skills they have been taught to defeat this enemy. You pick up your radio, and yell, "GO!" Victory is not gained by those who hide behind rocks.

Today, your mind races with a moral dilemma. You face a hill controlled by the sweeping gun of immorality. The Holy Spirit has spoken. You must take out this nest of sin. To ignore it is hurting those you live beside, and it is gnawing away at your own conscience. But you fear the cost of being righteous, of taking a stand and so you quaver in the muck of indecision. For God's sake, do what is right. If the immorality is your own sin, come clean. If it is the tolerated evil of someone else, speak up! When God identifies a moral issue, that is the time to act. To procrastinate is to give the enemy that many more opportunities to hurl his grenades. Don't be blown up!

Acts 15:22—Then the apostles and elders, with the whole church, decided to select men who were among them and to send them to Antioch with Paul and Barnabas: Judas, called Barsabbas, and Silas, both leading men among the brothers.

The Jewish Church Council in Jerusalem realized the moral dilemma Gentile believers faced. Overzealous Jews approached these new believers to impose their own religious convictions. The Council carefully discussed the issues, prayerfully approached God and decisively acted to send Paul and Barnabas with a letter to help clear up the confusion. Their ability to make a God-honoring decision did much to encourage the Gentile churches Paul and others had planted. They took the moral high ground, thereby crippling the misguided cause of reckless legalists.

What hill would God have you climb? If He has revealed what is wrong, don't be afraid to do what is right. He'll give you the strength to be holy because He *is* holy. Decide!

Flexible

August 25

Imagine being told you are headed to Iraq and you may not see your family for a year. You are trained with specific skills and given an important mission. Once you get past the emotional struggle of leaving your family you focus in on the task ahead of you. But everything changes. Instead of deploying overseas, your unit ends up at Fort Lewis and you and your fellow combat engineers are assigned to work as gate guards for the installation. Meet SSG Osborne! Such was the fate he and his fellow National Guardsmen from Oregon encountered.

Every time I drove onto Fort Lewis I was met by courteous, professional soldiers. Aside from their shoulder patches and a sign which proclaimed their unit, there was no way to differentiate between these men and the active Army military police who normally guard the reservation. If they were disappointed in their duty, it did not show. And that got me to thinking . . .

Acts 16:6-8—They went through the region of Phrygia and Galatia and were prevented by the Holy Spirit from speaking the message in Asia. When they came to Mysia, they tried to go into Bithynia, but the Spirit of Jesus did not allow them. So, bypassing Mysia, they came down to Troas.

Paul hoped to take the gospel into the province of Asia. Do you think he was frustrated when twice his plans were blocked? What discussion do you think his team held when God stopped them from going where their strategy dictated?

The key to flexibility is the ability to understand the big picture. How does an engineer remain cheerful checking ID cards at a gate despite the fact that this was not what he was trained to do? He understands that military police are in short supply and are greatly needed to maintain order and discipline in a dangerous environment elsewhere. His sacrifice is for the greater good of the organization.

How do we remain cheerful when our best plans are blown to smithereens and nothing seems to go the way we intended? We remember that we are serving an <u>Almighty</u> Father! We wear a godly attitude with Christ-like character to further the gospel which supersedes our agenda and personal need. Flexibility reveals contentedness which in turns testifies to a strong faith in God. Inflexibility reveals a need for control which spanks of pride and faithlessness. Are you willing to live "semper gumby" (always flexible) or would you rather simply grumble?

Inspiration ✝✝✝

This is the primary characteristic of obedience: eyes on God.—Margaret Thatcher in *The Freedom of Obedience*

Storms

August 26

As hurricane Irene approached the eastern coast of the U.S., the media were concerned the category 3 storm would inflict catastrophic damage from North Carolina to New England. My quiet time passage for August 26, the day before the hurricane was to hit, was Psalm 107. Verse 29 reads, *"He made the storm be still and the waves of the sea were hushed"* (ESV). Reminded of God's awesome power, I prayed, Lord, *You have many people who love You in that region, please calm the storm and hush the waves, spare our country the enormous damage that large hurricane might inflict.*

Perhaps millions of people prayed to God about Irene. Not surprising, her winds significantly decreased and what could have been the costliest disaster on record actually was much tamer than predicted. *Irene, goodnight.*

Psalm 109:4—In return for my love they accuse me, but I give myself to prayer. (ESV)

The Bible is packed with stories and reminders that God is involved in our lives and cares about what happens on our planet. One of the most prominent figures in Scripture to illustrate this is King David. Twenty seven of the 66 books of the Bible reference David. He is mentioned by name 974 times. In Psalm 109, David described what he did when wicked people lied about him, accused him, and responded to his good-hearted love with evil behavior. Instead of letting people-instigated storms overwhelm him, he redoubled his time in prayer. Approximately 88 times the Bible portrays David engaging God in prayer.

Trouble is a great reason to go to God! Are you worried sick by impending disaster? Are people attacking you for your moral stand or wrongly slandering you? Share your heart with your all-loving Savior. It amazes me how many steps we take to fix problems before we recognize that we ought to ask the Lord for His assistance. Isn't that sick!

Don't think that God is too busy to deal with your challenges or that you are unworthy of His attention. That is defeatist thinking and it does not square with Scripture. Jesus said in Matthew 11:28, *"Come to Me, all of you who are weary and burdened, and I will give you rest."* How can we come to the One who is in heaven, except through prayer and who is coming—those burdened! We wrongly focus on conditions when we should instead draw on faith! *"I assure you: Anything you ask the Father in My name, He will give you. Until now you have asked for nothing in My name. Ask and you will receive, that your joy may be complete"* (John 16:23b,24).

Ron's Phone Parable

August 27

Four of us were enjoying an informal time of fellowship when the topic came up of how we identify with Christ around others. One of the men pulled out his cell phone and showed how it had an icon of Christ as his background photo. Ron said he had also had a picture representing Christ on his phone. He pulled it out to show us, but all we could see was icons of missed calls that blocked the picture underneath.

Acts 21:21—But they have been told about you that you teach all the Jews who are among the Gentiles to abandon Moses, by telling them not to circumcise their children or to walk in our customs.

The Apostle Paul gave a report to James and the elders of the church in Jerusalem. He related in detail all he had done among the Gentiles through his ministry. When he finished, the elders glorified God and then shared with Paul of the thousands of Jews who had become believers. That report was followed by concern that these new Jewish converts were also zealous to keep the law. They were hearing reports that Paul was teaching Jews who lived among Gentiles to abandon obeying Moses or walking according to Jewish customs. This report was harmful to Paul's reputation. So the elders finished by instructing Paul what to do to dispel the incorrect perception.

Is it possible we think we are modeling Jesus to people but in fact the picture we present is distorted by misread things in our lives? People wrongfully assumed Paul was telling Jews to disregard the law. Perhaps they overheard a discussion and misinterpreted it. Perhaps they didn't like Paul's style and were just looking for a chance to slander him. It doesn't take much to trip people up. It is pretty easy for confusion to envelop clarity.

Just as the elders saw the problem and gave Paul a clear solution, so occasionally we ought to ask people to whom we are accountable to give us feedback on how we are doing in sharing Jesus. Am I engaged in something that is keeping others from focusing on Christ? Are others troubled by a perception of which I am unaware? Tell me! It's easy if it's my phone—I just click on the icons and they go away revealing the background photo. It's not quite so simple for life—all the more reason to be responsive.

By the way, when Paul obeyed the elders advice, Jews from Asia who despised him, assumed he brought Greeks into the Temple area. They wrongfully accused him in and created a riot. Don't be discouraged if you suffer setbacks trying to do what is right. Jesus was crucified as our perfect Savior.

Tested

August 28

He saw me sitting in the car and it seemed by the way he kept looking over at me like something was on his mind. When I exited the vehicle, he walked up and introduced himself to me. He said he was one of the new instructors in the Supervisor Course I was attending. Then he said he hoped he wouldn't offend me, but that he felt it was a breach of protocol to require general officers to take the end-of-course exam. He said he talked to the course managers about his concerns but that he was acting alone. Then he handed me two manila folders—one for myself and one for the other general attending the course. He asked me to sign the document and turn it in on Friday.

I walked into the building, went to my desk, shared with Dave, the other general, what had just happened, and then, in his presence, opened up the folder. In front of us was a test with all the answers circled. Dave looked and me and said, "No way!" Glad to see he was of the same mindset, I found that instructor and handed him the folders, declining to use them. He looked at me and said, "You're a good man."

Acts 24:16—I always do my best to have a clear conscience toward God and men.

Why did that instructor think it was a violation of protocol for two generals to take the same test as 49 other attendees? Did he think it was beneath us because of our rank and experience? Or was he testing us? I really don't know. But I do know this. There was no way I could rationalize cheating and leave that course with a clear conscience. I wonder if this is where so many leaders go astray—they determine they are somehow above the law or merit special favors.

God gave us each a conscience for a reason. His intent was that we would have an internal check to warn us not to err. Most testing is not so blatant as having someone hand out an exam with all the answers already circled! More often we are tested in subtle ways: to quibble with facts; to manipulate circumstances or compromise to gain unfair advantage; or to take positions that are popular at the expense of keeping God's truth.

How's your conscience? Is it taking a beating because you find it hard to do what is right? Is it silenced because you would rather not be bothered by its inconvenient beeping? Or are you living well, knowing that before the Lord and people you are doing what is right? The world does not see the value of Jesus in shady followers. If we are to be His effective ambassadors, we must in His strength do our best to maintain a clear conscience!

Inspiration †††

Testing puts muscles on your soul.—Paul White

Called a Slave

Romans 1:1—Paul, a slave of Christ Jesus, called as an apostle and singled out for God's good news.

Doesn't seem very flattering to be called a slave, does it? I don't want to be a slave to anyone. I want to be free—to do whatever I feel like doing, whenever, however. I want the right to control my life. I want the ability to choose my circumstances, pick my fun, and decide when to work, and nobody should be able to make me violate my own will. Do you see the trend? "I want . . ." And just how well does my plan work?

Life isn't free is it? You may have great plans for a career and find out no one is hiring. You may see a successful man you want to marry but he falls in love with someone else. You may plan to drive to see friends and get smashed by a drunk driver. You may be a superb athlete but aging robs your skills. Even your own thoughts cannot be corralled by a nature that is inherently selfish. Reality? None of us have the liberty we crave.

The Apostle Paul made a decision and stuck with it until he died. He chose to live in obedience to the will of Christ Jesus. He made himself a slave to God's Son. To do this he had to give up his successful career as a respected religious leader. He had to admit his zeal was wrong. He had to go from a position of power to enduring humiliation. His former friends hated him and some went to the extreme of plotting his assassination.

Paul knew that it was better to be a slave to Jesus and live under His authority than to be a slave to religious leaders and die for a hopeless cause. He knew trying to control himself was a non ending exercise in frustration (Rom. 7:15,19). He knew what it was like to be *"sold into sin's power"* (7:14). In essence, Paul recognized that everyone is a slave to something or someone and so he chose bondage to Christ.

Life can be free! This is the great paradox. When we choose to be slaves to Jesus, we find freedom. He rescues us from slavery to sin and pays our corrupt debt. He gives us an eternal inheritance and frees us from death. He gives us the knowledge that though we may suffer on earth, by obeying Him we can look forward to pain-free bodies and total liberation when God brings heaven. He rewards us.

The result of slavery to anything besides Jesus is ultimately meaningless. How sad that people chase religion, pleasure, power, recognition or possessions only to find out that what they thought would make them happy or give them freedom left a great void. I prefer this *sentence.* Dan, a slave of Christ Jesus, called as a saint and singled out for God's good news. How about you, will you submit your name and obey the Lord of All?

Covered

August 30

It was a classy show of sportsmanship. Tiger Woods walked into the gallery and was met by Jack Nicklaus, arguably the world's greatest golfer. Jack complimented him for his performance—his winning score of 67 matched Jack's own record. And then he told Tiger that his birdie on the 16th hole was one of the greatest shots he had ever witnessed.

Why was this conversation so remarkable? For the simple reason that Jack knew the heinous sins of Tiger. He witnessed the planet's most popular golfer meltdown morally and behave in ways that were a complete embarrassment to the sport. He rendered grace and dignity to an athlete he could deliberately have avoided.

Romans 4:7,8—How joyful are those whose lawless acts are forgiven and whose sins are covered! How joyful is the man the Lord will never charge with sin!

Paul never watched a golf tournament, but he understood a great deal about gracious behavior. He quoted King David's joy that comes to the person whose sins are covered by God. To the wicked King Jeroboam, God, through the prophet Ahijah, said, *"But you were not like My servant David, who kept My commands and followed Me with all of his heart, doing only what is right in My eyes"* (1 Ki. 14:8b). Huh? David murdered Uriah the Hittite, failed to discipline two sons—one a rapist the other a murderer, did nothing when his commanding general twice murdered a more honorable general, and took a census that greatly angered God. So what gave him cause to praise? God forgave him and blessed him with a powerful reign. He blessed David's faith and heart to follow Him.

Do you suppose Paul could relate to David? He participated in the slaughter of Jesus' followers. He directly opposed God's Son. To his young protégé Timothy, he wrote:

This saying is trustworthy and deserving of full acceptance: "Christ Jesus came into the world to save sinners"—and I am the worst of them. But I received mercy for this reason, so that in me, the worst of them, Christ Jesus might demonstrate His extraordinary patience as an example to those who would believe in Him for eternal life. (1 Ti. 1:15,16)

I don't know if Woods repented of his wrongdoing and I don't know the spiritual condition of Nicklaus. But I do know that God is willing to cover the sins of those who love and follow Him. He fills us with joy. We need to let go of the resentment we hold towards those who have wronged us. We need to stop living in fear of our past. We need to live joyfully! And we need to share what God has done for us. Contained joy is questionable. Radiated joy is the proof of covering!

Disposition

August 31

Guatemala is a beautiful land, vibrantly green and abundant with exotic fruit. Each day, we sensed the Lord's blessing in specific ways as we ministered to the people in Independencia. On day one we needed a translator. On the way to the village, we met a Cuban pastor from North Carolina who volunteered to help us all day! The next day we bought land from Arturo, a 79 year-old patriarch who loves the Lord. Arturo showed us his Bible. Inside was a picture of him standing next to my father. Then he told us his son lived in Japan. It turned out that Fernando and his wife, Makiko, were part of a Japanese church that heard about our ministry and months earlier, gave money to help us purchase property.

My disposition was joyful as I headed home. Pastor Eber, Arturo and Edgar accompanied me to Tapachula, Mexico to catch my plane. From there I flew to Guadalajara. I expected to be home before midnight. But a fire not far from the airport shut it down. By the time we lined up to board the plane at 1:00 a.m., the officials learned that customs at the Portland airport would close before we arrived so they cancelled the flight. Fortunately, I was able to catch a flight bound to Sacramento. At 4:00 a.m. I cleared customs and worked to get a 6:00 a.m. flight to Portland. But the Mexicana Airways official failed to enter into the computer my diverted schedule so I had to purchase a ticket with Horizon. I got on the plane hoping to be home soon. But the plane had a mechanical problem and we all had to disembark. An hour later, we flew on an Alaskan flight to Seattle. I caught another plane and after 26 hours of travel, arrived home.

Romans 8:11,12—And if the Spirit of Him who raised Jesus from the dead lives in you, then He who raised Christ from the dead will also bring your mortal bodies to life through His Spirit who lives in you. So then, brothers, So then, brothers, we are not obligated to the flesh to live according to the flesh.

Richard S. Taylor wrote in *A Right Conception of Sin,* "Let us remember, first, that God's quarrel is not with our humanity, but with our disposition to set our will against his."[71] Extended travel compounded by unforeseen disruption superbly tests one's disposition. I am happy to report that the Holy Spirit lives in me and lifted me beyond my natural nature. Rather than complain or find fault with my circumstances, I found cause to pray and rejoice. When my restless leg syndrome about drove me beyond sanity, I found grace in the journey. Twice God put me next to people I was able to serve. I knew beyond doubt that loving friends in prayer covered me. I am reminded again that when I fail, it is because my attention is on pleasing my old nature. When I succeed, it is because my attention is on pleasing my Savior. *O Lord, help me get it right as I follow You!*

On a Grassy Plain   September 1

Romans 8:19-21—For the creation eagerly waits with anticipation for God's sons to be revealed. For the creation was subjected to futility—not willingly, but because of Him who subjected it—in the hope that the creation itself will also be set free from the bondage of corruption into the glorious freedom of God's children.

    On a grassy plain thousands of hungry elk dine.
Massive bear fill their bellies with berries while squirrels leap overhead.
A red-tailed hawk swoops to snare a careless hare.
Trees play tag with a clever breeze;
the child of wind carries the seeds of cedar.
    Schools of fish swim through plant condominiums;
Both unmatched for their brilliant color and stunning patterns.
Who painted these graceful forms that live below,
That decorate murky waters and hidden reefs?
Or did they just evolve?
    Slabs of stone and mounds of dirt beneath the sheets of snow;
What magnets do mountains hold that pull admiring souls?
Who can tame an earthquake?
Lava beds, ocean waves, forests of triple canopy, desert grandeur,
Cranberry sunsets, puffed thunderclouds, arched rainbows
    When the bumblebee takes off in flight is the ant amazed?
Rains fill streams that carve rock as prized sculptures
while forming pools for thirsty creatures.
Lightning awakens gnarled pine in a signature of terror
Brush that choked its competition is burned away 'til new green emerges.
    What therapy provides the honest, unconditional love a dog shares?
Its tail and tongue and paw and eyes resound as faithful!
A purring cat brings calm.
The sun rises to gorgeous songs little birds create.
Dawn is the daily breath of newness to inhale. Is life a sentence or a gift?
    Pride will not admit a Maker for that would mean submission.
Yet unbelief cannot erase His handiwork and power to commission.
Can man control the weather, overcome decay or count all the stars?
Futility is defined by rejecting what is obvious to affirm what is hopeless!
A pagan man drowning yells, "Save me Lord!" because he knows!
    Creation is the visible expression of an invisible Maker.
The pathway to His lordship is built by the reality of life and suspense of death.
He gave us senses to lead us to know Him: the huckleberry and honey suckle . . .
the scent of rose . . . a warming fire . . . a bubbling brook . . . the aurora borealis.
    If an amazing creation groans now with the agony of sin, imagine what
its liberation will bring for those who believe in God's Son!

He is the image of the invisible God, the firstborn over all creation. For everything was created by Him, in heaven and on earth, the visible and the invisible, whether thrones or dominions or rulers or authorities—all things have been created through Him and for Him. (Col. 1:15,16)

Inspiration † † †

To say that the universe was created by chance is to say that it came from nothing. That is intellectual madness.—RC Sproul in *The Holiness of God*

Not According to Knowledge   September 2

Romans 10:2—I can testify about them that they have zeal for God, but not according to knowledge.

They come to our house at least twice a year. They are polite and clearly on a mission. If I told you they travel in pairs, often on bicycles wearing white shirts and ties, you would instantly know I meant Mormons. If they handed out Watchtower magazines, you'd correctly guess Jehovah's Witnesses.

The central problem with these die-hard door-knockers is that their zeal is not based on a correct understanding or application of God's Word. They have created doctrines that contradict or dismiss what the Bible teaches, while at the same time honoring it as sacred and valid. Yet in missing who Jesus is, they deserve the prayers of every Christian. They don't warrant the mocking, belittling or snide jokes that emanate from supposedly sanctified mouths. Such treatment in fact may spawn a dangerous broadcast—zeal is bad.

I have gone door-to-door in my city to invite people to church and if the opportunity arose, I would share the good news of Jesus. I took my children with me, and we had a great time. Many people we met had never had a Christian come to their door. Some actually shed tears and asked to pray with us. Unfortunately, my kids and I were unable to recruit anyone else in our church to help do what used to be called, "cold turkey evangelism." "We don't do door-to-door" was the common response.

Sometimes I wonder if zeal has become a word synonymous with wacky or fanatic. Yet, the Apostle Paul wrote to the Christians in Rome, *"Do not lack diligence; be fervent in spirit; serve the Lord"* (Rom. 12:11). The phrase *"do not"* is an absolute, not a suggestion. The issue is not whether we have knocked on stranger's doors. That is an action that should follow the prompting of the Holy Spirit and not the badgering of the pastor. The question is have we lost our zeal? When people see your life, do they conclude you are a devoted follower of Jesus? Do you stand out as different—in a God-honoring way?

We could learn a lot from the folks on bicycles. While we shake our heads, they are reaching people to their cause. If they can work so hard with a misguided zeal, shouldn't we be passionate to zealously share the Savior who changed our lives?

Inspiration † † †

If our knowledge about God is not charged with the life and power of God, mere knowledge becomes an idol in our mind.—Francis Frangipane in *Holiness, Truth and the Presence of God*

Wow

September 3

Romans 11:33-36—Oh, the depth of the riches both of the wisdom and the knowledge of God! How unsearchable His judgments and untraceable His ways! For who has known the mind of the Lord? Or who has been His counselor? Or who has ever first given to Him, and has to be repaid? For from Him and through Him and to Him are all things. To Him be the glory forever. Amen.

We do not know what He knows—His wisdom is beyond human comprehension, beyond measuring and unlimited in value. Take all the collective knowledge of the world and give it to one person and he or she would pale in comparison to God.

His judgments are resolute, trustworthy and accurate. The One without sin is perfect in every pronouncement. Who can judge how He judges? Who can find the source of His reasoning?

Who can predict His next act, define His previous actions or plot His doing now? He is invisible yet marks us, hidden yet inside us, working but doing what? He knows every thought, word and deed of ours and this ought to elicit from us a "wow!"

Tell me God's thoughts? Can you? Explain His mind. Give reason for His mercy when punishment is deserved, His grace when we are so deficient, His love while we ignore or disobey Him, His patience through our complaining, and His direction when we wander.

Do you advise the omniscient One? What is your resume that gives you the right to direct His ways? Who can add anything to the Maker of everything?

What contribution have you made that heaven's messengers dispatch God's IOU? At the first thought that you deserve better have you considered that you deserve nothing? The Creator who made all, more than the largest telescopes can see and rocket-born cameras discover, knows no debt. The word He deserves is "wow!"

A sinner named Saul knew the shame of his fall
    When the voice of His Savior delivered the call
And a saint named Paul left his blindness to bow
    To the Son of the Father, the Lord of the Wow!
For from Him and through Him and to Him all things
    To Him be the glory forever we'll sing! Amen.

Tom Capps wrote in *Pray and Plan*, "Genuine praise has a way of changing our focus from self to God, from problem to solution, from disappointment to great expectation, from depression to joy, from despair to hope."[72] Certainly Paul saw reason to marvel at God. So might we!

How to Become a Living Sacrifice   September 4

Romans 12:1,2—Therefore, brothers, by the mercies of God, I urge you to present your bodies as a living sacrifice, holy and pleasing to God; this is your spiritual worship. Do not be conformed to this age, but be transformed by the renewing of your mind, so that you may discern what is the good, pleasing, and perfect will of God.

In Romans 12 Paul gives us a beautiful blueprint from God in how we become living sacrifices—holy and pleasing to Him (v. 1).

I. Be Holy: Don't be conformed to the world; detest evil; do not be conquered by evil but conquer evil by good; do not repay evil with evil; cling to what is good.

II. Renew Your Mind: Discern what is the good, pleasing and perfect will of God; think sensibly in proportion to the faith God gives you; joyful in hope; patient in affliction; rejoice with those who rejoice; weep with those who weep.

III. Be Humble: Have a sober estimate of self; do not be proud; associate with the humble; do not be wise in your own estimation; don't avenge yourselves.

IV. Serve the Lord: Use the gifts God gave you according to His grace; be fervent; be diligent; persistent in prayer.

V. Love Others: Without hypocrisy; show family affection with brotherly love; outdo one another in showing honor; bless those who persecute you; do not curse.

VI. Be Generous: Share with the saints in their need; pursue hospitality; if your enemy is hungry or thirsty, give him something to eat or drink.

VII. Be Unified: Be in agreement with one another; do what is honorable in everyone's eyes; live at peace with everyone

Jesus perfectly modeled how to be a living sacrifice, the perfect model of spiritual worship. Before He died, Jesus prayed, *"I have glorified You on the earth by completing the work You gave Me to do"* (John 17:4). He followed His Father's plan and expected the same of those who followed Him. God never asks us to do what He will not equip us to perform—the key is our willingness to obey and pursue Him! To help us, the Holy Spirit acts as our Counselor to guide us in the truth and to empower us!

The beauty of our spiritual worship is that it pleases God, blesses us, and furthers the Lord's work in reaching more people with His love *as they see our transformation* (John 17:21). There is no greater pursuit in life than to pursue God—to bless Him through our surrender and to be blessed by Him forever. For this we climb higher . . . in reveration!

Inspiration ✝✝✝

To attempt to worship God in only the narrow sense of praising Him without seeking to worship Him in our whole way of life is hypocrisy.—Jerry Bridges in *The Joy of Fearing God*

In Reality   September 5

I once had a new boss that soon after taking command of our company, called me and two other subordinate leaders in for a meeting. I cannot remember anything he had to say except for one remark. He told us that one day he would be the Chief of Staff of the Army, a four-star general. The reason I remember that remark is that when the three of us got together afterwards, we all laughed. While his youthful passion was understandable, he overreached and by doing so, lost our respect. We knew enough about him to know his dream was not realistic and sure enough within several years he had left the service.

Uncontrolled zeal is fanaticism—a condition never endorsed in the Bible. Unfulfilled verbiage is hype—a first cousin to hypocrisy. We become unreal when we have all the right answers but the wrong applications. Most people quickly learn to spot smoke devoid of fire.

Jesus calls us to follow Him. If we want to be spiritually real, we must do just that! It does no good to *just talk* about following Him. It is hollow to brag about how well we *once* followed Him. We can project to others all kinds of goals and aspirations but if we are not currently living in obedience to God's will, we are just kidding ourselves and losing the respect of those around us.

God gives us open access to His presence. Will we share our hearts with Him? He quietly directs our conscience through the Holy Spirit. Do we submit to His lordship? Reality is defined by the word faithful. Never walk toward the future off the path of yesterday. Think sensibly. Live with humility. Walk after God in the present and in reality.

Romans 12:3— For by the grace given to me, I tell everyone among you not to think of himself more highly than he should think. Instead, think sensibly, as God has distributed a measure of faith to each one.

Inspiration † † †

Overmuch earnestness blinds the life to reality, earnestness becomes our goal. We bank on the earnestness and zeal with which things are said and done, and after a while we find that the reality is not there, the power and presence of God are not being manifested, there are relationships at home, or in business, or in private that show when the veneer is scratched that we are not real.—Oswald Chambers in *Studies on the Sermon on the Mount.*

Success

September 6

Bruce Thielemann tells the story in *Christus Imperator* of a king long ago who organized a great race within his kingdom. All the young men in the land participated. A bag of gold was to be given to the winner, and the finish line was within the courtyard of the king's palace. During the race the runners were surprised to find in the middle of the road leading to the king's palace a great pile of rocks and stones. But they managed to scramble over it or to run around it and eventually to come to the courtyard.

Finally all the runners had crossed the finish line except one. But still the king did not call the race off. After a while one lone runner came through the gate. He lifted a bleeding hand and said, "O King, I am sorry that I am so late. But you see, I found in the road a pile of rocks and stones, and it took me a while, and I wounded myself in removing them." Then he lifted the other hand, and in it was a bag. He said, "But, Great King, I found beneath the pile of rocks this bag of gold."

The king said, "My son, you have won the race, for that one runs best who makes the way safer for those who follow."[73]

Romans 12:10—Show family affection to one another with brotherly love. Outdo one another in showing honor.

Each day we must choose whether to live for ourselves or for our King. If we run for ourselves, we move to achieve all we have desired, planned or attempted—success is defined by the finish line. An honest person will soon admit the euphoria of crossing first ends in the emptiness that asks "is there not more in which to live for?"

If we race for God, it is not the tape draped across the road upon which we fix our eyes. No, we look to Jesus. Our aim is to be faithful as He was faithful. In the process we learn that success is really all about honoring others above ourselves. So if your hands are tired from moving stones that others ignored, be of good cheer. In your Father's eyes, you already are a success!

Inspiration † † †

True success is determined by how well we achieve the purposes for which God created us.—Bill Gothard in *Achieving Daily Success*

Meddling

September 7

I met Russ in a professional course we were both taking. We went to church on Sunday and had lunch together. Russ was a Captain in the Navy and a Delta pilot. He and I found we shared many things in common. Our time fellowshipping was quite enjoyable.

Russ mentioned that while in college he once led a time of worship at a spiritual rally. Afterwards, one of the ministry leaders commented that he seemed to thrive and to really enjoy song-leading. Russ agreed and shared that he could see himself serving in this capacity in the future. Then the unexpected happened. The mentor asked Russ when he was going to let go of song leading and really get on with doing what was important. Wanting to please him, Russ dutifully set aside his guitar and never played again.

Romans 12:16—Be in agreement with one another. Do not be proud; instead, associate with the humble. Do not be wise in your own estimation.

Romans 12:3-18 teaches us that God specifically gifts His followers and that we are to be humble about the way we view ourselves and sensitive to what is true in the lives of fellow Christians. What happened to Russ happens too often in Christianity and it is one of several reasons why we as a body of Christ are ineffective in reaching our world. When our gifts are recognized, nurtured, and allowed to flourish, team development is fabulous and local communities see firsthand the power of God at work. Unfortunately, too often, well-meaning leaders suppress gifts or activity they view as secondary in importance.

Minimizing or suppressing the giftedness of a brother or sister may very well constitute meddling. Meddling is involving oneself in a matter without right or invitation; it is interfering and intrusive. It does not matter if it is well-intentioned, the results can be harmful. To meddle is to be a junior holy spirit.

People meddle as a means to control, which is truly a symptom of insecurity. For others, it is a fixation on a narrow band of truth that is exclusive of God's broader band and bigger intentions. Still others fail to appreciate what they misunderstand. To suggest that someone should set aside leading worship for other activity is blatantly unscriptural. God made us to worship Him! Instead of praising God for gifting Russ and encouraging him, his leader was wise in his own estimation, demeaning the Spirit's creative infusion. Only if moved by the Holy Spirit do we have the right to prescribe. Otherwise, we are scratching stones instead of polishing gems. Don't meddle.

Authlicism

September 8

Often when I am driving on the road for long periods of time, I will tune in to listen to different radio talk shows. I have observed a pattern across the spectrum of those who claim to represent conservative America. Often they speak disrespectfully of politicians with statements like "he is an idiot" or "she is a moron." They mockingly belittle the mental competency of their intended targets or accuse them of evil motives. Several of these hosts skillfully move between humor and anger and it is easy to be sucked into the emotion-charged airwaves.

Romans 13:1,2,4—Everyone must submit to the governing authorities, for there is no authority except from God, and those that exist are instituted by God. So then, the one who resists the authority is opposing God's command, and those who oppose it will bring judgment on themselves . . . For government is God's servant for your good. But if you do wrong, be afraid, because it does not carry the sword for no reason. For government is God's servant, an avenger that brings wrath on the one who does wrong.

While it is okay to speak out against corruption or question policy, we must be wary that we don't become disrespectful and ugly towards those who are in positions of authority. For by judging and smearing those appointed to lead us, we give up the high ground of spiritual nobility for the sleazy soil of slander. By speaking against leaders, we may unwittingly speak against God for as the wise prophet Daniel noted, *"He [God] changes the times and seasons; He removes kings and establishes kings. He gives wisdom to the wise and knowledge to those who have understanding"* (Dan. 2:21, brackets mine).

We know the world is an evil place—this is not some shocking revelation. Ought we not to pray for those in power? Shouldn't we cry out to God to work His will, to redeem the unholy, to fix what is broken and to give us opportunity to be His rightful ambassadors? No government officials will find Jesus in the language of smear and vitriol spoken by those who claim to be His followers. Why wouldn't authorities look to marginalize and hurt those engaged in destroying them verbally? Jesus said, *"bless those who curse you, pray for those who mistreat you"* (Luke 6:28).

Not only should we pray for those who rule, we are expected to *"Submit to every human authority because of the Lord, whether to the Emperor as the supreme authority or to governors as those sent out by him to punish those who do what is evil and to praise those who do what is good"* (1 Pe. 2:13,14). Paul coached Titus in a time of great governmental corruption to share with those he taught the following:

> *Remind them to be submissive to rulers and authorities, to obey, to be ready for every good work, to slander no one, to avoid fighting, and to be kind, always showing gentleness to all people. For we too were once foolish, disobedient, deceived, enslaved by various passions and*

pleasures, living in malice and envy, hateful, detesting one another. (Tit. 3:1-3)

God never asks us to submit to laws or obey decrees that violate His moral and higher authority. For example, we have the right to refuse unlawful orders or lawful orders that put us in direct violation of what God commands. Peter respectfully reminded his Jewish authorities who ordered him not to mention the name of Christ, *"We must obey God rather than men"* (Acts 5:29).

Our challenge as God's children is not to engage in conduct unbecoming of saints. There is no glory in ruler-bashing or attacking leaders with saber-sharp language. I call this *authlicism*—criticizing those who are in positions of authority with disrespectful language. We don't have to find satisfaction from our tongue; we should be living in victory through the One in our hearts who is Lord of all and who helps us in our journey!

74

Cheyenne Disaster

September 9

Romans 13:14—But put on the Lord Jesus Christ, and make no plans to satisfy the fleshly desires.

Tom walked in to see his friend the Commander of Hunter Stuart Air Force Base. As he sat down, the colonel asked the young major if he knew anything about the Cheyenne. Tom knew it was a special gunship designed to help with the war effort in Vietnam. The colonel said to him, "Wouldn't you like to know who it is who will pick the team to fly this 'hot item?'" Tom almost fell out of his chair when the colonel then said, "You're looking at him." Then he further stunned Tom by telling him that after looking at his record Tom was not only qualified to fly the Cheyenne, he was the colonel's choice to lead the team. After Tom said he would be honored to take the assignment, the commander picked up the phone and called the Department of the Army to confirm his choice. Then he told Tom, "Well, your career has just been set for the next ten years."

After their meeting Tom and his wife Carolyn drove to the Georgia coast to get some personal time. While reading through the book of Esther, they concluded that Tom should turn down the assignment. They further concluded that God was calling them into ministry. So after returning to Fort Benning, Georgia, he resigned his commission. Shortly thereafter, while a civilian, he read in the *Stars and Stripes* newspaper that the Cheyenne helicopter project was cancelled for cost overruns. He and Carolyn were thankful for the decision they made.

Twenty-five years later a former military friend came out to visit. As Tom and his Army buddy talked, he asked Don if he had ever shared with him the story about the Cheyenne helicopter. When his friend said "No," Tom proceeded to tell the story. When he got to the part about being offered to lead the project, Don's face turned "white as a sheet." Don asked Tom if he knew why the project was cancelled. Tom answered because of cost overruns. Don shook his head and said, "I was the Chief Investigating Officer on the case. On its first Army test run the ship came apart in midair and ALL ON BOARD WERE KILLED!!!" Then Tom's face turned white. Had he taken that assignment he undoubtedly would have been on that aircraft.

So often we make decisions based on how we perceive we will gain prestige, profit or pleasure. The Bible warns us not to satisfy fleshly desires. What we see as gain may actually be a trap or result in disaster. To *"put on the Lord Jesus Christ"* simply means to follow Him, to do what He asks. Are you willing to give up what will burn to gain what is eternal?

Inspiration † † †

It is the man who is entirely consecrated to God and His will who will find the power come to claim everything that His God has promised to be for him.— Andrew Murray in *With Christ in the School of Prayer*

Alone with God

September 10

To be alone can have two different meanings. It can signify the solitary state of life devoid of contact with anyone else. Or it can mean unique, being without equal.

There are times when we feel separated from all other people. The crush of humanity may press against our very flesh yet we feel emotionally or mentally isolated. It is as if we are tuned to a radio frequency no one else is receiving. In such times, depression can easily transcend from stranger to first-name basis. To be alone, to sense no one else understands or cares may choke the very joy out of living.

Romans 14:7,8—For none of us lives to himself, and no one dies to himself. If we live, we live for the Lord; and if we die, we die for the Lord. Therefore, whether we live or die, we belong to the Lord.

Pearl S. Buck is credited for writing:
The person who tries to live alone will not succeed as a human being. His heart withers if it does not answer another heart. His mind shrinks away if he hears only the echoes of his own thoughts and finds no other inspiration.

Are we truly alone? If we belong to the family of God, there is no separation from Him! His Holy Spirit resides in us (1 Co. 3:16). Jesus wants us to understand this. He shared with the Jews in John 8:29, *"The One who sent Me is with Me. He has not left Me alone, because I always do what pleases Him."* Just as God did not abandon Jesus when He left heaven to serve on earth, so He will not abandon us when we place our trust in Him. Though you may feel alone, God promises He is with you.

We are always alone in our uniqueness. No one else shares my fingerprint, my personality, my looks, my thoughts or my soul. I either thank God He loved me enough to make me this way or I complain, unappreciative of His creative work. God also is alone. We discover in Rev. 15:4, *"Lord, who will not fear and glorify Your name? Because You alone are holy, for all the nations will come and worship before You because Your righteous acts have been revealed."*

Are you alone? Thank God for it! He's right there with you!

Inspiration ✝✝✝

Great eagles fly alone; great lions hunt alone; great souls walk alone-alone with God.—L. Ravenhill

Valor

September 11

Brian Birdwell in his book *Refined by Fire* wrote, "We all face personal fires—those life-changing, traumatic times when the course of our lives are altered."[75] On September 11, 2001, terrorists hijacked and crashed American Airlines Flight 77 into the Pentagon. MAJ Brian Birdwell was so close to the impact area that the ensuing explosion burned 60% of his body. He endured over thirty surgeries, fought off numerous life-threatening infections and suffered continuous horrific pain to the point that he "begged God constantly to let me die."

The natural response for most victims to catastrophic suffering is bitterness. "Why me?" is the two-word cry screamed to heaven. Yet while Brian struggles to forgive the terrorists who took 125 lives at the Pentagon and almost 3000 lives from the four coordinated attacks, he refused bitterness and chose *betterness*. "They see my scars. That's authenticity." The authenticity that Brian writes about is the living proof that God exists and that His grace is ample in taking us through the worst trials we could imagine.

John 16:33—I have told you these things so that in Me you may have peace. You will have suffering in this world. Be courageous! I have conquered the world.

Brian is a man of valor. The proof of courage is not when we fight from a position of strength, but rather the ability to proceed in weakness. Jesus warned we would face suffering in the world. He was not concerned by this reality. His intent was that we would grasp two things—courage and peace. Courage comes from believing that ultimately no matter what we face, Jesus wins. Peace comes from the belief that God <u>is</u> in control. This is why Brian could say, "In those seconds inside the Pentagon when I was on fire, going from the struggle to survive to acknowledging the reality of my death, I went from panic to calm. Who else can provide that except Christ?"

The Apostle Paul, no stranger to suffering, wrote in his letter to the Corinthians, "*So I take pleasure in weaknesses, insults, catastrophes, persecutions, and in pressures, because of Christ. For when I am weak, then I am strong*" (2 Co. 12:10). "*Because of Christ*"—those three words separate us from defeat, define our heritage, glorify the Author, and imbue us with valor.

Inspiration † † †

Meaning can give us strength and meaning can give us courage.—Steven M. Southwick & Dennis S. Charney in *Resilience*

Love sweetens pains. And when a Christian loves God, he can suffer for His sake, joyfully and courageously.—Brother Lawrence & Frank Laubach in *Practicing His Presence*

Pursuing Peace   September 12

Romans 14:19—So then, we must pursue what promotes peace and what builds up one another.

One of the greatest hindrances to the deepening of relationships is our propensity to want to change those around us. While our motives may seem pure, in fact, if we are not careful, there is an ever subtle danger that our distilled rationale for fixing others is in fact for our own betterment. Much of the time what we want from others or even for ourselves is not necessarily what God wants.

Let's suppose I aim to invite someone over for dinner for the purpose of fellowship. I call my wife and inform her of my intentions and she responds that the date is not a good time for her. She projects a busy day and does not feel she could prepare adequately. Immediately I am agitated. I question her priorities and remind her that we are to put others before ourselves (missing that I just put myself before her). I remind her that my schedule is much busier and this is the only convenient date I can meet with the person. She now feels guilty and acquiesces to my will. Do you see the problem?

If my motive is to promote peace and build up others, that motive cannot exclude the people closest to me. The moment my wife objects to the plan and date I proposed I should remember that my responsibility is to build *her* up. Pursuing peace means I thank her and work to reschedule. If I am still agitated, it means I probably have unresolved issues I need to settle with her. Rarely are we put off or irritated with a person for a single reason. Now it is time to go to the Lord in prayer and ask Him to reveal what is causing my irritation. Trying to fix another person is fraught with hypocrisy. In truth, I have many things that need fixing—selfishness, impatience, insecurities, hidden agendas, etc.

One reason our effort to correct others so often ends badly is because they see through our exhortation a pattern or act of manipulation that is to our advantage. This in turn can cause them to take *their* focus off of pleasing God. When my intent is to honor God, I am able to pursue peace. I begin to see people as He sees them. I can relax. I can overlook what bothers me and instead look to encourage another. When my resolve is to build up another with God-centered motives, I can correct in a spirit of love in God's timing if needed. Pursuing peace is often a matter of getting me out of the way!

Inspiration ✝ ✝ ✝

Fighting for your convictions is important. But finding peace is paramount. Knowing when to fight and when to seek peace is wisdom.— Wes Moore in *The Other Wes Moore*

Endurance and Encouragement   September 13

A runner sees endurance as vital to finishing a race; a parent sees endurance as the ability to shepherd a child to adulthood. Endurance originates from the compound Greek word: hupo (under) + meno (to remain) to give us the concept *continuing under pressure*.[76] It is much more than a physical resolve, it is a mental resolve. Without sufficient *why*, the *what* loses meaning and we are more prone to quit.

Romans 15:4—For everything that was written in the past was written to teach us, so that through the endurance taught in the Scriptures and the encouragement they provide we might have hope. (NIV)

God inspired men to write words teaching endurance and encouragement thousands of years before you existed to give you hope! Wow—that thought should produce goose bumps. If you are pressed to make a key decision by picking up and studying the Bible, the Holy Spirit is able to directly speak to your situation with direction. During a period of discouragement the Word of God is able to uplift you. When you feel conflicted, the Word brings peace. When you feel confused, the Word brings clarity. When you feel unstimulated, the Word brings vision. When you are in sin, the Word rebukes. When you feel attacked, the Word routs the enemy. This is exactly why I am so saddened that so many Christians disdain the habit of regularly reading their Bible.

Paul taught in 2 Timothy 3:16, "*All Scripture is inspired by God and is profitable . . .*" That word profitable is directed to you and me. But without investment there can be no profit. If God so carefully constructed a living document for our edification, shouldn't we see the wisdom and establish the habit to maintain divine appointments?

So I hear the objection, "Well sometimes I read the Word and it is boring?" *Really*! Do you always eat exciting food? Consider that what is boring this morning, the Holy Spirit may bring to your mind at a later date to help you endure and give encouragement. Another says, "I'm just too busy!" *Truly*! So you would rather maintain your frenetic chaos at the cost of reading the book that would amplify, rectify, codify, simplify, clarify, and purify your life for your betterment? Still another says, "The language is archaic and I don't understand it." *Ridiculous*! Get a modern translation. Yet another says, "The Bible is controversial and not politically correct." *Snobbish*! Are you impressed with the way the world operates and feeling encouraged? Which ground would you rather build your house on—relative ground or absolute ground? Finally another says, "I'm not sure I can trust such an ancient document?" *Hmmm*! Not reading it makes that self-evident. But if you cannot trust God's Word, you cannot trust God. Is that the path you truly want to take?

The world is full of hype God's Word is full of hope. If I could persuade you today, I would persuade you to persistently invest in Scripture. Make it your passion and objective and with firm resolve dedicate time to the book your Father inspired to give you hope.

Inspiration †††

Endurance is patience concentrated.—Thomas Carlyle

Manifestation

September 14

Would you agree it is quite enjoyable to watch people grow spiritually? Yet often the growth that is so evident to us goes unnoticed by the one being observed. I suppose in one respect it's similar to watching the changes in my children as they extend vertically. On the white painted wall behind our bedroom door is a ladder of pencil marks each proclaiming a new climb in inches. Periodically they will ask my wife or me to measure them to see how they are doing in their quest for height. Without that pencil-marked wall, each of my three kids would have a tough time gauging their growth.

1 Corinthians 1:4-6—I always thank my God for you because of God's grace given to you in Christ Jesus, that by Him you were enriched in everything—in all speech and all knowledge. In this way, the testimony about Christ was confirmed among you. John 1:14,18—The Word became flesh and took up residence among us. We observed His glory, the glory as the One and Only Son from the Father, full of grace and truth ... No one has ever seen God. The One and Only Son—the One who is at the Father's side—He has revealed Him.

If we believe that spiritual advancement is validated by the Lord manifesting Himself to us, we are apt to become discouraged. So many Christians crisscross the planet to wherever God is performing live to experience first-hand His power and presence. While this may render mountain-top experiences, it suggests a denial or misunderstanding of God's valley-workings and His ever quiet omnipresence.

By conceptualizing a God who must perform signs to prove He is at work in us we are tempted to worship the signs and miss God altogether. The power of our Father is less often grasped in visible dynamic expression. Yet His invisible dynamic impression is constantly occurring. So, if someone you know cannot apprehend the changes God has wrought in his or her life and you can, be a wall marker! Share the character changes you've seen the Master Artist sculpt for His glory.

Inspiration †††

We look to God to manifest Himself to His children: God manifests Himself in His children, consequently the manifestation is seen by others, not by us. It is a snare to want to be conscious of God; you cannot be conscious of your consciousness and remain sane.—Oswald Chambers in *God's Workmanship*

Song Selection

September 15

While flying back to Portland, I sat next to a man who worked for JDRUM (not its real name), a Christian-owned corporation of radio stations that play Christian music. Because of my passion for worship and experience listening to JDRUM, I queried him about how they chose the songs they aired. He told me that songs were selected according to the interests of the listeners. I challenged him on the accuracy of that statement. In essence, big labels sign artists and promote their music. While the public as a purchasing body has a say in what is popular, in fact, companies (targeting youth) sign artists based on what their market analysis determines will be well received by "young listeners."

How wise is it to pick songs based on the interests of youth—the age at which spiritual formation is still weak and immature! Repeatedly the Bible warns us against adopting worldly values (see Jam. 4:4 and 1 Jo. 2:15,16). Am I safe in concluding the world influences us more than we influence the world?

Embracing what is secular to attain what is spiritual is a faulty premise. If I was a non-Christian, my argument would be, "Why should I become like you if you are so intent on copying me?" Should we take drugs to better relate to our friends who are "high?" If we want to attract people to Christ, we must be Christ-like, not world-like. If we can't understand the "Christian lyrics" of a song screamed by an artist to a beat that is damaging to the eardrums, explain how it glorifies God. The test to determining whether our interests and tastes are valid can only be answered affirmatively if God is glorified.

1 Corinthians 3:1,2—Dear brothers and sisters, when I was with you I couldn't talk to you as I would to spiritual people. I had to talk as though you belonged to this world or as though you were infants in the Christian life. (NLT)

My intent is not to bash Christian radio stations. I love the unashamed manner in which they share the gospel and have prayer lines with counselors open to their listeners. Many songs they play certainly honor God. But I do question their approach and philosophy in music-selection. Too often I hear songs that are me-centric and not God-centric. Too often Christianity is defined by what is popular as opposed to what is Spirit-led. Too often music that should uplift listeners through love and reverence for God is garbled by silly jingles and values that affirm the world and not the Maker of the world. I don't think Jesus is preoccupied with how good I feel. He commands us to die to the world and to what the world values. Shouldn't the goal of Christian music stations be to draw listeners to Jesus?

Memorial

September 16

In September 16th 2011, I celebrated my 30th reunion with hundreds of other West Point classmates who graduated in 1981. We met in the Cadet Chapel for a memorial service remembering our deceased classmates. Darryl read twenty two names and then finished with Daren Hidalgo, a 2009 graduate killed in Afghanistan. Daren is the son of our classmate Jorge. Somber air marked the mention of each friend. But in the hush of those granite, shadowed halls it was a different hurt that saluted a son of our own.

We do well to acknowledge the pain that grips our heart with the passing of those we treasure. King Solomon once wrote, *"Grief is better than laughter, for when a face is sad, a heart may be glad. The heart of the wise is in a house of mourning, but the heart of fools is in a house of pleasure"* (Ecc. 7:3,4). How does grief make a heart glad? Perhaps the recognition that we are still living should make us thankful. Maybe it is our opportunity to make more of what was lost; to gain understanding from those who left us. Perhaps it is the recognition of soul searching; of looking inward and revaluing what matters most. Maybe it is the knowledge that those who died are free of pain or turmoil.

My memories reach back to Brian Haller, my best friend and fellow commander, the one whose name lives forward in our oldest son. He is the only man I have ever known who could read me and discern if something was wrong. He will be one of the first of friends and family I look forward to hugging in heaven.

Exodus 12:14,26,27—This day is to be a memorial for you, and you must celebrate it as a festival to the LORD. You are to celebrate it throughout your generations as a permanent statute ... When your children ask you, "What does this ritual mean to you?" you are to reply, "It is the Passover sacrifice to the LORD, for He passed over the houses of the Israelites in Egypt when He struck the Egyptians and spared our homes." So the people bowed down and worshiped.

Memorials preserve our memories of both people and events. And while with people it is death that we recognize, it is life that we honor. What is profound is not what decays or passes from the ranks of the living but the fact that the past marches forward.

Jesus, the world's most celebrated and controversial Rabbi offered His followers a promise when He said to them, *"In a little while the world will see Me no longer, but you will see Me. Because I live, you will live too. In that day you will know that I am in My Father, you are in Me, and I am in you"* (John 14:19,20). The world would not visibly see Him because He would die, yet how many invisibly see Him because He lives? The paradox is not in what we see but in what we don't see. If we are honest, as we remember those who are gone, we must ask ourselves are we living to die or dying to live? How we answer that question says much about us and about how and who we honor.

Is it fate that wraps its arms around us in death, or faith we wrap our arms around in life? Perhaps old mourning is not such a bad thing and this morning—renewed time to celebrate.

Inspiration ✝✝✝

Should it be ours to drain the cup of grieving
Even to the dregs of pain, at thy command
We will not falter, thankfully receiving
All that is given by thy loving hand.—Dietrich Bonhoeffer in *The Cost of Discipleship*

WIZDUMB

September 17

Driving Highway 101 from Fort Hunter Liggett to San Jose, I experienced an epiphany. Whoa, was it a boat rocker! It came via a clever California license plate in front of me—WIZDUMB. It caused me to reflect on the two kinds of wisdom that exist.

Wisdom = Understanding of truth as revealed by the Holy Spirit. True insight when applied by we humans which leads to awesome living.

Wizdumb = Understanding of truth as revealed by human thought that is ignorant or disdainful of God's revelation. Earthly insight originates from imperfect minds with the result that every wiz ends up being very dumb!

I'm indebted to the owner of that car in front of me for the spiritual wake-up. I don't want to go through any day without relying on God! I don't want to pretend my self-propelled thoughts and views are sufficient for successful living. Wizdumb is choosing my thoughts over His thoughts and I personally am never thrilled with the results. That's a good reason for us to agree with what the Apostle Paul prayed for the Christians in Ephesus: *"I pray that the God of our Lord Jesus Christ, the glorious Father, would give you a spirit of wisdom and revelation in the knowledge of Him"* (Eph. 1: 17). May our views be His view!

1 Corinthians 3:19,20—For the wisdom of this world is foolishness with God, since it is written: He catches the wise in their craftiness; and again, The Lord knows that the reasonings of the wise are meaningless.

Inspiration †††

If Jesus Christ is not revealed to us, it is because we have views of our own, and we want to bend everything to those views. To realize Christ we must come to Him.—Oswald Chambers in *Making All Things New*

Responsibility

September 18

I sit before a quiet screen in a well-lit study where the only noise is a blowing fan. A neon sign flashes repeatedly across my mind—"Faithful," "Faithful," "Faithful." Am I faithful to the One who called me?

Is my responsibility to please myself in a world that applauds personal achievement? Or, do I live to obey and honor the will of the One who sacrificed His Son to reach me? Tears provide the answer—so far to go, so much to learn, so hard to be responsible for that which matters most. In the journey of life, what's inside the suitcase reveals much about the traveler.

1 Corinthians 4:2—Now it is required that those who have been given a trust must prove faithful. (NIV)
John 4:34—"My food is to do the will of Him who sent Me and to finish His work," Jesus told them.

Randy Alcorn wrote in *Heaven*, "God is grooming us for leadership. He's watching to see how we demonstrate our faithfulness."

Inspiration ✝✝✝

Liberty means responsibility, that is why most men dread it.—G.B Shaw

Marriage

September 19

The story is told of a conversation between a teenager and his grandfather. The young man said, "Gee, Grampa, your generation didn't have all these social diseases. What did you wear to have safe sex?" The wise old gentleman replied, "A wedding ring."

1 Corinthians 7:3,4— A husband should fulfill his marital responsibility to his wife, and likewise a wife to her husband. A wife does not have the right over her own body, but her husband does. In the same way, a husband does not have the right over his own body, but his wife does.

Recently I ran across the term HPV—Human Papillomavirus. It is known as the "wart virus" and it is one of the most common human infections. Dr. Ray Fowler writes:

> By now, as many as 90% of cases of cancer of the cervix can have detectable HPV in the cancerous cells. The correct conclusion to draw seems to be that HPV can 'cause' cervical cancer. It is even proper to conclude that 'unprotected intercourse can lead to cancer of the cervix.'[78]

The number of people infected with sexually transmitted diseases today is shocking. Why do so many people put their physical, emotional and spiritual health at great risk by living promiscuously?

Fault-finding is a well-honed art. The loss of satisfaction in one's mate can easily lead to infidelity. Yet, until we get to heaven there is no such thing as a perfect spouse. Unless the one we are married to is in unrepentant adultery or engaged in unlawful abusive behavior, we should do all we can to preserve and enrich the marriage union.

Criticism tears the fabric of marriage. Picking apart a mate, using acid-laced sarcasm or constantly haranguing brings death to a union. Ruth Bell Graham says, "A good marriage is the union of two forgivers." Forgiveness and a willingness to invest in each other motivates healthy growth. When I see and communicate value in my spouse, I am investing in her worth.

Compliments and good listening strengthen the fabric of marriage. Giving of ourselves to please our mates helps prevent Hollywood's version of marriage which resembles sanitation work with its weekly dumping. We don't put an iron ring around our finger because iron rusts. We invest in gold—which serves as a reminder of our promise to hold our consummation sacredly.

Inspiration † † †

One of the main reasons marriages fail is that the husband or wife does not seek the other's bests interest.—Stormie Omartian in *The Power of a Praying Husband*

Demons

There are those who scoff at the reality of demons. The notion of religion or the existence of God seems like relics of an antiquated belief system. Tell that to the four men who on September 20, 2011 stood around Vlad* and prayed for him, watching as he writhed on the ground as one and then another demon left him. Two days later Vlad called Dad and said he was again under attack. So the two met near my parent's home and walked together up a nearby mountain.

Again Dad challenged Vlad with the test of 1 John 4:2,3—*"This is how you know the Spirit of God: Every spirit who confesses that Jesus Christ has come in the flesh is from God. But every spirit who does not confess Jesus is not from God . . ."* Vlad lunged at him, his eyes full of evil, stopping as if hitting a wall inches from his face. A voice taunted Dad that he did not have the authority to cast him out. He responded that by himself he did not have authority but by the name of Jesus Christ and in His power he held authority. He then commanded every demon in Vlad to leave.

The most horrible, foul cursing filled the air and again, Vlad was thrown to the ground where he coughed and wrestled with his unseen tormentors. This time, they all came out. Vlad was in his right mind and was filled with peace. That same day he finally put his faith in Jesus.

Luke 1:1-4—Many have undertaken to compile a narrative about the events that have been fulfilled among us, just as the original eyewitnesses and servants of the word handed them down to us. It also seemed good to me, since I have carefully investigated everything from the very first, to write to you in an orderly sequence, most honorable Theophilus, so that you may know the certainty of the things about which you have been instructed.

We should be encouraged when we read in Scripture that Luke wrote two books in the Bible, Luke and Acts, so that his friend Theophilus would *"know the certainty of the things"* taught him. The Bible is not fiction. It is not the fabrication of deluded men or the conjecture of superstitious simpletons. It is an amazingly accurate narrative of eyewitnesses. When it tells us that demons exist and torment people, we should take notice. When it reveals they must flee before the name and authority of Jesus Christ, we should feel empowered (Luke 9:42, Acts 16:18).

There are Vlad's all around us. In most parts of the world, people are very aware of demons—they know what it is to live in fear of evil spirits. In America, demons are far more subtle. They hide in plain sight fed by the sophisticated lie that they don't exist. *"That you may know the certainty,"* confront those seeking help from inner demons in Jesus' name.

*Not his real name.

Manny

September 21

Pound for pound, Manny Pacquiao may be the best boxer ever. Manny is not just a Filipino fighter; he is also a politician, musician and actor. Given his popularity, he may be his country's president someday. Manny is the first boxer to become an eight-division world champion. The Boxing Writers Association of America named Manny the "Fighter of the Decade."[79]

For a long time, life was difficult for this Filipino hero. The fourth of six children, Manny watched his mother divorce her husband after discovering he was living with another woman. At the age of 14 he dropped out of high school and moved to Manila where for a brief period he lived on the streets. Today he is married to Maria Geraldine "Jinkee" Jamora, and they have four children. Not surprising, "Pacquiao is also a military reservist with the rank of Sergeant Major for the 15th Ready Reserve Division of the Philippine Army."[80]

Boxing fans love watching Pacquiao because he gives his all when he competes. His professional record is 53-3-2. When asked the key to his success, this humble man gives all the glory to God. A devout Roman Catholic, every time he returns from a successful fight abroad, he attends a thanksgiving Mass in Quiapo, Manila to kneel and pray.[81]

1 Corinthians 9:25-27—Now everyone who competes exercises self-control in everything. However, they do it to receive a perishable crown, but we an imperishable one. Therefore I do not run like one who runs aimlessly, or box like one who beats the air. Instead, I discipline my body and bring it under strict control, so that after preaching to others, I myself will not be disqualified.

Four times I fought in a ring and three times I lost. One time I faced a leftie and the referee had to stop the fight I was getting beat so bad. If I had to make my living boxing, my family would starve. But in the ring of life, I don't ever want to be disqualified. When I live in such a way that I know God is displeased, it hurts. My goal is to receive an imperishable crown. So I train hard by disciplining my body, my mind, and my spirit to serve Jesus, the Savior of the world. Like the Apostle Paul and like Manny, I give Him all the credit for my being and doing. The One who gave His Son for me deserves full allegiance and respect. He is the One who makes life worth living! How about you? For what are you competing?

Inspiration †††

Nobody trains without a purpose.—Stuart Briscoe in *Spiritual Stamina*

Sacrament

September 22

It was the beginning of day four of a head cold that felt like a nonstop faucet leak through my eyes. I went through enough Kleenex to carpet a football field. Now it is standard practice in my Army organization to offer chapel service to any interested soldiers on Sunday. For some reason, our higher headquarters did not plan a service for this conference. So not only was my body weak, I was spiritually hungry for time with other saints to worship.

My Jewish Brigade Commander, David, has remarkable people skills. He walked up to me and handed me a small plastic container with what looked like grape juice inside. David had approached a group of people in our hotel that were getting ready to have a worship service. I saw them passing out the containers to their members in the lobby and concluded they were going to celebrate communion. I didn't think to ask them for one since I would be in meetings and could not join them. But David's thinking was much clearer. He asked for one and gave it me and encouraged me to have my own communion.

After our meeting, I had some time alone in the lobby. I pulled off the top of the container and to my surprise, it held not just juice but also a thin white wafer. As I silently prayed and thanked the Lord for His unbelievable sacrifice for me on a cross, I was immediately encouraged by His presence. Communion chills far surpass cold chills!

1 Corinthians 11:25,26—In the same way, after supper He also took the cup and said, "This cup is the new covenant established by My blood. Do this, as often as you drink it, in remembrance of Me." For as often as you eat this bread and drink the cup, you proclaim the Lord's death until He comes.

Twice the phrase *"as often"* graces the passage above. It reminds me that the sacrament of communion is not just about remembrance it is also proclamation. In that South Carolina Marriott hotel, brothers and sisters of an unknown church came to proclaim the unique message that makes our belief distinct for profound reasons. Our God loves us so much that He sent His Son to die for us. Who else does that? What makes fellowship sweet is the sourness of the cost shared from the mouth of One who knew His blood would flow in the most horrible fashion yet announced it beforehand with the encouragement *as often*!

My friend David encouraged me to celebrate my Savior Jesus. How profound that the one who does not yet know Jesus, brought Him to me in sacrament. More often should I thank my Lord, with this visible sign of His invisible grace! He is worthy—we are witnesses.

Symphony Orchestra September 23

In 1798 the U.S. Marine Band was born. Its primary mission is to provide music for the President of the United States and the Commandant of the Marine Corps. President John Adams gave the band its charter but Thomas Jefferson coined its lasting title, *"The President's Own."* Marine Band musicians appear at the White House more than 200 times annually. Their music thrills the ear and uplifts the heart.

1 Corinthians 12:12,27—For as the body is one and has many parts, and all the parts of that body, though many, are one body—so also is Christ . . . Now you are the body of Christ, and individual members of it.

Do you realize that we who place our faith and follow Jesus Christ are *God's Own*! We are a symphony orchestra under the direction of the Holy Spirit.

For an orchestra to sound beautiful *unity* is essential. Each member of the body holds an important part. If one person faithfully executes his or her piece, everyone celebrates. If one musician insists on playing too loudly, incorrectly or not at all, the song is degraded and the entire band suffers. Likewise, if we as Christians disdain playing the parts God gives us, we jeopardize the performance of the entire body. If you disagree, simply think of what happens when a believer publicly falls into sin—those who do not know Christ find occasion to label us (as a whole), as disgusting hypocrites. Our notes fall flat and turn off the ears of potential listeners.

For an orchestra to inspire there must be *humility*. When the piccoloist disdains her small part and plays on, she mars the expression of a song. She, along with each member, must believe the whole is greater than the one. Perfect blending comes when wind, percussion, and string sections focus one eye on their music and the other on their director. There is no place for viewing each other. So we must keep one eye in God's Word and one eye on the leading of the Holy Spirit.

If we are displeased with the parts God has given us to play, we do not understand the sound that He is trying to produce. God rewards us for faithfully doing what He asks us not for what position we hold within the orchestra. There is an entire world desperately yearning to hear the salvific notes of God's redeeming grace! The sound of truth presented in love by transformed musicians is unsurpassable! So play! Play! For God's glory, play!

Inspiration ✝ ✝ ✝

Christ has no body on earth but yours, no hands but yours, no feet but yours. Yours are the eyes through which Christ's compassion for the world is to look out; yours are the feet with which He is to go about doing good; and yours are the hands with which He is to bless us now.—Saint Teresa of Avila

The Great Advancer of Power September 24

1 Corinthians 13:4—Love is patient, love is kind. Love does not envy, is not boastful, is not conceited.

One of the saddest notions of humanity is the belief that unprincipled acts are justified if they prolong power. Every week in the world, a village is ravaged, some family is made homeless, crops are burned down, an idealist is imprisoned, and an opponent is slandered to further the causes of those who would inflict their will on others. The exercise of evil never engenders loyalty or the favor of people—instead it produces bitterness, resentment and suspicion. It fertilizes seeds of revenge that one day bear the fruit of treachery.

When we experience injustice, our natural response is to attack. In the name of justice we are quite capable of becoming ugly. Yet is it ever right to engage in immoral actions to protect what we hold as sacred? Those, who in God's name do evil things, will never reach ungodly people. Which action is more likely to bring a mother contemplating abortion to Christ—offering to help provide adoption or picketing a clinic while chanting inflammatory slogans? What leads a president burdened with immoral actions to repentance—believers praying for him or deluging his office with hate mail?

We Christians desperately want the world to like us. We want our nation to behave morally. As our land slips deeper into spiritual bankruptcy we are more prone than ever to rallying behind politicians we trust to save us. But God said in His Word that we would be hated because of Him. He already told us that the world is not going to get better. We are not the ones who are being rejected—God is. People unwilling to yield their hearts to Jesus take out their animosity on us—and we are surprised! The more we fight for our rights the more susceptible we are to missing our opportunities to truly reach people with the good news of Christ. What makes us different as God's children is not our political might but rather the grace that God extended to us to change our lives—the same grace He wants us to model to reach others. *"And be kind and compassionate to one another, forgiving one another, just as God also forgave you in Christ"* (Eph. 4:32).

The great advancer of power is love expressed as kindness. God proved this truth when He chose to sacrifice the very One He loved the most, His Son. Jesus refused to call the legions of angels at His service. Instead He hung in agony while forgiving the very ones who had Him murdered. He extended mercy, not wrath, to demonstrate that His power was made complete by love.

If we want to be effective messengers of the gospel, we must look for opportunities to exercise kindness. People yearn for the peace that surpasses understanding. To lead them to Jesus we must be visible expressions of grace in action. When we practice kindness in the name of Jesus, we minister to hearts. Therefore we ought to ask God to give us the sensitivity and discernment to see opportunities to minister to those around us and the courage to follow through.

Inspiration ✝ ✝ ✝

Kindness is a language the dumb can speak and the deaf can hear and understand.—C.N. Bovee

The measure of all love is its giving.—J.I. Packer in *Rediscovering Holiness*

Doors

September 25

Sandra, the leader of Jennifer's home Bible Study, informed the women of her job promotion with Key Bank. As a result, she would be moving to another state. While the women cheered her good fortune, they immediately wondered what would happen to their group when she left. At first, there was quite a bit of discouragement. Jennifer was personally going through a rough time in her life as a parent and Sandra's advice was often invaluable and encouraging.

1 Corinthians 16:7-9—I don't want to see you now just in passing, for I hope to spend some time with you, if the Lord allows. But I will stay in Ephesus until Pentecost, because a wide door for effective ministry has opened for me—yet many oppose me.

The Apostle Paul changed his travel plans because God presented him with significant opportunity to extend his ministry in the city of Ephesus. We can see in Paul's letter that he recognized that how he spent his time was subject to God's permissive will. He understood this required an open mind to observe what God was doing in his life and around him and a sensitivity to maximize divine providence.

Paul's writing reveals personal frustration he sometimes felt in trying to be an effective minister. Even while God opened a wide door for him to minister in Ephesus, people opposed him. Why? Perhaps some felt he should not spend as much time there. Maybe, his presence threatened leaders with their own agendas. Possibly, Paul faced purely secular threats—people purposely opposed to his sharing about Christ.

Often, God allows change to open our hearts to other options and opportunities, or, to test our resolve in proving faithful in what He provides. Sandra called Jennifer and asked to meet with her a week before moving. To Jennifer's surprise, Sandra shared that she saw God's hand at work in her friend's life and sensed that the Spirit was orchestrating events so that Jennifer could exercise leadership. Sandra separately prayed with the other women and they collectively agreed Jennifer was the right one to teach the study. What looked initially discouraging turned into a blessing.

God allows or arranges circumstances to lead us to a different place. He brings us to a door we are to walk through by faith. If we miss His handiwork, we see only walls. If we take counsel of our fears, we fail to turn the knob. If the door is before you and the Spirit beckons, walk through it and experience the joy of knowing your journey is a sanctioned adventure!

Inspiration † † †

The door we fear going through the most may be the very one where we will meet God most profoundly.—Erwin Raphael McManus in *Chasing Daylight*

Three Good Men   September 26

One night I came home with a sour attitude. I suspect I was not alone. What was unusual about this occasion was that I actually considered what had put me in such a funk. Actually, the answer was simple. A negative person cornered me in the presence of others and orally festered for thirty minutes venom towards a coworker he despised. I could not get away fast enough. In truth, I was infected. My cheery spirit was trampled by a bitter person's slander. I thought of how one bad apple can ruin a barrel of good apples. That analogy made good sense.

The next morning this same individual spotted me and said to a colleague, "We make a good team. You see the good in people and I see the bad." He then extended his hand to me perhaps to make amends for the previous evening or to justify the verbal pounding he gave a coworker.

1 Corinthians 16:17,18—I am pleased to have Stephanas, Fortunatus, and Achaicus present, because these men have made up for your absence. For they have refreshed my spirit and yours. Therefore recognize such people.

Can you almost feel the enthusiasm Paul is feeling towards three men who made a big difference in his life and in the lives of others? If our intent is to love God and to love people, we become like Stephanas, Fortunatus, and Achaicus. We become ministry multipliers!

The behavior we model each day matters. What we say and do broadcasts loud and clear our vision of God and what place He plays in our lives. Our intent ought to be to help those who are confused or discouraged. We bless by bringing energy and hope to those who are tired and frayed. Kouzes and Posner report in *Encouraging the Heart* that a whopping 98% of executives think they would perform better with encouragement. Just think what would happen if three good men became millions of good men and women committed to refreshing the spirits of others!

Inspiration † † †
Behavior is contagious. —Chip Heath & Dan Heath in *Switch*

The Reality of Trouble   September 27

Bad doctrine is like poisoned food. It may taste good. It may leave the stomach feeling full. But in the end it will cause indescribable agony. Have you ever turned on your radio or television and heard a preacher promise you that if you will put your trust in Jesus, your troubles will leave you? Perhaps you've been scolded for lacking faith because you struggle with issues. Has anyone suggested that all you need to do is claim in Jesus' name the solution you want, and trouble will not visit you? So why then did Jesus say, "*I have told you these things so that in Me you may have peace. You will have suffering in this world. Be courageous! I have conquered the world*" (John 16:33)? Who was James writing when he penned, "*Is anyone among you suffering? He should pray.*" (Jam. 5:13a)?

2 Corinthians 1:3,4—Praise the God and Father of our Lord Jesus Christ, the Father of mercies and the God of all comfort. He comforts us in all our affliction, so that we may be able to comfort those who are in any kind of affliction, through the comfort we ourselves receive from God.

If we think that life in Christ means trouble-free living, we're going to be disheartened with our loving Father. God never promised us that life in Jesus would be affliction-free. Quite the opposite—Scripture warns us that if we follow Jesus, we can expect trouble. Our hope is not that today will be free of problems! Our hope is that our Lord is greater than anything that can be thrown against us!

Are you in the swamp of sickness—God still loves you. You may die. But you will live forever healed with Jesus if He is your Lord. Do you suffer at the hands of corrupt people? You are not alone—conniving religious leaders crucified the Messiah! Are you weary, tired of trauma and exhausted with ordeals that suggest God has it out for you? Rest assured, He's your Father and like any loving dad, He will quickly comfort you if you'll let Him. No trouble I've experienced, no matter how tragic, has ever come remotely close to negating the ever-powerful love of God.

Now we have this treasure in clay jars, so that this extraordinary power may be from God and not from us. We are pressured in every way but not crushed; we are perplexed but not in despair; we are persecuted but not abandoned; we are struck down but not destroyed. We always carry the death of Jesus in our body, so that the life of Jesus may also be revealed in our body. For we who live are always given over to death because of Jesus, so that Jesus' life may also be revealed in our mortal flesh. (2Co.4:7-11)

Ethics

September 28

A home improvement con artist swindled a 100 year-old blind woman. Unsolicited, he rang the woman's bell to offer to do any repair work needed. The woman told him that for years she had struggled with a door that was difficult to open because it rubbed against the rug. To fix the problem, she agreed to pay the man $8,000, to jack up her house.[82]

2 Corinthians 1:12—For this is our confidence: The testimony of our conscience is that we have conducted ourselves in the world, and especially toward you, with God-given sincerity and purity, not by fleshly wisdom but by God's grace.

Ethics may be defined as a system of moral principles essential in guiding a person to be trustworthy, dependable, fair, and honest. God built in each of us a moral compass that allows us to determine right from wrong. Ethics encompasses those moral principles meant to guide us.

So why is this important? Does it seem to you that increasingly we live in a world focused on blurring the line between right and wrong? Which traits are easier to find: integrity and evenhandedness or, dishonesty, cruelty and shrewd manipulation? A reporter for India Times noted most qualified doctors do not teach ethics to medical students in college. As institutions in the U.S. and other nations disdain the need to teach ethics is it any surprise that there are financial, business and moral scandals among leaders and employees who should know better?

So what do we do? Those of us who are older must teach our children and the younger generations the meaning and importance of ethics. As Christians, our example is to reflect the moral principles God expects. When we live out those principles, we offer the world a direct example of Jesus and the value of holiness.

It was David who refused to kill King Saul even though the evil king was bent on destroying him. David would later write, "*I will praise the LORD who counsels me—even at night my conscience instructs me*" (Psa. 16:7). It was Paul, the stalwart follower of Christ who proclaimed, "*I always do my best to have a clear conscience toward God and men*" (Acts 24:16). "*Instead, we have renounced shameful secret things, not walking in deceit or distorting God's message, but commending ourselves to every person's conscience in God's sight by an open display of the truth*" (2 Co. 4:2). As Marcus Aurelius taught, "If it is not right, do not do it; if it is not true, do not say it."

Inspiration † † †

Ethical fitness makes ethical thinkers.—Rushworth M. Kidder in *How Good People Make Tough Choices*

Naked Mole Rats   September 29

It was a bright and hot Saturday outside Palm Springs as my family wandered through the Living Desert. Inside one of the exhibits we encountered a fascinating tunnel system full of *Heterocephalus glabers*—naked mole rats. These pale rodents are the only known mammals that live in a truly social system. All members of the group huddle together when sleeping in colonies that may consist of 20-300 creatures. Like bees, ants and termites, naked mole rats divide into classes of hierarchy. First in order is the dominant queen who may have up to five litters in a year with 1-27 newborns. Next, there are one to three breeding males followed by two to three soldiers who protect and care for the colony. Finally, there are the many workers. These asexual workers exist to dig the tunnels and find food. A mole rat can live 15-20 years in captivity and has the strongest jaw muscles for a mammal its size.

In a world infatuated with pleasure and strength it would be unsurprising to belittle the workers. But, if it were not for them, the queen and her entourage would not survive! Even God commends workers. God's need has always been for people committed to obeying Him and doing what He wills. Instead of supernaturally positing truth in the hearts of all mankind, God uses people to spread His message.

2 Corinthians 1:24—I do not mean that we have control of your faith, but we are workers with you for your joy, because you stand by faith.

If you are doing what God wants you to do, then you are surrounded by opportunities to expand His kingdom. Why be enamored with the position or status of others and bemoan your own circumstances? You can make an eternal difference right where you are by determining to let God work through you today and tomorrow. Heaven will be full of stories from people we never heard of wearing radiant crowns for their faithful work in the valleys where light was sparse, fog was thick and suffering a familiar acquaintance. May you be a worker who hears the Lord's commendation—"Well done!"

Inspiration ✝✝✝

When you do your work faithfully, your faith will be seen at work.—George Muller

Healthy Devotion   September 30

2 Corinthians 6:3-10—We give no opportunity for stumbling to anyone, so that the ministry will not be blamed. But as God's ministers, we commend ourselves in everything: by great endurance, by afflictions, by hardship, by difficulties, by beatings, by imprisonments, by riots, by labors, by sleepless nights, by times of hunger, by purity, by knowledge, by patience, by kindness, by the Holy Spirit, by sincere love, by the message of truth, by the power of God; through weapons of righteousness on the right hand and the left, through glory and dishonor, through slander and good report; as deceivers yet true; as unknown yet recognized; as dying and look—we live; as being disciplined yet not killed; as grieving yet always rejoicing; as poor yet enriching many; as having nothing yet possessing everything.

Spiritual burnout is not caused by being overly devoted to God. It is caused by being overly devoted to ministry, to people, to one's reputation and self-worth. In fact, I don't believe it is possible to be too devoted to God. Whenever I find someone no longer in ministry and angry or bitter towards God and His followers there is always a trail that leads back to misplaced devotion. How easy it is for us to start off in love with God and become more enamored somewhere along the way with what we are doing for Him. Once we dissemble our devotion we are vulnerable to defeat. Hard times come along and Satan sends his demons of doubt to feast on our table of self-pity. He whispers his sly message, "God let you down. You served Him and look what happened. He really doesn't care."

To whom or to what are you devoted? Now when life is good and circumstances are favorable, devotion seems easy—no big deal. But what about tomorrow when your safe world is shocked by unforeseen tragedy, or your trip on the mountain top ends? Will you find you were more loyal to your circumstances than to your Creator? Will your devotion be locked in the Redeemer or unlocked by the deceiver? Devotion comes at the time of crisis because it was forged on the plains of daily commitment.

O God, may we be Your devoted branches. Thank You for our freedom. For our prosperity, we acknowledge Your generous hand. We are a blessed people in the midst of turbulent times. Keep our eyes on You. May we hold to Your Vine when the wind of adversity comes and whips us in every direction. Deepen our joy when the moss of unjust treatment smothers our limbs. Nourish us in Your Son when the invidious pests of suffering and discouragement gnaw on our character. May we be wholly devoted to You for Your unending glory.

Inspiration † † †

Loyalty and devotion lead to bravery. Bravery leads to the spirit of self-sacrifice. The spirit of self-sacrifice creates trust in the power of love.—Morihei Ueshiba

Priorities

October 1

2 Corinthians 8:9—For you know the grace of our Lord Jesus Christ: Though He was rich, for your sake He became poor, so that by His poverty you might become rich.

Rather incredible isn't it? The Lord of the universe willingly disrobed of the heavenly splendor that was His.

- He set aside His royal power to be mocked, slapped, spit on and spiked to a cross—put to death by the very people He came to save.
- He let go of omnipresence to walk in sandals across dirty roads to preach to hungry hearts.
- He turned off omniscience to take instruction from His Father in the sacred mission of becoming Savior to a lost planet.
- He left heaven to experience hunger, thirst, pain, fatigue, disappointment, anger, frustration and the incessant onslaught of temptation.
- He vacated His majestic throne to encounter the invidious attitudes and self-indulging lifestyles of the religious, the immoral and the rebellious who had no clue to the depth of His love.

When the rich young ruler asked Jesus what good thing he should do to get eternal life, Jesus said, *"If you want to be perfect," Jesus said to him, "go, sell your belongings and give to the poor, and you will have treasure in heaven. Then come, follow Me"* (Mat. 19:21). When he turned away in sadness on account of his great wealth, he had no idea what splendor Jesus had set aside. No idea!

If the thought of setting aside riches to follow Jesus makes us defensive, the proof of our misplaced priorities is self-evident. Have we considered that the poverty Jesus embraced is the richness of our salvation? *"The poor in spirit are blessed, for the kingdom of heaven is theirs"* (Mat.5:3).

Inspiration † † †

A leader who says "I've got ten priorities" doesn't know what he's talking about—he doesn't know himself what the most important things are.—Larry Bossidy & Ram Charan in *Execution*

Giving Wisely

October 2

Jonathan Martin wrote the best book I have ever read concerning Biblical principles on giving wisely. The title of his book is *Giving Wisely?*

2 Corinthians 8:14,15—At the present time your surplus is available for their need, so that their abundance may also become available for our need, so there may be equality. As it has been written: The person who gathered much did not have too much, and the person who gathered little did not have too little.

During times of economic uncertainty, many Christians struggle with how to handle their money. My wife and I wrestle with how to best invest the resources God gives us towards His Kingdom. There are more needs than we can help and we regularly receive requests for financial assistance. On top of those requests are our own financial challenges. So what does God want us to do?

Jonathan shares five principles in the acronym RAISE to guide in helping us give locally or internationally in a God-pleasing manner.

R = Relationship. Jonathan notes, "The healthiest giving is best done at a relational level, not merely the emotional level." Too often we give out of a guilt complex that we have more than someone else, or because we feel manipulated emotionally by an appeal. It takes more work to form a relationship with someone but the end result is almost always better than resorting to a handout.

A = Accountability. Jonathan's church, Good Shepherd Community Church, does not support nationals directly. They give through organizations. This creates accountability and protects against fraud, misunderstanding and abuse. Is it wise to give a person money for food who has cable television, indulges bad habits and runs up debt?

I S = Indigenous Sustainability. Sometimes our giving directly sabotages the motivation of a local ministry to meet its needs. Our giving should not create dependency or stifle the creativity and responsibility of another body to fix its problems and grow local solutions.

E = Equity. Our giving should not inappropriately raise another above the local standard of living. As we see in the passage above, balance in the body is a good thing![83]

Notice Jacob's example in Genesis 43. His family was in the midst of a severe famine and they badly needed food. Despite the harsh and bizarre manner his sons were treated by Joseph (whom they did not recognize), Jacob sent them back to Egypt with the finest products of their land and additional money. He chose to be a blessing in the face of suffering. As Christians, we can always give something! Too often, we let our circumstances determine our action or inaction instead of trusting God.

Give because God gave you His best, Jesus. Help others so as to bless them and you in turn receive a blessing. Just don't forget to share wisely! God does not just expect us to be generous, He expects us to use discernment with His resources!

Inspiration † † †
This is not tithing, where God is given 10 percent and we keep 90 percent of what we make. This is gratitude expressing itself in miraculous generosity. One hundred percent giving is normal behavior in the kingdom. All that we have is placed at God's disposal. We are entrusted to manage His resources for Him.—Jan David Hettinga in *Follow Me*

The Dentist

October 3

Driving down the road on the back of a motorcycle in India is an experience any thrill-seeker would love. Picture weaving through vehicles and pedestrians on narrow, worn roads where there is almost no margin for driver error. Fortunately, I was seated behind Dr. Kester Frederick, the only driver among hundreds with a helmet on.

Kester is a Jesus-loving dentist. He took me about 20 km outside the city of Salem in TamilNadu to his clinic in a rural village; there he graciously cleaned my teeth. Kester works alone without the benefit of a dental hygienist. Once or twice a month he leaves his practice and travels a day's journey to help people too poor to afford a dentist. He has treated as many as 500 people in one day!

Our first cause is to love God and often the way we express our love to Him is by helping people. We don't just tell them about Jesus who came to save them. We look for opportunities to serve them so that they can firsthand experience His love working through our lives. Loving God sets in motion awesome opportunities!

Every time Kester travels south to minister, he goes without pay and at the cost of his own practice. While he is working on people's teeth, he is sharing about Jesus Christ.

2 Corinthians 9:13—They will glorify God for your obedience to the confession of the gospel of Christ, and for your generosity in sharing with them and with others through the proof provided by this service.

Are you willing to ask God how He could use you in your job (or whatever your life-situation) to further His kingdom? How many day's wages will you give up each month to invest in furthering the gospel? Are you willing to share your time and energy uncompensated to serve whomever God brings across your path? I hope so! Kester is making an eternal investment. God will richly bless him in heaven for what he is doing without fanfare and at personal cost on earth.

Inspiration † † †

Never testify with your lips what your life does not back up.—Oswald Chambers in *He Shall Glorify Me*

A Tiny Seed   October 4

A tiny seed fell years ago and grew into a pine tree. But alas, she rose in a place surrounded by firs and a healthy maple. The earth rotated and the sun shone but other more mature trees absorbed the light the struggling pine craved. Slowly, her lower limbs died. Her meager green needles only accentuated her brown gnarled plight. So with the help of Gary and Jim, the sickly pine in the corner of my yard came down.

A tree's destiny is determined by the place in which its seed falls. A man's destiny is determined by his ability to choose. If he chooses to surround himself with those who disdain the Light, he will decay inside with the sure disease of moral rot. If he hardens his heart against the voice of God and sets his face like steel, he will weather the seasons of life in coldness, rusting, growing brittle, 'til the breath of Life disdained becomes the icy blast of judgment. If he feeds for a time on God's good Word but turns away, forgoing the nutritious Bread of Life and Living Water and preferring his own buffet of self-pleasing items, his plate of lust and cup of pleasure will quench his spiritual appetite. He will not grow in righteousness because he chose to bloat in covetousness.

We cannot choose our race, our color or the place of our birth. A seed has no say in such matters. But in matters of destiny we are not helpless. What right have we to accuse God of being unjust because He damns those who refuse Him. Where does the created find the audacity to condemn the Creator? He offers Son-sacrificing love to reach us. He extends heaven to those who wonder how hell could be much worse than earth. He demands obedience knowing the grave consequences of sin. He flies the banner of sovereignty yet extends the scepter of free will. If we experience fruitless branches and wither, it is not because we are the victims of a prefabricated destiny. It is the evidence that we ignored grace, forsook truth, and abandoned the fear of God. Jesus Christ offers each and every person life-fulfilling grace. It is not a force-fed grace. We must elect who our savior will be. Our destiny is determined by our choice. Choose this day whom you will serve . . .

2 Corinthians 11:14-15—And no wonder! For Satan disguises himself as an angel of light. So it is no great thing if his servants also disguise themselves as servants of righteousness. Their destiny will be according to their works.

Inspiration ✝✝✝

To be accountable is to be subject to the consequences of our choices.—General Stephen Lorenz in *Lorenz on Leadership*

Failure

October 5

2 Corinthians 13:5,6—Test yourselves to see if you are in the faith. Examine yourselves. Or do yourselves not recognize that Christ Jesus is in you?—unless you fail the test.

Contemplation should be the precursor to provocative observation. Failure ending in disappointment with God often begins on a trail of good intentions.

- A businessman started a homeless shelter only to see it collapse after five hard years. Today he ignores the Heavenly Father who he mistakenly believed was not there for him.
- A journalist won't read her Bible or be seen in any gathering of Christians because her best Scripture-quoting friend gossiped and she has been shamed. How could a loving God permit such back-stabbing!
- A grandfather is bitter. His eyes hang below his mouth with the unmistakable look of defeat. He was defrauded by Christian businessmen more interested in his money than in his heart. Again, from his perspective God let him down. His pride refuses to look back up.

Could failure be the result of falling in love with the wrong god? If my ministry surpasses my relationship to Jesus, what distinguishes it from idolatry? If my reputation matters more than my Savior, what defines love? If my well-being and motivation are staked to the quality of life I enjoy, how do I view God when a tornado strikes? If family comes first, where do I turn when my teenager rebels?

My motivation when I wake up must be to love Jesus with all my heart, mind, soul and strength. Anything short of that propels me to ruin. My victory when I turn out the lights must be Christ, or my perspective is already jaded. Don't let your mind assume what your heart insists is best. God may graciously crush your dreams to enable you to see Him. The heart can be deceitful.

My goal was to be a missionary. I spent my life preparing to go. God rearranged my ambition through the slow fangs of a brain-stem tumor in my oldest son. He mercifully stripped me of what was good so that I could understand what was best. The potential loss of Bryan helped me see with new eyes God's loving Son. Could I serve Him if Bryan died? Could I live joyfully on His terms?

Failure often feeds on success—Satan is no dummy. What matters most is not family or career, health or prestige, work or recreation, but soul-sincere, heart-embracing, integrity-laced, truth-clutching, gut-inspiring, sin-quenched, chill-producing, worship-inducing, love for God. We dare not allow failure to avert our eyes from Jesus.

Inspiration † † †

Failure is a part of God's environment for shaping our character. —Erwin Raphael McManus in *Chasing Daylight*

Building Up

October 6

There is a marvelous tool called StrengthsFinder 2.0. I purchased the book and with the enclosed code answered questions on a website that then listed my top five strengths. I have used this tool with several organizations and with my own family. The beauty of Strengthsfinder is that it reveals what people are good at doing/being. By discovering people's strengths I am better able to position them where they are best utilized and most satisfied. This is fantastic for team building and for raising morale in any organization where leaders and workers previously focused on weaknesses to their own detriment.

2 Corinthians 13:10—This is why I am writing these things while absent, that when I am there I will not use severity, in keeping with the authority the Lord gave me for building up and not for tearing down.

I find it profound that the Lord gave the Apostle Paul authority to build up and *not* to tear down! He understood that God empowered him to improve and strengthen the body of believers. And doesn't this make sense? Who wouldn't prefer to be encouraged, edified and improved instead of being criticized, scolded and beat down? But if we are honest, I wonder if we would confess that building up is rarely the ministry of choice.

By our nature it is easier for us to point out faults in people. We can readily disparage others when we are hurt or disappointed. Our competitive nature gains a perverse satisfaction in noticing deficiencies in others. If we admit it, it feels good to be the controller or corrector. It takes more work and I would contend thoughtfulness to build others up. Plus the results are so much more favorable and enduring.

Instead of hunting for faults try hunting for successes. Take the time to find in those around you the strengths God has built in them and exploit those strengths for everyone's benefit. There is an undeniable buzz created in environments where people can work out of their strengths and utilize those around them who compensate where they are weak. Help a person find their strengths and applaud them. Notice how Paul applies his authority in the very next verse. *"Finally, brothers, rejoice. Become mature, be encouraged, be of the same mind, be at peace, and the God of love and peace will be with you"* (13:11).

Inspiration ✝✝✝

Effective executives build on strengths—their own strengths, the strengths of their superiors, colleagues, and subordinates; and on the strengths in the situation, that is, on what they can do.—Peter Drucker in *The Effective Manager*

Strategic

October 7

Nigeria is a nation of over 152 million people—the highest populated country in Africa. It comprises more than 250 ethnic groups.[84] Over twice the size of California, the nation is located on the Gulf of Guinea and shares borders with Benin, Cameroun, Chad and Niger. Our team ministered in the city of Jos (literally means Jesus Our Savior). Jos is in the Plateau State (Nigeria has 36 states) in the middle of the country.

Manasseh Wakawa, the advisor to the State Governor shared with us the strategic importance of the Plateau State. Nigeria is over 50% Muslim with the majority of its adherents located in the north. The Muslim goal is to convert the Christian population and for those who resist, to degrade their influence in the Plateau State. If that were to happen, the nation would decidedly turn Muslim and Wakawa believes because of the influence Nigeria has in Africa it would be a pivotal shift in making Africa an Islamic continent.

Since our team's visit to Jos, Muslim extremists have brutally attacked local Christians on three separate occasions. Followers of Jesus understand that their freedom to worship cannot be taken for granted and that they face countrymen determined to forcibly convert them to Islam or drive them from the state. Consequently, there is a commitment to Christ and fervor in pursuing Him decidedly different from the "easy-believeism" too often evident in America. Christians in Jos understand what living on the spiritual frontlines of a dangerous war entails.

Galatians 1:3-5—Grace to you and peace from God the Father and our Lord Jesus Christ, who gave Himself for our sins to rescue us from this present evil age, according to the will of our God and Father. To whom be the glory forever and ever. Amen.

When Jesus died on the cross, He fulfilled a strategic move by God to provide redemption from sin for a world full of evil doers. When He rose from the dead, He strategically squashed Satan's dominion over the earth, giving every person the right to believe in His lordship. Jesus is a rescuer. Every generation needs salvation from a present evil. The challenge for those of us who live in a relatively free society is to remember that we are in a spiritual war. Unless we understand this, we will take our liberties lightly, worship our Savior casually, and over time suffer a horrific cost. The consequence of compromise and failure to reproduce God-fearing leaders is spiritual sterilization. If you don't believe me, just ask your brothers and sisters in Africa.

Inspiration †††

Above all else, a warrior has a vision, he has a transcendence to his life, a cause greater than self-preservation.—John Eldredge in *Wild at Heart*

Outsiders   October 8

Have you ever wanted to be part of a group but found yourself excluded? Whether it be a school, church, club, team, a political party or affiliation most of us recognize the existence within any organization of an inner ring. Many people spend their whole lives seeking acceptance and entrance into these cliques or groups. No one wants to be left out.

Galatians 2:11-13—But when Cephas came to Antioch, I opposed him to his face because he stood condemned. For he regularly ate with the Gentiles before certain men came from James. However, when they came, he withdrew and separated himself, because he feared those from the circumcision party. Then the rest of the Jews joined his hypocrisy, so that even Barnabas was carried away by their hypocrisy.

What caused Peter and Barnabas to act in a manner they knew was wrong? Jews, affiliated with Jesus' brother James, came to Antioch from Jerusalem. These men undoubtedly voiced concerns to Peter that by eating with Gentiles he was setting up the Jewish Christians in Jerusalem and elsewhere for persecution from the circumcision party—a nationalistic group deeply committed to Jewish laws. Peter was afraid enough of this group to stop eating with the Gentiles.

Peter wanted approval from James and the men who came from Jerusalem. Whether he desired to be part of their team, we don't know. What we do understand is that he hurt the Gentile believers by pulling away from them. Peter forgot that when he accepted Jesus as his Lord, he became part of the only team that would ever matter—the Outsiders.

Would you agree the need for acceptance runs deep through our veins? We want to be part of a group or at least gain their approval for a number of reasons: power, status, security, safety, recognition, belonging, and/or privilege. The need to join an inner ring can be so compelling that a person will violate his or her own conscience and do the wrong thing. Consider what a person will do or not do to join a sorority. Can you think of a time in your life when peer pressure or the dictates of a club led you to engage in behavior you knew was wrong? It is often teens desperately seeking acceptance and ignored by the popular kids at school, who join gangs of misfits to engage in immoral behavior. The need to be included is more powerful than the ability to stand alone and risk rejection.

Outsiders are no longer of this world. Outsiders never put an organization or group above loyalty to Jesus Christ because they know that people will surely let them down. Outsiders do not need or look for membership in an inner ring to bolster their self-esteem. They are already family with the Inner Ring that truly matters—God the Father, God the Son, and God the Holy Spirit! Outsiders gain their confidence from being IN

Christ. Outsiders build their faith and function confidently because they know God loves them unconditionally and secured for them an eternal place in His presence.

If you are one of those influenced by the pack, or who feels the constant need to be a member of the "in crowd," ask yourself, "Who am I truly serving?" Better to be an outsider obedient and centered on God than an insider pursuing what cannot last and ultimately will not matter. I am not suggesting teams are unimportant—they are vital and essential to fellowship. But we must beware of seeking approval and inclusion wherever God's work and name are dishonored or hindered.

Inspiration †††

I believe that in all men's lives at certain periods, and in many men's lives at all periods between infancy and extreme old age, one of the most dominant elements is the desire to be inside the local Ring and the terror of being left outside.—C.S. Lewis in *The Weight of Glory*

Identification

October 9

Galatians 3:27—For as many of you as have been baptized into Christ have put on Christ like a garment.

A tabard is a tunic, a garment much like a cape that was worn by a knight over his armor. Emblazoned on the tabard was the knight's coat of arms. A similar garment was worn by a herald also bearing his lord's coat of arms.

Today this middle-aged tradition still lingers. Soldiers wear a cloth patch on the left upper arm of their uniform identifying the organization in which they serve. But it is not just soldiers who bear tabard-like markings. Many people wear a cross on a necklace, or wrist bands. The original purpose in wearing a cross was to enable others to see that the wearer was a Christian—someone committed by faith to following Jesus Christ.

Perhaps it would be a good thing if tabards came back into style. We would have to be more careful about what we said and did if we walked out of our homes each day as heralds wearing the coat of arms of the Son of God. There is no greater honor or privilege than to be identified with the King of Kings, the One who came to earth and lived a sinless life. He allowed Himself to be slaughtered as an innocent Lamb to save guilty wolves. He conquered death as a roaring Lion. He sits at the right hand of God—the greatest position of honor—our Champion and Messiah. What greater symbol of love could we wear than the cross? What deeper promise could we make than to serve Him and strive to be holy?

I have no right to wear God's tabard. I am completely unworthy to be clothed in His colors. Yet this cloth He invites me to wear is woven with the fabric of grace stitched together by unbreakable threads of mercy. The One I serve forgave my sin, embraced me in love and invited me to put on His luminescent tunic of power. When I march with Him, wearing His coat of arms, I go, knowing there is no opponent in existence capable of defeating Him. I go, believing that only He is able to save people from the penalty of sin. I go, committed to the task of making Him known to a world desperate for a Savior. I go, encouraged by the truth that He has changed me, given me purpose in life and joy in living. Therefore, when people see me, they should see Him. This is what it means to be identified with Christ!

Inspiration ✝✝✝

The proof that I have been through crucifixion with Jesus is that I have a decided likeness to Him.—Oswald Chambers in *My Utmost For His Highest*

COG Card

October 10

One year I flew almost 150,000 miles on airplanes (almost equivalent to circling the world six times). I try to have everything laid out the night before I travel because it speeds up getting ready to go the next day. On one occasion, I had trouble checking in online. I phoned an airlines agent and found out my ticket was deficient; I was scheduled but the fare was unpaid. I called up my deputy and after some research she was able to find out the cause of the problem and fix it. Because she helped, I was able to print my ticket.

Because I left at 0515 a.m. instead of 0500 a.m., I cut my travel time too close. I parked the car just in time to catch the bus but because I hurried I forgot to grab two items, a Garmin for getting to my destinations, and coins to give out to deserving Soldiers. The bus took on an extra load of passengers and I began to wonder if I would be able to check my bag on time. Because a young Japanese dad graciously moved his suitcases out of the way, I was able to grab mine and dash to the ticket counter. Because I was on government orders, the ticket agent immediately took my suitcase and checked it without charging me $20. Because of my MVP status with Delta, I was able to go through the express security line. As I walked up to the gate I joined the line of boarding passengers to Boston and breathed thanks to the Lord that I made the flight. There were many *becauses* to contemplate but the Holy Spirit reminded me of *status*. Had I not had official orders and MVP standing it is doubtful I would have made my flight.

Galatians 3:28,29—There is no Jew or Greek, slave or free, male or female; for you are all one in Christ Jesus. And if you belong to Christ, then you are Abraham's seed, heirs according to the promise.

Perhaps in addition to a tabard, those of us who follow Jesus ought to carry around a COG card. A **C**hild **o**f **G**od has status. No matter what stresses we encounter in life, (so long as we are not sinning), the Holy Spirit is our committed Advocate and Counselor. When hell blows its smoke at us and Satan does all he can to harm us, it does not matter! We may die but we certainly will LIVE. Our blood-paid status already affords us places in the JPH complex (Jesus-Prepared Homes). The next time you stand in line, or forget something, or feel like screaming because of uncontrollable circumstances, take a deep breath, pull out your COG card and have a praise session. What really matters is not the aggravators but rather the Redeemer. Jesus sent the Holy Spirit to remind us that we have eternal standing and restoration!

Inspiration † † †

The value of each human soul considered simply in itself, out of relation to God is zero. —C.S. Lewis in *The Weight of Glory*

Distortions

October 11

David, a local writer, slammed the U.S. President in an editorial in *The Oregonian* for falsely portraying events in a Middle Eastern country. He mocked the President for ignoring the reality of life *as the media portrayed it*. Shame on the Commander-in-Chief for believing the direct eyewitness account of soldiers and statesmen instead of the six o'clock news!

Because I was privy to inside information to a wide array of events in that land, I was dismayed by the biased and distorted view David and most of the media presented. It was poor journalism to daily report the number of casualties and castigate the administration for every misstep while selectively ignoring positive developments in the rebuilding of a nation's broken infrastructure. If loss of life was truly the media's concern, why not tally and print the number of Americans killed each day in traffic accidents in the United States, or the thousands of Mexicans killed by drug lords? Could it be that deeper principles were at work? I'm convinced the media is not about reporting information; it is about selling philosophy—truly bad news for everyone.

Galatians 4:17,18—They are enthusiastic about you, but not for any good. Instead, they want to isolate you so you will be enthusiastic about them. Now it is always good to be enthusiastic about good—and not just when I am with you.

Distortions are a part of daily life. There will always be people eager to win us over to their cause just as we are motivated to bring others to our way of thinking. If we want to protect ourselves from embracing or propagating distorted views, there are three key things we must do.

- First, we must be people of the Word. See 2 Ti. 3:16,17. By devoting ourselves to studying and obeying the Word, we learn to discern God's perspective towards life.
- Second, we must pray. See Col. 4:12. When we talk and listen to God, we receive His guidance. Often after praying my perspective towards things changes.
- Third, we must guard our hearts. How we spend our time eventually defines who we are and what we become! Distortion is fed by a worldly diet. See Pro. 4:23 and Gal. 6:8; 5:24,25.

Are you feeling twisted? Keep your eyes on Jesus for balance and heaven's perspective!

Inspiration †††

Envious persons are skilled in making what is praiseworthy seem despicable by means of unflattering distortions . . . the envious avert their gaze from the brightness in life and the loftiness of good actions and fix their attention on rottenness.—St. Basil

Gori   October 12

Eighteen of us sat around the circular table in the conference room of the Military Academy located in Gori. For several hours we met with different deputies from the Ministry of Defense and listened as they shared the challenges of living within field artillery range of Russian guns. Their fear of angering their neighbor and again losing their freedom is fueled by Russia's occupation in 2008 of Abkhazia and South Ossetia—two secessionist territories within Georgia.

Georgia was first unified as a kingdom under the Bagrationi dynasty in the 9th to 10th century. In 1243 her land was conquered by Mongol invasions. Hundreds of years later she was conquered by the Ottoman Empire. Then she was annexed by the Russian Empire in 1801. The Democratic Republic of Georgia sought to be independent from 1918-1921 but eventually the Soviet Union enveloped her, forcing her people to live under communism. It was not until 1991 that she became a free nation.

Georgians understand that should they be attacked, they cannot resist their northern neighbor's overwhelming military superiority without help. So they work hard to eliminate anything that might weaken their independence—like firing all 1700 corrupt police officials, shutting down the mafia, and eliminating a culture of bribery. They are not lackadaisical or timid in taking action. Their resolve to establish a safe, free nation was a reminder to our U.S. team of the preciousness of our independence.

Galatians 5:1—Christ has liberated us to be free. Stand firm then and don't submit again to a yoke of slavery.

When Jesus rose from the grave, He did not just conquer death, He also provided a path to freedom. He liberated us from legalism, from tyranny, and the consequences of our own sin. But never was it His intent that His costly death would permit us to be complacent. He called us to a freedom that demands self-denial; that is sacrificial. He called us to be ambassadors of this freedom not tenants of self-centeredness. We are responsible for sharing the hope that we have with any who are trapped in hopelessness.

We may or may not dwell under the shadow of a power that can strip away our ability to live as we choose but always we live under the shadow of the lord of darkness. He encourages rebellion from God and his rage to destroy mankind runs unabated. Perhaps we need to wake up and remember who it is that opposes us and how important it is to stand firm and proclaim truth. The toll road to slavery begins at the gate of apathy.

Inspiration † † †

If my brother hungers and I do not help him, I am a thief. And if my brother dies of hunger, I am a murderer, too.—St Ambrose

Revelation

October 13

You walk outside to pick up your mail when a brilliant flash momentarily blinds you. Before you hovers a Being of glorious light—it is the Lord. You reach out your hand and welcome Him and ask Him to come inside. "How exciting!" you think, a chance to show your Savior your home. So you walk Him around. "Look, Lord, at the beautiful wallpaper we used in our family room. Oh, you must come up and see the Jacuzzi—our favorite hangout. In here is where the kids sleep. Watch out for all the toys—I really wish they'd pick up after themselves. By the way, check out the new wheels I got in the garage. Isn't this a sweet SUV?" Time out.

If God descended in bodily form, the first thing you and I would do is go from the vertical to the horizontal with the greatest sense of awe and unworthiness that one could muster. When the Lord, in His kindness, reached down to pick us up, the last thing we would think about is our possessions! Would we think of work or the great meal we just cooked? Come on! All that would matter is the fact that He is present. Our every breath would hang on His next word and action. The whole experience would leave us exhausted—just look at the behavior of Daniel and John (Dan. 10; Rev. 1:17).

Revelation that does not bring us closer to God and make us more aware of our need for Him is most probably not from God and ought to be carefully scrutinized. Spiritual light does more than just part the darkness—it leads us to the King of Brilliance. So if we are mesmerized by mystical experience and constantly on the hunt for new manifestations, we've missed the boat. We've given more value to what we feel than to God Himself. If we're enchanted by dynamic dreams but our walk with God is no deeper, then their value is as rich as vapor.

The absence of revelation is no hilltop for prancing. Does the Holy Spirit speak to you from the Word, through God-fearers, by His gentle voice? If not, aside from divine purpose, is something blocking Him—like disobedience or fear? Revelation has not ceased! God spoke to me in the desert—audibly! The problem is never in His revealing. The problem is with our hearing. So much noise gets in the way. Are you hungry for a word from the Lord? Great—that's the first essential step. The second is . . .

Ephesians 1:17—I pray that the God of our Lord Jesus Christ, the glorious Father, would give you a spirit of wisdom and revelation in the knowledge of Him.

Inspiration †††

The revelation of God always brings us to our knees in contrition and reverence . . . —J. Oswald Sanders in *The Pursuit of the Holy*

Flying

October 14

He pulled out a large, black Bible, a beautifully gold tabbed one, and grabbed a pen. I watched from a row behind and to the left of him. Twice on our flight from Philadelphia to Atlanta, he pulled out his Bible and read—not just a cursory reading, I could tell he was intent on what he was studying. He wore neatly pressed tan slacks and a polo shirt—I would guess he was in his fifties.

I conversed with another man sitting next to me for quite some time. He worked for a petroleum company based in Santiago, Chile. He and his wife have two boys that are polar opposites. He graduated from a college in Boston and is a big Red Sox baseball fan. He was dressed in fatigue-patterned shorts and wore a casual shirt. I liked his easygoing demeanor. I would guess he was in his mid thirties but his boyish looks made him look much younger. He ordered an alcoholic drink, pulled out his laptop and went to work as we winged our way south.

Two very different men by age, dress, and probably by conviction bound for the same city but what kind of an eternity? When I got off the plane, I caught up to the Bible reader. I put my hand on his shoulder and said, "You have to tell me your name." He looked startled, pulled back from me and asked, "Why?" I told him I was impressed with his reading material on the plane. He grinned and said, "Rick." I told him my name and gave him my **First Cause** business card and told him I would enjoy praying for him, and that I lived near, Portland, Oregon. He thanked me and found his own card and handed it to me. He shared that he and his wife would be in Portland in a week. I noticed from his card that he is the CEO of a company located in Stone Mountain, Georgia. On my next flight, I pulled out my Bible—thankful for Rick's example.

Ephesians 3:7,11,12—I was made a servant of this gospel by the gift of God's grace that was given to me by the working of His power . . . This is according to His eternal purpose accomplished in the Messiah, Jesus our Lord. In Him we have boldness and confident access through faith in Him.

I'm flying. These words in my headphones written by Tim Hughes resonate in my heart: "Here I am to worship. Here I am to bow down. Here I am to say that You're my God."[85]

I'm flying. *Lord, I'm surrounded by men and women, little children crying, flight attendants working in the cramped space of a craft flying 35,000 feet above the earth, each one precious in Your sight. Please help me to be Your choice ambassador. Let the joy in my heart overflow upon some parched soul. Let me love You so passionately that I radiate Your presence.*

Dunamis

October 15

When we arrive in heaven, will there be a Hall of Fame? Will we find an interactive display manned by select angels who share the stories of those living legends who served God exceedingly well? While Adolf Hitler wrought great tyranny in Europe, his countryman Dietrich Bonhoeffer honored God. This German Lutheran pastor and theologian sacrificed a safer ministry in the United States and Great Britain to return to Germany.

Some have debated the ethical merits of Bonhoeffer's participation in the unsuccessful plot to assassinate Hitler. He paid for his resistance at the hands of the Gestapo who executed him by hanging just 23 days before the Nazis surrendered.[86] The world lost a brilliant theologian but it also watched a man whose courage inspired countless Christians. His willingness to stand against strong opinions began early in life. Against the advice and desires of his parents, Bonhoeffer decided as a teenager to become a pastor. His older brother told him not to waste his life in "such a poor, feeble, boring, petty bourgeois institution as the church." Fourteen year-old Dietrich replied, "If what you say is true, I shall reform it."

Perhaps his greatest contribution to Christendom came from his book, *The Cost of Discipleship*. In this study of Jesus' Sermon on the Mount, Dietrich provides a powerful warning against cheap grace. It is a must read for every Christian serious about his or her walk with God.

Ephesians 3:20—Now to Him who is able to do above and beyond all that we ask or think according to the power that works in us—to Him be glory in the church and in Christ Jesus to all generations, forever and ever. Amen.

Dietrich Bonhoeffer endured adversity and inspired his countrymen because the power he drew from God bettered that of his fascist nation. What we do or don't do in life is defined by our source of strength. The Greek word for power in Eph. 3:20 is *dunamis*. Preachers often associate this word with dynamite. While dunamis certainly can be defined by explosive strength, there is an oft-overlooked primary definition of dunamis. This power is "inherent power, power residing in a thing by virtue of its nature . . . moral power and excellence of soul.[87]

God's power is not just a physical force, it is His supreme character. In the presence of His holiness we fall to our knees undone. Did you know that by holding fast to virtue you radiate power? The reason God asks us to be holy as He is holy is He knows that in doing so we will be powerful!

Costly Grace

October 16

Ephesians 4:7—Now grace was given to each one of us according to the measure of the Messiah's gift.

Ephesians gives us a powerful apologetic for the true meaning and application of grace. Too often we hear preached the message "God loves you and *all* you have to do is tell Him you are sorry for your sins, place your faith in Jesus and you will be saved." This statement by itself is incomplete and if not explained can imply to the listener—"Don't worry about your sin, God has taken care of it. You just do the best you can. God wants to bless you. You don't need to suffer anymore. Just claim your blessing and live your dreams." Both messages are well-received and both carry with them an implied assurance that so long as we believe in Jesus we can live our lives in pursuit of whatever pleases us. But watch the progression of truth about grace the Apostle Paul teaches the Ephesians and see if it differs profoundly from what we often hear taught.

2:8—*"For you are saved by grace through faith, and this is not from yourselves; it is God's gift."* To properly understand grace we must understand faith. Nowhere in the gospels (with the obvious exception of the thief on the cross) is it implied that saving faith constitutes a one-time statement of trust in Jesus. Faith is an *ongoing process* whose authenticity is established by our willingness to believe in Jesus as our Savior <u>and</u> Lord. A single declaration followed by a lifetime of ignoring Him is an impotent Savior-formula and does not demonstrate faith or lordship. That this is so is demonstrated by His words in Mat. 7:23 to those who on their own terms considered themselves His followers—*"Depart from Me, you lawbreakers!"* Grace is God's gift applied to sincere (persevering) faith. Never presume God will give grace to one who initially trusts Him only to live out willful disobedience and wanton disregard for His authority.

3:8—*"This grace was given to me—the least of all the saints—to proclaim to the Gentiles the incalculable riches of the Messiah."* Paul understood God's grace was extended to him (who formerly pursued Christians to have them killed) and that he now had a life-long obligation to share God's grace with the Gentiles.

4:1—*"Therefore I, the prisoner for the Lord, urge you to walk worthy of the calling you have received . . ."* No one walks with one step. Walking is evidenced by continuous directional progress. The point of grace is a life walked in worthiness to God's extended calling.

4:17-19—*"Therefore, I say this and testify in the Lord: You should no longer walk as the Gentiles walk, in the futility of their thoughts."* Paul makes it clear that to be a follower of Christ, one must not live an impure, immoral life. Grace never excuses or sanctions sin. Grace insists that we walk in a manner that is God-honoring. This does not mean that we will never sin. It means that we will not consciously justify sin and continue to err in defiance of God's commands.

4:22-24—*"you took off your former way of life, the old self that is corrupted by deceitful desires; you are being renewed in the spirit of your minds; you put on the new self, the one created according to God's likeness in righteousness and purity of the truth."* To put on the new man, is to identify and live like Jesus, the New Man. One receives grace from sin to put off sin. One receives grace to walk as Jesus walked.

6:24—*"Grace be with all who have undying love for our Lord Jesus Christ."* The evidence of grace at work in a person's life is "undying love" for Jesus. Notice the whole purpose and point of a person clothed in grace is to love and obey the object of love—Jesus Christ!

> Cheap grace is the deadly enemy of our Church . . . Cheap grace means the justification of sin without the justification of the sinner . . . Cheap grace is the preaching of forgiveness without requiring repentance, baptism without church discipline, Communion without confession, absolution without personal confession. Cheap grace is grace without discipleship, grace without the cross, grace without Jesus Christ, living and incarnate.[88]

If you hear taught from any platform that you can sin without worry because grace is without limit, that you can live as you please because grace covers your life, that you should never suffer as a child of God, RUN or stand up and rebuke the false teacher! This is not the message that Jesus taught His disciples to teach the world. This is the heretical teaching of those who make a mockery of the spilt blood of Christ to provide a false application of grace over their sinful junkets.

True grace is costly. We embrace faith. We renounce identification with the world and our right to live as we please so as to identify with Christ and obey Him! This grace does not justify sin, it justifies the sinner. "The only man who has the right to say that he is justified by grace alone is the man who has left all to follow Christ."[89]

Don't be a Sledge Hammer! October 17

If we are only true to a doctrine of Christianity instead of to Jesus Christ, we drive our ideas home with sledge-hammer blows, and the people who listen to us say, 'Well that may be true'; but they resent the way it is presented. When we follow Jesus Christ the domineering attitude and dictatorial attitude go and the concentration on Jesus comes in.[90]

Ephesians 4:14,15—Then we will no longer be little children, tossed by the waves and blown around by every wind of teaching, by human cunning with cleverness in the techniques of deceit. But speaking the truth in love, let us grow in every way into Him who is the Head—Christ.

The Apostle Paul was known for his keen intellect. He studied under the famous teacher Gamaliel and was thoroughly versed in the law (Acts 22:3). We can be assured that the same passion Paul brought to serving as a Pharisee, he retained in serving in Jesus. The major difference was that before knowing Jesus, Paul was willing to put to death any who strayed from what he considered orthodox teaching (read that as Christians). After having his life changed by Jesus, Paul recognized the importance of applying love to truth.

We can be so confident that we are right that we come across as arrogant or intent on passing our agenda at the expense of communicating in a way that is sensitive to the situation and needs of our listeners. Always we must be careful that we are not drawn away by false teaching and that we protect those we know from a similar fate. But we must also be sure that we don't become preservers of doctrine at the expense of loving people and keeping our focus on Christ.

Light in the Bible often stands for truth or the representation of God. Jesus taught His followers to be lights that shone so that people were attracted. He did not teach them to be lasers that burned so that people would be seared! If we are in love with Jesus, our light will shine at the right intensity. If we are in love with doctrine, watch out—our light may repel the very people we seek to reach.

Inspiration ✝✝✝

Sin is "the claim to the right to myself"—and therefore "the claim to my right to my view of things"—and therefore the root of a profound and inescapable relativism.—Os Guinness in *The Call*

Changing of the Guard October 18

Stockholm Palace is located on Stadsholmen in Gamla Stan (the old town). The first building was a fortress with a tower built in the 13th century by Birger Jarl to defend Lake Malaren. Ever since the early 16th century, the palace has been guarded by members of the Swedish Armed Forces. Several times a week a special changing of the guard is observed by the public.

At 1:00 p.m., I listened to the sounds of a drum and bugle corps approaching on the cobblestone road. Slowly and precisely they marched into view, crossed the stone floor in the central plaza, and took their assigned place. Then the incoming unit relieved the outgoing unit. As the leaders barked out their commands the drummers struck up the beat that allowed each formation to keep in step as they moved to their new positions. It was a well-practiced drill that the crowd enjoyed. At the conclusion of the changing of the guard the band marched forward and performed a concert of three songs.

Ephesians 4:15,16—But speaking the truth in love, let us grow in every way into Him who is the head —Christ. From Him the whole body, fitted and knit together by every supporting ligament, promotes the growth of the body for building up itself in love by the proper working of each individual part.

If there were no band, it would be hard for the units to keep in step as they moved into position. If there were no units, the playing of the band would be pointless. In essence, both parts are essential or the ceremony would be as interesting as attending a horse race with no jockeys. Each soldier and band member fill an important role. Some are quite visible while others remain hidden in the ranks. Similarly, we each play a role in serving each other for the good of God's Kingdom.

What is important is not whether the crowd recognizes you and me for our contribution but rather that we understand that our presence and actions are valuable. God is glorified by the whole of our contribution and man best sees Him when we best fulfill the role He gives us. Whether we are guards in reserve, the trumpet section, officers barking the orders, or drummers, what we do matters. So be encouraged—God is watching and unlike people, He sees everything! *"Therefore, whether you eat or drink, or whatever you do, do everything for God's glory"* (1 Co. 10:31).

Inspiration ✝ ✝ ✝

Never, in peace or war, commit your virtue or your happiness to the future. Happy work is best done by the man who takes his long-term plans somewhat lightly and works from moment to moment "as to the Lord."— C.S. Lewis in *The Weight of Glory*

Purpose

October 19

Twice in my life I have experienced periods where I had no clue what God's purpose for my life entailed. The first time this occurred, I had graduated from seminary firmly believing that God was calling me to the mission field. He did not. He blocked the door and called me into launching a church in another state and pastoring it—something for which I had no experience. I spent a restless year before the Lord made His purpose clear that I was to pastor.

A danger in this time of waiting is to conclude that God does not care. He does. But often His will takes us in directions we would not have chosen or understood. Often He must work on our character or teach us vital lessons we will need for the next phase of our journey.

The second danger is to think that what makes us important is what we do. It is not. Our value to God is in who we are. What matters most is not that we draw esteem from our work but that we grow in our relationship to Him. It is this very truth that sustains and encourages me during a time of running a race where I have no clue where the road will go next.

The third danger is to grow tired of waiting for God to reveal His purpose and to launch ahead on my own. Solomon wrote in Proverbs 3:5,6, "*Trust in the Lord with all your heart, and do not rely on your own understanding; think about Him in all your ways and He will guide you on the right paths.*" Wisdom's child is Patience. Wisdom counsels "wait on God and move as He leads." Why? Because the days are evil and my own understanding is flawed.

If you, like me, are in a period where more question marks fill the jar than answers, be encouraged. We learn what God's will is by listening and by faithfully spending time with Him. Never despair of finding His purpose. If we seek Him, He will be found. If we knock, He will open the door. If we ask, He will answer. That's a promise of Christ, not a marvelous maybe.

Ephesians 5:8-10, 15-17—For you were once darkness, but now you are light in the Lord. Walk as children of light—for the fruit of the light results in all goodness, righteousness, and truth—discerning what is pleasing to the Lord . . . Pay careful attention, then, to how you walk—not as unwise people but as wise—making the most of the time, because the days are evil. So don't be foolish, but understand what the Lord's will is.

Inspiration ✝✝✝

If you agree with God's purpose he will bring not only your conscious life, but all the deeper regions of your life which you cannot get at, into harmony.—Oswald Chambers in *My Utmost For His Highest*

Humanism   October 20

Ephesians 6:7,8—Serve with a good attitude, as to the Lord and not to men, knowing that whatever good each one does, slave or free, he will receive this back from the Lord.
Revelation 4:11—Our Lord and God, You are worthy to receive glory and honor and power, because You have created all things, and because of Your will they exist and were created.

Scripture brings immense truth to ponder. Whenever we champion humanism we plummet down Folly Hill. Eventually, every king of a manmade mountain tumbles. If we render service to people as our *highest value*, look what happens:

- We serve for our own betterment (self-centeredness).
- We serve to avoid unfavorable treatment (self-preservation).
- We serve for attention (pride).

Each of these *may appear* to buy us better life but these all end in death. There is no exception.

The boat of humanism always breaks apart on the reef of sin. We find ourselves in competition because our hierarchy of humanistic causes differs from one group to the next. The *only* solution to this mess is to serve God. When we put Him first, it results in our betterment, our preservation and our satisfaction, for He blesses us and His blessing and His favor is eternal. He is supposed to always be first because He is our Creator! By His will we exist and He is worthy of all kudos.

We must be careful about championing causes or political parties. Slowly, the cause displaces the Causer. Subtly, we find ourselves wrapped around platforms and our need to be right replaces obedience to the Holy Spirit. We judge others and lose our perspective because we are serving the wrong master. Likewise, we must avoid putting our hope in people. No man can save the world except God's Man. The temptation to find a new messiah to free us from all our woes is as misguided as asking a television to raise our children.

If God is not first, we are worse for the wear, and the glory we gain is not worth the blessing we lose. Should we be passionate? Should we work hard for those in whom we believe? Yes—but in balance! Our track record as people is terminally weak—consider the first bad choice—when God took second place to a piece of fruit. Satan is all about humanism—he knows when we serve ourselves, we are furthering his agenda.

Inspiration ✝✝✝

If I am only devoted to the cause of humanity, I will soon be exhausted and come to the point where my love will falter . . . –Oswald Chambers in *The Place of Help*

Spiritual Fitness

Okay, I admit it. There are days I just don't feel like working out. However, if I want to have good muscle tone, a healthy heart, and a strong body, I have to exercise. Physical fitness doesn't just happen. It takes *consistent* work. As Dr. John George notes, if I want to be physically fit I need to eat right, manage stress, and do SAFE exercises (Strength, Aerobic, and Flexibility exercises). We all know what occurs when we don't exercise regularly. One workout (jogging, weight-lifting, aerobics class) per week will not make me physically fit! Unfortunately, it's be fit or be fat.

Isn't it just a little bit ludicrous to think we can stay in shape spiritually by working our spiritual muscles only on Sunday mornings? To be spiritually fit, we must be *in the Lord* and *in His mighty power*. He is the Coach! If we want to be strong, we have to hang with Him. He's given us a spiritual circuit plan for spiritual growth: time in prayer, time in the Bible and time in fellowship. Spiritual workouts are generally private—just me and God. But to increase my strength capacity lifting weights, I need a spotter. (It's not good to have barbells hanging over your chest and not be able to lift them!). In the same way, we need fellowship. Other Christians can lift weights we are trapped underneath, provide insight for improving worship, and offer gifting and encouragement we need to keep at it.

Muscles and sniveling are mutually exclusive! Who's challenging you? Are you spiritually fit? If not, will you allow me to say, "Get after it! Be strong *in the Lord*. Quit sniveling or procrastinating! The awesome God of the Universe has given you an unlimited supply of divine appointments. What would keep you from building your relationship with Him?"

Ephesians 6:10—Finally, be strengthened by the Lord and by His vast strength.

Prayer Walk Report October 22

Ephesians 6:18—Pray at all times in the Spirit with every prayer and request, and stay alert in this, with all perseverance and intercession for all the saints.

Nigerian Prayer Walk Report[91]—October 2008

I want to testify that God is already at work in us to both will and do His good pleasure! Prayer walk groups are springing up everywhere in the city [Jos] and across the nation [Nigeria]. We are glad to be part of this move of God. It is spreading like wild fire! Perhaps, God will use you to further spread it as you read our testimonies.

Most of the prayer walk groups wake up as early as 5am and pray for an hour or more. More than 15 groups are consistently prayer walking every morning and about 3 groups every night at different locations. The result of the prayer walk is amazing! *Let every believer wake up and prayer walk.*

Praise Report

During our prayer walk in one of the communities, the Lord put in our hearts to pray against evil and controlling powers in the community. We prayed for God to expose evil in that community. The following morning:

1. God convicted an elder in a local assembly and he stood before the congregation, confessed and repented of his sins. He revealed that he had buried some charms in the church, so he could continue to weaken the church members and manipulate their lives through witchcraft. He also revealed that he was responsible for the mysterious deaths of some church members. He killed a number of them through automobile accidents and sickness. He did those things through diabolical means.

2. Another fetish man in the community was exposed through the power of God a day after we prayed. He sent a snake, which had two heads to a family to kill a girl. A woman spotted the snake on the girl's foot and neighbors killed it. It was observed that after the snake was killed and burnt, the man became furious. When he was questioned, he revealed another thing—a fetish box, hidden in a hole, the size and shape of money saved. He used that to "lock up" people's success and to swallow up their wealth (Job: 20:15). He had done this for several years. (The above reports may be unbelievable to some of our readers but they are TRUE! God is exposing evil, bringing some to repentance!)

We prayed for conversions among Muslims and idol worshippers. A man named Danladi, got born again from Islam and is being discipled. He is up every morning, prayer walking. He began to pray for the wife's conversion too! This morning he testified that she has yielded! Praise the Lord! Danladi is reaching out to his friends—one of them is Sani (Muslim). The word has been planted in Sani's heart, may the Holy Spirit convict him. Amen.

Praise the Lord God has restored marriages; God is healing many of different sicknesses and diseases. God is at work! God is breaking denominational walls! The members of the prayer walk teams come from different denominations—Charismatic/Pentecostal, Baptists, Catholics, Anglicans, etc.

Spiritual Battle   October 23

O Lord! The smell of smoke, unending pressure, ferocious jaws of confusion and fear, ear-splitting cries of others wounded . . . adrenaline rushes like some careening jet. A quick glance around reveals that this battle is extensive and the combatants as diverse as one could imagine:

- A mother's nerves are severely tested by the incessant wail of a stubborn child while two older siblings clamor for her attention . . . she yearns for quiet, depressed . . .
- A mechanic is asked to forge documents by his boss, his job feeds five mouths . . .
- A teenage class president hears her peers suggest she is weird—a loser if she won't get beer for their party . . .
- A family worships in secret; the threat of imprisonment hangs like a heavy fog . . . neighbors lost their home to rampaging thugs . . .

Spiritual battle is as certain for God's children as the orange ball that ascends and descends. We cannot live in a world clutched by Satan and not feel the squeeze. We are naïve and in grave danger if we think we can follow the narrow path Jesus paid for and not see our faith tested.

Philippians 1:14—Most of the brothers in the Lord have gained confidence from my imprisonment and dare even more to speak the message fearlessly.

Jerry sent an email from Nigeria. He was beaten almost to death by five men and they robbed his house. Fortunately his wife and daughter were not there. He had to leave that unsafe neighborhood and find another place to live. Yet in the midst of pain, Jerry praised God. His courage and faith lifted those around him. His example of faith despite adversity made a difference.

Do you want to succeed in battle? Then you must prepare! Faithfully love God first and foremost, stay immersed in the Bible, seek and value godly fellowship, pray with devotion, avoid evil with uncompromising integrity, and serve others with humility and sincerity for the sake of the gospel. Those who fake, compromise, neglect, or ignore any of the above invariably suffer acute damage and often have little stomach for what God would see them through. Before the chains there must be good mettle!

Inspiration ✝ ✝ ✝

At the beginning of any extended prayer time or prayer battle, feed deeply on the Word of God.—Wesley L. Duewel in *Touch the World through Prayer*

Retirement

October 24

I rise up from my bed today with thoughts beyond attire,
    To serve with every breath I take to please my Lord and Sire,
I know that obstacles may come, temptations from the liar,
    But they cannot put out the Flame, my everlasting fire!

I cannot work to work no more for that would make life dire,
    I will not quit because His grace has taught me to aspire.
He placed a new song in my mouth of praise and deep desire,
    Many will see and worship Him, the sellers and the buyers.

The race goes on I'm full of hope yearning for the wire,
    I hear the cheers of those who ran and now make up God's choir.
Infused with love, I see His cross atop a million spires,
    So stoked by what He did for us, O how could I retire?

Philippians 1:20—My eager expectation and hope is that I will not be ashamed about anything, but that now as always, with all boldness, Christ will be highly honored in my body, whether by life or by death.

    Did you know the word *retirement* does not exist in the Bible? Nowhere do Jesus or His disciples preach on reaching a certain age and then calling it quits. The reason for this is that we do not live life for ourselves, we live for Christ. So long as we have breath, we can pray! So long as we are alert, we can encourage and exhort others of the importance of faith and to persevere in the faith. God may use you more for His Kingdom in your senior years than at any other time in your life. If we will simply trust Him and give Him each day, what a difference that day can make!

    Do you know people advanced in age and discouraged about living? Encourage them with the truth that God is not finished with them yet and can do marvelous things through them if they will just give Him each day. My dad never talks about being retired—that is because he does not recognize the concept. Each day he looks for new opportunities to serve God. Each day I know he is praying for me. He is constantly climbing higher . . . in reveration!

Inspiration ✝✝✝

    Jesus Christ never encourages the idea of retirement.—Oswald Chambers in *My Utmost For His Highest*

Worthy of the Gospel   October 25

Philippians 1:27,28a—Just one thing: Live your life in a manner worthy of the gospel of Christ. Then, whether I come and see you or am absent, I will hear about you that you are standing firm in one spirit, with one mind, working side by side for the faith that comes from the gospel, not being frightened in any way by your opponents.

There are some words we can easily gloss over in reading Scripture. The words *"worthy of the gospel"* ought to jump right out and seize us. We tend to feel good about those battles in which we emerge victorious after saying "no" to temptation. But what about those times we choose to engage in activities that are good but have nothing to do with where the Holy Spirit would take us? I may watch a movie and miss the leading of the Spirit who has opened an opportunity for me to share with my neighbor about Christ.

Being worthy of the gospel, implies being sensitive to and obeying the leading of the Holy Spirit to leave that which I rationalize as good to obey what He dictates as best. The measure of how we live is not authenticated on our standards or according to our estimate but rather in accordance with God's Word and obeying His leading. Adolf Hitler once stated, "I believe today that my conduct is in accordance with the will of the Almighty Creator." First he was a pagan. Second, he had no intention of yielding his life to God's sovereign control. He did not work for *"the faith that comes from the gospel,"* but rather to build his own kingdom.

Ernest Bramah noted, "A reputation for a thousand years may depend upon the conduct of a single moment." There is no appropriate time to live our lives in an unworthy manner. As Randy Alcorn wrote in *Heaven*, "A man who sees himself seated with Christ in Heaven, in the very presence of a God to whom the angels cry out, "Holy, holy, holy," won't spend his evenings viewing Internet pornography."[92] The test for us as believers is that we learn to yield each moment each day to living for the glory of God.

Benjamin Disraeli stated, "Circumstances are beyond human control, but our conduct is in our own power." While we look to God for His leading regarding His will, He looks to us to act wisely. Our conduct is *our* responsibility. Too often believers blame their reactions on the actions of others or the conditions in which they find themselves. In truth, our power is made complete by God's power! Therefore we have no place for excuses for poor conduct. When we live *in* Christ, we live in the highest of ways for the good of His glory!

Inspiration ✝✝✝

... obedience must be understood as the outworking of faith.—Robert Coleman in *The Master Plan of Discipleship*

Seeing Others First   October 26

Russ and Marianne Lambert are the kind of couple I imagine almost everyone would want living in their neighborhood. Russ was my High School principal at Faith Academy in the Philippines. Not only did he take a personal interest in us as students, he worked to relate to us at our level—not an easy task with teenagers. Marianne, like her husband, was immensely popular and very gracious—like a den mother to a pack of—well we weren't wolves, but you get the idea!

So, it hit a lot of us grads hard to see Marianne afflicted with a brain tumor. It's difficult to think of a more special couple suffering as they are. Yet, when I spoke with Russ, he spent little time dwelling on their situation. Instead, he asked me about my family and how we were doing. He inquired about my folks. When we did get back to Marianne's health, he commented on how they were blessed. Blessed—an interesting choice of words during the hardest trial of his life.

When Jesus Christ is Lord of our lives, no matter what our circumstances, we can with say conviction that we are blessed. When Jesus is Lord, we don't gravitate towards selfishness; we rightly prioritize life and relationships. When Jesus is Lord, we clue in to the people God brings alongside us and minister to them from the heart. When Jesus is Lord, we don't curl into a ball and wilt before fear, we look adversity in the eye and thank God that through His Son we are overcomers. When Jesus is Lord, God is honored and everyone knows it. I can tell you, Jesus is Lord in the Lambert's lives.

Philippians 2:3-4—Do nothing out of rivalry or conceit, but in humility consider others as more important than yourselves. Everyone should look out not only for his own interests, but also for the interests of others.

How's your world? Do you find yourself continuously gravitating towards personal needs? Does it seem you are fixated on problems that just won't evaporate? If so, it's important to schedule personal time to fellowship with God. When He is first, it truly is amazing how balance is restored. You'll see those people that climb under your epidermis with a different set of eyes. The Holy Spirit will give you insight in how to minister to those you encounter. Jesus enables us to see the interests of others and care. From my vantage, there are a whole lot of people that need caring. So let's make a difference one life at a time—like the Lamberts have done for over forty years.

Inspiration † † †

Service isn't just a kind act. Service is an indescribably beautiful picture of Jesus.—Bill Perkins in *the Jesus experiment*

Kenosis

October 27

Philippians 2:5-8—Make your own attitude that of Christ Jesus, who, existing in the form of God, did not consider equality with God as something to be used for His own advantage. Instead He emptied Himself by assuming the form of a slave, taking on the likeness of men. And when He had come as a man in His external form, He humbled Himself by becoming obedient to the point of death—even to death on a cross.

Can You See?
When He looked down from above, tell me what He felt
For One so strong and mighty lying helpless as a babe?
While Mary held her baby boy, God was holding earth.
Joseph fed his newborn son the One who'd be our Bread.

Can you see that Love believed enough to be our grace?
Can you see inside your heart that Jesus took your place?
Can you know if angels came and shepherds saw the sight
That heaven opened up its doors so you would see His Light?

This Child born one awesome night, a gift unwrapped in joy
Became a Man of Sorrows for every girl and boy.
Every year He lived as man, the Son in suffering grew
Until He died for broken hearts and rose to make them new.

Now the stars hang silently, and centuries have gone.
And still across the land are those who've never heard His song.

Do you see that Love believed enough to be our grace?
Do you see inside your heart that Jesus took your place?
Do you know if angels came and shepherds saw the sight
That heaven opened up its doors so you would see His Light?
©2009 Daniel York See His Star ARR

We declare that the one selfsame Christ, only begotten Son and Lord, must be acknowledged in two natures, without any co-mingling, or change or division or separation, that the distinction between their natures is in no way removed by their union, but rather, that the specific character of each nature is preserved, and they are united in one person and one hypostasis.—Portion of the *Creed of Chalcedon* 451 A.D.*

*This Creed was formulated by the Church to defend against several additional heresies that denied either Jesus' full humanity or deity.

Grumbling

October 28

Philippians 2:14,15—Do everything without grumbling and arguing, so that you may be blameless and pure, children of God who are faultless in a crooked and perverted generation, among whom you shine like stars in the world.

Harry is a phenomenal Command Sergeant Major. His dedication and his uncompromising zeal are inspiring. When I think of him, I am reminded of Paul's challenge to the Philippians in the passage above.

Harry instituted a weekly police call. Wednesday afternoons, junior officers and noncommissioned officers working in the headquarters are expected to go out into the parking lot and pick up trash—especially cigarette butts! At first the senior leaders did not think he was serious and they did not send out their troops with bags. That did not last long when Harry made them pick up the trash and hand carry it to dumpsters. It only took one tongue thrashing from CSM Estabrooks to get a leader's attention that he was committed. Because he leads by example, Harry turned negative attitudes into willing support. Our organization received lots of compliments from visiting leaders for the cleanliness of our area.

Harry insisted that every soldier exercise three times a week and held them accountable to show up for formation. Lots of grumbling followed this edict. Next came numerous excuses for people to skip working out. But Harry faithfully lifted weights and ran and demanded that our team improve their physical condition. Not surprisingly, our team won local running races and had more soldiers max their physical fitness test than any other unit on post.

People ask me, "How can I share my faith when I am not articulate and I'm afraid I'll say the wrong thing?" Refrain from grumbling and arguing. Grumbling is a contagious disease. It was the very thing that caused God to exercise great wrath against the Israelites. Instead of trusting and obeying Him as He miraculously fed and cared for them, they turned grumbling into an art form (Num. 11:1).

The next time someone asks you to do something unpleasant or not on your "fun-to-do list," before complaining, *stop* and remember who you serve. Jesus did not come to be the Lord of grumblers. He came to change us to be like Him, the humble King who undeservedly picked up the cross, took the whip, absorbed the scorn and hate, and died without a word of complaint. The reason we argue with God is because at heart we don't trust Him. The reason we grumble is because we think our plan is better. The proof that our logic is faulty is the planet—look around at the world. What a perverted mess. Let's change our attitude and praise God without murmuring—that's moving towards purity.

Inspiration † † †

To complain against God is in effect to deny His holiness and to say He is not fair.—Jerry Bridges in *The Pursuit of Holiness*

Pura Vida October 29

Walking up the road from our hotel on our way to dinner, a young man walked up to me and handed me a grasshopper he made from a palm leaf. He said, "Pura vida! Welcome to Costa Rica." Intrigued by his friendliness, I conversed with him while he tried to show me how to create a palm grasshopper. The rest of the family joined us and prompted by the Lord, I invited Carlos to join us for dinner. Because Sarah and Mark are fluent in Spanish, we enjoyed interacting with him at a nearby restaurant.

Carlos shared with us about having to leave school to work because of the multiple operations his mom underwent for a serious back problem. For a period of time his father was unemployed and Carlos and his brother and sister had to work to pay the bills. Listening to this articulate seventeen year-old, I asked if he would be interested in hearing Bryan's story to which he readily agreed. He was amazed to hear how God had miraculously healed Bryan from his brain-stem tumor.

We asked Carlos what his dream was and his eyes lit up as he shared about his desire to become a pilot. Shortly before we finished eating, he invited us to his house for dinner, sharing that his mom made terrific tortillas. We set a date for the following Sunday to go to his house.

Philippians 4:8—Finally brothers, whatever is true, whatever is honorable, whatever is just, whatever is pure, whatever is lovely, whatever is commendable—if there is any moral excellence and if there is any praise—dwell on these things.

Pura vida means *pure life*, but "Pure life" in Spanish would be "Vida pura." The real meaning is closer to "full of life," "this is living," or "cool!" It serves as a greeting and a farewell, to convey satisfaction, to politely express indifference when describing something, or even to say "Thank you." Costa Ricans use the phrase to express a philosophy of strong community, perseverance, positive resilience in overcoming difficulties, enjoying life slowly, and celebrating good fortune.[93] As we traveled Costa Rica many people spoke these two words to us. We found them written on billboards, shirts and handicrafts.

Reading Paul's words to the Philippians, I think of *pura vida*. Through the Holy Spirit we are able to live life to its fullest! By His help we discern God's will for expending our time and energy on whatever pleases Him.

Inspiration † † †

Life is the sum total of what you do with the moments given you.—Erwin Raphael McManus in *Chasing Daylight*

Bee Stings October 30

Dinner with Carlos and his family turned out to be quite extraordinary. We arrived looking to encourage them with our Hope and instead enjoyed rich fellowship. Francisco, Rocío, and their three children all have a strong faith in God. While eating Rocío's incredible Tamales, I asked Francisco how he came to meet the Lord.

As a child, Francisco worked for a farmer. One day this man was badly stung by bees on his head. Francisco waited to see him swear and raise a commotion but nothing of the sort happened. The farmer despite his pain remained calm and amazingly serene. Francisco asked him how this was possible when he had been so unfairly attacked and stung. The farmer responded by sharing that God made the bees and they were His creatures. He went on to share that it was because of God's Son, Jesus that he was able to live with the power not to lose his composure and become angry. Francisco was so amazed that he determined that day to place his faith in such an amazing Savior. The farmer proceeded then to help him become a follower of Jesus.

Philippians 4:9—Do what you have learned and received and heard and seen in me, and the God of peace will be with you.

The power of the gospel is not complex. It is the manifestation of simple appropriation of God! He offers freely His Son. When received, heaven's Gift of Life changes our lives. We knew this soon after entering the threshold of Carlos' home. His parents radiated joy and the peace that is not purchased in super markets. Francisco regaled us with story after story of God working in their lives. We gained special friends and we left with a work of art Francisco painted that was both beautiful and touching.

Bee stings! How we react to intrusive attacks reveals what we have learned and received and heard from the Truth. Someone once said, "The bubbling brook would lose its song if you removed the rocks." What music plays from your speakers? May the God of peace reside in you that others may see His presence and want what you have! Truth to trust to tranquility to triumph—the way is paved by the love of our Father who gives us His strength to live nobly!

Joseph Aldrich wrote in *Gentle Persuasion,* "Open or closed, the response to the Christ of the Bible is often determined by the material found in the book of our lives."[94]

Inspiration † † †

Open or closed, the response to the Christ of the Bible is often determined by the material found in the book of our lives.—Joseph Aldrich in *Gentle Persuasion*

Glue

The earliest known discovery of humans using an adhesive is linked to spear stone flakes glued to wood with birch-bark-tar found in central Italy. In Sibudu Cave in South Africa humans used compound glues from plant gum and red ochre thousands of years ago. Similarly six thousand-year-old ceramics show evidence of adhesives made from horse teeth. Native Americans of the eastern United States used a combination of spruce gum and fat to create waterproof seams in their birch bark canoes.[95]

Today, most of us are big fans of Cyanoacrylate. Were it not for this product in my house my kitchen chair would fall apart! We call this product "Super Glue" or "Krazy Glue." Cyanoacrylate is used as a forensic tool to capture fingerprints. Those who work with models or who do wood-working know how important super glue is because of how fast it dries and bonds. Did you know rock climbers and stringed musicians use cyanoacrylate to protect their fingers?[96]

Colossians 1:17—He is before all things, and by Him all things hold together.

When Paul wrote the Colossians that Jesus existed before all things and that all things are held together by Him, he had no knowledge of the yet-to-be-invented super glue. Yet, he understood that the greatest adhesive is our Lord. The body (corporately and individually) may suffer pain, but His love is our sure bond. Satan may attack God's creation but he cannot defeat the grip of Jesus. He is our Sustainer. What a Friend—this One who holds all things together.

"*He is also the head of the body, the church; He is the beginning, the firstborn from the dead, so that he might come to have first place in everything*" (1:18). The idea that Christ is before all things is not just a tribute to His preceding it is also a tribute to His superiority—He is preeminent. He is most excellent. He is the Lord of the church. It is a testimony to His superiority that He is able to impart meaning, sustain life and deserve our worship. Why would we not cling to Him? Why would we not recognize that our very purpose and hope is defined by this grand Vine from which we extend? Francis Frangipane wrote in *Holiness, Truth and the Presence of God*, "The Lord wants us to be rooted in Him, not rooted in our ideas about Him." Let us make Him first in everything for in so doing we will experience incredible fruit and joy to His delight!

Inspiration ✝✝✝

God took to Himself our flesh so that He might be our way back.—St. Augustine

Mindset

November 1

Generally speaking I love the color green, but in this case I'll make an exception. I put a Koi pond in my backyard looking forward to spending time each day sitting by the pool to pray and enjoy watching beautiful fish grow. But I can no longer see the fish! Algae proliferates despite the fast current the pump creates. If I don't do something drastic soon, the green goop will kill the fish, the mosquitoes will breed and I will coin a new word, *pond·tif·i·cate*, which mean "to hold opinions or judgments clouded by stale thinking."

Colossians 3:1,2—So if you have been raised with the Messiah, seek what is above, where the Messiah is, seated at the right hand of God. Set your minds on what is above, not on what is on the earth.

Twice Paul delivers the message—focus on heaven, not on earth. Having a spiritual mindset is not easy; we're born on the earth, raised on the earth and eventually become earth. Our only escape from earthly (sinful) things is to find a champion who can deliver us from sin and death. The Bible tells us *"Enoch walked with God; then he was not there, because God took him"* (Gen. 5:24). Elijah was taken to heaven alive on a fiery chariot—2 Ki. 2:11. These two men escaped death but neither was sinless and therefore qualified to save mankind.

Jesus willingly suffered crucifixion as a perfect Son of Man to atone our sin penalty. He overcame death to triumphantly rise into heaven. He made a way for us to join Him. We do this by placing our faith in Him and by putting to death whatever belongs to our earthly nature: *"sexual immorality, impurity, lust, evil desire, and greed, which is idolatry"* (Col. 3:5). Paul promises that when Christ, *"who is your life, is revealed, then you also will be revealed with Him in glory"* (v. 4).

My Koi cannot conquer the algae in their pond. It is too strong! The only way they can be saved is for me to completely change the water and treat it. So also, I cannot change my condition on a polluted earth. My only hope is for God to replace my dying water with His Living Water. But, unlike the helpless Koi, God gives me the right and ability to request the saving help of His Son and the right to determine my behavior by adopting a heavenly mindset! I'm so glad God sent Jesus to save me! I'm amazed He gave me the right to love Him. I've set my heart and mind on things above! How about you? Are you washed in the blood of the Lamb to live in the will of the Lion?

Inspiration † † †

We cannot go to either heaven or hell with both in our heart.—Richard S. Taylor in *A Right Conception of Sin*

Infatuation

November 2

Jamaal and Hannah spend hours each day playing video games. Their mother Roxanne,* says it is "okay"—at least they are not doing drugs or out on the street involved with the wrong crowd. Today we have Jamaals and Hannahs in their mid-thirties who devote hours each day to gaming. Their spiritual lives are mediocre and their contribution to advancing heaven's agenda is abysmal. Their parents let them feed their infatuations when they were younger, so long as the obsession was "harmless." But there is no such thing as a harmless infatuation.

Colossians 3:5—Therefore, put to death what belongs to your worldly nature: sexual immorality, impurity, lust, evil desire, and greed, which is idolatry.

No lust-less people have ever inhabited our planet. The Colossians did not have high tech games to become enslaved to but they fed their appetites with other pleasures. Sexual immorality, impurity, lust, evil desire and greed are all related and each rooted to the world. Jesus' devoted disciple, John, said, *"the lust of the flesh, the lust of the eyes, and the pride in one's lifestyle—is not from the Father, but is from the world"* (1 Jo. 2:16). Peter, also part of Jesus' inner circle, warned, *"Dear friends, I urge you as strangers and temporary residents to abstain from fleshly desires that war against you"* (1 Pe. 2:11). Notice the word choice—"war"; the very word screams that our survival is threatened.

The Apostle Paul explains for us what bad and good infatuation looks like:

For those who live according to the flesh think about the things of the flesh, but those who live according to the Spirit, about the things of the Spirit. For the mind-set of the flesh is death, but the mind-set of the Spirit is life and peace. For the mind-set of the flesh is hostile to God because it does not submit itself to God's law, for it is unable to do so. Those who are in the flesh cannot please God. (Rom. 8:5-8)

Later, Paul instructs his readers, *"But put on the Lord Jesus Christ, and make no plans to satisfy the fleshly desires"* (Rom. 13:14).

We see why Peter chose the word, "war" when we understand from Paul that what the flesh craves leads to death and is opposed to God. For this reason even a minor fixation must be crushed. There is no such thing as permissible idolatry. Therefore we cannot afford to make allowance for anything that captures our heart and is linked to the world. We are either in flesh or in Christ the two do not coexist. Do you find your motivation to follow Jesus ebbing? What fills your mind and has your heart?

There are things I would like to do that I cannot do because I know how weak I am. If I make exception for my flesh and its desires, five things consistently happen:

- My time with God is rushed, dry, and I do not gain His blessing or presence.
- My spirit is agitated such that I am insensitive or impatient towards others.
- I carry guilt for not pleasing God.
- The fruit of my self-interest is of no value.
- I miss opportunities to invest in God's kingdom.

I know that I cannot eliminate infatuation by my strength. The flesh is too strong. The only way I can stay in Christ is to rely on the Holy Spirit for help and to be accountable to saints who will ask me the tough questions and assist me in rooting out any behavior or activity that is meant to burn. I suspect the same is true for you. So what are you putting to death?

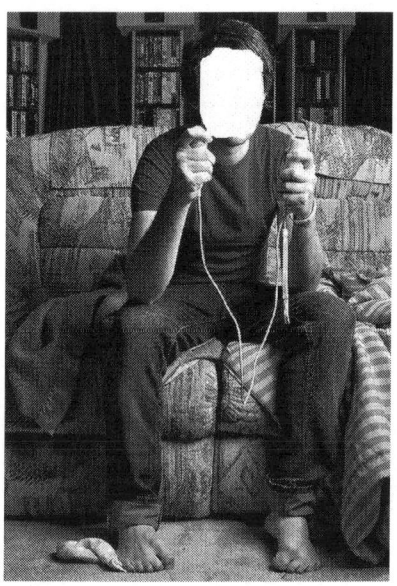

Inspiration † † †

The very effort of the church to appease fleshly expectations makes her unattractive.—Robert Coleman in *The Master Plan of Discipleship*

*Fictitious names

The Three P's   November 3

Colossians 3:5,8,12,13—Therefore, put to death what belongs to your worldly nature: sexual immorality, impurity, lust, evil desire, and greed, which is idolatry . . . But now you must also put away all the following: anger, wrath, malice, slander, and filthy language from your mouth . . . Therefore, God's chosen ones, holy and loved, put on heartfelt compassion, kindness, humility, gentleness, and patience, accepting one another and forgiving one another if anyone has a complaint against another. Just as the Lord has forgiven you, so you must also forgive.

I received a call from a distressed young man. Kafar's marriage was about to end. His wife told him she no longer loved him and she wanted a divorce. Distraught and resolved not to lose Angela, he wanted advice. In the few days since Angela made clear her intentions, Kafar had time to reflect. She made him meals before he went to work. He did nothing for her before her shift. She paid the bills, took care of the house and put time into meeting his needs. He slept, drank too much alcohol and was pretty selfish.

A desperate man will cry for help; a broken man will listen to advice. God looks for those whose hearts are soft and His Word is full of great medicine. In Colossians, the Apostle Paul shares with us three p's that are essential for anyone who wants to live a Christian life. These p's also happen to be essential in preserving marriages. First, one has to *put to death* his worldly nature. Coveting anything that pleases the flesh and displeases God is a sure recipe for disaster. Second, one has to *put away* or take off five behaviors that are sure to alienate his partner. Anger, wrath, malice, slander and a filthy mouth all cause deep wounds, are forms of abuse, and create an unsafe environment.

Third, anyone who wants to have a healthy marriage must *put on* or put into play the seven traits that Paul shares with the Colossians. I have never seen a woman in her right mind leave a compassionate, kind, humble, gentle, patient, accepting and forgiving husband! Unless her own disposition is foul, she will thrive with such a loving partner.

Before Kafar can win back Angela, he will need God's help to get his spiritual life in order. Often the one who is afraid of losing a spouse resorts to a change in behavior but without the necessary change in heart. Unless God has our first love and we are committed to obeying Him it is impossible to change ourselves and apply the three p's. The only time I have ever seen a failed marriage restored was when the Lord of creation became the Lord of the marriage. Two hearts committed to Him make one enduring love song!

Inspiration † † †

Life for the flea is all about how you affect me. The flea is totally focused on changing the other person.—Craig Hill in *two fleas & no dog*

Outlook

November 4

Friday I drove with Normi for five hours to Spokane unsure of Aunt B.J.'s condition. At the age of 83, it would be bad enough to have one intestinal surgery, but she was now recovering from the second operation within a week with no food in her system and a weak heart. Her second surgery removed a blockage the size of a football. It was not surprising that she was very tired when we finally arrived on the 10th floor of Deaconess Hospital and walked into her room. B.J. wanted one of us to stay with her so Normi spent the night in her room while her other daughter Vicki and I took turns the next day.

Colossians 3:15—And let the peace of the Messiah, to which you were also called in one body, control your hearts. Be thankful.

Saturday, B.J. felt and looked much stronger. Towards late afternoon as I held her left hand (in the process of adjusting her pillow), she immediately began praying. She mentioned to God that while unsure why He wanted her to go through what she was suffering she was nevertheless thankful to Him for His help and desired to be a testimony to others. Then she proceeded to pray at length for me!

Lying in a hospital bed is anything but a pleasant experience. It was hard for B.J. to sleep because nurses or doctors almost hourly entered her room to run tests, check vitals, treat her body or adjust her environment. Craving food, fighting pain, low on rest and high on worry are not conditions that build tranquility. Yet, B.J. steadily maintained a thankful demeanor. She filled her anxious cup with faith and found serenity. One of her nurses commented, "If every one of my patients were like you, I would do this job for free!"

When tubes run in your nose and arms, and noise is unabated; when your blood pressure rises as your body throbs in pain; when life seems more like death and lungs are filled with fluid; when *why* is missing reason, and *when* cannot be measured, can you be thankful? What's your outlook when the prognosis is stormy? If you can pray for others when *your* need is greatest, you have the peace of the Messiah, and He has control of your heart!

Inspiration † † †

My mind and heart are at peace; Jesus Christ is my all sufficient savior.— COL Joshua Chamberlain before his Brigade's Civil War fight at the battle on Little Round Top

Lengkat

November 5

Riding from Abuja to Jos, Nigeria, David Joel, pastor of *Agape Communion Church*, shared with me an amazing story. There was a military coup in Nigeria in February 1976. Jurbe, a Captain in the Nigerian Army, was implicated in the coup. Despite his innocence, the authorities tried and executed him. Paul Wakkies, his younger brother, took his death hard. But on November 5, his wife, Kurnyang, bore him a daughter. They named her *Lengkat*, which means, "*Don't Worry!*" Paul took solace in the fact that, although He allowed the death of his brother, God provided new life.

While speaking to youth at Evangelical Church West Africa (ECWA), David spotted Lengkat and was immediately attracted to her. After worship, he gave her his business card and asked her to call him. She called, and they continued to communicate until David, sensing God's confirmation, proposed. On April 5, 2003, David married her. Today, they have three children and a wonderful ministry in Jos. David is a mighty man of prayer that God is using to impact key people around his nation.

Philippians 4:4-7—Rejoice in the Lord always. I will say it again: Rejoice! Let your graciousness be known to everyone. The Lord is near. Don't worry about anything, but in everything, through prayer and petition with thanksgiving, let your requests be made known to God. And the peace of God, which surpasses every thought, will guard your hearts and your minds in Christ Jesus.

No matter how difficult things get, we don't have to worry—God is in control. David illustrated this principle in profound ways. You see, all week while he blessed us with his presence and heart for people, he was also mourning the loss of his mother, who graduated to be with Jesus. Lengkat is a concept we can all apply. We rejoice! We offer graciousness! We have a thankful heart at peace because we believe that God truly guards our hearts and minds in Christ Jesus.

Inspiration † † †

Worry does not empty tomorrow of its sorrow; it empties today of its strength.—Corrie Ten Boom

Cleaning Toilets

November 6

Colossians 3:23,24—Whatever you do, do it enthusiastically, as something done for the Lord and not for men, knowing that you will receive the reward of an inheritance from the Lord. You serve the Lord Christ.

I had an interesting conversation with a retired Marine Master Sergeant. Mike leads the men's retreats for his church. Periodically he is called by men who ask him if they can be involved with the men's leadership team. Mike will then invite the inquiring person to join him on Saturday morning to help him as he helps the janitor clean toilets. Not surprisingly, his offer is declined whereby Mike informs the applicant that his services on the leadership team are not needed. I think the Apostle Paul would like Mike's selection technique.

Recently I was visiting one of my units in New York. As I was exiting the restroom I noticed the trash can was overflowing with paper towels. Instead of someone dumping the garbage, soldiers just threw their excess paper on the floor. This building was shared by multiple units and on this day the place was crowded. So I called the sergeant escorting me and asked him where the dumpster was so I could dump the trash. He was embarrassed and said not to worry, he would get someone to take care of it. But I assured him I didn't want him to get anyone else because it was now my responsibility to dump the trash. You can learn a lot about organizations from their rest rooms and mentor accordingly.

Whether it be cleaning toilets or taking out the trash, the task can be enjoyable if our motivation is to serve the Lord. Conversely, if we are not willing to do serve, because it is either beneath our pay grade or considered too unpleasant, then perhaps that says something about our pride and priority. Consider Paul. He was an elite apostle, gifted by God, given visions no one else was privy to, and arguably one of the most important leaders in the early church. Yet, he considered it a privilege to make tents to earn money so that he was not a burden on others. Paul worked for God. Therefore, instead of becoming power-driven, title-enamored, or pleasure-focused, he was able to remain Christ-centered.

Whatever you do, do it with enthusiasm—from the soul! Are you a homemaker? Make your home Jesus-honoring. Are you a student? Learn with gusto. Beware of obsessing on people-pleasing. Don't work hard when the boss is watching but slack off when no one notices or you lose the privilege of honoring God who sees everything. If you do the little things well, you'll find it easier to do the big things well. The Lord sees the heart, so be hearty and act with the passion that pleases your Father and leads to eternal dividends.

Falling Away   November 7

Karl and Joe* accompanied me on a missions trip. We had a great time together sharing Jesus with people who had never heard of Him. We laughed at ourselves as we struggled to speak the language of our hosts. We enjoyed the adventure of braving rush hour on motorcycles and eating strange but delicious foods. We bonded as a team as we shared in hardships and victories in the journey of serving God.

Decades later, Karl is still serving the Lord and making a difference in the lives of people. Joe is wrapped around the pursuit of making money and climbing the corporate ladder. He likes to be seen in church on Sunday while the rest of the week he works to pursue *the good life*.

Colossians 4:14—Luke, the dearly loved physician, and Demas greet you.

The only mention of Luke being a doctor in the New Testament is recorded in the verse above. Luke was not just the author of one of the gospels and the book of Acts, it is apparent that he was a beloved man. He faithfully accompanied Paul on his missionary journeys and he made an indelible mark on the lives of the people to whom he ministered.

Demas also was part of Paul's team. At the time when Paul wrote the Christians in the city of Colossae, Demas evidently had good standing with them. But something went very wrong as Paul neared the end of his life. In 2 Timothy 4:9-11 we read, *"Make every effort to come to me soon, for Demas has deserted me, because he loved this present world, and has gone to Thessalonica. Crescens has gone to Galatia, Titus to Dalmatia. Only Luke is with me . . ."*

Luke faithfully remained with Paul. Demas took off. The word "desert" is a strong word. It means Demas abandoned Paul when there was an expectation that he was needed and should stay. It means he failed his mission. Clearly, in Paul's eyes, Demas was more in love with the world than with the Maker of the world. Thessalonica was a city of 200,000 people who mainly worshipped idols, Greek and Roman gods, and the Roman emperor himself.[97] This was not a destination Demas needed to reach and certainly not at a time when Paul needed him.

So what makes one man faithful while another falls away? The answer is found in the eyes. When our eyes are on Jesus, we do what is right. The team benefits and the gospel flourishes. When our eyes are on the world, we become selfish. The team languishes and the gospel is ridiculed. This is precisely why the Apostle John wrote, *"Do not love the world or the things that belong to the world. If anyone loves the world, love for the Father is not in him"* (1 John 2:15). Check your eyes. Is your desire to do your own thing or are you zealous to serve those God places around you? Wrong motivation in the heart is a sign the eyes are distracted. I know how easy it is to focus on earthly things. To bless others and stay on track, I must focus on Jesus. I need frequent eye exams! How about you?

Inspiration ✝ ✝ ✝

I choose faithfulness...Today I will keep my promises. My debtors will not regret their trust. My associates will not question my word. My wife will not question my love. And my children will never fear that they father will not come home.—Max Lucado

*Not their real names.

Letter to You

November 8

1 Thessalonians 1:2—We always thank God for all of you, remembering you constantly in our prayers.

I am writing a letter to you to encourage you in your faith. There are four things that leap from my heart as I remember you. First, I want to pass on how faithful God is to me and what a huge difference He makes in my life. My goal is to pass on His Word and to be a blessing to others as He is a blessing to me. I love Him so much! Second, please prepare for persecution. Our nation is increasingly hostile to God's standards and rebellious towards His will. The more we align ourselves with Him the more we can expect to suffer. Third, never give up the pursuit of holiness—abstain from sin and treat others with love. This is God's will for us and He will reward us for such conduct. Fourth, be highly encouraged with the truth that Jesus is coming back. The anticipation of being united with Him ought to give us a joyful hope!

I'm so thankful for you. You are a reflection of God's creative handiwork and a unique story of grace. Thinking of you brings a smile to my face. To remember you in prayer is a privilege.

Incidentally, I patterned this letter from Paul's missive to the Thessalonian believers.[98] The four things above are the very points he made to his friends in Thessalonica. And the last point ought to really charge our batteries. Jesus' return is mentioned in every chapter of Paul's letter. Reading his words one can sense how much he wanted the Thessalonians to look forward to seeing Jesus (1:10, 2:19, 3:13, 4:15-18, 5:2,10,23). Are you excited about coming into the presence of our awesome Savior? What a fantastic day that will be!

Paul thought so much about his brothers and sisters in Greece that he sent his good companion Timothy to check on them and encourage them (3:2). Timothy brought back a great report on their faith and love (3:6). No wonder he was thankful for them and remembered them in prayer. How about you? Who comes to your mind when you think of fellow believers? Who do you pray for? And how would you feel about writing a letter—a message from your heart to those you care about and cheer on to be faithful? A letter from the heart is good medicine.

Inspiration † † †

I have so fixed the habit in my mind that I never . . . seal a letter without putting a word of prayer under the seal . . . never change my classes in the lecture room without a minute's petition for the cadets who go out and for those who come in . . . —General Stonewall Jackson

Be a Blessing! November 9

1 Thessalonians 3:11,12—Now may our God and Father Himself, and our Lord Jesus, direct our way to you. And may the Lord cause you to increase and overflow with love for one another and for everyone, just as we also do for you.

Context: My predecessor seldom left her office. She didn't walk around and meet the employees in her organization. She was not a bad person, she was just not engaged. Her style of leadership was completely "hands off."

The Army is reeling from too many soldiers taking their lives and we were ordered to do a "stand down" day to discuss suicide prevention. I wasn't excited to attend the first battle assembly after taking command to address this morbid subject with all of our headquarters personnel. Before I started speaking I walked around the room to meet each employee and shake as many hands as I could. Then I went in front of them and shared from my heart why I believe suicide is a spiritual problem. I don't think the audience expected to hear such words in our increasingly secular environment. We ended up having productive dialogue before I turned the time over to the facilitator.

Later that day, I learned that one of our captains broke down (emotionally expressing to others that he considered taking his life). But because I shook his hand, he felt encouraged enough that he mattered and decided to open up. My deputy encouraged me to meet with him and I was able to learn much about this young officer's struggles. Fortunately, because he was honest we were able to get him help and avert what could have been a tragedy.

The simple act of shaking someone's hand made a difference. I was profoundly reminded of how important it is for us who are loved by Jesus to be a blessing to others. Your words and actions carry great weight. Take the time to thank those you work with (and perhaps take for granted) and share your appreciation for them. If you are married, pass on a blessing to your spouse. Tell your children how much you love them. May the Lord direct you to those you know whom you might encourage.

God's love is not finite. We have His power inside us to increase our love for one another. Andrew Murray wrote in *With Christ in the School of Prayer*, "It is when we give ourselves to be a blessing that we can specially count on the blessing of God."[99] Thank you for who you are you. Thank you for what you do that honors our Father. Thank you for loving the Lord and for wanting to be more like Him. Thank you for inspiring me to inspire others. You are a blessing.

Inspiration †††

The word for bless in the Hebrew is barak. It means "to bend the knee."—Dr. Bill Gothard in *How to Conquer Habits and Addictions*

Tribute

November 10

One of the things I appreciate most about memorial services is learning about the lives of those who have departed through the eyes of those who knew them. Mike walked up to the microphone and paid tribute to our departed classmate John Hennessey, a fellow member of his company.

As a plebe, Mike was in danger of failing boxing (something many of us non-boxers can appreciate). John happened to be his last graded opponent. Before they went into the ring, John told Mike just to aim for his chin. During the fight, Mike threw a punch to John's exposed chin and John immediately fell to the mat. Mike was amazed that John would let him knock him down thereby enabling him to win the bout and pass the class. It was a selfless act of kindness that typifies a class whose motto is "Strength As One."

2 Thessalonians 1:11,12—And in view of this, we always pray for you that our God will consider you worthy of His calling, and will, by His power, fulfill every desire for goodness and the work of faith, so that the name of our Lord Jesus will be glorified by you, and you by Him, according to the grace of our God and the Lord Jesus Christ.

I would venture that all of us in attendance at the memorial service were touched by the tributes given to our departed friends. If we, as imperfect beings, can find ways to give tribute to each other here on earth, can you imagine what it will be like to stand in heaven one day and be honored alongside our Savior, Jesus Christ? Our singular motivation to live good lives ought to be to bring Him glory. Paul prayed that the Thessalonian Christians would live a life worthy of their Lord's calling.

What is His calling for us? I believe Scripture teaches that we are to live holy lives, to be obedient to God's will, to love our enemies and treat our neighbors the way we would want to be treated, to accomplish God's purposes for us and to have an attitude that is built on faith that God's power can enable us to accomplish whatever He prompts us to do!

When we live according to God's calling, we honor the name of Jesus. God promises that we in turn will be honored thanks to His fantastic grace. So let's live so that our actions and character, attitude and conduct are a living tribute to Jesus. In the end that never ends, we will receive a heavenly tribute! Amen!

Inspiration † † †

The call to the "extraordinary" is the inevitable risk men must take when they follow Christ.—Dietrich Bonhoeffer in *The Cost of Discipleship*

Enlightened

November 11

Veteran's Day is an American holiday that commemorates those brave men and women serving and defending their nation in the Armed Forces. A nation without veterans would be an impoverished state. They possess a patriotic fervor and misty-eyed love for the flag that transcends what many feel. Theirs is the rigid posture of respect when the national anthem plays. Theirs was the taking of oaths and the understanding that they might die on some forsaken soil, work for marginal pay and benefits, serve away from family and follow costly orders. Sacrifice has a way of making us appreciate what we take for granted and better understand what we possess. I wish every spoiled, flag-burning, nation-degrading American given the right to protest was shipped overseas under the tutelage of a drill sergeant. They might think twice before bashing. They might learn from those who can spell P-A-T-R-I-O-T-I-S-M.

Growing up with a father who was wounded fighting in Korea, whose valor was recognized by the awarding of a silver star, gave me an intense desire to serve.

Philemon 6—I pray that your participation in the faith may become effective through knowing every good thing that is in us for the glory of Christ.

As much as I love my nation, there is a greater calling than defending national values. There is a greater citizenship than what any nation, no matter how powerful or wealthy, can bestow. If we should learn from the example of vets, how much more should we gain from those who take up their cross daily to serve in a war that is far greater in scope and magnitude—one that has raged for as long as mankind has known the gift of breath? To lose this war is to lose everything for eternity. To fail to follow the Creator-in-Chief, heaven's leader, empowers his enemy, Satan, to the peril of billions.

I fear we have become silent about our faith when we should be bold in sharing Jesus. Could it be that we are more inclined to be content than convicted to be obedient? If we don't feel the need to tell people about the saving grace of Jesus, then by our very inaction we accept their citizenship in hell. The cure to spiritual stagnancy is found in purposeful sharing. Paul exhorted Philemon in the passage above to actively share his faith. He knew by experience that when we stand up for what we believe in, we are more fully enlightened in just how blessed we are in Christ. Do you really know every good thing you have in Jesus?

Inspiration † † †

If your personal faith in Christ has no positive outward expression, then your faith—and mine—has a hole in it.—Richard Stearns in *The Hole in our Gospel*

I Grabbed a Rifle

November 12

Guards stopped us at the entrance to Forward Operating Base (FOB) Ho Chunk and checked our IDs before allowing my Command Sergeant Major (CSM) and me to walk into the camp where several units trained. As we inspected the premises we saw unmade beds and gear strewn haphazardly inside tents. Soldiers walked by us out of uniform. I ducked inside a tent and noticed several unsecured weapons so I grabbed an M16 and slung it on my shoulder. Soon after, warning sirens sounded and a quick response force rushed by us to meet the threat. I wondered what soldier was running around trying to find what happened to his M16! The captain in charge of the FOB (known as the mayor) approached us and spoke to us for several minutes. Amazingly he completely missed the fact that I was carrying a rifle—not something generals do.

As we departed Ho Chunk, the guards failed to notice I was armed. Before we drove off, the CSM opened up the snatched weapon. It was filthy and rusted in several places. This M16 had not been cleaned in a long time. Steam ascended from Harry's head and his eyes bore the glare of disgust. He strode back inside the FOB and notified the nearest leader that they had a missing weapon and that he expected the entire chain of command to report to his office the next morning. It would be a long night for several embarrassed leaders participating in our training exercise.

A soldier failed to clean his weapon and left it unsecured. But it was first line leaders who failed to inspect and instill discipline. Irresponsible units die before a determined enemy. It is our job and duty to make sure that never happens.

2 Thessalonians 3:11—For we hear that there are some among you who walk irresponsibly, not working at all, but interfering with the work of others.

Irresponsibility is always linked to a lack of discipline. Fat feasts on excessive food without exercise. Fatigue impairs those who stay up too late. If a person is backsliding spiritually, you can be sure he or she is weak in the spiritual disciplines. Sadly, slackers don't just hurt themselves, they discourage those around them.

How responsible are you? If your life is a mess, something is amiss. It is those who are strong in discipline and who master the basics that win on the battlefield. If negligence and apathy characterize those around you, what are *you* doing to make a difference? Sometimes we have to grab a weapon to get the attention of a soldier. Get engaged and make a difference! Paul did not ignore the report of irresponsible Thessalonians, he commanded them to get back to work if they expected to eat.

Suicide

November 13

Every day for about eight months I received emails from the Pentagon with news of a soldier taking his or her life. Some days there were multiple messages. The reports were concise and heartbreaking. Once after three consecutive emails I just had to cry. A colonel facing retirement put a gun to his head and pulled the trigger; a female captain hung herself; a sergeant overdosed on drugs; a private threw himself in front of traffic; and, a specialist leaped from a bridge. Relentlessly these bitter messages invaded my Blackberry.

What is wrong with people that they so despair of life? And consider that I am just talking about one segment of our society—the Army. According to the Centers for Disease Control and Prevention, "In 2009, the rate among the 25 to 64 year age group was 16.25 suicides per 100,000."[100] The projected population of the United States in early October 2012, was 314,535,408.[101] According to these statistics (assuming the most recent 2009 rate), 51,112 people will commit suicide this year. The size of my city Tigard is about 49,000. Imagine a city lost every year! Tragically, about 140 people in our nation take their lives every day.

1 Timothy 1:15,16—This saying is trustworthy and deserving of full acceptance: "Christ Jesus came into the world to save sinners"—and I am the worst of them. But I received mercy for this reason, so that in me, the worst of them, Christ Jesus might demonstrate His extraordinary patience as an example to those who would believe in Him for eternal life.

The Apostle Paul faced times in life so distressing he considered dying. *"For we don't want you to be unaware, brothers, of our affliction that took place in Asia: we were completely overwhelmed—beyond our strength —so that we even despaired of life"* (2 Co. 1:8). On top of persecution he faced enormous guilt. Prior to his conversion, he facilitated the death of Christians, he used his keen intellect to oppose God's work, and he brashly acted to make Jesus' followers miserable. Yet neither present persecution nor past fault led him to take his own life. How did he persevere?

It was Paul who wrote the Colossians, *"He [Jesus] erased the certificate of debt, with its obligations, that was against us and opposed to us, and has taken it out of the way by nailing it to the cross"* (Col. 2:14). We have an epidemic in our land that will not be cured by drugs, by noble speeches, or by persistent monitoring. The only cure is mercy because the real problem is spiritual. When men and women come to the end of themselves, the message they need to hear is not that they are being selfish or cowardly if they choose to embrace death. The message they need to hear is that *God loves them* and offered Jesus to erase their debt. God is not fazed by their vile guilt; unsympathetic to their continuing shame; critical of their bottomless depression; clueless to their mistakes; or, blind to their dilemmas.

Jesus mercifully took every bad thing we could do, every evil thought and vain imagination, every sense of uselessness and fear and obliterated them by His blood. He embraced death so we wouldn't be left holding a sin debt we could never pay. It was knowing this that gave Paul the courage to serve the Savior he formerly slandered. Grasping mercy, he withstood hell's worst attacks. We have that same compassion that flows from eternal love.

Find a person who cannot bear to live. Share with him Jesus who already died. Even believers need reminders. When our land wakes up and chooses again to worship its risen Savior and to share His love, the needless deaths will stop. Until then, we have a formidable challenge and the emails will continue.

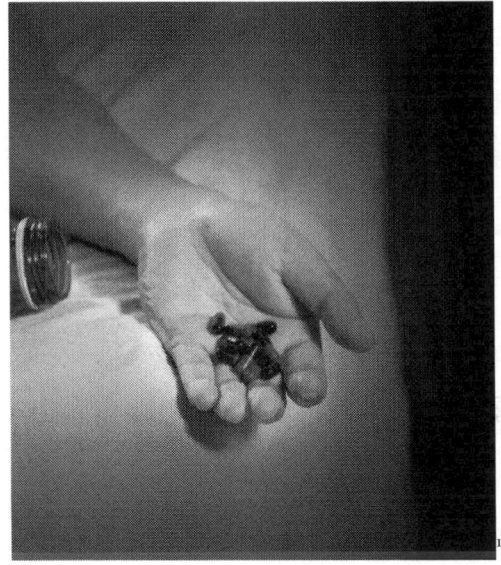

A Noble Work   November 14

In the Army Reserves, it is becoming increasingly difficult to find officers willing to serve as company and battalion commanders. One would think that the opportunity to command would be the sort of challenge many would relish. But the opposite is true. Fewer officers want the risk associated with leading because if they do not do well, their careers are in jeopardy. Also, the burden of command requires more work and sacrifice—neither of which is an attractive proposition for those with busy jobs or a comfortable rhythm of life.

1 Timothy 3:1—This saying is trustworthy: "If anyone aspires to be an overseer, he desires a noble work."

Paul encouraged Timothy to raise up more leaders (2 Ti. 2:2). That past need is still a present reality. Too many churches are pastor-centric and pastor-dependent and consequently in trouble. Just as the Army needs competent leaders, so also, God's family requires a team of gifted leaders to care for fellow Christians. Their job description is spelled out in 1 Ti. 3:1-13. But don't misunderstand those qualifications. Paul did not say that a person had to be perfect to be a leader—that would have disqualified everyone! Show me a parent with no struggles and I will show you a parent with no children. There is not an elder alive who does not make a mistake.

Do you want to be rewarded by God for a splendid exertion? If you have leadership abilities and the aspiration to serve, step up! Don't let the challenge of exhorting fellow believers to grow spiritually, the necessity of serving and the demand of living a respectable life scare you. Don't let the need to please yourself rob you from the opportunity to make a difference in the lives of people. Don't let the unholy roar of competing voices dissuade you. Don't run if the faithful Father has called you. Don't be intimidated by the office. God will give you the strength, the grace and the wisdom to do what He asks of you. And if you have no leading to lead, but you love the Savior, encourage those you know who should be leading. Give them your support. Your gentle nudge may be the very thing God uses to bring forward a hesitant spectator.

Dave Kraft wrote in *Leaders Who Last:* "A Christian leader is a humble, God-dependent, team-playing servant of God who is called by God to shepherd, develop, equip, and empower a specific group of believers to accomplish an agreed-upon vision from God." A noble work with needy people in a wicked world—seems like a nice recipe for His glory!

Inspiration † † †

The only real training for leadership is leadership.—A. Jay

Better to cultivate ten works than the work of ten.—Carl George in *Prepare Your Church for the Future*

Fearing Failure

November 15

Instant communication comes with a price. Imagine if a leader made a mistake before 1845. People living hundreds of miles away might never hear of the gaffe. With the invention of the telegraph by Samuel Morse on in 1844 and the implementation of thousands of miles of wires, people could more quickly hear news. But it cost money to send telegraphs and it took time for mailed letters to reach their destination. Now, anyone in the world with access to the internet can watch video footage of another human's accident or meltdown.

A young girl who purposely kneed an opposing player in the face on the soccer field was embarrassed to see the footage on Yahoo. Virtually the whole world capable was capable of seeing her bad sportsmanship. The second-order effect of tweets and posts and texting is universal embarrassment for the person who fails.

Terry Bragg, who leads a company called Peacemakers Training, wrote, "Fear of failure is one of the greatest fears people have." Leaders in industry are discovering that this seems to be an ever-increasing problem among young adults. Young adults are not coping well when they make mistakes. They are too devastated by errors and lack confidence that they can overcome their mistakes, thereby becoming risk-aversive.

2 Timothy 1:7—For God has not given us a spirit of fearfulness, but one of power, love, and sound judgment.

Winston Churchill said, "Success is not final, failure is not fatal: it is the courage to continue that counts." We often learn far more from our mistakes than we do from our victories. It is important that we who are older and understand that defeats are a means to growth communicate this to our children and to those whom we have opportunity to mentor. The fact that *more* people may know of our shortcomings does not negate our ability to learn and overcome!

Man's technological advances do not limit God's attributes. Nor does the increased magnitude of what people may know about us, restrict the measure of what God can do in us. He does not want us to be afraid of failure He wants us to live in the abundance of His indwelling Holy Spirit! If more people know we have failed, then, by God's grace, may even more know that we persevere to succeed.

Paul wanted Timothy to be *encouraged* that he was a prisoner for Christ. He knew what it meant to depend on God's power (1:8). We cannot rely on a need to be perfect, we can rely on our perfect Lord while we climb higher . . . in reveration!

Learned, Received, Heard, and Seen November 16

There is almost an intoxication that comes with preaching the Word from a pulpit to a listening crowd. But I do not believe this is the kind of preaching Paul is challenging Timothy to perform. If anything, I have found over the years, that little results from Sunday morning sermons. Yes, people may go away encouraged, challenged, thinking or offended, but do their lives change much? Are Jesus-followers created or is the crowd just expanding? Followers are not made by microphone messages to seated masses. This is why the building and Sunday-message-focused church is not winning the world for Jesus.

2 Timothy 1:13—Hold on to the pattern of sound teaching that you have heard from me, in the faith and love that are in Christ Jesus.
Philippians 4:9—Do what you have learned and received and heard and seen in me, and the God of peace will be with you.

I believe the teaching that Paul challenges the Philippians and Timothy to be engaged in is the delivery of Biblical principles to people who have indicated a desire to follow Christ. This is what he modeled. He met people where they were at whether in the work-setting or at home. We love winning people to our convictions. How much better to see them take God's truth and replicate it. The former results in spiritual nurseries the latter in a vibrant spiritual army!

Never say, "I cannot coach anyone, I don't know enough." You can coach someone else. Just commit to sharing what Jesus through His word is teaching you. If you are content in your spiritual life but are not sharing God's Word with others so they grow in their faith, you are missing the whole objective of Christianity—to go and make Jesus-followers! Rebel against complacency! Burn the creed "I'm too busy." Get after the most rewarding work God gave us—the privilege of spiritually reproducing! Such work results in eternal reward; most everything else will burn.

Inspiration †††

What would happen for God's kingdom if we did not consider our job complete when people confess their sins and say a prayer inviting Jesus to be their Redeemer, but would *use their new commitments to Christ as a launching pad for a lifelong quest to become individuals who are completely sold out—emotionally, intellectually, physically, spiritually—to the Son of God?*—George Barna in *Growing True Disciples*

Treasure Hunting

November 17

It was a bittersweet day. Although I earned my Expert Infantryman Badge (EIB) at Fort Benning, Georgia as a Second Lieutenant, I lost my West Point ring in the process. I have always thought it would be great to rent a metal detector and go searching for that lost treasure. The problem is, many decades later, I have no idea even what area to search!

Treasure hunting is big business. Hunters spend years on the water searching for buried gold and jewelry on sunken ships. Thousands of people buy metal detectors and make it their hobby to look for coins and artifacts on beaches or old battleground sites. Perhaps you can remember a time in your life when you found something and the discovery brought you great excitement. I remember as a youngster finding an old lamp used on miner's helmets in Idaho. Because my grandfather worked the mines it held special value.

2 Timothy 1:14—Guard, through the Holy Spirit who lives in us, that good thing entrusted to you.
Colossians 2:2,3—How I long that you may be encouraged, and find out more and more how strong are the bonds of Christian love. How I long for you to grow more certain in your knowledge and more sure in your grasp of God himself. May your spiritual experience become richer as you see more and more fully God's great secret, Christ himself! For it is in him, and in him alone, that men will find all the treasures of wisdom and knowledge. (J.B. Phillips)

The greatest treasure find is not gold, expensive gems, or antiques. It is not the acquisition of possessions, it is knowing the Possessor! As Paul wrote the Colossians, the treasures of wisdom and knowledge are found in Jesus Christ. The prophet Isaiah wrote his countrymen, *"There will be times of security for you—a storehouse of salvation, wisdom, and knowledge. The fear of the LORD is Zion's treasure"* (Isa. 33:6).

To worship, to fear, to know Jesus is to understand and to properly value life. So many people are searching for the wrong treasures! The world is full of false advertisements regarding what is important or matters. King Solomon wrote in Ecclesiastes 2:8-11:

> *I also amassed silver and gold for myself, and the treasure of kings and provinces . . . I became great and surpassed all who were before me in Jerusalem . . . All that my eyes desired, I did not deny them. I did not refuse myself any pleasure . . . When I considered all that I had accomplished and what I had labored to achieve, I found everything to be futile and a pursuit of the wind. There was nothing to be gained under the sun.*

Nothing brings peace, joy, fulfillment, and ultimately understanding like knowing God's Son.

Erwin Raphael McManus wrote in *Chasing Daylight* "One of the wonderful side effects of following Jesus Christ is that you get better at living." If Jesus sat next to you at a corner table in a warm coffee shop and asked, "What treasure are you hunting?" How would you answer? What if His next question was, "What would those who know you well say you are seeking?"

All the treasures are hidden in Him.

Inspiration †††
He who searches for pearls must dive below.—John Dryden

Refreshed

November 18

2 Timothy 1:16,17—May the Lord grant mercy to the household of Onesiphorus, because he often refreshed me and was not ashamed of my chains. On the contrary, when he was in Rome, he diligently searched for me and found me.

Almost nobody wants to be in the company of a loser. Clearly prisoners would constitute a class of society that many would gladly avoid altogether. If a person is behind bars, the natural inference is that he or she is for whatever reason a failure, a lawbreaker, or person not to be trusted. But what if God put *you* behind bars? What if He loved those unloved people so much that He made you His Cell Ambassador?

My good friend, Andre has languished in prison in his African home country for years. Prior to his arrest he was a counselor to the President and a very successful pastor. So imagine his pain when he was tried and convicted for a business mistake and thrown behind bars. Away from his wife and children, his friends and coworkers, if anyone had the right to be bitter, it would be this tall, winsome saint. But Andre is not bitter. He is lonely, hurting, often discouraged and so ready to be free. He is also sharing Christ with his fellow prisoners, training them in how to be followers of Jesus and maximizing his time as a convict to model holiness and humility. He chose to be like Paul and praise the Lord in prison.

Maybe you can think of periods of crazy busyness or quiet discomfort when you were lonely and wished someone would diligently search for you; for someone to make the time and effort to be an encouragement. If you have felt this way, imagine what Paul and Andre felt behind the cold, uncaring bars of isolation. Watchman Nee wrote in *Love not the World*, "To refresh the hearts of the saints is the kind of ministry which everyone can fulfil and which can reach everywhere. In the valuation of God it is without price."

Today would you take the time to ask the Holy Spirit to bring to your mind someone whom you could refresh? When you have the answer, go make a God-honoring difference. If by chance you are feeling alone and discouraged, the prayer below is for you:

Lord, please bring an Onesiphorus to remind my friend how important she is! Bring an Onesiphorus to let him know that he matters and that You love him. Let her be encouraged, let him be warmed beyond measure because You eternally care.

Inspiration † † †

If we are walking with God there is not a day when we may not, if we wish, be a refreshment to our brethren.—Watchman Nee in *Love not the World*

I Don't Know

November 19

In the Philippines it is culturally considered embarrassing to be asked a question and to not know the answer. So, if I am out driving and I ask a bystander for directions, I may get directions even if the person has no clue what the correct way is. Therefore, one must always beware of heeding advice and acting on it without getting a second or third opinion. Filipinos do not like to say "I don't know."

Ironically, this same desire not to appear uninformed also often afflicts the church. Consequently, Christians will weigh in with answers (educated or not) on vexing questions so as to appear that they are mature or knowledgeable. Some probably even think they do know the answer. But unlike in the Philippines where not saying "I don't know," is culturally understood and therefore not much of a problem, in the church when people weigh in with authority on what they do not really know, it can be very dangerous.

Let's suppose I go to a pastor and I say, "Pastor, I am concerned about what will happen to me when I die. Will I go to heaven?" The pastor replies, "Well Dan, have you prayed and confessed your sins and asked Jesus to be your Savior?" I nod my head yes. He then says, "Well then, you don't have to worry, you will go to heaven." Folks this is potentially a terrible answer.

2 Timothy 2:19—Nevertheless, God's solid foundation stands firm, having this inscription: The Lord knows those who are His, and Everyone who names the name of the Lord must turn away from unrighteousness.

First, as Paul taught Timothy, God is the One who knows who are His (saved). We dare not make claims that are not ours to make. Second, the pastor made an assumption that because I prayed a "verbal formula" I am therefore saved. This is dangerous on two accounts. As Paul notes in the verse above, all who profess the Lord's name are required to flee from sin. If I am living in sin, I have not met God's requirement therefore, why would I be saved? *"This is how we are sure that we have come to know Him: by keeping His commands"* (1 Jo. 2:3). If I am not keeping God's commands, I don't have the truth in me (v. 4). If I love the world or the things that belong to the world, I don't have love for the Father in me (2:15). The absence of truth and God's presence is a clear indicator I am not saved. Furthermore, if I do not love others, I don't know God (4:8). *"The one who remains in love remains in God, and God remains in him"* (4:16b).

Rather than pronounce me saved, the pastor should have asked me more questions to find out my circumstances, convictions, and behavior. Finally, the honest admission is to say God is the one who determines if I am saved and Scripture provides clear instruction, as noted earlier, to help me evaluate my condition. By making a pronouncement without really knowing, the pastor in this case could send me away thinking I am "good to go" when, in fact, I may not be walking with God at all and not be part of His "fold." This is not only presumptuous on the part of a leader, but he will also stand accountable to God for his actions.

There is an important doctrine that is oft not taught in theology. It is the doctrine of "I don't know." Scripture often uses the word *mystery* to describe things the prophets did not understand about God and His ways. There are issues that only God understands and can answer. Here are just four examples:
1. Is a blind man's condition related to his sins? (John 9:2,3,34)
2. Jesus' sinless birth through Mary
3. Can a person lose his or her salvation?
4. If God is holy, how could He allow one of His angels to act as a deceiving spirit? (1 Ki. 22:22)

Rather than appear that we have solutions for every problem we would be far more helpful to admit that we don't know and will not know until we are united with God in heaven. This doctrine calls for humility. It encourages a person to rely on the Holy Spirit instead of human reasoning. Finally and most importantly—it is truthful.

103

Preparation

November 20

2 Timothy 2:20,21—Now in a large house there are not only gold and silver bowls, but also those of wood and clay, some for honorable use, some for dishonorable. So if anyone purifies himself from anything dishonorable, he will be a special instrument, set apart, useful to the Master, prepared for every good work.

J. Oswald Sanders wrote in *The Pursuit of the Holy* "There must be preparation before conquest." Let us consider what life looks like with and without preparation.

Scenario One

This week we will be tested. We will be offered the plate of sin and dine. We will be offended by the actions of the insensitive and let them know it. We will be pushed when we needed pulling, corrected when we desired encouragement, ignored but desirous of attention, and needing rest but too busy to sleep. We will bathe in self-pity while battling critical thoughts. We may be innocent before the eyes of those who see us, and yet be miserably impure inside. At the end of the week, we are morally beaten by the everyday storms of life and ticked off that God was nowhere near when we needed Him.

Scenario Two

This week we will be tested. We will be offered the plate of sin but refuse to eat. We will be offended by the actions of the insensitive and be gracious in our response. We will be pushed when we needed pulling, corrected when we desired encouragement, ignored yet sustained in God's love so that we find rest in the whirl. Though pressed on all sides, we will find joy in God's Word. We will resolve that as we see problems we will pray. We will not let the actions of others deter us from glorifying our Father in heaven. At the end of the week, we are amazed at how awesome God is and what a privilege it is to serve the King.

Inspiration †††

Preparation is not something suddenly accomplished, but a process steadily maintained. It is easy to imagine that we get to a settled state of experience where we are complete and ready; but in work for God it is always preparation *and preparation*. Moral preparation comes before intellectual preparation, because moral integrity is of more practical value than any amount of mental insight.—Oswald Chambers in *So Send I You*

Joseph

November 21

2 Timothy 4:1,2— I solemnly charge you before God and Christ Jesus, who is going to judge the living and the dead, and because of His appearing and His kingdom: Proclaim the message; persist in it whether convenient or not; rebuke, correct, and encourage with great patience and teaching.

Joseph is a handsome man with a distinctive white tuft of hair on his forehead that belies his deep wisdom. Joseph served as my interpreter each time I spoke. We were blessed by his humility and impressed by his skill in moving from English to Swahili. It was evident by testimony and crowd reaction that he was greatly respected.

Before Joseph met Jesus, he impregnated a woman he was in love with and she bore a child. He was still completing high school and the father and brothers of the girl were furious with him. As soon as the child was born, the brothers brought him to Joseph and ordered him to raise his son. Meanwhile, the father whisked his daughter to East Kenya and enrolled her in school, hiding her from Joseph.

Less than two years later, Joseph put his trust in Jesus and in answer to his prayers, the Lord provided him a wife to help him raise his son. Together they had five more children. Believing God called him to ministry, he started Trinity Baptist Church. Tragically, Joseph's wife became ill and passed away leaving him with six children to raise. Several women in the church helped him with the children, but six years as a single parent took their toll on the lonely shepherd. Joseph shared with his elders the desire to remarry and asked God to bless him with a wife to help him parent his children.

Somehow the woman who bore his first son found him. Rose wanted to see the child she never knew. Joseph agreed, but on the condition that she come to his church and not reveal her identity as the mother. So Rose came to Eldoret and met her son, now over 20 years of age. After the church service, Joseph confided to her that he still loved her. She shared similar feelings to his surprise and joy. So they determined to gain her father's blessing, and with his consent get married.

God miraculously provided Joseph with the funds for a wedding. He and Rose had another child and seven of them live in a small, two-bedroom, mud hut. His church, the students he teaches in Bible School and the surrounding community love this godly pastor. God is using this faithful servant to further His Kingdom in Eastern Africa.

When was the last time you considered that God wants to work through your proclaiming, persisting, rebuking, correcting, and encouraging for His glory?

Sound Beyond Reproach

November 22

Dr. Ben Carson, a pediatric neurosurgeon, spoke at the National Prayer Breakfast. Sitting just two seats away from the podium, President Barack Obama listened as this godly doctor shared observations about America's problems and his prescriptive ideas for changing the country for the better. It was a bold, uncompromising message delivered by a humble, God-fearing man. Some in the media castigated him for daring to speak openly against policies connected to the president. Prophetically, Dr. Carson emphasized the dangers of political correctness in his message.

Titus 2:8—Your message is to be sound beyond reproach, so that the opponent will be ashamed, having nothing bad to say about us.

Primarily we are to live holy lives because as Peter noted, "*The One who called you is holy, you also are to be holy in all your conduct*" (1 Pe. 1:15). Additionally we are to live holy lives because it deprives our enemies of ammunition to use against us. When we are "*sound beyond reproach*" in the way we live, we remove the ability of those who object to our message to buttress their argument by accusing us of a hypocritical lifestyle. While the president may not have agreed with the doctor, he certainly respected his character, and that opened up a marvelous door for truth telling. By addressing the issues and not mentioning or bad-mouthing the president and sitting politicians, Dr. Carson exemplified "what right looks like."

In the book of Cretans, Jesus told His disciples at an official's banquet, "I'm sick of Herod and his corrupt policies." To this Thomas replied, "Lord, what about the oppressive Roman rules Cesar forces us to endure?" Jesus answered, "Yes, he too needs to go. I've come for this very reason, to overthrow idiot leaders because I'm always right." Nathaniel asked him how he would get the Sanhedrin's support. Jesus shook his head and said, "This is why you are hardly ever mentioned in Scripture, do you really think I need them? Make blankets and embroider my name on them with the phrase, 'Cleaner of the Corrupt.' Place them on donkeys so people will know why I have come."

Thankfully there is no book of Cretans and that whole conversation never happened. Christ came to die for our sins and not to campaign for our votes. Never in Scripture does God call us to bash our leaders, to mock them, or to engage in complaining. He calls us to respect authority. He asks us to pray for our leaders and He compels us to tell the truth. When we live for Him first, we have not just the right, but the ability to dispense wisdom. Our audience may disagree with what we say, but at least we give them reason to reason when our lives are "*sound beyond reproach.*"

New Thought

November 23

I read a book called *Key To Yourself* by Venice Bloodworth. It was recommended to me by a nice man who felt I would find it inspiring. What I found was that it was immensely dangerous. The book could be summarized in a four word sentence near the beginning, "Psychology is the answer." Published in 1952, the book is a primer for New Thought. Dr. Bloodworth's contention is that we are all part of God and "your future is entirely under your own control."[104] What we need is to harness positive thinking which will then reap positive outcome. The reason we suffer ill fortune is because of the negative energy and thoughts we generate in our minds. "If the state of your health or finances is not all you desire, you must look within yourself for the cause."[105] Later she wrote, "Ignorance of the existence and power of the subconscious mind is the cause of all failures and near failures in the world."[106]

Dr. Bloodworth cites the Bible when it reinforces her position and conveniently ignores passages which contradict her theories. For Venice, Jesus is a positive genie who teaches us to rub our own bellies to obtain all we can think. She never mentions anything about His coming back to judge us or that God will hold people accountable for their sins.

Titus 3:5—He saved us—not by works of righteousness that we had done, but according to His mercy, through the washing of regeneration and renewal by the Holy Spirit.

So is psychology the answer? Dr. Bloodworth states, "We grow old or sick or feeble for no other reason than that we believe in old age and sickness . . . there is no principle of decay or death."[107] One has to wonder what was said at her funeral just four years after her book was published and why her casket would reveal rot!

The New Thought Movement is cleverly packaged old heresy. Positive thinking is great, as is indoor plumbing, but neither will save us from death. We can say we are all part of a universal life force and that we are divine but to do so pits us against a jealous Creator who guards His uniqueness and who does not take it kindly when the created claims His authority, power and space. Satan told Eve to eat the forbidden fruit for *"your eyes will be opened and you will be like God"* (Gen. 3:5). Opened eyes saw nakedness, separation and pain and entered a prison no self-thinking key could unlock. That is precisely why God sent Jesus. If thinking was capable of saving us, God would never have done the unthinkable! If regeneration was simply a matter of rearranging a mindset, we would not need the Holy Spirit or God's mercy. No, life is not fulfilled by self-fabricated psychology, and evil won't go away because we think less of it. *Think* God and follow His saving Son—*"so that having been justified by His grace, we may become heirs with the hope of eternal life!"* (Tit. 3:7). Eternal joy comes from a heavenly Father who loves us more deeply than we can ever love ourselves.

Inspiration †††

Truth never changes with the times, but heresy *always* does.—John MacArthur in *The Truth War*

Thanksgiving

November 24

1 Timothy 4:4,5—For everything created by God is good, and nothing should be rejected if it is received with thanksgiving, since it is sanctified by the word of God and by prayer.

Kathy was a hard worker—the kind of person who made everyone around her better. When she shook your hand, you knew you were in the presence of a strong woman! I remember many eggs, bacon, and toast she happily prepared for her husband Clay and me in their home in Newberg, Oregon. Now that her battle with cancer is finally over; it is nice to know she is with the Lord.

After Kathy's funeral service, I invited Clay to join my family for Thanksgiving. He politely declined. He had already made plans to serve Thanksgiving meals to homeless kids. Actually, I was not surprised because Clay is a big man with a huge heart. While his heart ached with the loss of his beloved wife, his hands brought joy to others because of his deeper spirit of thankfulness.

When I think about Thanksgiving, I think more about the sacrifice than the abundance. Jerry Wilson wrote:

The Pilgrims set ground at Plymouth Rock on December 11, 1620. Their first winter was devastating. At the beginning of the following fall, they had lost 46 of the original 102 who sailed on the *Mayflower*. But the harvest of 1621 was a bountiful one. And the remaining colonists decided to celebrate with a (3 day) feast—Including 91 natives who had helped the Pilgrims survive their first year. It is believed that the Pilgrims would not have made it through the year without the help of the natives.[108]

Perhaps it is wise to consider why we are able to give thanks. Jesus experienced humanity, not so He could go back to heaven and tell the angels what it is like to be a man. Rather, He cared so much about our pathetic condition, that He accepted catastrophic death. Through Divine eyes, He humanly saw beyond our selfishness something far deeper—souls created and made for fellowship!

Thanksgiving is a celebration of life; the unextinguished life made possible by Jesus. Thanksgiving is a process of faith, beyond the blessings of food, clothing, or shelter; our unseen Father will one day welcome His children into heaven. Thanksgiving is an act of worship, amplified beyond what we have, deserve or need, focused on the One who gets all the glory for what He did and does and will do!

Dividers

Titus 3:9-11—But avoid foolish debates, genealogies, quarrels, and disputes about the law, for they are unprofitable and worthless. Reject a divisive person after a first and second warning, knowing that such a person is perverted and sins, being self-condemned.

If I had to choose which type of leadership challenge is the most difficult, draining, and frustrating, I would weight most heavily those people who are dividers. Dividers can almost be described by one word—petty. Dividers are defined as those who willfully choose to ignore pressing issues to focus on their minor agendas. A good example in Christendom is a person who maintains with belligerence that only the King James Version is acceptable for Bible translations. God establishes His two main priorities with the two greatest commandments as read in Mark 12:30,31: *"Love the Lord your God with all your heart, with all your soul, with all your mind, and with all your strength . . . Love your neighbor as yourself."* The church struggles to do this and to live out the gospel. Meanwhile, Mr. Divider lost all sight of love in his quest to defend an archaic translation as the world's paramount issue.

Dividers are disloyal. Rather than build the team, they build their agenda. Dividers are corrosive, bringing disrepute to the reputation of their organization by their stubborn behavior. Dividers are proud. They camp on the turf they have staked on principle and run up their flag of cause expecting that one day everyone will salute their superior position. Dividers are antagonists looking for every opportunity to cast doubt on those they oppose and to harm anyone willing to stand in their way.

Jesus had no tolerance for dividers. Witnessing the ridiculous actions and positions of the religious leaders He blasted them for their pride and hypocrisy. Read His diatribe in Matthew 23:13-36. I suspect Paul had similar feelings about those who called themselves Christians yet went around subverting his ministry. His warning to Titus is a warning to us.

Avoid disputes that are not profitable for building up the church. Warn a divisive person once and then again. If the warning goes unheeded, reject that person—put him or her out of the fellowship. The cost of tolerating, placating or participating with a divider is too high a price for the body of Christ to bear. The mark of a great leader is not to put up with a divider but rather to put out the divider. God tossed Satan out of heaven for spawning rebellion. Do you think He will do any less for the person who insists on harming His church? William Barclay wisely noted, "More people have been brought into the church by the kindness of real Christian love than by all the theological arguments in the world."

Bernoulli's Spiral

November 26

Jacob Bernoulli was born in Basel, Switzerland. As a young man, he studied theology and entered the ministry. Later he studied mathematics and astronomy. Traveling throughout Europe from 1676 to 1682, Jacob learned about the latest discoveries in mathematics and the sciences.[109] First described by René Descartes, Bernoulli extensively investigated the logarithmic spiral. "This equiangular spiral or growth spiral is a special kind of spiral curve which often appears in nature."[110] Jacob called it *Spira mirabilis*, "the marvelous spiral."

Hebrews 1:10—And: In the beginning, Lord, You established the earth, and the heavens are the works of Your hands.

There is a deliberate order to creation. By investigating what fascinated Bernoulli, we discover God's calculus at work. As the size of a logarithmic spiral increases its shape is unaltered with each successive curve. The following are examples of such spirals in nature:
- A hawk's circular approach to its prey.
- The natural growth curves of plants.
- The arms of spiral galaxies.
- The cornea nerves in our eyes.
- The horns of many bovids like gazelles and shells of mollusks
- The arms of tropical cyclones (hurricanes).[111]

Did you know that engineers discovered that the optimal curve for highway turns is a logarithmic spiral? The Creator who took the time to meticulously plan the heavens and earth reveals how much He loves us! Even the human embryo displays an equiangular spiral. From our designed beginning we grow unique in appearance, personality and thought. The Father of perfect art finds even greater satisfaction in our souls! God created us for the purpose of fellowship. So we glory in His design and find joy in His companionship!

Jacob Bernoulli was so enthralled by "the equiangular spiral's self-reproducing properties," that he had the curve engraved on his headstone with the phrase "Eadem mutata resurgo" (Though changed, I rise again the same.)[112] Someday we will rise and have opportunity in person to thank our Creator for His awe-inspiring work!

Inspiration †††

A man can no more diminish God's glory by refusing to worship Him than a lunatic can put out the sun by scribbling the word, 'darkness' on the walls of his cell.—C.S. Lewis

Drifting

November 27

When navigating with a compass, if we don't keep on line with the precise azimuth, we get off course. Just walking across uneven land, over hills and through brush can easily cause us to get lost. I remember as a child in Japan, descending from the top of Mt. Fuji with two other boys. We left the sure circular path to take a short cut. But coming down the steep slope, we walked at an angle and ended up far away from our intended destination, lost and separated from the rest of our group.

Hebrews 2:1—We must, therefore, pay even more attention to what we have heard, so that we will not drift away.

Have you ever seen a child of such fierce temper that he will hold his breath and pass out? Even little children demonstrate the sin nature so prevalent in all of us. Morality is not something we easily attain and maintain on perfect course. And this is what the author of Hebrews communicates to his readers. We have a responsibility to pay attention to the truth God reveals to us. Otherwise, we will drift away.

Drifting objects in water are easy to spot. A piece of wood is caught in whatever is the strongest current and floats with it. In some ways, this illustrates what happens with followers of Jesus. At least five currents (often subtle) pull us away from God's course.

Many of us float with *distractions*. Instead of making time to be with the Lord, we fill our lives with other activities. We set aside what is best or right for what is alluring or convenient.

Some of us are misled by *deception*. We put greater stock in science, education, tradition or what is popularly deemed correct at the expense of faith, steadfastness and the willingness to listen intently to the leading of the Holy Spirit. The voice of the world holds more weight than the whispers of heaven or the words of Scripture.

Others of us drift because of *demands*. Jobs and relationships can suck the spiritual life out us if we let them. We become so busy needing to meet expectations or please people that we neglect to make time for spiritual nourishment. We stop looking to God and live by our calendars and the never-ending parade of events and projects.

Difficulties cause drifting. Sickness or sadness weighs us down. We become so absorbed in our pain that we doubt our Healer. Persecution and adversity cause us to fear standing with Jesus. We run confused like Elijah, far into the desert only to be burned in the process.

Certainly *disobedience* creates drift. Whenever we tell God "No!" and go our way should we be surprised when we can no longer feel His presence or experience His blessing?

Let us reset our azimuths. Let us keep *"our eyes on Jesus, the source and perfecter of our faith"* (Heb. 12:2). Let's paddle out of those foolish, twirling eddies and get back on track with our Lord. There is no fulfillment in deviating from truth on the road home!

Inspiration † † †

I find the great thing in this world is not so much where we stand, as in what direction we are moving: To reach the port of heaven, we must sail sometimes with the wind and sometimes against it, but we must sail, and not drift, nor lie at anchor.—Marjorie Holmes

What Causes Immaturity?   November 28

Racquel's company is struggling and she is discouraged. The majority of her problems are caused by a few employees who are persistent roadblocks to progress. They constantly go to Human Resources (HR) and complain about perceived double standards with the company's leaders. They bypass the company's open door policy to drop anonymous complaints to Racquel's parent company. If asked why they do this, they say it is because "No one listens to them or will fix the problem."

Because of the attitude and actions of a few immature people who have been with the company for many years, morale is poor, team dissension is an ongoing factor and first line leaders seem incapable of fixing the problem. Racquel would like to fire and rehire but this option is time consuming and costly.

Hebrews 5:11,12—We have a great deal to say about this, and it's difficult to explain, since you have become too lazy to understand. Although by this time you ought to be teachers, you need someone to teach you the basic principles of God's revelation again. You need milk, not solid food.

Whenever an author labels his readers as "lazy," we can be sure frustration is at work. If milk is the prescribed diet, it is apparent that immaturity is the spiritual condition. So what causes immaturity?

Laziness! To be lazy is to be so content with the status quo that tiny effort is expended to bring growth. A second cause of immaturity is selfishness. Rather than give leaders the trust they need and then work to fix things, it is easier to lodge complaints and justify personal substandard behavior by the "surrounding problems." Immature people are professional blamers. A third cause of immaturity is weak values. Rather than accept discipline and persevere, the juvenile person opts for pleasure and the path of least resistance.

So what is the fix? Wilhelm Stekel said, "The mark of the immature man is that he wants to die nobly for a cause, while the mark of the mature man is that is wants to live humbly for one."[14] In truth, three things can transform immaturity. In Racquel's case, if she can help her employees recognize that their actions and conduct are improper, that is half the battle. Next, if she can gain agreement that they will apply their attitude and action towards growth, it is possible that they will become encouraged and see the folly of returning to improper behavior. Finally, prayer is essential. If helping people mature was easy, we wouldn't be dependent upon God. In reality, He knows how to arrest the attention of the inattentive and sometimes that work begins in us.

Write Your Will

November 29

While I was in college my uncle had a massive heart attack and died. His death was far more tragic than necessary. Norm was a very wealthy man. Because he failed to write a will, when his heart collapsed, he left his wife and two daughters with no plan and protection. Because he did not train his sons-in-law how to run his business, they badly floundered. Soon a shyster appeared and proceeded to horrifically swindle my aunt and her family. Later, one of the sons-in-law died. He failed to write a will. The financial and emotional suffering caused by two men unwilling to prepare for death extends to this day.

Hebrews 9:16,17—Where a will exists, the death of the one who made it must be established. For a will is valid only when people die, since it is never in force while the one who made it is living.

There is much benefit in preparing a will. This exercise causes us to reflect and to take inventory of not just our living but our values. It is a stark reminder that we cannot take anything with us and a wise opportunity to determine what we leave behind. Jesus in Mat. 6:19-21 said:
> Don't collect for yourselves treasures on earth, where moth and rust destroy and where thieves break in and steal. But collect for yourselves treasures in heaven where neither moth nor rust destroys, and where thieves don't break in and steal. For where your treasure is, there your heart will be also.

To invest on earth is to speculate amidst three sure threats: creatures, calamities, and crooks. Why should we be overly concerned about what we will have on earth to the loss of what God would give us in heaven? The greatest gift we can leave those who follow us is a legacy of faithfully following Jesus. When we give God our hearts, our reward is protected and eternal. Does this mean we should not leave any money or possessions to our family members? The answer to that question is determined by the likely outcome. If money and possessions will compromise their hearts' love for God, cause them to flounder morally, and corrupt their time with maintenance and attention to stuff, then I should give everything away. If what I leave them enhances their ability to honor God and is a blessing, then may God give me exactly what I should give them.

None of us know the moment our lives will end. Not writing a will does not magically prolong one's life. It requires wisdom to carefully prepare for the lives of those we love when we have graduated. Where a will exists hopefully a blessing persists. Write your will!

Savonarola
November 30

Roman Catholic monk Girolamo Savonarola, (Sep. 21, 1452—May 23, 1498), was shocked by the immorality in Italy and by the corruption he observed within the church. As a teenager, he walked beside the River Po where he sang to God and wept over the condition of the people. At the age of 22, he wrote "Contempt of the World," comparing the sins of his time to Sodom and Gomorrah. Years later, while praying, the Holy Spirit gave him a vision in which he was told to announce to the people that hard times were coming to the church.

Savonarola obeyed God and was a powerful speaker against the evil he observed. Boldly, he prophesied that Florence's ruler, the pope and the king of Naples would die within a year because of their sins, and they did. For over eight years, he preached from the largest cathedral in Florence. Great revival broke out as people repented of their sins and sought to obey God. Heavily convicted, people brought their obscene pictures, wicked literature and anything associated with evil. Their possessions made a pyramid over sixty feet high and 240 feet in circumference. Someone lit the pile and as the huge bonfire burned, the people sang hymns.

Outraged by this upstart monk, the corrupt religious leaders eventually incited a mob which broke down the convent doors where Savonarola stayed. They tortured him, tied his hands and repeatedly hoisted him to a great height and dropped him dislocating his shoulders and tearing his muscles. But the faithful priest refused to recant. Eventually, with two other monks before thousands of onlookers, the three men were hung and their bodies burned. Savonarola's last words were, "Should I not die willingly for Him who suffered so much for me?" His life, ministry and death greatly influenced a young man who knew and observed him. We know this man as Martin Luther."[5]

Hebrews 11:13-16—These all died in faith without having received the promises, but they saw them from a distance, greeted them, and confessed that they were foreigners and temporary residents on the earth. Now those who say such things make it clear that they are seeking a homeland. If they were thinking about they came from, they would have had an opportunity to return. But they now desire a better place—a heavenly one. Therefore God is not ashamed to be called their God, for He has prepared a city for them.

Inspiration ✝✝✝

To kill us means to multiply us. The blood of martyrs is the seed for new Christians.—Tertullian

Endurance

December 1

Toxicity is an ongoing condition of antagonism which perpetuates open wounds. Toxic people are experts in creating hostile environments. For over a year now my son has put up with an older woman who badgers him and his fellow employees constantly. She whines, manipulates to get her way, criticizes, and uses sarcasm and mocking to tear down those around her. Why she is such an unhappy person, no one seems to know. But going to work is not fun for Bryan.

No one likes being bullied. A toxic person is like a boxer who repeatedly hits his opponent's body until he no longer has the mental or physical ability to resist. The ability to endure mental and emotional beatings is virtually impossible. But there is a way to escape this ring of hostility.

Hebrews 12:3—For consider Him who endured such hostility from sinners against Himself, so that you won't grow weary and lose heart.

According to the Gospel writers Jesus constantly faced criticism, accusations and threats from the religious and legal establishments. The very people who should have been noble instead were venomous. And from this tragic reality we find our solution to toxic people and hostile environments.

1. Don't let feeling unfairly treated ruin your attitude, focus and disposition. Consider that Jesus was perfect yet endured harassment.

2. If you *are* growing weary and losing heart, your focus is on the toxic person and personal hurt instead of on Jesus. Looking to Jesus brings healing perspective which builds the faith necessary to endure.

3. The fuel for endurance is faith in Jesus!
   Therefore, since we also have such a large cloud of witnesses surrounding us, let us lay aside every weight and the sin that so easily ensnares us. Let us run with endurance the race that lies before us, keeping our eyes on Jesus, the source and perfecter of our faith . . . (Heb. 12:1,2)

4. Like Jesus who asked God to forgive His accusers, we ought to have empathy for those who are noxious.

Dear Lord, I feel trapped in a toxic environment. Give me the strength to believe that You can bring me through this. Help me to see where my own sin might be contributing to the problem and welcome Your discipline. May your mercy and grace reach and transform the life of this one who is so bitter and mean without You. Thank You for Your example of endurance. May my eyes stay on You. Amen.

Climbing the Staircase

December 2

Climbing the staircase to Lieutenant Colonel Mark Armstrong's office, one cannot help but notice the words painted between steps: Loyalty, Duty, Respect, Selfless service, Honor, Integrity and Personal courage. These are seven key values the Army seeks to instill in all its soldiers. They are values that Mark takes seriously as the Battalion Commander of the 1st Battalion of the 46th Infantry.

Young men from around the nation assemble at Fort Knox, Kentucky. They enter companies a motley meld of self-centered individuals. Those who graduate Basic Training nine weeks later emerge as team-oriented soldiers, radically transformed before the eyes of their incredulous parents and friends.

Mark has ascertained first-hand why values are important. Each day he watches drill instructors work with men who often come from broken families. He sees self-centered rookies, grown children unaccustomed to persevering through adversity, privates whose idea of loyalty is looking out for #1, individuals who can barely define integrity or exemplify honor. If these men refused the challenge of embracing values or were part of an organization without a moral compass, they would help create a treacherous society bent on feeding untamed lusts. It is no wonder this seasoned officer's eyes fill with tears as he shares countless stories of changed lives. He cherishes imparting truth to a generation fed on materialism, relativism and intolerance for pain. He understands why it is necessary for soldiers to obediently low crawl in mud below barbed wire while life-ending tracers whiz overhead. He knows what happens at the other end.

Hebrews 12:4-6—In struggling against sin, you have not yet resisted to the point of shedding your blood. And you have forgotten the exhortation that addresses you as sons: My son, do not take the Lord's discipline lightly or faint when you are reproved by Him, for the Lord disciplines the one He loves and punishes every son whom He receives.

Values are not priceless because they come easy. We do not become godly by being lazy or righteous by pleasing our flesh. If we are serious about loving God, He will seriously work to test our mettle, to break what is corrupted to create what is incorruptible. Jesus taught that we must be robed in self-denial and refuse to leave the narrow path no matter how easy the broad road looks. Did Jesus struggle? Ask the centurion who watched Him die. Was His sacrifice worth it? Ask the sinner who understands what it means to be pardoned and given eternal life.

Inspiration † † †

It's not hard to make decisions when you know what your values are.—Roy Disney

He Never Played a Down December 3

I don't remember his name, which is somewhat profound. He was the cadet speaker at the Army Quarterback Luncheon before Army's game against Tulane. He was a senior and it was obvious that he had gained his coach's respect. What was so remarkable about this young man? He never played a down in a game for the Army football team in his four years at West Point.

This well-built scholar-athlete served on the Scout team, a squad whose members were cannon fodder for the varsity line to practice against each week. Imagine practicing for four years on a team you will never see action with! Imagine knowing you are too slow and not quite gifted enough to be on the field, yet never quitting! Why did this leader of the forgotten squad persevere? He believed in the team. He valued the camaraderie. He understood the bigger picture and realized his role, though without glamour, was essential nonetheless. He was a believer in Army football and his testimony was inspiring.

Hebrews 13:16—Don't neglect to do what is good and to share, for God is pleased with such sacrifices.

Do you long for recognition that never seems to come? Do you know what it means to wallow on the plains of drudgery while others bask in recognition? Be encouraged my friend! It is not the letter on the jacket that makes a person special. It is the willingness to serve unpretentiously for the greater cause. God looks for hearts that are committed to serve Him. *"You yourselves, as living stones, are being built into a spiritual house for a holy priesthood to offer spiritual sacrifices acceptable to God through Jesus Christ"* (1 Pe. 2:5). In the house Jesus builds, every stone is important.

Do you love God? Will you serve Him no matter how the world treats you? Your willingness to obey Christ at any cost is not just necessary, it is essential! Duty is not defined by glamour, or honor by position. It is a heart steadfastly set on following God at all costs that stands as the noble example. This heart understands and relishes the opportunity to be faithful for a perfect Coach on a team of followers intent on winning the game of life before a world of searchers that are far more observant than we think. Get up! Get dressed! Get on with the task of serving—you can do it in the strength of the Lord, for His glory and your joy!

Inspiration ✝✝✝

Are you and I here on earth, utterly committed, utterly given to God Himself?—Watchman Nee in *Love Not the World*

Maturity

December 4

Young Eric made quite an impression. This child from Tigard, Oregon gave a church full of people an earful of wisdom. During a time of thanksgiving, Eric bravely stood up and waited for the microphone. The youngster explained that although he was sad his family would be moving away, they would have a special opportunity to be missionaries to the people in the city where his dad now has a new job. As most of us know, leaving friends and the comfort of home to reside in another place is tough. But Eric had a heavenly perspective that didn't come from reading comic books.

Spiritual maturity is not necessarily proportional to age. The Bible clearly indicates that it is linked to our relationship with God. Anyone whose eyes look through the lens of faith and whose heart is linked with Christ can demonstrate maturity. This is precisely why children can utter such profound statements. A child in love with God often understands truth in a simple and meaningful fashion.

While experience is an indispensable asset and perseverance a great key to growth, the most mature people I have ever known are those who have a deep friendship with God. Their maturity is like a rich Persian rug woven with the royal fabric of sound character that demonstrates holiness, and by wisdom evidences an ability to discern the voice of the Holy Spirit.

We can test our maturity by evaluating our desires. Earthly (unspiritual) maturity is mostly defined by what is achieved. A logical pattern develops. Evil desires, when conceived, give birth to sin, which, when full-grown, result in death (Jam. 1:14,15). Heavenly (spiritual) maturity is mostly defined by what one is willing to lose in order to know God. Good desires are God-dependent and result in the peace of God which transcends all understanding and which guards one's heart and mind in Christ Jesus (Php. 4:7).

A child saw opportunity to honor His Father and in so doing gained a heavenly perspective. Sometimes it takes the voice of a child to remind us what really counts. Way to go Eric!

James 1:5—Now if any of you lacks wisdom, he should ask God, who gives to all generously and without criticizing, and it will be given to him.

Inspiration † † †

When we become mature in godliness God trusts His own honor to us by placing us where the world, the flesh, and the devil may try us, knowing that "greater is He that is in You, than he that is in the world."—Oswald Chambers in *Studies in the Sermon on the Mount*

More Than Intellectual   December 5

Perhaps one of the dangers of living in the "information age" is that we glorify the brain—our computer, library and communications control center. Misguided brain glorification can result in serious spiritual muscle fatigue. For example, knowing becomes more valuable than doing. Faith accordingly, is defined as knowing God. We have the cerebral awareness that our salvation comes through His Son, Christ. We determine that by reciting a formula in which we confess our sin and invoke the name of Jesus, we shall be saved. We therefore base our salvation on an intellectual assent to God's plan. But faith must be much more than an intellectual act.

James 2:14-17—What good is it, my brothers, if someone says he has faith but does not have works? Can his faith save him? If a brother or sister is without clothes and lacks daily food and one of you says to them, "Go in peace, keep warm, and eat well," but you don't give them what the body needs, what good is it? In the same way faith, if it doesn't have works, is dead by itself.

Faith is a matter of the heart! James challenges us with the reality that a faith that does nothing is dead. Doesn't faith engage the heart more than the mind? The mind identifies what must be done, but the heart is the responding agent. I can say that Jesus is my Lord with my mind but until I embrace Him with my heart do I really have faith?

The faith we see demonstrated in the Bible is a faith that responds obediently to an invisible Creator. God never affirms those who call Him Father but ignore His leadership. *"You believe that God is one; you do well. The demons also believe—and they shudder"* (Jam. 2:19). Faith that ignores observing God's will, that is entirely devoid of any evidence of a changed life, is not faith. The demonstration that I have faith is not that I call myself a Christian but that I *am* a Christian.

Oswald Chambers taught in *Approved Unto God* "Our Lord's word believe does not refer to an intellectual act, but to a moral act; with our Lord to believe means to commit." I know that my body must have water to survive. I believe it when I drink. If I don't drink, I become physically useless and all the knowledge I possess about liquid nourishment is irrelevant.

Inspiration ✝ ✝ ✝

I love the recklessness of faith. First you leap, and then you grow wings.—William Sloane Coffin

Negative Emails　　　　　　　　　　　　　　　December 6

Cassidy sent out an email to her boss citing several recent incidents that occurred and accused Konrad, a coworker and fellow executive, of harassing her and generally acting like a jerk. The boss was surprised because he had worked with Konrad for years and had never before received complaints like this about him or observed him acting in a way that was disrespectful to others. So he asked Cassidy to call him. When she did, he questioned her as to what exactly Konrad had done. In the course of conversation the boss realized that Cassidy was making several bad assumptions about her coworker. It especially galled him that she had not discussed her concerns with Konrad before sending him the negative report.

James 3:7-9—Every sea creature, reptile, bird, or animal is tamed and has been tamed by man, but no man can tame the tongue. It is a restless evil, full of deadly poison. We praise our Lord and Father with it, and we curse men who are made in God's likeness with it.

If James were alive and writing today, I believe he would cite negative emails as an extension to his teaching about the volatile tongue. They become a record of our rashness, live on as data bytes or printed material, and can be forwarded more destructively than an oral report. In essence they become a poison of greater magnitude.

Through our computer tongue, too often we say things that are negative about others that we later regret. When we criticize and judge the motives of others, we spread discord. We also reveal ourselves to be angry, insensitive, insecure, mean-spirited, vengeful and foolish. From a sick heart come sick words. James writes, *"The fruit of righteousness is sown in peace by those who cultivate peace"* (3:18). A heart at peace births kind, gentle, constructive, or fair-minded words—revealing wisdom.

Cassidy's boss confronted her for failing to speak first with Konrad. He reminded her that she would have been furious if he had treated her in such a shabby manner. Second, he admonished her for using strong language—words that imputed guilt and damaged Konrad's reputation. Third, he said she had no right to judge his motives simply because she resented his actions—none of which were unethical, illegal or immoral. Finally, he helped her determine that her wounded pride was the source of her spewing. From insecurity, she crafted hasty accusations. To her credit, she called Konrad and apologized. A contentious spirit became contrite and peace was restored.

*Not their real names; fictitious company.

Selfishness

December 7

Each year senior military officers attending the Army War College choose a gift to present to the school. Because of differing tastes, this exercise of selecting a gift proves to be the most contentious challenge each class will face. Typically, students pick a reputable artist and commission that artist to paint a historical event the class chooses. Civil war themes are by far the most popular and sell the most prints. One year when the artist revealed his sketch, one southern student on the selection committee complained that there were no confederate soldiers present. Another member objected that no black Americans were depicted. So they sent the artist back to his canvas. Imagine their surprise when the clever painter produced a beautiful portrait of black Union soldiers guarding sullen Confederate prisoners!

James 3:14,16—But if you have bitter envy and selfish ambition in your heart, don't brag and deny the truth . . . For where envy and selfish ambition exist, there is disorder and every kind of evil.
Psalm 119:36—Turn my heart toward your statutes and not toward selfish gain. (NIV)

Selfishness is like eating a steady diet of candy. It may feel good when we get what we want, but in the end, our rotted teeth and poor health testify to habitually making wrong choices. Selfishness is an internal fixation on meeting our own needs. Unfortunately, because we are already a fallen race, self-pleasing is inherently flawed. Everyone cannot get what they want without depriving someone else. What makes Jesus so awesome is that He came to earth and forfeited His divine rights, focused on the needs of those around Him, and ultimately gave up Himself to rescue us from ourselves (our sin nature). Find a person in love with Jesus, fueled by a desire to be like Him and you will find a selfless person. In contrast, those who continuously manifest a self-promoting agenda reveal an inability to trust God and a faculty for hurting others.

Selfishness at its core is an unwillingness to believe that obeying God is sufficient. He asks me to put <u>His will</u> over my own, to look at the needs of others before I concern myself with my own things. Jesus' paradoxical truth teaches me that when I die to self, that is when I truly become alive! Often we don't realize how subtle selfishness creeps in and corrupts. A good way to test how God-focused we really are is to measure how much of our time and thinking we give Him. Second, is our attitude more often acidic or angelic? There is a reason why God's perfect painting often differs from our ideas.

Hypocrisy

December 8

James Hewett, in *Illustrations Unlimited*, tells the story of an Irish priest, who decided to visit the Bowery—a haven of homeless alcoholics and other derelicts in New York City. While walking, he suddenly felt a gun against his ribs. Then he heard a raspy voice. "All right mister, gimme all your money!" As he quickly reached for his wallet the holdup man noticed his clerical garb. Overcome with shame the thief said, "Forgive me, Father. I didn't know you were a priest." The priest replied, "That's all right, son. Just repent of your sin. Here, have a cigar." The robber replied, "Oh, no, thank you, Father, I don't smoke during Advent."

1 Peter 2:1—So rid yourselves of all malice, all deceit, hypocrisy, envy, and all slander.

The *American Heritage Dictionary* defines hypocrisy as: "The practice of professing beliefs, feelings, or virtues that one does not hold or possess; falseness." Karl Rahner, quoted in the *Wittenburg Door*, said, "The number one cause of atheism is Christians. Those who proclaim God with their mouths and deny Him with their lifestyles is what an unbelieving world finds simply unbelievable." We all know hypocrites, and if we are honest, we see our own shades of falseness.

What causes whim and will to cavort towards flesh at the expense of walking holy? Hypocrisy is rooted in three things: ego, insecurity and immaturity. The first two are calculated and layered upon perception. Jewish religious leaders of Jesus' day were adept at looking good in the eyes of the people with their pious behavior and scholarly knowledge. But Jesus, looking into their hearts saw rotten, self-absorbed men. How God must grieve today looking down and seeing the same distorted pride flourish among many who call themselves His faithful followers.

Rhonda challenges her Tuesday class to love their neighbors. "This is a great way to reach them for the Lord," she intones. But she avoids the Iranian family next door. She knows the prejudice on her block toward these foreigners. Rather than reach out to them, she kowtows to the beat of the street. When our eyes are on the crowd and not focused on the Master, our lives will be a lie as we live behind the plaster. When we dedicate ourselves to knowing God and following after His Son, pretentious behavior becomes repugnant. We have no place for phoniness. A relationship riveted in truth, characterized by selflessness and frequently washed by Living Water shines and fills the air with the fresh unmistakable fragrance of purity. As the Chinese proverb states, "One foot cannot stand on two boats."

Lovemic

Chip and Dan Heath wrote a terrific book called *Switch*. If you are a leader or a worker in an organization undergoing change, this is a necessary read. Chip and Dan make a point that self-control is an exhaustible resource. They share an experiment that proves the point. Researchers divided college students into two groups and placed them in a room with two bowls: one contained chocolate-chip cookies while the other contained radishes. One group could only eat the cookies; the other group could only eat the radishes. The researchers then left the room to induce temptation. Fortunately, all the participants followed the rules. Next, each group received a series of unsolvable puzzles. The group that ate the chocolate spent nineteen minutes on the task making 34 attempts to solve the challenge. The radish eaters gave up after only eight minutes and 19 solution attempts. Why did this latter group quit so quickly? They used up self-control by not eating the chocolate!

1 Peter 4:8—Above all, maintain an intense love for each other, since love covers a multitude of sins.

It is time for a new coined word—*lovemic* (lov·e·mic). *Lovemic* describes a condition of feeble love, a degradation of love in desire and quality. That Peter had to encourage his fellow Christians to keep their love for one another at full strength implies that their affection was sometimes lacking. Similarly, Paul wrote the Thessalonians, *"Brothers, do not grow weary in doing good"* (2 Th. 3:13). The fuel for doing good is love as we learn from Paul's challenge to the Corinthian believers, *"Your every action must be done with love"* (1 Co. 16:14).

Do we agree that there are times when we are lovemic? So how do we keep motivated to love God and people? The two greatest commandments in Scripture require high-quality love (see Mat. 22:37-39). How do we avoid becoming weary of putting others before ourselves?

Jesus gives us the answer in John 15:9, when He says, *"As the Father has loved me, I have also loved you. Remain in My love."* Jesus' ability to love was at full capacity because He drew from the inexhaustible love of His Father. The key to our success is our reliance upon His Son! When we remain in His love, we are able to extend love. Are you tired and don't feel like loving? Are you frustrated and sick of dealing with sinful people? Call on Jesus—*draw your strength from Him*. Left to our own power, love like self-control is a diminishing commodity. Plugged into Jesus, we have a limitless charge.

Prison

December 10

Kim Jong Un, North Korea's youthful dictator pushes his nation towards the brink of war. Threatening a "'preemptive nuclear attack' on the United States, a 'final destruction' of South Korea, and a 'nuclear attack' on Tokyo" leaves much of the world holding its collective breath.[116] While we should pray that war does not break out, we should also remember that even bullies and police states cannot keep God from revealing His love in amazing ways.

1 Peter 4:16—But if anyone suffers a s a "Christian," he should not be ashamed but should glorify God in having that name.
Colossians 4:3,4—At the same time, pray also for us that God may open a door to us for the message, to speak the mystery of the Messiah, for which I am in prison, so that I may reveal it as I am required to speak.

Dr. James Kim is a businessman with a huge vision for providing education to North Koreans. While interviewed by Sheila Shuller Coleman he stated:
> I worked with the communist conflict in China and in North Korea for about 27 years. When I arrived in the communist country of China and North Korea, I declared myself I'm not capitalist, I'm not communist, but I'm a love-ist. When they asked me what is the meaning of a love-ist? I replied, Jesus-ist! I am just demonstrating Jesus' love, as He shared to others. I give love to the people who never had the kind of love as Jesus Christ's love.[117]

Kim, a South Korean and now U.S. citizen, traveled to North Korea in 1998 to donate food. His intentions were misunderstood and he was arrested by the secret police and accused of being a spy for the CIA. For six weeks he was imprisoned and threatened with death. Yet as he shares his story he relates being full of joy. When his captors tortured him, he did not feel any pain. When they asked him to prepare his will he bequeathed his body for medical study in Pyongyang and asked that his organs be used for transplants.[118] Then he wrote his relatives that "in the event of my death, don't seek revenge." Revenge was unnecessary for "My 'crime' was demonstrating God's love and I was merely misunderstood.'"[119]

When Kim Jong Il heard what Dr. Kim wrote in his will he was so amazed that he met personally with him. He asked him what he wanted and learned of his dream to build schools in North Korea to help the people. Amazingly, he was released from prison. Through his fundraising efforts and governmental permission the Pyongyang University of Science and Technology was founded. In 2011, while the colleges and universities across North Korea were closed, his university remained open. Christian faculty members from the United States and Europe model God's love in a place where worshiping Christ is forbidden.

In a dark dungeon where most perish, God blessed the courage of a man determined at all cost to shine as a light. Dr. Kim is a reminder to us all that what matters is that we give the love of Christ no matter the conditions or cost; for as Paul so nobly noted, "For *me, living is Christ and dying is gain*" (Php. 1:21). Are *you* shining?

Inspiration † † †

The surest test of the truth of Christianity is suffering. Suffering is the infinite dissatisfaction one realizes as he approaches nearer to God.— Norman Geisler in *Christian Apologetics*

Elders

As the Apostle Peter neared the end of his life he wrote powerful words of instruction to the leaders of God's people. He urged them to shepherd God's flock. Then he defined what their motives and attitudes should look like. His words of truth are just as applicable to us today.

1 Peter 5:1-4—Therefore, as a fellow elder and witness to the sufferings of the Messiah, and also a participant in the glory about to be revealed, I exhort the elders among you: Shepherd God's flock among you, not overseeing out of compulsion but freely, according to God's will; not for the money but eagerly; not lording it over those entrusted to you, but being examples to the flock. And when the chief Shepherd appears, you will receive the unfading crown of glory.

Elders must oversee people of the church free of compulsion and with sensitivity to knowing God's will. Their decision-making should not revolve around their biases, how the crowd feels, or because of peer pressure. They make decisions through listening to the Holy Spirit! For this motive to succeed requires quality time spent in understanding God's Word and frequent communication with Him in prayer.

Elders lead with enthusiasm and zeal, not for money or for benefits. The key to this motive ties into a correct understanding of treasure. Jesus taught this in Mat. 6:20-21.

Elders are not to be bossy, domineering chiefs over the people God gives them. The key to their authority is humility! Great elders bring a foot-washing mentality to those they are committed to helping spiritually grow. Beware of leaders enamored with title or position and who seem to need to dominate or control people so as to constantly get their way. Such leaders reject the cloth the Carpenter wore to don the robes of Pharisees.

Elders must serve as proper examples. This calls for an attitude of godliness fueled by love. Elders before acting or making major decisions should ask, "What would Jesus do?" They should value holiness, protect their character and God's reputation and be lifelong learners. Because they adore God, they live out a love for people that allows them to feel safe and valued in their presence. Have you noticed how gentle and kind those who walk with the Lord become as they mature? Godly elders are like honey that nourishes and leaves the eyes bright and the body healthy.

In return for providing godly leadership, God promises elders an unfading crown of glory. How much better to have heavenly splendor than earthly reward that vanishes with time!

Inspiration † † †

The central task of leadership is influencing God's people towards God's purposes.—Robert Clinton in *The Making of a Leader*

Koi

December 12

My youngest son Stephen and I went with some friends to a Koi/Goldfish show. It was the first time we'd ever attended anything like this. We were quite amazed. Koi come in a wide assortment of colors and shapes. It was obvious standing around the varied pools that most of these people knew a great deal about carp. Here are some facts I learned and lessons that jumped to mind:

1. If you buy Koi for their pattern and color design and the fish are less than three years old, don't expect them to look the same as they grow older. Only when the fish reach their maturation point will their pattern and coloration become fixed.

Lesson: We need to be careful we don't assume too much about children because of what we see when they are young. With growth will come change—not always what we expect—for good or for bad. Someone once said, "Don't judge the parenting until they reach thirty-five."

2. Koi may jump out of their ponds. I heard more than one fish story of a renegade carp found stiff as a board by its grief-stricken owner.

Lesson: God can give some people all they need to enjoy life and they may still do something wrong only to suffer dire consequences.

3. People travel all over the U.S. to Koi shows to buy or admire these fish! One English woman flew in from Great Britain, at personal expense, to serve as a judge. Koi can live as long as sixty years! People actually will their fish to younger family members or friends. How'd you like to go from cradle to grave with a fish pal?

Lesson: If we can love fish so much, imagine how great God's love is for us!

4. The physical size Koi attain depends largely upon the size of their pond or tank.

Lesson: Our spiritual growth is dependent upon how willing we are to let God stretch our boundaries. I hear folks ask why they aren't growing much. Often it is because they are unwilling to leave their safe confines.

5. Vigilant care must be given to maintaining their water environment! A slight change of PH (acidic vs. alkaline) can cause Koi to go belly up.

Lesson: A slight change in PH (Perfecting Holiness) will cost our health. If we sin or tolerate sin around us, we will get spiritually sick.

2 Peter 1:3—His divine power has given us everything required for life and godliness through the knowledge of Him who called us by His own glory and goodness.

Inspiration ✝✝✝

Men do not know that God is here. What a difference it would make if they knew.—A.W. Tozer in *The Pursuit of God*

Climbing Higher

December 13

2 Peter 1:19—So we have the prophetic word strongly confirmed. You will do well to pay attention to it, as to a lamp shining in a dismal place, until the day dawns and the morning star rises in your hearts.

There is a spur on the 11,239-foot Mount Hood where a small rock shelter stands firm against the winds of time. Atop this small ridge is a spectacular view of Mount Rainier, Mount Adams, Mount St. Helens, hundreds of square miles of valleys, streams, lakes, and hills carpeted with green forests. I love the high ground. There are few things in life more beautiful than standing in thin air to watch the sun rise in silent majesty over a glacier-covered volcano and all that surrounds it. It is not hard to understand why Oregon and Washington are called "God's country."

King Solomon wrote in Proverbs 4:18,19, *"The path of the righteous is like the light of dawn, shining brighter and brighter until midday. But the way of the wicked is like the darkest gloom; they don't know what makes them stumble."* Was it from his chariot on the heights of Jerusalem that he followed shafts of sunlight as they worked their way across the Kidron valley and formed an illustration in his mind?

"Your word is a lamp for my feet and a light on my path" (Psa. 119:105). The longer one travels the highway of morality, the clearer the way becomes. Righteousness refuses to wind in the confusing circles of rationalism. Virtue understands and avoids the eroding torrents of carnality. Virtue bypasses depravity's boulders.

Jesus who stated, *"I am the light of the world"* (John 8:12), enlightened His own followers. *"You are the light of the world . . . In the same way, let your light shine before men, so that they may see your good works and give glory to your Father in heaven"* (Mat. 5:14a,16). If we neglect to be moral people, we hide our light. *"Now those who belong to Christ Jesus have crucified the flesh with its passions and desires. Since we live by the Spirit, we must also follow the Spirit"* (Gal. 5:24,25). Purity matters and the higher we climb the better we see the way and all the better for the world to see the glorious light Christ calls us to be!

Inspiration † † †

Purity is not a question of doing things rightly, but of the doer on the inside being right . . . No man is born pure: purity is the outcome of conflict. The pure man is not the man who has never been tried, but the man who knows what evil is and has overcome it.—Oswald Chambers in *Studies on the Sermon on the Mount*

Change

December 14

1 John 3:2,3—Dear friends, we are God's children now, and what we will be has not yet been revealed. We know that when He appears, we will be like Him because we will see Him as He is. And everyone who has this hope in Him purifies himself just as He is pure.

Change is the recognition of our inadequacy. By myself I am incapable of holiness. I see a beautiful woman and impure thoughts spring to life. A driver cuts in front of me almost causing an accident. My normal reaction is to be frustrated and to utter unkind words. What hour goes by that there is not something in me that could improve and be more Christ-like?

Change is the avowed enemy of complacency. If we resist changing, we don't understand *"we are God's children now"* and we certainly don't understand our Father's plan. A perfect Jesus prayed, *"Not my will, but Yours be done"* (Luke 22:42b). If perfection required change, what makes us think we should be left alone?

Change is hard. Kim Cameron and Marc Lavine cited a study of people who had recently undergone heart bypass surgery in *Making the Impossible Possible:*

> They were given a choice by their physicians of changing their lifestyles or of dying. A consistent result over several decades, including thousands of patients, is that only about 10 percent actually make the change. More than 90 percent of people choose death rather than implement major changes in their lives. Opposition to change is universal and persistent.[120]

1 John 5:19 reminds us *"that we are of God, and the whole world is under the sway of the evil one."* Though it is a challenge to modify our thoughts and behavior, with God all things are possible.

Change is the proof of hope. Hope, by its very meaning, implies there is something or someone better! *"What we will be has not yet been revealed."* God is going to make us different from how we are now. Jesus wants us to be like Him. John asserts that when He appears, we *will* be *like Him.* Right now we can only see Him through earthly lens smudged, scratched, and fogged by our flawed condition. Change is coming!

Change is a requirement of transformation. *"Everyone who has this hope in Him purifies himself."* Purification requires alterations! Max Lucado writes in *The Applause of Heaven*, "You change your life by changing your heart."[121]

Inspiration † † †

If you change the path, you'll change the behavior. —Chip Heath & Dan Heath in *Switch*

Intimacy

December 15

Why do followers of God go through the motions of Christianity shallowly in love with their Father? What does it mean and look like to have an intimate walk with Jesus? Spiritual intimacy can be defined as a growing *I can't live without You relationship* with God that is our first cause, our abiding joy and our natural expression.

1. To <u>value</u> intimacy, we must work to understand who God is and how much He loves me! As my mentor, Paul Drake likes to say, "What is love? GOD!" 1 John 4:16 teaches, *"And we have come to know and to believe the love that God has for us. God is love, and the one who remains in love remains in God, and God remains in him."* John 3:16 reveals the depth of God's love for us and 14:16-17 shows love applied. God does not just talk about loving us, He chooses through His Spirit to indwell us!

And I will ask the Father, and He will give you another Counselor to be with you forever. He is the Spirit of truth. The world is unable to receive Him because it doesn't see Him or know Him. But you do know Him, because He remains with you and will be in you." (John 14:16-17)

2. To <u>attain</u> intimacy, God must be part of our daily lives and we cannot take Him for granted. Expecting to gain a cherished friendship with God just through church attendance is as silly as thinking a few meals a week will keep our bodies healthy! We need a regular love language that saturates our soul.

Lord, I love You! Thank you for today and the privilege of serving You. Help me to know You better. Lord, what would You have me learn about You today and what do You want from me?

3. To <u>protect</u> intimacy, we must follow God's clear leading. We learn in Deu. 6:5 and 10:12 that He expects us to love Him with all our heart, soul and strength; to fear Him, walk in His ways and worship Him. Intimacy requires valuing what He says and doing what He asks. Jesus said in John 14:15, *"If you love Me, you will keep My commands."* Holiness, which is a great indicator of intimacy, comes through godly obedience.

- It is impossible to be intimate with a hard heart!
- It is impossible to be intimate while living in sin!
- It is impossible to be intimate with conflicting loyalties

So many people give up on the possibility of a deep relationship with God because of sin, after all, how could God love anyone contaminated! Yet, each of us understands that the way to get rid of dirt is to bathe. Is it any different spiritually? If we sin, we need to clean up what is wrong, repent and ask God for His restoring forgiveness.

In Luke 7:37,38 we discover a sinful woman who sought out Jesus. She stood behind Him weeping and then washed His feet with her tears. She wiped them with her hair, kissed them and then anointed them with expensive perfume. Her focus was completely on Jesus. Her heart was honest and broken. She didn't care what the religious people thought. This is the stuff of intimacy!

4. To <u>sustain</u> intimacy we must steadfastly commit to a God-centric life mission! My life mission is to do my best to advance in love with God (worship), be a godly husband and father; wisely serve people and treat them as Jesus would; and correctly discern and walk in alignment with God's will for my life.

Too often, I run into folks who lost their friendship with Jesus to misplaced priorities. Paul Drake shares, we can be so busy in the work of the Lord that we neglect the Lord of the work! Too often dashed dreams, unrealized hopes, or lives bashed upon the rocks of misfortune kill one's resolve to know Christ. Don't let this happen. Pursue God passionately as you would seek water for a famished tongue. Climb higher . . . in reveration!

Inspiration † † †

Everything that God does in our lives is designed to promote intimacy with Him, to have us know Him so completely on an experiential basis that we will never doubt His presence with us.—Tom Capps in *Pray and Plan*

Paper and Ink

December 16

2 John 12—Though I have many things to write to you, I don't want to do so with paper and ink. Instead, I hope to be with you and talk face to face so that our joy may be complete.

While attending a class on cyber security in November of 2012, I was amazed to learn that 4.8 billion people own a mobile phone, which surpasses the 4.2 billion people who own a toothbrush. Fascinating! Just imagine if all of those people could connect via a twitter account—the ability to pass information instantaneously is staggering.

Jesus' beloved friend John, the son of Zebedee, lived the longest of the twelve disciples. Our Bible contains five books he authored through the inspiration of the Holy Spirit—the Gospel of John, three letters and Revelation. What it was like to sit down in his presence before he died and listen to the amazing stories he recalled from his time with the Messiah and a life lived in serving Him? He was a kind, humble and warm-hearted man full of love and reverentially committed to God.

John wrote often about the topics of love and truth. What establishes sincerity in his words to me though is his statement regarding paper and ink. John was not satisfied to just write down his thoughts and send them via messenger to those he knew in the church. He wanted to physically be in their presence. He knew that the best kind of joy comes from face-to-face fellowship. There is an important lesson in his observation.

Information for the sake of information is rather empty. A twitter-fed frenzy of what is happening in life is not LIFE; it is a snapshot in time quickly lost in our always-in-need-of-a-new-buzz world. Eric Schmidt the CEO of Google notes, "Every two days now we create as much information as we did from the dawn of civilization up until 2003." When my youngest son Stephen was born, Google was not even a word!

Speed in passing information is certainly valuable. Leaders make better decisions by capturing relevant data. But if we just live for amassing and passing information, we have lost sight of what really matters. Take the time to go and hug someone you care about and tell them you love them. Sit and listen to what they have to say. Truth and love are best learned by being there. There are men and women in Africa and South America today who walk days just to be able to attend spiritual gatherings. We think, "What a pity that so much time was wasted having to travel!" They think, What a joy to be able to journey!" If we treasure the flurry of information and exalt the speed at which it travels, we may miss the greatest most valuable lesson of all—the joy of presence in the beauty of fellowship.

Tracks

December 17

Kevin and I prayer walk an asphalt trail that is about 3/4 of a mile around a church, a wooded area and large field. This morning I noticed big paw tracks from a dog that extended for quite a ways along the trail. If I were trained, I could tell by the size of the prints the approximate size of the dog that left its mark. Instead I could only see the obvious—a dog walked in a muddy field and then wandered across the path we were walking.

3 John 3,4—For I was very glad when some brothers came and testified to your faithfulness to the truth—how you are walking in the truth. I have no greater joy than this: to hear that my children are walking in the truth.

Every day, you and I leave tracks; most of the time we are oblivious to this. But unless we are isolated, someone sees us or notices the sign that we were there. The best "tracks" we can leave come from a steadfast adherence to the truth. When we live according to the way Jesus desires, we positively impact people. Our holy footprints testify that we are faithful.

There is an African proverb that says, "If you think you are too small to make a difference, try spending the night in a closed room with a mosquito." God does not just love us because it is a godly thing to do. He loves us so that we are transformed. He wants us to follow His truth because He knows that when we obey Him, our lives are fulfilled and become an encouragement to others. We can and should walk in such a way that a blessing is left far beyond our actual presence. Someone cleverly noted, "People don't listen to you speak; they watch your feet."

Lord, help us walk in Your truth so that even when we are gone, people still see the signs that You were there!

Inspiration † † †

When a Christian walks free from need to be reproved, his enemies have nowhere to fasten their teeth on him, but are forced to gnaw on their own malignant finger.—Robert Layton

Partnership—A Better Perspective

December 18

3 John 5-8—Dear friend, you are showing faithfulness by whatever you do for the brothers, especially when they are strangers. They have testified to your love in front of the church. You will do well to send them on their journey in a manner worthy of God, since they set out for the sake of the Name, accepting nothing from pagans. Therefore, we ought to support such men so that we can be coworkers with the truth.

Kathleen and I often receive letters with requests for money from friends or family members who are preparing to go on a mission trip. We particularly enjoy when the request is from a teenager or young adult. God often uses mission trips both to bless those who are ministered to and to expand the faith of those responding to His call. I have seen my children, nieces and nephews, and the children of friends return blessed by the people they communed with and more deeply committed to serve Christ.

I am far less excited by requests for money from strangers or people I hardly know who want to journey to other countries. Most of the time I ignore them. I fail to honestly pray whether I should respond. So I find the passage above in John's letter to his friend Gaius to be encouraging, convicting, and enlightening.

First, John commended his friend Gaius, apparently for physical and monetary help he provided to fellow Christians (probably strangers). Gaius was glad to do it. This encourages me to be more perceptive to opportunities around me that require assistance from those whom I don't necessarily know who are serving the Lord.

Second, I am convicted about lacking empathy and for not being perceptive to meet the needs of those who require assistance. I need an attitude adjustment. These men John mentions refused to receive any help from pagans. They would not let credit for their efforts go to those who were not following Christ. What a great statement of fidelity! We who are believers need to take care of our own.

Third, I am enlightened by several gems John reveals. Gaius didn't just help strangers; his actions encouraged the whole church! John recognizes that those who serve God should be treated *"in a manner worthy of God."* Ill-equipped Christians who go out to serve the Lord are a poor reflection on the church and may end up dishonoring God. At stake is not just a mission enterprise, but the very glory of the Lord they serve! Finally, John noted that Gaius' actions made him a coworker with the truth. By giving, Gaius became a partner in the propagation of the gospel. You and I may be unable to journey to another land to share about Jesus but we can go vicariously by supporting those able to travel. We show our faithfulness by whatever we do for our brothers and sisters, *"especially when they are strangers."*

Taps

December 19

Every evening at sundown, 78 year-old Don Brittain stands on his back porch, places his trumpet on his lips, and plays Taps. At the first sound of the 24 notes his neighbors stop what they are doing and walk outside to stand at attention. Most of them have never served in the military. Nor has Don, who suffered polio as a child. Yet, like this aerospace worker who chooses to honor our military veterans, they are gripped and inspired by the solemn music he so carefully plays. And as much as his ritual is for the military, it is also for his neighbors.[122]

Daily Mr. Brittain contends for the honor of those who uphold our liberty. His unwavering commitment reminds me of the Old Guard who stand watch over the Unknown Tomb regardless of the weather conditions. His thirty-six seconds of music wash over his Tacoma, Washington neighborhood every evening in the form of a sacred proclamation.

Jude 3—Dear friends, although I was eager to write you about the salvation we share, I found it necessary to write and exhort you to contend for the faith that was delivered to the saints once for all.

Jude exhorts his readers to contend for the faith. Evil men had come in and corrupted the gospel message. No doubt the brother of Jesus, who knew firsthand the validity of his Messiah, was outraged to see a holy faith attacked by stealthy frauds (v. 4). It is no different in our age. We constantly face those who distort the gospel truth or who deny Christ. But in order to contend we must have a plan and methods and motivation.

If I could play the bagpipes, I'd walk outside at dawn and play Amazing Grace. Now is not the time to get so busy in our hectic living that we miss opportunities to shine as lights. Now is not the time to complain about leaders, to gripe about corruption, or to bury our heads in the sands of indifference. Plenty of people already do these things.

Who will *stand* and *play the notes*? Someone can write. Someone can speak. Someone can listen. Someone can fix what is broken. Someone can give. Someone can bring food to the hungry. Someone can pour water for the thirsty. Someone can sing. Everyone can pray. Should we not always listen for the Master's clarion note to contend? If a song for the dead can be so powerful, imagine what a choir for the living would do!

Inspiration † † †

A candle loses nothing of its light by lighting another candle.— Proverbs and Wise Sayings Paul Vithayathil

Choices

December 20

I grew up in a pornography-free environment. My parents love God and they made sure that we were raised in a house that allowed no such filth. During my second year of college, I had a roommate who kept in the second drawer on the left side of his desk a stack of Playboys and other adult magazines. He owned a stereo and loved to play music that glorified sex and championed lust. I condemned his reading material and protested his choice in music. But he did not value my values or agree with my convictions. Slowly, my resistance wore down until the day came when I submitted to the raging temptation to look inside those magazines. No one ever saw me but I was observed. No one ever caught me but I was imprisoned. I endured a miserable semester of inner guilt and gained immeasurable insight into what the Apostle Paul meant when he wrote:

> *For I know that nothing good lives in me, that is, in my flesh. For the desire to do what is good is with me, but there is no ability to do it. For I do not do the good that I want to do, but I practice the evil that I do not want to do . . . What a wretched man I am! Who will rescue me from this dying body? I thank God through Jesus Christ our Lord! So then, with my mind I myself am a slave to the law of God, but with my flesh, to the law of sin.* (Rom. 7:18,19,24,25)

Many would say that what I did wasn't so bad. I was the victim of an environment over which I had little control. I was exercising my natural curiosity and no one else was involved so what difference did it make. Some would go so far to say that with my experience I gained valuable insight useful for helping others who have struggled most of their lives with pornography.

We live in a society that has mastered the art of making excuses. We flourish at ignoring God's laws when they are not in synch with our own appetites. We rationalize immorality by attacking moral absolutes as restrictive and judgmental. We condone the actions of those who are genetically conceived with peculiar tastes while missing the reality that everyone is wired to sin. We succumb in the war of evil because we have lost sight of the battle of choice. As Pro. 4:18,19 reveals, *"The path of the righteous is like the light of dawn, shining brighter and brighter until midday. But the way of the wicked is like the darkest gloom; they don't know what makes them stumble."*

Righteousness—doing right, is something we must choose. Wickedness—doing wrong also requires us to choose. So life is made up of choices. I decide:

- to pay for merchandise or shoplift
- to speak the truth or deceive
- to honor authority or be disrespectful;
- to love or hate
- to serve or be selfish
- to listen or ignore
- to confront or feign ignorance

- to be patient or impatient
- to persevere or give up
- to obey God's commandments or disobey Him
- to spend time with family or live at work
- to care for the body or wear it out
- to exercise moderation or consume carelessly
- to speak kindly or tear down
- to think pure thoughts or harbor resentment and envy

If you are caught in behavior that God forbids, there is a way out.
1. Be honest enough to call wrongdoing sin. Confess it before God!
2. Stop rationalizing wrong behavior.
3. Cry out to Jesus who endured temptation, knows what you are going through (Heb. 2:18), and will rescue you!
4. Choose to do what is right.

Dr. John George reminds us, "We are not born with character; it is the result of the decisions we make every moment of our lives. What you are to be, you are now becoming."

Jude 24,25—Now to Him who is able to protect you from stumbling and to make you stand in the presence of His glory, blameless and with great joy, to the only God our Savior, through Jesus Christ our Lord, be glory, majesty, power, and authority before all time, now and forever. Amen.

Inspiration † † †

I don't think most of us have even begun to understand how big a factor personal purity is in the fruitfulness of our ministries.—Christopher Adsit in *Personal Disciple-Making*

Bold Despite Their Fear

December 21

In Stephen's senior year of high school, his drama teacher would not allow them to use the words, "Merry Christmas" for an upcoming drama presentation. The reason the teacher gave him was that the school did not want to offend anyone.

When a school official bans students from saying "Merry Christmas," with whom or with what is that official's identity linked? Ironically, that educator could be a Christian, yet, in succumbing to political correctness, chooses not to be identified as a Jesus-follower. Jesus said in Luke 9:26, *"For whoever is ashamed of Me and My words, the Son of Man will be ashamed of him when He comes in His glory and that of the Father and the holy angels."* What we are willing or unwilling to say or do gives people a framed picture of our identity.

Ezra 3:3—They set up the altar on its foundation and offered burnt offerings for the morning and evening on it to the LORD even though they feared the surrounding peoples.

There is deep meaning in the verse above. The Jews who were exiled to Babylon for over 70 years returned to their land. In the seventh month of their liberation, they gathered from their towns to meet in Jerusalem and celebrate the Festival of Booths as prescribed by Moses. When Jeshua and his priestly brothers along with Zerubbabel and his brothers began building the altar, they were making a definitive statement. Burnt offerings make smoke! In this case, that smoke was devoted to their Lord. In essence, the priests were saying, *"We are back and we are determined to worship God!"* But they were no longer the power brokers. They established their identity as Yahweh-followers amongst a population of pagans. They feared the surrounding residents, because those people had the capability of destroying them. They knew what it meant to be conquered and shamed and the thought of provoking attack generated angst. Nevertheless, they did a courageous thing. On an altar made of stones, burnt offerings ascended morning and evening to God.

You and I don't offer burnt offerings. Instead of us earning God's forgiveness through the blood of animals, our faith in His Son is sufficient. But what kind of smoke do we give off each morning and evening? Is it the fragrant aroma of lives unalterably linked to Jesus, our Lord and Savior? Or do we wear the smell of compromise, the odor of Satan the world's presumptuous ruler? I'd rather make a statement than be made a statement. "Merry Christmas"—two great words that deserve sharing.

Inspiration † † †

Courage is an outgrowth of who we are.—Max Lucado in *The Applause of Heaven*

Loving-Kindness

December 22

"Merry Christmas!" she says as the customer picks up his bags. Her store seems to explode with activity as people rush to buy gifts. Jingle bells lag behind the more familiar ka-ching of cash registers. Yuletide music is light and cheery with the hope the holidays communicate. How many college students will fly home to be with family? How many children will stoke the fire of merriment as school is set aside? Freshly cut green trees adorn the tops of vehicles making their way home. For weeks they will stand beautifully adorned by ornaments, and lights, underneath the gaze of a metal angel or some priceless figurine.

But not every house will blink with lights or play songs of a Savior wrapped in swaddling clothes. In every town and city are those who sit at home bereaving a spouse, a child, a parent, a friend who left the world on an eternal hiatus. Stress, grief, and memories of pain will suppress many hearts just hoping to endure this time of long nights.

God never changes. He is not pumped by the beat of the rapper or depressed by a polluted environment. He is not incapacitated by the sins of a spinning globe. He is not paralyzed by the hatred of those who mock His existence. He will not turn His back on those who seek Him, though for a season He may not be found. He is immutable. During a season of great contrasts this reality is gigantic.

God never changes. His loving-kindness extends from the farthest reaches of unseen galaxies to this very page you are reading. His loving-kindness is better than life; for without it we could not live. His loving-kindness is capable of taking our joy to a deeper dimension. His loving-kindness is available to cover us with comfort. It brings understanding to confusion; rest to anxiety; refuge to fear; meaning to emptiness; value to worthlessness; hope to despair. God loves us so much! Perhaps it is during the very hustle of holidays that we need to remember this truth the most. Jesus takes us inside the shadow of the El-Shaddai! In the refuge of His love we find blessing.

Psalm 36:5-7—LORD, Your faithful love reaches to heaven, Your faithfulness to the clouds. Your righteousness is like the highest mountains; Your judgments, like the deepest sea. LORD, You preserve man and beast. God, Your faithful love is so valuable that people take refuge in the shadow of Your wings.

Inspiration †††

God wishes to give Himself utterly to every creature that names His name.—Jeanne Guyon in *Experiencing the Depths of Jesus Christ*

When They Saw the Star

December 23

Matthew 2:9,10—After hearing the king, they went on their way, And there it was—the star they had seen in the east! It led them until it came and stopped above the place where the child was. When they saw the star, they were overjoyed beyond measure.

It seems rather preposterous! What rational, intelligent men would climb aboard camels loaded with gifts and trek for who knows how long to worship an unknown king simply because a special star was spotted in the sky? They came from the east to Jerusalem in faith and caused quite a commotion with their heartfelt question, "Where is He who has been born King of the Jews?" (Mat. 2:2a). Their faith was rewarded. Their journey was not in vain. They were afforded the privilege of bowing before God—the Creator of the Universe who willingly chose to become like us. How fitting that a star should herald His arrival.

We need no star today. God in His infinite wisdom chose to make those who would follow His Son, light to a darkened world. The proof that Jesus is God's Son, the greatest Man who ever lived on earth is demonstrated in the lives of those changed by the Savior. Our globe is continuously punctuated by shining followers who offer themselves as living sacrifices—gifts worth more to God than gold, frankincense and myrrh.

We become lights as we surrender our hearts to Jesus and worship Him who alone gives peace to replace turmoil, hope to erase despair, love to eliminate emptiness and faith to live beyond death. So let your light shine! Forget about those tiny bulbs wrapped around your Christmas tree. Your bulb is far more important for all the world to see! If you will let the Son influence you, your luminescence will be inspirational! May God's blessings be upon you this season and forever.

Inspiration ✝✝✝

Jesus Christ is, beyond all reasonable question, the greatest Man who ever lived. The greatness of a man is to be estimated by two things; first, by the extent of his influence upon mankind, and secondly—for no one is altogether great who is not also good—by the purity and dignity of his character. Tried by both these tests, Jesus is supreme among men. He is at once the most influential and the best of Mankind.—P. Carnegie Simpson in *The Fact of Christ*

Joy and Sorrow

December 24

We sat in church and celebrated a Christmas Eve service with hundreds. There was good music and message and the proverbial ending replete with candles lit and singing *Silent Night*. Then we went home. I thought about how easy it is to be joyful when no one is shooting at you and when the most treacherous aspect of the holidays is negotiating icy-snowy roads. How different it is for my friends in India, Kenya, and Nigeria who have experienced the sudden upheaval of violence, barely escaping the hate of those who despise Christians.

Is it important to understand that in celebrating the birth of Jesus we must remember the cost it entailed and the warning that preceded it by the prophet Jeremiah? *"A voice was heard in Ramah, weeping and great mourning, Rachel weeping for her children; and she refused to be consoled, because they were no more"* (Mat. 2:18).

Matthew 2:16—Then Herod, when he saw that he had been outwitted by the wise men, flew into a rage. He gave orders to massacre all the male children in and around Bethlehem who were two years old and under, in keeping with the time he had learned from the wise men.

Bible scholars estimate at least twenty babies were slaughtered in and around Bethlehem by the edict of a cruel ruler bent on ensuring no king would grow up and challenge his throne. Why did God allow this carnage to happen? How do you think the mothers and fathers of those murdered children felt? Do you suppose any of those parents were still alive when Jesus went south from Galilee to minister. If they figured out the timing and disputed His *messiahship*, how could they look at Him and not feel anger that *His* life meant their innocent son's death! Do you suppose *they* might have yelled, "*crucify*," with heartfelt anger?

Is it possible that we have an incomplete picture of Jesus' arrival on earth? We readily make mangers but who constructs a memorial? Who sings songs of lament for babies unfairly eliminated and their inconsolable mothers?

The gift of Jesus came with a price tag. Babies died because an evil ruler lived. God knew Herod's heart and sent Joseph, Mary and Jesus to Egypt so His Son would live. Does that mean God didn't love those families that lost their babies? He heard the severe wailing in Bethlehem. He knew the grief they felt.

Often when holiness confronts contamination there is a cost and pain. Noble Abel died at the hands of Cain. Lying Ananias fell dead before an offended Holy Spirit. Angels gave a joyful tribute. Mothers sang a Ramah dirge. Sorrow is fleeing Bethlehem in the middle of the night knowing that many of your new acquaintances will suffer unbearably.   In the course of celebration remember the cost. Sorrow is the cross foreshadowed by a feeding trough. Sorrow is the love that propels the Almighty to cover the sins of His children with the blood of His Son. And sorrow is an important part of the Nativity painting. As C.S. Lewis wrote in *Surprised By Joy*, "The hardness of God is kinder than the softness of men, and His compulsion is our liberation." [123]

Inspiration † † †

The hardness of God is kinder than the softness of men, and His compulsion is our liberation.—C.S. Lewis in *Surprised By Joy*

Ransom

December 25

I spent an hour and a half trying to travel two miles after an ice-storm struck Portland and stranded Christmas shoppers. Storms have an amazing ability to put things into perspective. What fragile creatures we truly are! In a power outage, people quit arguing over the appropriateness of "Happy Holidays" versus "Merry Christmas" and start thinking about staying warm. Buying presents takes a back seat to getting home without skidding off the road. The real meaning of Christmas is LIFE! In the gathering storm, can we see that our survival is what God is after and not our need to enjoy His Son in diapers? Can we recognize that our happiness came at a horrific cost—a holy ransom?

Psalm 49:7,8—Yet these cannot redeem a person or pay his ransom to God—since the price of redeeming him is too costly, one should forever stop trying.
Mark 10:45—For even the Son of Man did not come to be served, but to serve, and to give His life—a ransom for many.

We come to a season where reason is heated,
    and arguments rise to the top of the charts.
The crib with its Child if honored in public
    turns some into snarling, unhappy hearts.
Their holiday wish is to leave out religion
    and not have to listen to carolers sing.
They care not for wise men or Bethlehem manger,
    just leave them with Santa and all that he brings.

We come to a season where none can offend,
    so nothing is gained and nothing is won.
Convictions are muted to ruffle no feathers
    'til soon Silent Night will no longer be sung.
Lost in the battle for who should be heard
    is the very foundation of what gives us might
Freedom to worship in pure, humble expression
    is what turns our land to a beacon of light.

Maybe the Baby is the source of our focus
    but surely the Lord is the need of our souls.
He came to this earth with a mission to save us,
    a ransom that only He could pay in full.
In the midst of our tidings of yuletide and cheer
    we ought to remember the cost God endured.

For Jesus the King did not come to be served
    but to give up His life as a payment secured.

We live in a season with war all-surrounding
    and now is the time when the battle is here;
To raise up the standard that most holy guidon;
    proclaim to the world that His coming is near.
For God who so loved us that He offered His Son,
    calls us who believe Him to go out and share.
At issue is not whether ears are offended
    but that sin is conquered in answer to prayer.

This Christmas, let's thank God for giving us life and for sending His Son to ransom us.

Busyness   December 26

The cockpit of a C17 military transport aircraft is amazing. As the two young Air Force Captains went through their preflight checklist, I was astounded by all the instruments they and their crew chief had to monitor and operate before we could taxi down the runway in Stockholm. While I watched from my rear perch, I listened on headphones to the tower. The chatter from the air traffic controllers to incoming and outgoing aircraft was virtually nonstop. As our pilots were busily engaged the tower called their call sign and passed instructions. The captain asked his copilot if she heard what was said and she shook her head no. Because I was undistracted and heard the message, I was able to convey what they missed. Each time they received instructions they repeated them back to the controller to ensure the transmission was accurately understood. This was a great failsafe for everyone involved and reinforced how important it was to listen.

Revelation 3:20—Listen! I stand at the door and knock. If anyone hears My voice and opens the door, I will come in to him and have dinner with him, and he with Me.

I confess that too often my bandwidth is so full of activity that I fail to hear God's voice. This is like determining to fly my plane without taking instructions from the tower! Shouldn't I be engaged in discerning what flight path the Lord would have me take and then fellowshipping with Him as I fly?

What happens if we persist in our busyness at the expense of listening? Bill Hybels notes in *Too Busy Not to Pray*, "But if we don't follow up on the Holy Spirit's leadings, he may see no reason to continue speaking."[125] I often wonder if this is not the state of Christendom in America. Little fruit, much apathy, and prolific complacency are three indicators of our busyness. Without effort, we may find ourselves constantly surrounded by noise and in danger of missing a word from our Father. I would hate to find out that He knocked and I was too busy to hear Him or that He had a word for me that was missed in all the chatter.

Inspiration † † †

But if we don't follow up on the Holy Spirit's leadings, He may see no reason to continue speaking.—Bill Hybels in *Too Busy Not to Pray*

Mortification

December 27

Do these words make sense? "Of not of glorification innermost soul the but God cry is appeasement the self for the." Hardly—they contain only a convoluted truth because they are not pieced together properly. So it is with our lives when we give ourselves haphazardly to God. We display a message of devotion—but one filled with syntax errors which at best are confusing, at worst, entertain the vast skepticisms of a doubting world and surely hurt the heart of our Father.

What keeps us from giving ourselves fully to a God who does not need us yet whose love for us is immeasurable? We can boil the gist of the problem to selfishness but that may be overly harsh. Perhaps what we lack is courage. The Apostle Paul eloquently wrote, *"My eager expectation and hope is that I will not be ashamed about anything, but that now as always, with all boldness, Christ will be highly honored in my body, whether by life or by death"* (Php. 1:20).

John MacArthur teaches that "The true gospel is a call to self-denial. It is not a call to self-fulfillment." Jonathan Edwards taught:

> But whoever has tried self-denial can give in his testimony that they never experience greater pleasure and joys than after great acts of self-denial. Self-denial destroys the very root and foundation of sorrow, and is nothing else but the lancing of a grievous and painful sore that effects a cure and brings abundance of health as a recompense for the pain of the operation.

Let us rise off our couches of fear. Let us not be afraid to kill those passions that quench our thirst for our Almighty Friend; that keep us from living for Christ—dying for gain. The innermost cry of the soul is not for the appeasement of self but the glorification of God.

> Any fool will give up wrongdoing and the devil, if he knows how to do it; but it takes a person in love with Jesus Christ to give up the best he has for Him. Jesus Christ does not demand that I give up the wrong, but the right, the best I have for Him, namely, my right to myself.[126]

Revelation 3:21—The victor: I will give him the right to sit with Me on My throne, just as I also won the victory and sat down with My Father on His throne.

Inspiration ✝✝✝

Mortify whatever there is that remains of your corrupt affections and desires; mortify your own will; mortify your taste, your disposition, the things you are naturally inclined to; mortify your habits.—Jeanne Guyon in *Experiencing the Depths of Jesus Christ*

Worship

December 28

Revelation 15:4—Lord, who will not fear and glorify Your name? Because You alone are holy, for all the nations will come and worship before You because Your righteous acts have been revealed.

My favorite devotional is *My Utmost For His Highest* by Oswald Chambers. One of my favorite quotes from that outstanding work is the following:

> Worship is giving God the best that He has given you . . . The measure of the worth of our public activity for God is the private profound communion we have with Him. Rush is wrong every time, there is always plenty of time to worship God. Quiet days with God may be a snare. We have to pitch our tents where we shall always have quiet times with God, however noisy our times with the world may be.

May I invite you to stop what you are doing. In the midst of your busy world, imagine that beside you sits a beautifully crafted silver case. Open it and choose at least four of the golden tent pegs of love, reverence, faith, obedience, holiness, joy, peace, and hope that sit in that case. Next pull out the royal purple cloth and its four golden ropes attached to each corner. Grab the bronze hammer and fasten each cord to the ground you occupy. Now in the holy hush of anticipation you might consider sharing the following words with your Heavenly Father who loves you and takes incredible joy in your heartfelt offering:

Lord, I have come to worship You and to open up my heart.
I am not deserving of Your grace or
Of the blood You freely shed when You hung there in my place.
Forgive me Lord for my sins and all my wrongs
By Your Spirit make me holy for the glory of Your Name.
For Your body that was broken I give thanks to You O Lord.
For Your blood You offered up as a fragrant sacrifice
For Your mercy that brings healing and life forever more.
For Your love that has no limits I'm amazed and filled with joy
I am are so blessed to be Your friend.
To glory in Your promise that our love will never end.   Amen.

Inspiration ✝✝✝

Worship is the adoration and praise of that which delights us. We praise what we enjoy, because praise completes the enjoyment. We worship God for the pleasure to be had in him.—Pastor John Piper

War

December 29

Revelation 17:14—These will make war against the Lamb, but the Lamb will conquer them because he is Lord of lords and King of kings. Those with him are called, chosen, and faithful.

The world does not get safer as man gets smarter. New technologies do not usher in everlasting calm. Stately planes become ferocious missiles. Man may clone, unlock the genetic code and discover new cures for old diseases. He may call for universal gatherings of like-minded people to meditate for peace and create a New World order. But, he cannot eliminate war. Why? Because he refuses to cry heavenward for mercy. He rejects God's gift of Jesus.

Spiritual people may find in disaster and conflicts the opportunity to implore for revival—spiritual awakening in violence-soaked lands. But without true repentance every society is at war against the Lamb. Tumultuous days will come. Why? Does not the Bible warn us to expect such events? Until Jesus returns the earth will only get more chaotic.

War is competing ideologies. It is the offspring of pride. War makes a wounded nation wring its heart in sorrow and spawns countless questions. What will grow from our anguish? From the mounds of ash and rubble who will fix our course of trouble?

Let us not lose perspective. No jihad will prevail against Jesus. The greatest danger mankind faces is not the threat of terrorists but the rejection of God's Son. He offered His life in love to save us from our sin. He alone provides eternal security. Jesus warned in Luke 12:4,5:

> And I say to you, My friends, don't fear those who kill the body, and after that can do nothing more. But I will show you the One to fear: Fear Him who has authority to throw people into hell after death. Yes, I say to you, this is the One to fear!

Jesus came to save us from that hell. Let us be faithful to proclaim that great truth!

Inspiration † † †

The question is on the lips of people today, "Is war of the devil or of God?" It is of neither. It is of men, though both God and the devil are behind it. War is a conflict of wills, either in individuals or in nations. As sure as there is will versus will, there must be punch versus punch.—Oswald Chambers in *The Love of God*.

Mutiny December 30

On December 30, 2007, President Kibaki, of the Kikuyu tribe, was again sworn in as the winner of the Kenyan Presidential election. According to most reports and the opposition candidate Raila Odinga, of the Luos tribe, the election was rigged and the incumbent should have lost. Immediate fighting broke out across the country. In Eldoret, gangs of youth set fire to an Assembly of God church killing fifty Kikuyus seeking refuge there. This was the first reported attack of a church in Kenyan history.

My friend pastor Joseph Shikokoti, with his entire family, fled their home in Eldoret and hid for two days. They slept out in the cold, fearing for their lives. Thugs tried to break into the cybernet café of an orphanage dependent upon that business for funds. Commerce shut down, and it was not safe to go out. By God's grace they were able to return home and their house and church were unscathed.

1 Kings 12:18,19—Then King Rehoboam sent Adoram, who was in charge of forced labor, but all Israel stoned him to death. King Rehoboam managed to get into the chariot and flee to Jerusalem. Israel is in rebellion against the house of David until today.

Thousands of years earlier, a Middle Eastern king assumed the throne. His people asked him to give them relief from the heavy-handed leadership of his father. The elders told him to listen to the people. But Rehoboam's young friends counseled him to take an even sterner posture. He took their advice and in the process of foolish policy spawned a mutiny. People do not like to be cheated, bullied, mistreated or punished. Rebellion is sure to occur against such behavior if the right opportunity exists. But let us not be so naïve as to confine sedition to tyranny.

Satan did not like God's authority. Even serving the Perfect Leader, he chose to rebel rallying with him a great number of angels. Mutiny was born in the heavens and earth was not unscathed. We humans are quite adept at resisting God's law, scorning Jesus' salvation offering, and grieving the Holy Spirit. The seeds of mutiny are in us! Only grace and mercy can set us free.

Inspiration †††

Mutiny, a rise against authority, comes from persecution. There is any amount of weakness in us all, but deep down there is red-handed rebellion against the authority of Jesus Christ—"I'll be damned before I yield."—Oswald Chambers in *Servant As His Lord*

Come

December 31

Revelation 22:17—Both the Spirit and the bride say, "Come!" Anyone who hears should say, "Come!" And the one who is thirsty should come. Whoever desires should take the living water as a gift.

It is the last day of the year and fittingly I am reading from the final chapter of the Bible, Revelation 22. I'm struck by a simple word, *"come."* I hope that kind word of invitation never grows old to my eyes.

Imagine for a moment. The unfathomable Creator custom designed us (Psa. 139:13). Before you or I can think it, God already knows the words we will say (139:4)! There is no place to hide from the omnipresent One. There is no power that can defeat Him. There is no argument to overcome His standards or means to live purer than His holiness. Yet, from cover to cover, the all-time best selling Life Manual consistently reveals the ultimate Lover's desire for us! He wants us. He calls us. His Spirit says, *"Come!"*

Isn't it fitting that the author bolsters the invitation with the example of one who is *thirsty*? What human has not experienced thirst? Every dried out one of us can relate to the simple joy of gulping down water. Are you thirsty? God says, *"Come!"*

I was four years old when I heard His invitation and responded. More than fifty years later, I cannot think of one moment I wished to undo that decision. In the most distressing trials, He has fortified me. In the loneliest, most gut-wrenching periods of pain, He has kept me under His arms. In times of blessing and joy, I've seen His fingerprints. He is more real than any reality I have ever known. As His child, I love His word, *"Come!"*

Jesus says to us, *"The one who believes in Me, as the Scripture has said, will have streams of living water flow from deep within him"* (John 7:38). Max Lucado noted in *The Applause of Heaven*, "Admission of thirst doesn't come easy for us. False fountains pacify our cravings with sugary swallows of pleasure." As we end another year, let us quench our thirst with the Living Water. We are exceedingly blessed by the One who invites us and refreshes us with His eternal presence! We are called to come by the One who leads us to climb higher . . . in reveration!

Inspiration †††

There is not one biblical hero who did not come in to the presence of God on a regular basis.—Jack Deere in *Surprised By The Power Of The Spirit*

Bible Marking Code—36 + Themes

Colors & Symbols

Gray = Prophecy   Orange = Healing   Pink = Fasting
Teal = Humility   Yellow = Prayer, Light

Brown Color Marking: Obedience, Compliance, Follow
Brown Symbols:
π = Altar, offering   B = Book of Life
+ = Discipleship   S = Serve, servant, minister

Black Marker for Notes
Black Symbols:
Ω = Idols, Idolatry   ✓ = Salvation
★ = Key Verse;   ①= Verse of the Year
J—Judgement; Jc-Conditional; Jf-Fulfilled; Jp-Predicted;
Jv-Vengeance; Ju-Just, Justice; Ju/ = injustice

Blue Color Markings: Light Blue = Love;
Dark Blue = Holiness, Holy Spirit, Pure
Blue Symbols:
☐ = Apologetics (box around vs #)   ₽= Leadership
^ = Truth   __ = Memorized   ⟶ = Key Thought

Green Color Marking: Faith, hope, trust
Green Symbols:
O = Christ's return (circle around vs #)   🍎 = Fruit
G = Grace; GB = Blessing; GF = Favor
$ = Money, giving, generous
P—Promise; Pc-Conditional; Pf-Fulfilled; Pr-Remembered

Purple Color Marking: Worship, Praise, Thanksgiving
Purple Symbols:
! = Joy, Excitement   Δ = Trinity
♪ = Music, singing, Instruments,   __ = God's Name
W—Wisdom: Knowledge, Learning, Understanding, Discerning, Teaching, Instruction

Red Color Marking: Fear of God
Red Symbols:
♡ = Heart   ♥ = Wholehearted   # = Pride, Arrogance
⊗ = Power, Strength, Might, Fortress, Stronghold
☹ = Adversity, Suffering, Pain, Hardship, Misery

WHY FIRST CAUSE?

God put a new song in our mouths, a hymn of praise to Him so that people would see and revere Him and put their trust in Him (Psalm 40:3). This is what First Cause is all about. Our goal is to share the inspired songs (not just music but also a metaphor for written and spoken words) to all who God will bring us in contact with so that they too might have the deep love and trust for Him that makes life rich with meaning and joyful. He is our First Cause and we love sharing His message.

WHAT WE DO

We emphasize three ministries: prayer, coaching and providing resources designed to help people grow spiritually. Our goal is to help those who are hungry for purpose and meaning in life to be successful spiritually, physically, emotionally and socially.

To learn more about First Cause, to access or sign up for free weekly devotionals, or to order our products, visit http://www.firstcause.org.

Other Books and Music by Daniel York

Lost on Mount Fuji

Something to Think About in **Reveration** Vol 1

The Strong Leader's Hand

To order go to **www.firstcause.org** and click on products

All songs are original compositions

Where Were You?   See His Star (Christmas)

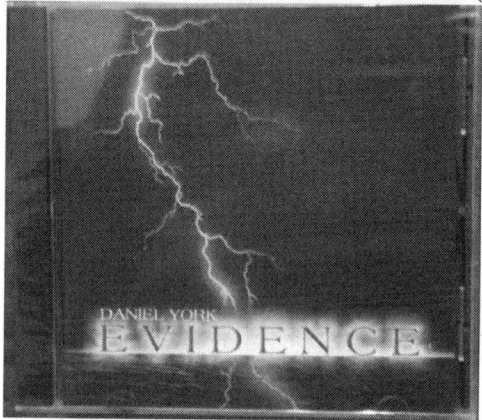

Evidence

Of Seen and Unseen   Choices

To order go to **www.firstcause.org** and click on products

About the Author

Daniel York grew up as a missionary kid, the son of Ron and Betty York. He lived in Okinawa, Korea, Japan, the Philippines, and throughout the United States. In 1977, after graduating from Faith Academy in the Philippines, he spent four years as a cadet at West Point. Following his graduation from West Point in 1981, he served with the 101st Airborne (Air Assault) Division before joining the Army Reserves in 1986. Dan served on staff with The Navigators for ten years, during which time he received a Master of Divinity from Bethel Seminary (West) in San Diego, CA, before moving with his family to Oregon in 1991 to plant and pastor Horizon Community Church. In 2000, he started the nonprofit First Cause, an organization committed to worship and leadership training. He has authored seven books and recorded seven albums of original music.

Dan was promoted to Major General in 2012. As of 2013, he serves as the Division Commander of the 76th Operational Response Command headquartered at Fort Douglas, UT. He is married to Kathleen over 30 years and is the father of three children: Bryan, Sarah and Stephen. Sarah is married to Mark Tegtmeier and gave Dan and Kathleen their first grandson Jadon.

Dan's life verse is Psalm 40:3—"*He put a new song in my mouth, a hymn of praise to our God. Many will see and fear and put their trust in the Lord.*"

ENDNOTES

[1] Jim Loerhr and Tony Schwartz, *The Power of Full Engagement*, (New York: Free Press, 2005)
[2] Image courtesy of xedos4/FreeDigitalPhotos.net
[3] www.greatdreams.com/masters/ascended-masters.htm
[4] Erwin Raphael McManus, *Chasing Daylight*, (Nashville: Nelson Books, 2002)
[5] http://www.daveroever.org/roeverstory.php
[6] Jack Deere, *Surprised By The Power Of The Spirit*, (Michigan: Zondervan, 1993)
[7] http://en.wikipedia.org/wiki/Jacques-Louis_David
[8] Henry T. Blackaby, Richard Blackaby, *Spiritual Leadership: Moving People on to God's Agenda, Revised and Expanded*, (Nashville: B&H Publishing Group, 2011)
[9] George Mueller, *The Autobiography of George Mueller*, (Pennsylvania: Whitaker House, 1996)
[10] Joe Rojas-Burke in *"Antidote for illness comes with life goals"* The Oregonian Thursday March 11, 2010
[11] http://www.reformation-scotland.org.uk/articles/fear-of-god/
[12] Oswald Chambers, *The Pilgrim's Song Book*
[13] http://rabbielimallon.wordpress.com/tag/ashrei
[14] Oswald Chambers, *The Shadow of an Agony*
[15] Max Lucado, *A Gentle Thunder: Hearing God Through the Storm*, (Nashville: Thomas Nelson, 2012)
[16] Andrew Murray, *With Christ in the School of Prayer*, (Michigan: Zondervan, 1983)
[17] Brennan Manning, *The Ragamuffin Gospel*, (Oregon: Multnomah Books, 2005)
[18] http://dictionary.reference.com/browse/wisdom
[19] *The American Heritage® New Dictionary of Cultural Literacy*, Third Edition (Houghton Mifflin Company, 2005)
[20] Image courtesy of Evgeni Dinev/FreeDigitalPhotos.net
[21] C.S. Lewis, *Christian Reflections*, Edited by Walter Hooper, (Michigan: William B. Eerdmans, 1994)
[22] C.H. Spurgeon, *Sermons on Proverbs*, A sermon (No. 1418) delivered on Lord's Day morning, June 9th, 1878, at the Metropolitan Tabernacle, Newington
[23] http://en.wikipedia.org/wiki/Turtle_ship
[24] http://www.dictionary.com
[25] http://www.aasianst.org/eaa/connor.htm
[26] *Proverbs and Wise Sayings* by Paul Vithayathil (India, 1999)
[27] Os Guinness, *The Call*, (Nashville: Word Publishing, 1998)
[28] http://www.academia.org/keeping-communism-down/
[29] Oswald Chambers, *My Utmost For His Highest*
[30] http://www.brainyquote.com/citation/quotes/quotes/f/francoisra400191.html?-ct=Francois+Rabelais
[31] http://www.biblestudytools.com/lexicons/hebrew/nas/rasha-2.html
[32] Email received from a friend—unknown author
[33] Image courtesy of Victor Habbick/FreeDigitalPhotos.net
[34] http://en.wikipedia.org/wiki/Book_of_Nahum
[35] John Calvin, *John Calvin's Commentaries on St. Paul's Epistle to the Romans*
[36] Image courtesy of think4photop/FreeDigitalPhotos.net
[37] HCSB Study Bible, 2010, pp. 1608,1609
[38] Francis Frangipane, *Holiness, Truth and Presence of God*, (Iowa: Advancing Church Publications, 1986)

39 http://www.oocities.org/zonejennyx/funnythings2.html
40 Bruxy Cavey, *The End of Religion*, (Colorado: NavPress, 2007)
41 Jeanne Guyon, *Experiencing the Depths of Jesus Christ*, (Georgia: SeedSowers, 1975)
42 George Barna, *Growing True Disciples*, (Colorado: WaterBrook Press, 2001)
43 https://forrestgeneral.com/HIL/main3708.htm
44 Ayn Rand, *Atlas Shrugged*, (New York City: Signet, 1996)
45 www.dictionary.com
46 http://www.biblegateway.com/passage/?search=luke%201:57,58&version=HCSB
47 Susan Martins Miller, *Jim Elliot: Missionary Martyr*, (Ohio: Barbour Publishing, Inc. 1996)
48 http://en.wikipedia.org/wiki/Jim_Elliot
49 Robert E. Coleman, *The Master Plan of Evangelism*, (New Jersey: Fleming H. Revell Company, 1980)
50 Watchman Nee, *Spiritual Authority*, (New York: Christian Fellowship Publishers, Inc., 1972)
51 John Thornbury, *Five Pioneer Missionaries*, (Pennsylvania: Banner of Truth, 1965)
52 *Holman Study Bible*, ©2010, Nashville, TN
53 Dietrich Bonhoeffer, *The Cost of Discipleship*, (Nashville: B&H Publishing Group, 1998)
54 http://dictionary.reference.com/browse/stewardship?s=t
55 Donald Joiner, *Creating a Climate for Giving*, (Nashville: Discipleship Resources, 2003)
56 http://www.wikipedia.org/wiki/Universalism
57 http://www.carm.org/religious-movements/universalism
58 http://lavistachurchofchrist.org/LVarticles/images/Trinity.gif
59 http://en.wikipedia.org/wiki/Vasa; information also taken from Museum handouts
60 J.I. Packer, *Evangelism & The Sovereignty of God*, (Illinois: IVP, 2012)
61 Wesley Duewel, *Ablaze For God* (Michigan: Zondervon, 1989)
62 Oswald Chambers, *So Send I You*
63 http://en.wikipedia.org/wiki/Process_theology
64 Charles Hartshorne, *Omnipotence and Other Theological Mistakes* (Albany: State University of New York, 1984), 32-36
65 C. Robert Mesle, *Process Theology: A Basic Introduction* (St. Louis, MO: Chalice Press, 1993), p. 106
66 http://www.processandfaith.org/resources/Cobb%20On%20Process%20-Theology.shtml
67 http://veritasdomain.wordpress.com/2010/03/28/a-critique-of-process-theology%E2%80%99s-epistemology-and-doctrine-of-revelation/#_ftn4
68 James Rutz, *Mega Shift*, (Colorado: Empowerment Press, 2005)
69 C.S. Lewis, *The Weight of Glory*, (Michigan: William B. Eerdmans Publishing Company, 1974)
70 http://martinvance.blogspot.com/2011/11/james-brother-of-jesus-christ.html
71 Richard S. Taylor, *A Right Conception of Sin*, (Missouri: Beacon Hill Press, 1945)
72 Tom Capps, *Pray and Plan*, (Oregon: VMI Publishers, 2004)
73 Bruce Thielemann, "Christus Imperator, Preaching Today, no. 55
74 Image courtesy of imagerymajestic/FreeDigitalPhotos.net
75 Brian Birdwell, *Refined by Fire*, (Illinois: Tyndale House Publishers, Inc. 2004)
76 http://www.bible.ca/ef/expository-2-peter-1-6b.htm
77 Image courtesy of Evgeni Dinev/FreeDigitalPhotos.net
78 http://www.herpes.org/human-papillomavirus/
79 http://en.wikipedia.org/wiki/Manny_Pacquiao
80 Ibid
81 Ibid

82 http://www.ethicsineducation.com/intro.htm
83 Jonathan Martin, *Giving Wisely*, (Oregon: Last Chapter Publishing LLC)
84 www.cia.gov/library/publications/the-world-factbook/geos/ni.html
85 http://www.lyricsmode.com/lyrics/t/tim_hughes/here_i_am_to_worship.html
86 http://en.wikipedia.org/wiki/Dietrich_Bonhoeffer
87 http://www.studylight.org/lex/grk/view.cgi?number=1411
88 Dietrich Bonhoeffer, *The Cost of Discipleship*, (New York: The Macmillan Company 1963)
89 Ibid
90 Oswald Chambers, *Studies in the Sermon on the Mount*
91 David Joel wrote this Reveration Prayer Report
92 Randy Alcorn, *Heaven*, (Illinois: Tyndale, 2004)
93 http://en.wikipedia.org/wiki/Culture_of_Costa_Rica
94 Joseph C. Aldrich, *Gentle Persuasion*, (Oregon: Multnomah Press, 1988)
95 http://en.wikipedia.org/wiki/Adhesive
96 http://en.wikipedia.org/wiki/Super_glue
97 HCSB Study Bible, 2010
98 HCSB Study Bible 2010, p 2065
99 Dave Kraft, *Leaders Who Last* (Illinois: Crossway, 2010)
100 http://www.cdc.gov/ViolencePrevention/suicide/statistics/trends02.html
101 http://www.census.gov/population/www/popclockus.html
102 Image courtesy of Naypong/FreeDigitalPhotos.net
103 Image courtesy of domdeen/FreeDigitalPhotos.net
104 Venice Bloodworth in *Key To Yourself*, (DeVorss Publications 1952), p. 33
105 Ibid, p.12
106 Ibid, p.22
107 Ibid, pp. 82,83
108 http://wilstar.com/holidays/thankstr.html
109 http://en.wikipedia.org/wiki/Jacob_Bernoulli
111 http://en.wikipedia.org/wiki/Logarithmic_spiral
111 Ibid
112 http://online.redwoods.cc.ca.us/instruct/darnold/calcproj/fall98/darrent/equiangularspiral.html
113 Image courtesy of Cecelia/FreeDigitalPhotos.net
114 *The Autobiography of Wilhelm Stekel : The Life Story of a Pioneer Psychoanalyst* edited by Emil Arthur Gutheil, (New York: Liveright Publishing Corporation, 1950)
115 Wesley L. Duewel. *Revival Fire.* (Michigan: Zondervan Publishing House, 1995)
116 http://www.cnn.com/2013/04/13/opinion/ghitis-north-korea/index.html
117 http://www.hourofpower.org/interviews/detail.php?contentid=6971
118 http://www.nytimes.com/2001/07/31/news/31iht-a4_34.html?pagewanted=1
119 http://www.hourofpower.org
120 Kim Cameron and Marc Lavine, *Making the Impossible Possible*, *(California:* Berrett-Koehler Publishers 2006)
121 Max Lucado, *The Applause of Heaven*, (Texas: Word Publishing, 1990)
122 Steve Hartman http://www.cbsnews.com/video/watch/?id=7425136n&tag=strip
123 C.S. Lewis, *Surprised by Joy*, (Calfornia: Harcourt, Brace, Jovanovich, 1966)
124 Image courtesy of dan/FreeDigitalPhotos.net
125 Bill Hybels, *Too Busy Not to Pray*, (Illinois: IVP 2008)
126 Oswald Chambers in *The Shadow of an Agony*

Made in the USA
San Bernardino, CA
03 April 2018